Arbitration in Africa under OHADA Rules

ARBITRATION IN AFRICA UNDER OHADA RULES

States Parties to the OHADA Treaty

1 Benin
2 Burkina Faso
3 Cameroon
4 Central African Republic
5 Chad
6 Comoros
7 Congo
8 Democratic Republic of Congo
9 Equatorial Guinea
10 Gabon
11 Guinea
12 Guinea Bissau
13 Ivory Coast
14 Mali
15 Niger
16 Senegal
17 Togo

≃ 20 Arbitration Centers, including the center of the CCJA.
Area: 9,124,233 km^2, ≃ 29.985% of Africa.
Population: 287,716,192 ≃ 22.241% of African population.
Source for area & population: https://www.populationdata.net/, accessed June 2, 2020.
Source for the map: Daniel Dalet, https://d-maps.com/carte.php?num_car=737&lang=fr, accessed June 30, 2020.

Arbitration in Africa under OHADA Rules

Mahutodji Jimmy Vital Kodo

Wolters Kluwer

Published by:
Kluwer Law International B.V.
PO Box 316
2400 AH Alphen aan den Rijn
The Netherlands
E-mail: international-sales@wolterskluwer.com
Website: lrus.wolterskluwer.com

Sold and distributed in North, Central and South America by:
Wolters Kluwer Legal & Regulatory U.S.
7201 McKinney Circle
Frederick, MD 21704
United States of America
Email: customer.service@wolterskluwer.com

Sold and distributed in all other countries by:
Air Business Subscriptions
Rockwood House
Haywards Heath
West Sussex
RH16 3DH
United Kingdom
Email: international-customerservice@wolterskluwer.com

ISBN 978-94-035-0942-6

e-Book: ISBN 978-94-035-0981-5
web-PDF: ISBN 978-94-035-1025-5

In loving memory of my late father, Christophe Maurice Kodo, who inspired me for amazing things from a very early age.

Where there was once vacuum, there is now an illuminating and enlightening book ... from an Africa-driven initiative, in Africa, for the benefit of all who desire to expand their knowledge of arbitration ... in Africa.

Justice Edward Thorgbor[1]

1. In *The Transformation of Arbitration in Africa. The Role of Arbitral Institutions* xxvii (E. Onyema ed., Kluwer Law International 2016).

About the Author

Dr. Mahutodji Jimmy Vital Kodo is an independent arbitrator and a leading OHADA expert and practitioner with over fifteen years of experience. He has been appointed arbitrator by the African States in investment disputes, and regularly represents parties in complex litigation and arbitration proceedings as well as appeals before the Common Court of Justice and Arbitration (CCJA), the Court of Final Appeal for the seventeen African States Parties to the OHADA Treaty.

Fluent in English and French, he obtained a Master's degree in Business Law from the University of Abomey-Calavi, Benin, an L.L.M. in Corporate Law from the University of Lille and a Ph.D. *summa cum laude* in African Business Law (OHADA) from the University of Paris-Est Creteil, France. The Ph.D. thesis of Dr. Kodo, which was published in 2010, constitutes the only comprehensive study of published OHADA jurisprudence and has contributed to the development of the Treatise on OHADA (*Code Pratique OHADA*) published by Editions Francis Lefebvre since 2013 and of which Dr. Kodo is the director since 2016.

Dr. Kodo has been the Technical Advisor to the President of the CCJA from 2014 to 2016, the only attorney to have held such office. Prior to becoming the Technical advisor to the President of the CCJA, Dr. Kodo was an adjunct professor of law at the University of Paris-Est Créteil (France). Dr. Kodo is an expert trainer in OHADA law and has acted in that capacity for the OHADA Superior Regional School of Magistracy (ERSUMA).

In addition to his arbitration and litigation practice, Dr. Kodo has published extensively on OHADA-related topics and has been a speaker at various institutions, such as the World Bank and the American Society of International Law (ASIL). He has also been a speaker on OHADA-related topics in the United Kingdom, China, Canada, Israel, Ethiopia, Nigeria, and Ghana.

He has been invited as a guest lecturer at many foreign universities, such as the University of Cape Town in South Africa, Howard University and George Washington University in Washington, D.C., U.S.A. In addition, Dr. Kodo delivered the keynote speech at the *26th Fulbright Symposium on International Legal Problems* on April 7, 2016 at Golden Gate University in San Francisco, California.

A Fellow of the Chartered Institute of Arbitrators (London, United Kingdom), Dr. Kodo is a certified arbitrator of the CCJA and is listed on the Arbitrator Roster list of many institutions around the world (*inter alia,* MIAC - Mauritius, Lagos Court of Arbitration - Nigeria, CACI - Ivory Coast) and most recently, on the list of the Arbitrators of African Descent with a U.S. Nexus. He is currently a Member of the Singapore International Arbitration Court (SIAC) Users Council.

Table of Contents

Foreword

by Dr. Won Kidane

Tagged along with the adoption of the two major legal systems of the world, the doctrine, culture, and practice of international arbitration have developed in Africa in two parallel tracks crossing paths far too infrequently. All seventeen Member States of the Organization for the Harmonization of Business Law in Africa (OHADA) (with the partial exception of Cameroon that follows both) have adopted a brand of the civil law legal tradition in its various forms. While, in the post-World War II era, Europe has by comparison remarkably succeeded in harmonizing substantive rules and eliminated most jurisdictional obstacles by creating robust and functioning international arbitration regimes that complement an already developed transnational judicial system, Africa is just getting started on both fronts; the most notable effort in that direction being OHADA. The cultural and linguistic differences have, however, significantly contributed to OHADA's relatively isolated existence and development.

Dr. Jimmy Kodo's *Arbitration in Africa under OHADA Rules* book-length appraisal of the two OHADA international arbitration systems is a highly welcome bridge that connects the rest of the world with OHADA and shares its experiences with the rest of Africa and beyond.

Dr. Kodo's contribution is most notable in at least four respects.

First, at the doctrinal and practical levels, he methodically goes through the twofold arbitration system under OHADA consisting of the Uniform Act on Arbitration (UAA) and institutional arbitration under the auspices of the Common Court of Justice Arbitration (CCJA). Not infrequently confused, this book clarifies the distinctions and the specific features of each of these two systems. Under the same rubric, Dr. Kodo methodically analyzes matters ranging from the frontend issues of the validity and enforceability of the arbitral agreement to the backend issues of the form, content, annulment, and enforceability of arbitral awards. In so doing, not only does he scrutinize the rules on their own accord but also puts them in a comparative context (for example, in annulment context, he profiles rules in Benin, Burkina Faso, Cameroon, Congo, Ivory Coast.)

Second, he introduces the OHADA system itself for a broader audience. At the risk of overgeneralization, outsiders' frequent impression of the OHADA system is that it is one of the most successful but obscure supranational efforts in Africa. Dr. Kodo demystifies it.

Third, dissatisfied with the quality of the English versions of the rules currently available (although technically English, along with Spanish and Portuguese are official languages), he usefully translated and appended a clear English version of the rules.

Finally, and perhaps more importantly, he takes the most informed and the least informed practitioner on a very informative step-by-step practical journey through the two OHADA arbitration systems. In that sense, it is an extraordinarily useful practice advisory.

I cannot think of a better scholar and practitioner than Dr. Jimmy Kodo for this work. With over fifteen years of scholarship and practice in the area of international arbitration with the benefits of excellent linguistic and cultural facility of both the French and English-speaking world, he brings academic excellence, practical refinement, and cultural nuance to bear in a work of this size and complexity. At the most basic level, his work is not only profoundly credible as a matter of fact but also exceedingly useful as a matter of practice guidance. It is a rare cultural bridge between common law and civil law, between Francophone and Anglophone, and more importantly, between OHADA and the rest of Africa and the world. I wish to extend Dr. Kodo my deepest congratulations for this wonderful work and highly recommend the book to all practitioners, students, and academics of international arbitration around the world.

Dr. Won Kidane

He is a professor of law at Seattle University School of Law in Washington State admitted to practice law in the District of Columbia, Illinois, and Washington State and founding partner of the Addislaw Group. He regularly represents states and other entities in investor-state arbitration and international commercial arbitration. He is the author of *The Culture of International Arbitration* (Oxford University Press, 2017), *China-Africa Dispute Settlement* (Kluwer 2012), two more co-authored books, and more than forty law review articles and book chapters.

Preface

by Professor Emmanuel Gaillard

The fourteen West African States that signed the treaty creating the Organization for the Harmonization of Business Law in Africa (commonly abbreviated as OHADA, from the organization's name in French) on October 17, 1993, in Port Louis, Mauritius, entrusted this organization with an ambitious objective: to encourage foreign investments in the OHADA region by creating a harmonized legal environment. Specifically, OHADA was tasked with developing legal instruments governing relevant areas of business law and directly applicable in all Member States. Accordingly, starting in 1997, OHADA adopted several Uniform Acts regulating areas ranging from General Commercial Law and insolvency proceedings to the taking of security interest and accounting principles.

In keeping with OHADA's supranational aims, very early on, the architects of this structure established arbitration as one of its central pillars. In fact, the legalization on arbitration that was enacted in March 1999 allows parties to arbitrate under two separate regimes: ad hoc (and sometimes institutional) arbitration pursuant to the Uniform Act on Arbitration (UAA) and institutional arbitration administered by the Common Court of Justice and Arbitration (the highest juridical body within OHADA) under its Regulations on Arbitration (CCJA Arbitration Rules).

This dual arbitration system was distinctly modern, drawing from best practices in international arbitration. Core principles of international arbitration—including, party autonomy, autonomy of the arbitration agreement, *competence-competence* (including its indirect effect), the independence and impartiality requirement for arbitrators, and the tribunal's authority to grant provisional measures—were given unequivocal recognition in the UAA and CCJA Arbitration Rules. OHADA's arbitration framework was further enhanced in November 2017, when the UAA and CCJA Arbitration Rules were revised to bring them in line with most current practice in international arbitration. Over the past twenty years, the OHADA arbitration framework has been tried and tested in proceedings before arbitral tribunals, Member States' courts, the CCJA, as well as courts in Western countries in the context of enforcement proceedings.

In light of this accumulated experience, and amid growing calls for greater coordination and integration on arbitration matters between Africa's sub-regions, OHADA arbitration can and should serve as a reference point for ongoing efforts to promote arbitration in Africa. Instead, and much as Anglophone and Francophone African countries have held back on fully engaging with each other on arbitration matters, OHADA arbitration still suffers from not being widely accessible to non-Francophone Africa or Africans not conversant with the civil law legal system. Indeed, there are no official translations from French to the English language of the UAA or the CCJA Arbitration Rules. Moreover, the vast majority of studies, commentary, and practical guides on OHADA arbitration are published only in French.

Dr. Jimmy Kodo's *Arbitration in Africa under OHADA Rules* takes a resolute step in the right direction. His book, for the first time, provides the arbitration community with a complete treatise in English on the OHADA arbitration system. Dr. Kodo methodically dissects every aspect of the OHADA arbitration system, both under the UAA and the CCJA Arbitration Rules. He also critically examines the implementation of these instruments by the courts of the Member States and the CCJA. At every relevant juncture, Dr. Kodo shines the light on the singular traits of the OHADA arbitration system and comments on areas requiring further improvement following the 2017 revisions. The book is also complemented by revised and annotated versions of the unofficial English language translations of the UAA and the CCJA Rules published on OHADA's website.

This treatise is practitioners' and academics' long-awaited gateway to OHADA arbitration. That Dr. Jimmy Kodo decided to take on this challenge should not come as a surprise. Dr. Kodo has devoted his entire career to the advancement of OHADA law. His doctoral thesis, published in 2010, remains the only comprehensive study of published OHADA case law. His work in this respect contributed to the subsequent development of the reference guide on OHADA law—*Code Pratique OHADA*—published by *Editions Francis Lefebvre* and regularly updated since 2013. Dr. Kodo has served as an instructor on OHADA law at the OHADA Superior Regional School of Magistracy (ERSUMA) and previously acted as Technical Advisor to the President of the CCJA from 2014 to 2016. He is also a certified arbitrator of the CCJA and regularly represents parties in proceedings before that court. It is this unique combination of skills—scientific knowledge and practical experience in Arbitration in Africa under OHADA Rules—that Dr. Kodo has brought to bear in his treatise. No one would have been better qualified to perform this task. Any stakeholder who wishes to engage with OHADA arbitration is now adequately equipped to do so.

Professor Emmanuel Gaillard
Global Head of International Arbitration Practice—Shearman & Sterling
Visiting Professor, Yale Law School & Harvard Law School

List of Abbreviations

ACHR	African Court of Human Rights
ASECNA	Agency for Aerial Navigation Safety in Africa and Madagascar (Agence pour la Sécurité de la Navigation Aérienne en Afrique et à Madagascar)
All ER	All England Law Report
APA	American Psychological Association
App.	Application
Ass. plen.	Assemblée plénière
AU	African Union
Austl.	Australia
CACI	Cour d'Arbitrage de Côte d'Ivoire
CAMC-O	Centre d'Arbitrage, de Médiation et de Conciliation (Burkina Faso)
CAMEC-CCIB	Centre d'Arbitrage, de Médiation et de Conciliation à la Chambre de Commerce et de l'Industrie du Bénin
Cass.	Cassation
CATO	Cour d'Arbitrage du Togo
CECAM	Centre de Conciliation et d'Arbitrage du Mali
CEMAC-CCIAD	Centre d'Arbitrage, de Médiation et de Conciliation de la Chambre de Commerce et d'Industrie de Dakar
CEMACO	Centre de Médiation et d'Arbitrage (Congo)
CEMAN	Centre de Médiation et d'Arbitrage de Niamey
CMAG GICAM	Centre de Médiation et d'Arbitrage du Groupement Interpatronal du Cameroun
CCJA	Common Court of Justice and Arbitration
Civ.	Civil (chamber of a court)
Civ. & com.	Civil & Commercial Chamber (of a court)

CJ ECOWAS	Community Court of Justice of the Economic Community of West African States (ruling in matters of Human Rights)
CEO	Chief Executive Officer
CFO	Chief Financial Officer
Chr.	Chroniques (JurisClasseur)
CHRO	Chief Human Resource Officer
Chron.	*Chroniques (Dalloz)*
Collins dic.	Collins Dictionary
Com.	Commercial (chamber of a court)
ConLR.	Construction Law Report
D.	Recueil Dalloz (France)
ECHR	European Court of Human Rights
Ed.	Edition
Eng.	England
Eur. Ct. H.R	European Court of Human Rights
EWHC	England & Wales High Court
FCFA	Franc cfa
FAA	Federal Aviation Administration (USA)
Gaz. Pal.	Gazette du Palais (France)
GICAM	Groupement Interpatronal du Cameroun
IBA	International Bar Association
IBA Rules	International Bar Association Rules on the Taking of Evidence in International Arbitration
ICC	International Chamber of Commerce
JCP E.	Juris Classeur Entreprises (France)
Lloyd's Rep.	Lloyd's Reports
Ltd	Limited
NSWCA	New South Wales Court of Appeal (Australia)
NSWSC	New South Wales Supreme Court (Australia)
Obs.	Observations
OHADA	Organization for the Harmonization of Business Law in Africa (*Organisation pour l'Harmonisation en Afrique du Droit des Affaires*)
OAU	Organization of African Unity
PA	Petites Affiches (France)
PAPA	Publication Manual of the American Psychological Association
Para.	Paragraph
Prague Rules	Rules on the Efficient Conduct of Proceedings in International Arbitration
QB	Queen's Bench
Rev. arb.	Revue de l'arbitrage
SA	Société anonyme

Scot CS	Scottish Court of Session
Somm.	Sommaires
TCC	Technology & Construction Court (England)
TGI	Tribunal de Grande Instance
TPI	Tribunal de Premiere Instance
UAA	Uniform Act on Arbitration
UACCGR	Uniform Act on Contracts for the Carriage of Goods by Road
UAM	Uniform Act on Mediation
UAOCPWOD	Uniform Act Organizing Collective Proceedings for Wiping Off Debts
UAOHCAS	Uniform Act Organizing and Harmonizing Company Accounting Systems
UAOS	Uniform Act Organizing Securities
UAOSRPME	Uniform Act Organizing Simplified Recovery Procedures and Measures of Enforcement
UARCC	Uniform Act Relating to Cooperative Companies
UARCCEIG	Uniform Act Relating to Commercial Companies and Economic Interest Group
UARGCL	Uniform Act Relating to General Commercial Law

Acknowledgments

I thank my Heavenly Father for giving me the ability to write this book and, more importantly, for allowing me to share my passion for African law through this book. As a practitioner, mainly in France and Africa, regularly speaking at conferences and in universities across the USA, it has occurred to me that there was no book in English on this topic of increasing importance worldwide. That inspired me to write this book.

I would like to thank the following persons from Kluwer: Mr. Simon Bellamy, Ms. Eleanor Taylor, and Ms. Kiran N. Gore, to whom I am very grateful for her availability, her patience and her guidance throughout the publication process. I am also thankful to *Editions Francis Lefebvre*, for their kind permission to translate and reproduce specific comments I published in the *Code Pratique Francis Lefebvre. OHADA 20-21* in this book.

Special thanks to Ms. Rose Rameau, FCIArb, Esq., for her constant support and advice. It was a great pleasure to receive insightful suggestions and comments from a leading arbitration practitioner, truly engaged in African legal issues; Mr. Marius Anoh Koffi and his team from *Akama Groupe* (Abidjan, Ivory Coast) for their help in the making of the illustrative map which I designed; and Ms. Zaenab Nassirou for her precious suggestions.

My mother, Afiavi Thérèse Capo, has always provided unconditional support and love for all of my endeavors, including this book, and I can never thank her enough. Finally, this book is also a tribute to Ms. Laurence Lucas, my first English teacher in my freshman year of high school and to everyone interested in arbitration in Africa.

Introduction

Almost twenty-seven years have passed now since several African States, from different regions of the continent, have signed the Treaty creating the "Organization for the Harmonization of Business Law in Africa"[1] (the Treaty) to stimulate foreign investments and foster economic growth. In the preamble of the Treaty, the signatories' heads of States and Governments declared themselves "*willing to promote arbitration as an instrument for resolving contractual disputes*"[2] after affirming their determination "to build a stream of confidence in their countries' economies to create a new development hub in Africa."[3]

Later revised[4] and currently in force in seventeen African countries,[5] the Treaty is open to all African States, whether or not they are members of the African Union

1. The Treaty creating the Organization for the Harmonization of Business Law in Africa (commonly abbreviated as "OHADA," from the French acronym), the Treaty, or OHADA Treaty, was signed by fourteen African Heads of States on Oct. 17, 1993 in Port Louis (Mauritius). Parts of the historical background of OHADA presented in this introduction have first appeared in my former publication: B. Mercadal, M.J.V. Kodo & Y. Agboyibo, *OHADA Member States*, in *International Bank and Other Guarantees Handbook: Middle East and Africa* 411-454(Y. Aubin, L. de Longeaux & J.C. Vecchiatto eds., Kluwer Law International 2011 (Mercadal, Agboyibo & Kodo, *OHADA Member States*, 2011). Unless otherwise specified, "the Treaty" refers to the OHADA Treaty throughout the entire book.
2. Official Journal of OHADA, N° 4, Nov. 1, 1997, p. 1 [Emphasis added]. (OHADA, 1997).
3. *Id.*
4. The OHADA Treaty was revised on Oct. 17, 2008 in Quebec (Canada).
5. In the order of ratification, the OHADA Member States are: Bissau Guinea (Jan. 15, 1994), Senegal (Jun. 14, 1994), Central African Republic (Jan. 13, 1995), Mali (Feb. 7, 1995), Comoros (Feb. 20, 1995), Burkina Faso (Mar. 6, 1995), Benin (Mar. 8, 1995), Niger (Jun. 5, 1995), Ivory Coast (Sep. 29, 1995), Cameroon (Oct. 20, 1995), Togo (Oct. 27, 1995), Chad (Apr. 13, 1996), Congo (May 28, 1997), Gabon (Feb. 2, 1998), Equatorial Guinea (Apr. 16, 1999) and Guinea (May 5, 2000). *See* Jacqueline Lohoues Oble, *Traité du 17 Octobre 1993 Relatif à l'Harmonisation du Droit des Affaires en Afrique*, in *OHADA: Traité et Actes Uniformes Commentés et Annotés,* 63 (J. Issa-Sayegh et al., eds., 2nd ed., Juriscope 2002). Democratic Republic of Congo (DRC) is the last country to sign the Treaty on OHADA, under the Law n° 10/002 on adhesion of Democratic Republic of Congo to OHADA, promulgated on Feb. 11, 2010: http://www.droit-afrique.com/upload/doc/rdc/RDC-Loi-2010-02-adhesion-OHADA.pdf, accessed Aug. 26, 2020. See also http://www.ohada.com/actualite/1614/depot-des-instruments-d-adhesion-de-la-rdc-a-l-ohada-dakar-13-juillet-2012.html, accessed Aug. 26, 2020.

(AU). Even non-AU countries are explicitly eligible to ratify the treaty, so long as the existing members approve their membership.[6]

The Treaty creates a dual legal system, where national laws coexist with the business legislation[7] instituted by OHADA. OHADA laws supersede national laws that cover the same subject matter. Thus, OHADA has limited jurisdiction, and it trumps only business laws, including procedures relating to OHADA laws. Adoption of the OHADA treaty modernizes business legislation in the member states by the process of unification, which substitutes the new legislation for preexisting national laws in relevant areas of business. Harmonization is also mentioned in the treaty since OHADA is an "organization for the harmonization of law." Harmonization integrates community law within the framework of national laws. It can be effected by replacing preexisting national laws with new laws, or by setting a framework within which non-identical national laws must be oriented to reach a common goal.[8] The law-making body of OHADA has used these two techniques of harmonization by fostering the enactment of new laws by coordinating with non-conflicting national legislation that remains applicable. The Treaty unifies business law by making the Uniform Acts as an integral part of the national legislation of the Member States without the necessity of further action by national parliaments. The Uniform Acts created under the Treaty[9] automatically and directly repeal all preexisting contrary legislation and supersede any future legislation in the covered areas.[10]

6. Under Article 53 of the revised OHADA (Oct. 17, 2008), The African Union (UA), current successor to the Organization of African Unity (OAU), may also be a party to the OHADA Treaty although not a sovereign nation.
7. "Business Legislation" in OHADA system, under Article 2 of the OHADA Treaty refer to "all the rules relating to corporate law and the legal status of traders, debt collection, security interests and enforcement, companies receivership and judicial liquidation, arbitration law, labor law, accounting law, sales and transport law, and any other matter that the Council of Ministers would unanimously decide to include, in accordance with the purpose of this treaty and under Article 8."
8. For more details, *see* J.A. Yakubu, *Community Laws in International Business Transactions*, in *Unified Business Law for Africa: Common Law Perspectives on OHADA*, 4 (C. Moore Dickerson ed., GMB Publishing 2009) (Yakubu, 2009). Although harmonization is mentioned in the Treaty, OHADA, in fact, unifies business law, and the word "harmonization" was used instead of "unification" consciously and for political reasons.
9. To date, ten Uniform Acts have been enacted, ratified and are enforceable: the Uniform Act Relating to General Commercial Law (Apr. 17, 1997, revised Dec. 15, 2010); Uniform Act Organizing Securities (Apr. 17, 1997, revised Dec. 15, 2010); Uniform Act Relating to Commercial Companies and Economic Interest Group (Apr. 17, 1997, revised Jan. 30, 2014); Uniform Act Organizing Collective Proceedings for Wiping Off Debts (Apr. 10, 1998, revised Sept. 10, 2015); Uniform Act Organizing Simplified Recovery Procedures and Measures of Enforcement (Apr. 10, 1998); Uniform Act on Arbitration (Mar. 11, 1999, revised Nov. 23, 2017); Uniform Act Organizing and Harmonizing Company Accounting Systems (Mar. 22, 2000, revised Jan. 26, 2017); Uniform Act on Contracts for the Carriage of Goods by Road (Mar. 22, 2003); Uniform Act Relating to Cooperative Companies (Dec. 15, 2010) and the Uniform Act on Mediation (Nov. 23, 2017).
10. OHADA Treaty, Art. 10. For an application by the CCJA, *see* Yovo v. Societe Togo Telecom, N° 043/2005, Decision, Common Court of Justice and Arbitration [C.C.J.A.] (Jul. 7, 2005), http://www.ohada.com/jurisprudence/ohadata/J-06-32.html.

Under Articles 27-31 and 41, the institutional framework of the organization consists of the Conference of Heads of States,[11] the Council of Ministers,[12] the Common Court of Justice and Arbitration (CCJA), the Permanent Secretary and a Regional School of magistracy. The CCJA is a supranational Court aimed at ensuring that the Uniform Acts are interpreted and applied uniformly, thereby further ensuring the unification of business laws across the OHADA Member States. The jurisdiction of the CCJA includes:[13]

1. review, as a supranational cassation Court, of decisions and rulings of Appellate or High Courts, Courts of appeal and non-appealable decisions rendered by any national court of Member States, but only in cases involving the application of the Uniform Acts. In most cases, after overturning or quashing a judgment of a lower court, the CCJA performs de novo review of the case, which is the main difference between the CCJA and other supreme or cassation courts, such as the Cassation court of France;
2. issuance of advisory opinions upon requests from Member states, the Permanent Secretary and any national court before which an OHADA-related case is pending;
3. administration of institutional arbitration proceedings under the CCJA Arbitration Rules.

As an appellate Court, the CCJA has the power to render final decisions in the cases brought before it. It has the same powers and acts as National Supreme Courts of the Member States of OHADA in the fields of OHADA Legislation. The CCJA has final and exclusive jurisdiction, and its decisions and rulings have the authority of a final judgment (res judicata) and are immediately enforceable in each Member State.[14] The CCJA has jurisdiction and is competent as long as any challenged decision of a national court contains issues or questions relating to the Uniform Act.[15] Therefore, the *CCJA has the final word regarding interpretation and application of the Uniform Acts*, except for criminal offenses.[16] However, in some limited cases, the CCJA can be flexible in its decisions.[17]

11. Under Article 27 of the Treaty, the Conference of Heads of States has exclusive jurisdiction to rule on any issue pertaining to the OHADA Treaty.
12. Often referred to as the "*Community legislator*, which is made up of all the member states of OHADA each with a different judicial organization from each other" (*see* Thales Security Systems v. Kattie, N° 034/2012, Decision, CCJA, 2^{e} ch. (Mar. 22, 2012) [emphasis added], the law-making body of OHADA, or the "OHADA Legislator" designates, under Articles 8 and 27 of the OHADA Treaty, mainly the Council of Ministers of OHADA and incidentally the Conference of Heads of State when it gathers to modify provisions of the Treaty.
13. OHADA Treaty, Art. 14.
14. *See id.* Art. 20.
15. Banque Internationale pour l'Afrique Occidentale—Côte d'Ivoire v. Societe Ivoirienne de Produits et de Negoce, N° 059/2005, Decision, [C.C.J.A.] (Dec. 22, 2005), http://www.ohada.com/jurisprudence/ohadata/J-06-36.html.
16. The subject matter jurisdiction (jurisdiction *ratione materiae*) of the CCJA is limited. The CCJA does not have jurisdiction to hear criminal cases, even if they are linked to cases brought before

This book is aimed at presenting in detail the two arbitration systems under OHADA Rules, equipping the practitioners with everything they need to know to conduct arbitral proceedings efficiently. It was much needed because there was no English publication on the topic in the world, while there is an increasing need for it. The Treaty covers a geographic scope of 9,124,233 km^2 and a population of 287,716,192 inhabitants, probably the largest and most populated regional integration Treaty on the African continent. Many of the States Parties to the Treaty in Africa are known for their mining of natural resources, many of which are part and parcel of many industries across the planet,[18] with some countries of the OHADA geographic zone owning more than 50% of the worldwide reserves of some rare minerals.[19] Many multinational companies that deal in minerals sign agreements with investment arbitration clauses within the OHADA States Parties, and it is important that the people who advise those companies are aware of the new arbitration regime currently in force in those seventeen countries, both for commercial and investor-state arbitration.

The OHADA Arbitration Rules having been recently revised, it was the right time for writing this book, with which practitioners would need to be acquainted if they are to provide good value arbitration services to their clients wherever they are situated across the planet and whatever their position (investors, governments, etc.).

The role of the CCJA both as an arbitral institution and the Court of Final Appeal for arbitral awards has been presented in the past,[20] and the focus of the present book

---

it and it cannot issue penalties. Member States have exclusive jurisdiction to issue and enforce penal sanctions per domestic criminal laws (*see* OHADA Treaty, Articles 5 and 14-3).

17. It can overrule its own prior decisions when there is a clerical error or a misinterpretation. A clerical error or scrivener's error is an error resulting from a minor mistake or inadvertence, in writing or copying something on the record, and not from judicial reasoning or determination. *Black's Law Dictionary* (B.A. Garner ed., 9th ed., WEST 2009) (Garner, 2009). For example the CCJA corrected a wrong date in a decision (Côte d'Ivoire Telecom v. Publistar, N° 015/2003, Decision, [C.C.J.A.] (Jul. 1, 2003), http://www.ohada.com/jurisprudence/ohadata/J-04-109.html, and overruled a decision which wrongfully ordered a winning party to pay costs (Office des Produits Vivriers du Niger v. Societe Nigerienne de Banque, N° 018/2007, Decision, [C.C.J.A.] (Apr. 26, 2007), http://www.ohada.com/jurisprudence/ohadata/J-08-235.html). An example of interpretation of Article 32 of the Uniform Act Organizing Simplified Recovery Procedures and Enforcement Measures can be seen in (Karnib v. Societe Generale de Banques en Côte d'Ivoire, N° 002/2001, Decision, [C.C.J.A.] (Oct. 11, 2001), http://www.ohada.com/jurisprudence/ohadata/J-02-06.html, www.ohada.com, Ohadata J-02-06), overruled by (Societe d'Exploitation Hôteliere et Immobiliere du Cameroun v. Societe Generale de banques au Cameroun, N° 012/2003, Decision, [C.C.J.A.] (Jun. 19, 2003), http://www.ohada.com/jurisprudence/ohadata/J-04-104.html).
18. This is the case of DRC, which is believed to be the second producer tantalum (coltan) worldwide, an indispensable mineral for the manufacture of mobiles phones and some other devices. *See* Amanda Kay, *5-Top Tantalum-Mining Countries*, https://investingnews.com/daily/resource-investing/critical-metals-investing/tantalum-investing/2013-top-tantalum-producers-rwanda-brazil-drc-canada/ [accessed May 8, 2020, at 16:15] (Kay, 2018).
19. DRC is also the first producer of cobalt, another key mineral for the electric automobile industry, with an estimate of more than 100,000 metric tons produced in 2019. *See* M. Garside, "Major countries in worldwide cobalt mine production from 2014 to 2019," https://www.statista.com/statistics/264928/cobalt-mine-production-by-country/ [accessed May 8, 2020, at 15:58] (Garside, 2020).
20. Mahutodji Jimmy Vital Kodo, Narcisse Aka, *The CCJA as a Regional Arbitration Institution*, in *The Transformation of Arbitration in Africa: The Role of Arbitral Institutions*, 47-59 (E. Onyema ed., Kluwer Law International 2016) (Kodo Mahutodji Jimmy Vital, 2016).

is to provide the reader with a clear and detailed presentation of the arbitration mechanisms available under OHADA Rules.

The most important thing to keep in mind while going through this book is that there are two different sets of Rules leading to two different procedural paths that must not be mixed.

In other words, the arbitration system is twofold under current OHADA Rules:

1. there is mainly ad hoc arbitration governed by the Uniform Act on Arbitration (UAA), which was revised on November 23, 2017 and entered into force on February 23, 2018;[21]
2. and an *institutional arbitration* under the aegis of the CCJA governed by the following Rules:
   - 2.1. Articles 21-25 of the Treaty;[22]
   - 2.2. The CCJA Regulation on Arbitration, which was revised on November 23, 2017 and entered into force on February 23, 2018, as well as its appendixes which are, to date, nine as follows;[23]
   - 2.3. Arbitration Bylaws of the CCJA of June 2, 1999;
   - 2.4. Prescriptive Decision of the CCJA N° 004/99/CCJA of February 3, 1999 on Arbitration Costs;[24]
   - 2.5. Prescriptive Decision of the CCJA N°020/2013/CCJA/ADM/ARB of March 14, 2013 Setting the Time Limit for Paying the Provisional Advance on Arbitration Costs;
   - 2.6. Prescriptive Decision of the CCJA N°022/2013/CCJA/ADM/ARB of March 14, 2013 Setting the Terms for the Advance Grant on the Arbitrator's Fees;
   - 2.7. Prescriptive Decision of the CCJA N°030-Bis/2004/CCJA/ADM/ARB of August 16, 2004 Setting the Terms of Allocation of Fees Among Arbitrators;
   - 2.8. Prescriptive Decision of the CCJA N° 50/2011/CCJA/ADM/ARB of October 10, 2011 Setting the Personal Costs of the Arbitrators and the Costs of the Arbitral Tribunal;
   - 2.9. Prescriptive Decision of the CCJA N°0198/2017/CCJA/ADM/ARB of December 18, 2017 on the Appointment of Administrative Secretaries and the Setting of Their Duties;
   - 2.10. Prescriptive Decision of the CCJA N°068/2018/CCJA/ADM/ARB of April 18, 2018 Setting the Terms and Conditions of Registration on the Arbitrators' List of the CCJA and its Updating;

---

21. *See* Appendix III, *infra*. At times, arbitration governed by the UAA may be institutional, especially where it is organized by a national or local arbitration center of any of the 17 States Parties to the OHADA Treaty.
22. *See* Appendix I, *infra*.
23. *See* Appendix II, *infra*.
24. OHADA Official Journal, No 8, May 15, 1999, pp. 21-22 (OHADA, 1999).

2.11. Prescriptive Decision of the CCJA N° 069/2018/CCJA/ADM/ARB of April 18, 2018 Setting the Costs of the Procedural Acts of the Court in Matters of Arbitration.

All but one of the States Parties to the Treaty are civil law countries, Cameroon being the only OHADA jurisdiction that also includes a common law tradition because it has both legal systems. Since March 21, 2010, when the revised version of the Treaty came into force,[25] all the four official languages of the States Parties (French, English, Spanish and Portuguese) became the working languages of OHADA.[26] Even though French is the prevailing language of the organization,[27] it has been specified, since the revised Treaty is enforceable, that no party to proceedings before the CCJA can be precluded from submitting briefs and exhibits in any of the four official languages.[28] The Treaty and most of the Uniform Acts were recently translated into English,[29] but there is, to date, no official English version of the new statutes enacted by the organization in November 2017 and which are the subject of the present book, namely the UAA and the CCJA Regulation on Arbitration. This situation raises some organizational and conceptual problems because of the prevalence of French in the Treaty. As a legal scholar from Cameroon puts it:

> Implicitly, any document in English or any other language would be a translation from French to English or Spanish or Portuguese. Most of the texts in translation have been criticized for being literal, inadequate and rather nebulous. They are simply approximations, and in many cases there are no legal equivalents in English. There is a need for co-drafting of future OHADA Uniform Acts in order to avoid translation. Furthermore, it would be desirable to have a co-revision team to work together on the existing Uniform Acts. This team should employ contextual meanings of terminologies and the adaptation approach to translation. Member States should develop an OHADA lexicon of words, phrases and concepts. This would go a long way, clarifying the misunderstandings of legal jargons and terminologies.[30]

The lack of an official English version, combined with the need for revision of the existing Uniform Acts, as highlighted by Ms. Tumde above, and the existence of some substantial inaccuracies in the non-official English version of the revised UAA and the

---

25. Newsletter, *OHADA.com*, (Mar. 4, 2010), http:// www.ohada.com/newsletter.php?news=040 32010-848# (UNIDA, 2010).
26. Revised version of OHADA Treaty, Art. 42, Oct. 17, 2008.
27. Under Article 42 of the Treaty, all the statutes and some other documents already published in French are fully enforceable before their translation into English, Spanish and Portuguese; and where there is a difference between the French version and one of the other languages, French prevails.
28. Trigon Energy Ltd v. Banque Commerciale du Sahel, N° 031/2011, Decision, [C.C.J.A.], 3e ch., (Dec. 6, 2011), http://www.ohada.com/jurisprudence/ohadata/J-13-167.html.
29. Official Bulletin of OHADA, Nov. 24, 2016, http://www.ohada.org/index.php/en/component/content/article?id=1848:official-bulletin-of-ohada-special-edition-nov-2016 (OHADA, 2016).
30. Martha Simo Tumnde, "OHADA as Experienced in Cameroon: Addressing Areas of Particular Concern to Common Law Jurists," in *Unified Business Law for Africa: Common Law Perspectives on OHADA*, 2 ed. C. Moore Dickerson (London: GMB Publishing, 2012), 84 (Tumnde, 2012).

CCJA Regulation on Arbitration available on the official website of the organization,[31] have prompted me to carry out a full revision of those versions of the two statues *before* starting to write this book. Alongside that, some editorial policy decisions have had to be made for the purposes of clarity, simplicity and consistency.

For example, Under Article 12, paragraph 2 of the UAA in my improved version, "The legal or contractual time limit for the arbitration may be extended, either *by* agreement of the parties, or at the request of one of the parties or of the arbitral tribunal, *by* the competent court in the State Party." "Or" has been removed before "by" because if not removed, the sentence would mean that the competent court in the State Party can also request the extension of the time limit, which is not what the original French version of the Uniform Act states.

In the CCJA Regulation on Arbitration, Article 3.2 of my improved version states that "Arbitrators may be chosen from the list of arbitrators drawn up by the Court and updated annually. The members of the Court *cannot* be included on the said list." "*May be*" has been replaced with "*cannot*" because the translated version "The members of the Court *may be included* on the said list" conveys exactly the opposite of the original French version, as well as Article 3 of the Arbitration Bylaws of the CCJA of June 2, 1999 under which *no member of the CCJA can be personally involved in arbitration proceedings* under the CCJA Rules.

I also restored the right content of the CCJA Regulation on Arbitration, Article 22.3 paragraph 3, which states "However, if *one or two arbitrators refuse* to sign the award, it must be mentioned and the award has the same effect as if it had been signed by all the arbitrators." "A *minority* of them refuses" has been replaced with "*one or two* arbitrators refuse." It is important to note that the French original version specifically refers to the refusal of "one or two arbitrators" ("*si un arbitre ou deux arbitres refusent de la signer*"). Therefore, this passage cannot be translated by 'a minority' because two arbitrators out of three are absolutely not a minority. I also added the missing parts of some provisions and reorganized the paragraphs as did the Legislator.[32]

In order to avoid any confusion in reference to the rules, I changed the title "*Arbitration Rules* of the Common Court of Justice and Arbitration" into the "*Regulation* of the Common Court of Justice and Arbitration on Arbitration" (the CCJA Regulation on Arbitration),[33] because as mentioned *supra*, institutional arbitration under the aegis of the CCJA is governed by a set of rules (currently 11), of which only one is the Regulation on Arbitration. Thus, calling that single rule "Arbitration Rules of the CCJA" would be confusing in singling out all the other ten rules that are part of the set.

Likewise, in the vast majority of cases where an obligation is expressed by the Legislator, I replaced "shall" with "must" in the UAA and the CCJA Regulation on

31. The unofficial revised English version of the CCJA Regulation on Arbitration is available at: https://www.ohada.org/attachments/article/2490/Reglement-Arbitrage_CCJA-English.pdf; and the UAA is available at: https://www.ohada.org/attachments/article/2490/Acte-uniforme-Arbitrage-English.pdf, both links accessed Apr. 9, 2020.
32. For example, the last paragraph (8th) was omitted at Article 26 of the CCJA Regulation on Arbitration and I added it. *See* Appendix II, *infra*.
33. *See* Appendix II, *infra*.

Arbitration to be in line with the rule in *Gutierrez de Martinez v. Lamagno*, where the U.S. Supreme Court held that "shall" means "may,"[34] and which is widely acknowledged across majors common law jurisdictions across the planet such as Australia, United Kingdom, and Canada where "certain drafters ... have determined that drafters cannot be trusted to correctly use the word 'shall' and have forbidden its use."[35] In few cases, "shall" has been replaced with the present indicative tense, which is widely known to convey an obligation or a mandatory rule in many major Civil Law jurisdictions such as Canada (because of Quebec)[36] and France,[37] as well as in the States Parties to the Treaty, as demonstrated by the ruling in *Ngot v. Dietsman Technologie Internationale*, where the Court of Appeal of Pointe-Noire (Congo) held that "*It follows from the use of the present indicative ... that these provisions [containing the present indicative] are mandatory and confer a public order character.*"[38]

I also simplified and clarified the style, for example by replacing "pursuant to" with "under" or "in accordance with," for reference to a provision of the rules and used gender-neutral expressions such as the singular "they" or "them" instead of "he" or

34. Gutierrez de Martinez v. Lamagno 515 U.S. 417 (1995), https://supreme.justia.com/cases/federal/us/515/417/ [accessed May 3, 2020, at 20:40].
35. Jery Payne, "The False imperative," http://www.ncsl.org/legislators-staff/legislative-staff/research-editorial-legal-and-committee-staff/volume-xxvi-issue-2-the-false-imperative.aspx [accessed Aug. 6, 2019, at 11:39] (Payne), citing Bryan A. Garner, *Garner on Language and Writing* 174-175 (2009) (Garner, 2009). *See also* the Federal Aviation Administration (FAA), "What's the Only Word That Means Mandatory? Here's What Law and Policy Say about 'Shall, Will, May, And Must'," available at: https://www.faa.gov/about/initiatives/plain_language/articles/mandatory/ [accessed May 2, 2020], stating that "'Must' is the only word that imposes a legal obligation on your readers to tell them something is mandatory" (Federal Aviation Administration, s.d.).
36. Under Article 24(1) of the Legislative Drafting Conventions of the Uniform Law Conference of Canada, "Verbs should appear in the present tense and indicative mood unless the context requires an exception." Department of Justice of Canada, *Legistics. Present Indicative,* https://canada.justice.gc.ca/eng/rp-pr/csj-sjc/legis-redact/legistics/p2p3.html [accessed May 3, 2020, at 17:10] (Canada).
37. In 2008, the Constitutional Court of France held that "the use of *the present indicative having imperative value,* the substitution of the present of the indicative for a wording formulated in terms of obligation does not remove their imperative character from the provisions of the new Labor Code" (Conseil Constitutionnel [CC] [Constitutional Court] Decision No. 2007-561 DC, Jan. 17, 2008, at No 17, https://www.conseil-constitutionnel.fr/decision/2008/2007561DC.htm [accessed May 2, 2020, at 16:12]). [Emphasis added].
38. Ngot v. Dietsman Technologie Internationale, CA Pointe-Noire, Jul. 7, 2005, N° 142, (Congo), http://www.ohada.com/jurisprudence/ohadata/J-13-127.html. The Court ruled that:

> *It follows from the use of the present indicative* in Article 170 paragraph 1 of the Uniform Act Organizing Simplified Recovery Procedures and Measures of Enforcement (UAOS-RPME) in relation to the form in which such challenges are brought before the competent judge, *that these provisions are mandatory and confer a public order character* upon the demurrer which is established there so that the first judge was bound to raise it ex officio. By not having done so, he violated the aforementioned Article 170 and Articles 142, 200 of the Code of Civil Commercial Administrative and Financial Procedure of Congo and the challenged order must be set aside in all its provisions. [Emphasis added]

"she" or "their" instead of "her" or "his," according to the most recent rules of the American Psychological Association (APA).[39]

While most of these changes were required to restore the exact meaning of the translated rules, some of these changes were simple editorial choices aimed at improving the style and without pretending having done a perfect job, I believe my improvements to the translated rules, which are all shown in italics in the Appendixes, will enhance the rules and ensure their efficient use by the readers, whatever their purpose may be.

The book is structured in five parts: **Part I** will present the arbitration agreement under the OHADA Rules. **Part II** will present the arbitration procedure; **Part III** will be dedicated to the arbitral award. **Part IV** will present the possible remedies and recourse against arbitral awards, and **Part V** will focus on recognition, enforcement and other effects of arbitral awards.

39. Woodworth, A. T., & Adams, A. A. (n.d.). *Publication Manual of the American Psychological Association* (7th ed., Woodworth & Adams, 2020).

PART I The Arbitration Agreement

The unique chapter of this first part of the book presents the basics of the arbitration agreement, which is the foundation and starting point of any arbitration proceedings.

CHAPTER 1

Formation, Validity and Legality of Arbitral Agreements

For arbitration to take place, there must first be a valid arbitration agreement. This chapter will present the requirements of the Rules with regard to the parties to an arbitration agreement (§1.01), acceptance of the agreement (§1.02), specific conditions for the validity of the agreement (§1.03), the effects of a valid arbitration agreement between the parties (§1.04) and finally the specifics of interpretation of arbitration agreements under the two sets of arbitration available under the OHADA Rules (§1.05).

§1.01 PARTIES TO THE ARBITRAL AGREEMENT

The essential information to be known about the parties to an arbitration agreement will be presented in this section for both the UAA (§1.01[A]) and the CCJA Arbitration Rules (§1.01[B]).

[A] Under the Uniform Act on Arbitration

The arbitration agreement may be in the form of either an arbitration clause or a submission agreement. The arbitration clause is the agreement by which the parties undertake to submit to arbitration disputes, which may arise or result from a contractual relationship. The submission agreement is the agreement by which the parties to an existing dispute agree to settle it through arbitration.[1]

Article 2 of the UAA states:

> Any natural or legal person may resort to arbitration with respect to any rights on which they have the free disposal.

1. UAA, Art. 3-1, para. 1-3.

> States, other public territorial authorities, public entities and any other legal person under public law may also be parties to arbitration, regardless of the legal nature of the contact, without being able to invoke their own law to object to the arbitrability of a dispute, to their capacity to submit to arbitration or to the validity of the arbitration agreement.[2]

Under Article 2 above, any type of person enjoying their rights and having legal capacity can agree to submit to arbitration under the UAA. That provision raises questions as to who can resort to arbitration, i.e., the types of persons (§1.01[A][1]) and for what type of disputes (§1.01[A][2]).

[1] Different Types of Persons Who Can Resort to Arbitration under the UAA

Natural persons (§1.01[A][1][i]), as well as States Parties to the Treaty (§1.01[A][1][ii]) can resort to arbitration under the UAA.

[i] Natural and Legal Persons

In a decision by the Court of Appeal of Abidjan, this rule has been applied to the representative of a corporation. The Court ruled that the UAA allows any individual or legal entity to resort to arbitration on the rights to which it has free disposition. It is, therefore, in vain that the representative of a newspaper raises the nullity of an arbitration clause in the partnership agreement binding them to the appealing party since it is the infringement of the rights ceded in that contract that is the cause of the referral to the Court and the action is also directed against the appealing party in that capacity. Therefore, national courts must decline jurisdiction and refer the parties to arbitration, in accordance with their contract.[3]

[ii] States Parties to the Treaty

A State Party to the Treaty cannot invoke its own laws to challenge the validity of an arbitration agreement signed by its Minister of Finance, since, in the circumstances of the signing of the agreement, the representatives of the other party could legitimately believe in the powers of that Minister, who was also the Monetary Authority of that State. Therefore, the arbitral tribunal was right in considering itself competent to rule on the dispute by rendering the challenged arbitral award.[4]

2. UAA, Art. 2. *See* the full text in Appendix III, *infra*.
3. CA Abidjan, Jun. 6, 2005, 1re ch. civ. & com., N° 585 (Ivory Coast), http://www.ohada.com/jurisprudence/ohadata/J-08-78.html.
4. République de Guinée équatoriale v. Commercial Bank Guinea Equatorial, N° 012/2015, Decision, [C.C.J.A.], 3e ch., (Nov. 29, 2015), http://www.ohada.com/jurisprudence/ohadata/J-13-142.html.

[2] Types of Disputes Likely to Be Resolved by Arbitration under the UAA

Contractual disputes (§1.01[A][2][i]) and disputes relating to the employment of some corporate executives (§1.01[A][2][ii]) will be handled below.

[i] Contractual Disputes

The arbitration clause inserted in a contract between two persons who are not traders is valid because the UAA does not require all parties to be traders. In the presence of such a clause, state courts do not have jurisdiction for disputes arising from this contract.[5]

[ii] Disputes Relating to the Employment of Corporate Executives

Apart from certain employment contracts of some executives of corporations, most countries, in general, do not allow employer-employee and all other related disputes to be submitted to arbitration. In a case involving retired executives of an international organization claiming some unpaid benefit, a Court of Appeal ruled that in the presence of an arbitration clause included in the Executive Employment Regulations of the Agency for Air Navigation Safety in Africa and Madagascar,[6] executives who have retired without receiving their severance pay are admissible to file a motion before the competent judge for interim measures[7] for the appointment of an arbitrator.[8]

[B] Under the CCJA Rules

In general, the rules regarding the parties to arbitration under the CCJA Rules are quite similar to those of the UAA with regards to the parties bound by an arbitration agreement. Article 9 of the CCJA Regulation on arbitration states:

> Where, prima facie, there is no arbitration agreement between the parties requiring the application of this Regulation on arbitration, if the respondent objects to the arbitration of the Court or does not file a response within the thirty (30) days referred to in Article 6 above, the claimant is informed by the Secretary General

5. CA Abidjan, Jul. 30, 2002, N° 1032 (Ivory Coast), http://www.ohada.com/jurisprudence/ohadata/J-03-28.html.
6. The Agency for Aerial Navigation Safety in Africa and Madagascar ("*L'Agence pour la Sécurité de la Navigation aérienne en Afrique et à Madagascar* (ASECNA)") is an air traffic control agency based in Dakar, Senegal. It is composed of 18 Member States; 17 African States and France (Benin, Burkina Faso, Cameroon, Central African Republic, Chad, Comoros, Congo, Ivory Coast, Equatorial Guinea, France, Gabon, Guinea Bissau, Madagascar, Mali, Mauritania, Niger, Senegal, and Togo). As an international public organization, it has a special status that allows its staff to submit to arbitration.
7. This refers to the "*Juge des référés.*" *See* the glossary & defined terms, *supra*.
8. CA Abidjan, Jul. 2, 2003, Ord. réf. N° 1435 (Ivory Coast), http://www.ohada.com/jurisprudence/ohadata/J-04-177.html.

> that he intends to refer the matter to the Court with a view to seeing it decide that arbitration cannot take place.
>
> The Court rules in light of the claimant's comments submitted within the following thirty (30) days if the latter deems them necessary.

Under exceptional circumstances, an arbitration agreement can be extended to a person who is not a party to the agreement. The ruling of the CCJA in *Compagnie Malienne pour le Développement des Textiles v. Société Inter Africaine de Distribution* provides a good illustration of this situation. A dispute arose between the claimants, two corporations, and the respondent, another corporation, about the supply of some herbicides. The respondent first sued the two claimants before state courts. The claimants declined the jurisdiction of state courts, alleging there was an arbitration agreement between the claimants that is applicable to the respondent. The state courts declined jurisdiction, and after the respondent referred the dispute to arbitration under the CCJA Rules, the two claimants argued that there was no valid arbitration agreement between them and the respondent justifying the arbitration proceedings. The CCJA decided that the arbitration will proceed under its arbitration rules. The arbitral tribunal rendered an award by which it determined it has no jurisdiction to handle the dispute. By another decision, the CCJA ruled that the arbitral tribunal did have jurisdiction, and the arbitral proceedings could resume at the initiative of the most diligent party. Twice, the two claimants petitioned the CCJA for review of its decision affirming the jurisdiction of the arbitral tribunal and were unsuccessful. The respondent applied for the resumption of the arbitration proceedings, and the CCJA appointed a sole arbitrator, who rendered a final award. The respondent then applied for *exequatur* of the award and the two claimants challenged the award, alleging, among other claims, that the award violated Article 10.3 of the CCJA Regulation on arbitration and was in breach of international public policy because the arbitrator determined they have jurisdiction on the sole basis of the ruling of the CCJA mentioned above, instead of ruling on their own jurisdiction under the *competence-competence* principle. The Court ruled that:

> The claimants, who themselves have inferred that the contract binding them must be extended to the respondent and for that reason, the dispute must be referred to arbitration, thereby raising the lack of jurisdiction of the state judges, which have been enshrined in final and binding decisions of the state courts, cannot validly challenge the arbitral award for breaching international public policy in that the arbitral tribunal extended the arbitration clause to the respondent who was not a signatory of the said clause; plea rejected.[9]

9. Compagnie Malienne pour le Développement des Textiles v. Société Inter Africaine de Distribution, N° 160/2016, Decision, [C.C.J.A.], Ass. plen., (Dec. 1, 2016), http://www.ohada.com/jurisprudence/ohadata/J-17-100.html.

§1.02 ACCEPTANCE OF THE ARBITRATION AGREEMENT

The specifics of acceptance of an arbitration agreement will be presented for the UAA (§1.02[A]) and the CCJA Rules (§1.02[B]).

[A] Under the UAA

The arbitration agreement is a contract by which the parties entrust the arbitrator with the mission to settle their dispute, and it must be assessed according to the common will of the parties. The fact that a party to a dispute did not react to the other party's proposal on a possible arbitration proves that it did not express its will to conclude the agreement, and for that reason, it did participate neither in the appointment of the arbitrator nor in the proceedings. This is particularly so since it appears from the memorandum of understanding signed by the parties that in the event of a dispute arising from the contract, they elect domicile with the courts. In the present case, the arbitration agreement, which was not accepted by all the parties, does not exist and results in the nullity of the award.[10] Likewise, the annulment of the authentic instrument, which served as the basis for an arbitral award, entails the annulment of that award, which no longer has any ground.[11]

It has also been ruled that the willingness to submit a dispute to arbitration must be clearly expressed in the parties' agreement. The clause that assigns jurisdiction to the state judge entails the waiver of the parties to the arbitration, and the order of the judge appointing an arbitrator under such circumstances must be retracted, at the request of the most diligent party, for breach of contractual will.[12]

[B] Under the CCJA Rules

Under *Etat du Mali v. Société CFAO*,[13] the CCJA has set an essential rule to be taken from Article 9 of the CCJA Rules above, namely that consent to arbitration is not presumed and in the absence of evidence of the oral consent of the opposing party, the arbitral tribunal ruled without an arbitration agreement, and its award must be annulled.

10. CA Centre, Sept. 30, 2009, N° 381/Civ., (Cameroon), http://www.ohada.com/jurisprudence/ohadata/J-10-33.html.
11. CA Littoral, May 16, 2008, N° 060/C., (Cameroon), http://www.ohada.com/jurisprudence/ohadata/J-19-124.html.
12. TPI Yaounde-Ekounou, May 6, 2013, Ord. N° 185, (Cameroon), http://www.ohada.com/jurisprudence/ohadata/J-14-125.html.
13. Etat du Mali v. Société CFAO, N° 039/2014, Decision, [C.C.J.A.], Ass. plen., (Apr. 17, 2014), http://www.ohada.com/jurisprudence/ohadata/J-15-130.html.

§1.03 VALIDITY OF THE ARBITRATION AGREEMENT

Regardless of the UAA of the CCJA Arbitration Rules, as a contract, the arbitration agreement must meet specific conditions under national laws applicable to contracts, such as consent and legal capacity, among others. A recurring issue in the arbitration is the validity of arbitration clauses incorporated by reference. The issue of whether arbitration clauses incorporated by reference are enforceable or not does not seem to have been handled under the CCJA Arbitration Rules yet, but it has been under the UAA. In *Atlantique Telecom v. Planor Afrique & Telecel Faso,*[14] the CCJA ruled on the issue that:

> It is a general principle of law that in international arbitration, the arbitration clause incorporated by written reference to a document containing it is valid, even if it is not mentioned in the main agreement, where the party to which the clause is opposed has had knowledge of the content of this document at the time of conclusion of the contract and had accepted the incorporation of the document into the contract. When, as in the present case, a Court of Appeal, after examining the various transactions between the parties, has determined with judicial discretion[15] and by a reasoned decision, that the arbitration clause contained in a shareholders' agreement is not enforceable against a party if it appears nowhere in the file that that party was aware of the said clause and expressed the will to be bound by the arbitration agreement, the argument against this judgment is devoid of merit and must be dismissed.

Likewise, it was held, in *Roger v. Fofana*, that:

> An arbitration clause stipulating that "any litigation which could arise from the interpretation, the execution and the termination of this contract" is binding as well on the judges of appeal as to the litigants including notably the defendant in the appeal, which, although not being signatory of the contract involved, necessarily finds in its object and enforcement the ground of their real or alleged quality of pursuing creditor or, at the very least, agent ..., to fetch a commission on the market defined by the aforementioned contract. Thus, by ignoring the arbitration clause, the Court of Appeal, ruling as it did, set out its decision to be quashed.[16]

14. Atlantique Telecom v. Planor Afrique, N° 041/2010, Decision, [C.C.J.A.], 1st ch., (Jun. 10, 2010), http://www.ohada.com/jurisprudence/ohadata/J-11-85.html.
15. In the original French case, there is a reference to the "*pouvoir souverain d'appréciation du juge,*" which is the equivalent of the "judicial discretion" as "A liberty or privilege allowed to a judge, within the confines of right and justice, but independent of narrow and unbending rules of positive law, to decide and act in accordance with what is fair, equitable, and wholesome, as determined upon the peculiar circumstances of the case, and as discerned by his personal wisdom and experience, guided by the spirit, principles, and analogies of the law" (*Black's Law Dictionary* Free Online Legal Dictionary (2nd ed., https://thelawdictionary.org/discretion/)). For an illustration, *see* Osborn v. United States Bank, 9 Wheat 866, 6 L. Ed. 204: https://www.courtlistener.com/opinion/85451/osborn-v-bank-of-united-states/.
16. Roger v. Fofana, N° 024/2010, Decision, [C.C.J.A.], 2e ch., (Apr. 8, 2010).

§1.04 EFFECTS OF ARBITRATION AGREEMENTS

A valid arbitration agreement is binding for the parties (§1.04[A]) and entails the lack of jurisdiction of any State court (§1.04[B]).

[A] Mandatory Nature of the Arbitration Agreement on the Parties

In both arbitration systems,[17] parties are bound by their valid arbitration agreement. Article 10 of the UAA states that parties are "committed to applying the arbitration rules" of the institution they have referred their dispute to unless they have waived some provisions of those rules where it is possible.[18]

By agreeing to resort to arbitration under the CCJA Arbitration Rules,[19] parties "submit *ipso facto*"[20] to those rules by which they are bound. The mandatory nature of the arbitration agreement is also emphasized by Article 10.1 of the CCJA Regulation on arbitration, which states that "If one of the parties refuses or abstains from participating in the arbitration, the arbitration takes place notwithstanding that refusal or abstention."[21]

[B] The Lack of Jurisdiction of Courts of Law

The second main consequence of the existence of a valid arbitration agreement is the lack of jurisdiction of any court to resolve a dispute the parties to a contract have agreed to refer to arbitration. Applying Article 23 of the Treaty in *Sow v. Aka*, the CCJA ruled that a court to which a dispute that the parties have agreed to submit to arbitration has been referred must decline jurisdiction when one of the parties so requests. Retaining jurisdiction to uphold the judgment under all of its provisions, on the grounds that the dispute here relates to the validity and therefore the very existence of the agreement and not to its application; in these conditions, the arbitration clause, which only operates in the execution of the agreement, cannot be enforced in the present case; it is, therefore, right that the first judge retained its jurisdiction, the Court of Appeal has erred in its application of Articles 23 of the Treaty, and its ruling must be quashed. Upon de novo review, the CCJA must set aside the judgment undertaken, decline jurisdiction because of the arbitration clause, and refer the case and the parties to the arbitration procedure provided for in their agreement.[22]

Similarly, the clause inserted in the articles of association of a company and stipulating that "for all disputes between the company and the shareholders, their heirs or representatives resulting from these articles of association, the appeal is submitted

17. Arbitration under the UAA and arbitration under the CCJA Arbitration Rules.
18. UAA, Art. 10 para 1.
19. It must be remembered that there is a set of rules governing the institutional arbitration under the CCJA Rules, as stated *supra*, in the introduction.
20. CCJA Regulation on arbitration, Art. 10.1.
21. *Ibid.*, Art. 10.2.
22. Sow v. Aka, N° 020/2008, Decision, [C.C.J.A.], 1st ch., (Apr. 24, 2008), http://www.ohada.com/jurisprudence/ohadata/J-09-46.html.

to the arbitration of the International Commercial Chamber" [sic], is well within the scope of arbitration under Articles 21 and 23 of the Treaty. In the presence of such an arbitration clause, the state judge had to decline jurisdiction as requested by one of the parties, and the Court of Appeal was right in affirming the judgment by which the lower court judge declined jurisdiction.[23]

The CCJA also applies Article 13 of the UAA to enforce the lack of jurisdiction of national courts in the presence of an arbitral agreement.[24]

However, in some rare cases, courts of law sometimes admit an exception to the lack of jurisdiction of courts of law in the presence of an arbitration agreement, notably because of the reckless behavior of a party who hindered the implementation of an arbitration agreement. In *Entreprise Ivoirienne de Construction Bâtiment v. Groupe Eoulee*, the CCJA held that while it is true that party autonomy legally expressed through an arbitration clause becomes the law for these parties, this autonomy must only be respected if it is based on the loyalty of the parties who cannot contradict themselves when, by their bad faith behavior, one of them makes the other party lose confidence. In the case at hand, the express, certain and unequivocal waiver of the appellant to the application of the arbitration clause can only be analyzed by a just sanction for the unilateral behavior of the appellee who has remained indifferent to all the steps taken by the appellant under the arbitration clause of the contract. Consequently, the waiver of the appellant, based on the behavior of the appellee, which triggered legal proceedings by the appellant before the Court of First Instance of Abidjan, must be examined by the judge and not by the arbitral tribunal. Therefore, the Court of law rightfully retained its jurisdiction.[25]

§1.05 INTERPRETATION OF ARBITRAL AGREEMENTS

The general "*competence-competence*" principle, by which an arbitral tribunal has jurisdiction to interpret the arbitration agreement on the basis of which the dispute has been referred to it, even if the decision of the tribunal on the meaning and the implications of the arbitration agreement may not be final,[26] is well established under

23. Gomez v. Banque de l'Afrique Occidentale, N° 035/2010, Decision, [C.C.J.A.], 2e ch., (Jun. 3, 2010), http://www.ohada.com/jurisprudence/ohadata/J-11-79.html.
24. Resocom v. Financial House, N° 230/2017, Decision, [C.C.J.A.], 3e ch., (Dec. 14, 2017). *See also* United Bank of Africa v. Grassfields Holdings Limited, N° 129/2016, Decision, [C.C.J.A.], 3e ch., (Juil. 7, 2016), where the CCJA ruled, under Art. 13 of the UAA, that in the presence of an arbitration agreement, the competent judge for interim measures can order only provisional or protective measures without prejudicing the merits and any ruling of such judge on the merits must be overturned; Société Générale de Surveillance v. La République Démocratique du Congo, N° 178/2020, Decision, [C.C.J.A.], 1e ch., (May 28, 2020).
25. Entreprise Ivoirienne de Construction Bâtiment v. Groupe Eoulee, N° 012/2012, Decision, [C.C.J.A.], 1e ch., (Mar. 8, 2012). In Transrail v. Canac Senegal, N° 040/2020, Decision, [C.C.J.A.], 1e ch., (Feb. 13, 2020), it was also held that since contracts result from the autonomy of the will of parties and must be performed in good faith, the trust which underpins the recourse to arbitration is undermined when a party to a chain of contracts is convicted of fraud.
26. Philippe Fouchard, Emmanuel Gaillard & Berthold Goldman, *Fouchard, Gaillard, Goldman on International Arbitration*, § 473, 254 (Kluwer Law International, 1999) (Fouchard, Gaillard, & Goldman, 1999).

OHADA rules and generally well enforced by state courts handling cases under the UAA (§1.05[A]), as well as the CCJA handling cases relating to the two arbitration systems under OHADA Rules (§1.05[B]).[27]

[A] Under the UAA

Under *Société Phondace Sarl v. Société Nationale des Eaux du Sénégal*, the Court of Appeal of Dakar, Senegal ruled that it follows from Article 11 of the UAA that the arbitral tribunal rules on its own jurisdiction, including all questions relating to the existence or validity of the arbitration agreement.[28] The same court then went further to specify that "it is inferred from Articles 2 and 11 of the UAA that the challenge relating to the capacity of a state-owned corporation[29] to sign an arbitration agreement is within the jurisdiction of the arbitral tribunal and not of the state court which must decline jurisdiction as soon as it finds the existence of an arbitration clause or a submission agreement. The judgment of the lower court, which declined jurisdiction for the benefit of the arbitral tribunal must be affirmed."[30]

[B] Under the CCJA Arbitration Rules

The power of an arbitral tribunal to interpret arbitration agreements under the CCJA arbitration rules is implied through the wording of Articles 10.3, 10.4 and 15.1.b, 5.e 6.b and 6.d.

First, Article 10.3 of the CCJA Regulation on arbitration states:

> Where one party raises one or more arguments relating to the existence, validity or scope of the arbitration agreement, the Court, having found prima facie the existence of this agreement, may decide, without prejudging the admissibility or the merits of these arguments, that the arbitration will take place. In this case, it will be up to the arbitral tribunal to make all decisions on its own jurisdiction.[31]

Where the CCJA, in its administrative capacity,[32] determines prima facie that there is an arbitration agreement, it decides the arbitration must proceed, and from that moment, the arbitral tribunal is empowered to make all relevant decisions including on its jurisdiction. In ruling on its jurisdiction, the arbitral tribunal will inevitably have to assess the agreement of the parties and some factual circumstances and evidence before making its determination. That process entails, to some extent, under the circumstances of each case, an interpretation of the arbitration clause or submission agreement of the parties. In light of this, the CCJA ruled that a tribunal which

27. Namely, the UAA and the CCJA Arbitration Rules, as mentioned in the introduction, *supra*.
28. Société Phondace Sarl v. Société Nationale des Eaux du Sénégal, N° n°339, Decision, CA Dakar, Jul. 7, 2018, unpublished.
29. For the expression translated as a state-owned or public corporation, *see* the glossary, *infra*.
30. Société Phondace Sarl v. Société Nationale des Eaux du Sénégal, N° n°339, *supra*.
31. CCJA Regulation on arbitration, Art. 10.3.
32. The CCJA acting under Art. 1 and 2 of its Regulation on arbitration as administrative body supporting the arbitration.

determined, on the ground of a ruling of the CCJA, that it had jurisdiction to resolve a dispute, ruled well on its jurisdiction in accordance with Article 10.3 of the CCJA Regulation on arbitration which it did not violate.[33]

Second, Article 10.4 clearly states that:

> The arbitral tribunal has *exclusive jurisdiction to rule on its own jurisdiction and on the admissibility of the request* for arbitration.
>
> Unless otherwise stipulated, *if the arbitral tribunal considers that the arbitration agreement is valid* and the contract binding the parties is null or nonexistent, the arbitral tribunal is competent to determine the respective rights of the parties and rule on their claims and submissions.[34]

In order to reach the conclusion that "the arbitration agreement is valid," the tribunal, which "has exclusive jurisdiction to rule on its own jurisdiction and on the admissibility of the request for arbitration," must interpret the agreement of the parties.

Finally, during the case management conference, which is an important step of the arbitration proceedings, the arbitral tribunal will have "b) to determine *whether an agreement exists between the parties on the issues listed in Articles 5(e) and 6 (b) and (d)* [of the CCJA Regulation on arbitration]. In the absence of such an agreement, the arbitral tribunal *determines* that the award will have to settle this issue."[35] The issues listed in articles 5(e), 6 (b) and 6(d) are pertaining to:

- "agreements between the parties on the seat of arbitration, the language of arbitration, the law applicable to the arbitration agreement, the arbitration proceedings and the merits of the dispute; in the absence of such agreements, the wishes of the claimant for arbitration on these various issues are expressed";[36]
- b) "confirmation or not of the existence of an *arbitration* agreement resulting from a contract or any other instrument *between the parties referring to arbitration under this Regulation*";[37]
- d) "the responses of the respondent *on all* the issues raised in the request for arbitration under paragraphs (d) and (e) of Article 5 above."[38]

Again, handling all the issues mentioned above will require the arbitral tribunal to do some interpretation work at some stage of the proceedings as the circumstances may require.

---

33. Compagnie Malienne pour le Développement des Textiles v. Société Inter Africaine de Distribution, N° 160/2016, Decision, [C.C.J.A.], Ass. plen., (Dec. 1, 2016), http://www.ohada.com/jurisprudence/ohadata/J-17-100.html.
34. CCJA Regulation on arbitration, Art. 10.4. [Emphasis added].
35. *Id.*, Art. 15.1.b.
36. *Id.*, Art. 5.e.
37. CCJA Regulation on arbitration, Art. 6.b.
38. *Id.*, Art. 6.d.

PART II The Arbitration Procedure

This second part on the arbitration procedure is formed of nine chapters, on the selection, challenge and replacement of arbitrators (Chapter 2), rights and duties of arbitrators (Chapter 3), selection of the arbitral seat (Chapter 4), the choice of the procedure by the parties (Chapter 5), evidence and discovery (Chapter 6), provisional measures(Chapter 7), consolidation, joinder, and intervention (Chapter 8), confidentiality (Chapter 9) and finally, legal representation and professional conduct (Chapter 10).

CHAPTER 2
Selection, Challenge and Replacement of Arbitrators

The four main sections of this chapter will deal with the number (§2.01) and selection of arbitrators (§2.02), their independence and impartiality (§2.03), as well as their challenge and replacement (§2.04).

§2.01 NUMBER OF ARBITRATORS

Under both arbitration systems, an arbitral tribunal can be made up of either a sole arbitrator or three arbitrators.

[A] Under the UAA

Article 5 of the UAA starts by specifying that "the assignment of an arbitrator can be performed only by a natural person."[1] Then it continues by stating that "the arbitral tribunal is made up of either a sole arbitrator or three arbitrators. In the absence of agreement between the parties, the arbitral tribunal is made up of a sole arbitrator."[2] In a UAA-governed arbitration, the parties will need to ensure that the number of arbitrators they want in a tribunal handling their dispute is specified in their arbitration agreement, whatever its form (arbitration clause or compromise agreement). Depending on the stakes of the dispute, especially financial, they may want to retain more control in the arbitration process by providing for a three-member tribunal, because their silence would result in the appointment of a single arbitrator.

One may wonder what would happen where parties would stipulate arbitration by only two arbitrators? Article 6 paragraph 2 of the UAA states that "where the parties have agreed to appoint two arbitrators despite the provisions of Article 5, paragraph 2

1. UAA, Art. 5, para. 1.
2. *Id.*, Art. 5, para. 2.

of this Uniform Act, the arbitral tribunal *is* supplemented by a third arbitrator mutually chosen by the parties. The same applies in the case of an appointment made necessary by reason of recusal, incapacity, death, resignation or dismissal of an arbitrator."[3]

A ruling of the CCJA in *Sarci Sarl v. Atlantique Telecom Sa* provides an interesting illustration of the answer. The arbitration clause of the parties stipulated that two arbitrators were to be appointed, and the arbitrators will have to appoint a third one only if the first two arbitrators could not agree on an award. The Court of Appeal determined that that stipulation of the parties, in the context of arbitration by two arbitrators, is flawed under Article 8 of the UAA, which governs arbitration and is contrary to the fundamental principle of the obligation to deliberate in an odd number in matters of justice. Those flaws, according to the Court of Appeal, invalidated the arbitration clause at issue and prevented the organization of an effective arbitration procedure. Thus, the Court of Appeal annulled the arbitration clause.

Instead of annulling the arbitration clause, the Court of Appeal should have used its powers under Article 8 of the UAA [which became Article 5] to appoint a third arbitrator, and that was the substance of the ruling of the CCJA:

> If the parties to an arbitration agreement appoint the arbitrators in an even number, the composition of the arbitral tribunal may be corrected in accordance with article 8 [which became Article 5][4] of the UAA. Where, like in the present case, the first two arbitrators appointed under the arbitration clause have supplemented the composition of the arbitral tribunal by appointing the third arbitrator without waiting for the precondition of their possible disagreement on a joint award, it is a tribunal of three arbitrators, not two, which has rendered the award at issue. By annulling the arbitration agreement, while the competent judge in the State Party has the power, under Article 8 of the UAA if the matter has been referred to him, to take measures to ensure that the arbitral tribunal is constituted in accordance with the odd number rule at paragraph 1 of that Article, the court violated the provisions of Article 8 of the UAA and its judgment must be quashed.[5]

Where it appears from the challenged award that the respondent served a request for arbitration to the claimant, informing the claimant at the same time of the arbitrator that the respondent had chosen and inviting the claimant to appoint their arbitrator within fifteen days otherwise the appointment would be made by the competent judge; that in the face of the claimant's lack of reaction, a judge appointed a second arbitrator and the two arbitrators chose the third arbitrator; that the registrar of the court notified the composition of the tribunal thus constituted to the claimant by serving them a writ and inviting them to participate in the preparatory meeting to be held on a specified date, the claimant who failed to produce evidence justifying their failure to participate

3. *Id.*, Art. 6 para. 2. [Emphasis added].
4. The ruling has been made under Article 8 of the UAA before the enactment of the revised version of November 2017 which turned Art. 8 into Art. 5.
5. Sarci Sarl v. Atlantique Telecom Sa, N° 044/2008, Decision, [C.C.J.A.], 1e ch., (Jul. 17, 2008), http://www.ohada.com/jurisprudence/ohadata/J-10-15.html.

in the arbitration proceedings cannot rightly raise the breach of adversarial principle as a defense in that the arbitration sessions were held in their absence.[6]

[B] Under the CCJA Arbitration Rules

The CCJA Regulation on arbitration simply states that "the dispute may be settled by an arbitral tribunal made up of a sole arbitrator or of three arbitrators."[7] Although the CCJA Regulation on arbitration does not specify it, like the UAA, only a human being can be appointed as arbitrator, since no legal entity can perform the mission of arbitrator, enjoy the rights it entails and be bound by the specific duties that go along with the task.

§2.02 SELECTION OF ARBITRATORS

It will be presented under the UAA (§2.02[A]) as well as the CCJA Rules (§2.02[B]).

[A] Under the UAA

The selection and appointment of arbitrators are governed by Article 6 of the UAA, the first paragraph of which states that "arbitrators are appointed, dismissed or replaced in accordance with the parties' agreement." Article 6 of the UAA also states in paragraphs 4 to 7:

> In the absence of agreement between the parties on the appointment procedure, or if their stipulations are insufficient:
>
> a) in case of an arbitration with three arbitrators, each party appoints one arbitrator, and the two arbitrators so appointed choose the third arbitrator; if a party does not appoint an arbitrator within thirty (30) days of receiving a request for arbitration from the other party, or if the two arbitrators fail to agree on the choice of the third arbitrator within thirty days (30) of their appointment, the appointment is made, upon the request of a party, by the competent court in the State Party;
> b) in case of an arbitration with a sole arbitrator, if the parties cannot agree on the choice of the arbitrator, the latter is appointed, upon the request of a party, by the competent court in the State Party.
>
> The decision to appoint an arbitrator by the competent court is made within fifteen (15) days of referral to the court, unless the laws of a State Party provides for a shorter time period. This decision is subject to no appeal.

This provision has led to many disputes, and from the available case law, three different situations regarding the appointment by the parties (§2.02[A][1]), by an arbitration center (§2.02[A][2]) or by the supporting judge (§2.02[A][3]) will be

6. CA Littoral, Apr. 28, 2010, N° 199/Civ., (Cameroon), http://www.ohada.com/jurisprudence/ohadata/J-12-73.html.
7. CCJA Regulation on Arbitration, Art. 3.1.

presented, followed by the consequences of the irregular appointment of an arbitrator (§2.02[A][4]) and the absence of an arbitration clause (§2.02[A][5]).

[1] Appointment of Arbitrators by the Parties

By far, the most natural way of appointing arbitrators is by the parties under their own stipulations. This subsection will tell us how the flawed composition of a tribunal is handled (§2.02[A][1][i]), answer the question of whether the appointment of an arbitrator in a submission agreement before a dispute arises is valid (§2.02[A][1][ii]) and emphasize the preference of the will of the parties in the formation of an arbitral tribunal (§2.02[A][1][iii]).

[i] Flawed Composition of the Tribunal

When the thirty-days' period given to a party to appoint their arbitrator expired on December 30, 2006, the formal notice given to that party for the purpose of appointing their arbitrator was not to be issued to them until December 31, 2006, in the case at that date, they had not made the appointment. The appointment of the second arbitrator by court order on December 18, 2006, on referral from the other party, before the expiry of the legal deadline, and the constitution of the ad hoc arbitral tribunal did not comply with the requirements of Article 5, paragraph 2, a) as to the deadline for appointing the second arbitrator,[8] and Article 9 as to the equal treatment to be enjoyed by any party to a trial since one of the parties was unable to exercise their right to appoint an arbitrator. It follows that the ad hoc arbitral tribunal was improperly constituted, and its award must be annulled.[9]

[ii] Validity of the Appointment of an Arbitrator in a Submission Agreement Before the Dispute Arises

The plea alleging the irregularity of the appointment of the sole arbitrator lacks merit and must be rejected when the parties have expressly and directly designated in the submission agreement a sole arbitrator in the person of the President of the Commercial Court of Pointe-Noire, who indeed was the arbitrator that rendered the challenged award.[10]

8. This ruling was made under Art. 5, para. 2, a) of the UAA of Mar. 11, 1999, which has become Art. 6 para. 5 since the enactment of the UAA of Nov. 23, 2017 which is currently in force.
9. Sarci Sarl v. Atlantique Telecom, N° 044/2008, *supra*, Chapter 2, fn. 5.
10. CA Pointe-Noire, Mar. 4, 2005, (Congo), http://www.ohada.com/jurisprudence/ohadata/J-13-73.html.

[iii] Preference of the Will of the Parties in the Constitution of the Tribunal

The provisions of Article 5 paragraph 1 of the UAA [now Article 6 paragraph 1] according to which "arbitrators are appointed, dismissed or replaced in accordance with the parties' agreement" enshrine the principle of the pre-eminence of the will of the parties in the constitution of the arbitral tribunal and the supplementary nature of the provisions of the UAA. In the presence of contractual stipulations that "the arbitral tribunal will be composed of three (3) arbitrators, two of which (2) will be appointed by each of the parties, the third arbitrator being chosen by the two arbitrators previously appointed. Each party undertakes to appoint its arbitrator within a maximum of fifteen days following the request for arbitration sent by one of the parties to the other, by registered letter with acknowledgment of receipt or by any proven means. Failing appointment by a party of their arbitrator and/or the third arbitrator, the arbitrators will be appointed at the request of the most diligent party by the president of the Libreville Commercial Court," which provide no other than the fifteen-day period given to the respondent to appoint their arbitrator, and the first two arbitrators appointed to appoint the third, the claimant has been able to exercise their right to appoint an arbitrator, and no breach of the equality of the parties in the composition of the said tribunal can be usefully raised, since the request for arbitration was notified to the defendant on March 06, 2014, and the order of the supporting judge was made on March 31, 2014, that is after the expiration of the fifteen (15) day period stipulated. Therefore, the argument lacks merit and will be rejected.[11]

This case illustrates the importance of a careful drafting of arbitration clauses. The parties had stipulated a shorter time limit than the thirty days under Article 6 paragraph 5 of the UAA for referring to the supporting judge for the appointment of an arbitrator. After receiving the notification of the request for arbitration and the appointment of their arbitrator by the claimant, the respondent, who was relying upon the thirty days under Article 6 of the UAA, failed to appoint their arbitrator within the fifteen days stipulated by the parties. In its decision, the CCJA determines that the provision of Article 6 paragraph 5 of the UAA is supplementary in nature and not mandatory; thus, the time limit freely stipulated by the parties must be enforced, even if it is less advantageous for the respondent.

[2] Appointment of Arbitrators by an Arbitration Center

This subsection deals with the annulment of an award resulting from the irregular appointment of an arbitrator (§2.02[A][2][i]) and highlights the mandatory nature of provisions of the rules of an arbitration center chosen by the parties and not waived by them (§2.02[A][2][ii]).

11. Le Bistro Family v. Rosace Marbrée, N° 196/2018, Decision, [C.C.J.A.], 2e ch., (Oct. 25, 2018).

[i] Annulment of an Award for Irregular Appointment of an Arbitrator

Where it follows from the submission agreement that the parties have given the power to the National Chamber of Arbitrations to appoint the President of the arbitral tribunal and no document has been submitted in the file to establish that the sole arbitrator has been appointed by the said chamber in the present case, the arbitrator self-proclaimed, thus exposing their award to annulment, as well as the resulting *exequatur*.[12]

[ii] Mandatory Nature of the Provision of the Arbitration Rules of the Center Chosen by the Parties and Not Expressly Waived by Them

Where the parties have agreed to submit any dispute between them to a specific arbitration center to be settled once for all under the arbitration rules of the center, without having expressly waived the provisions of said Rules relating to the formation of the arbitral tribunal, the Court of Appeal was wrong in annulling the challenged award by finding that "… the [arbitration center] appointed [X.] as President of the arbitral tribunal in violation of the relevant provisions of Article 5 paragraph 2 a) of the [UAA]." The ruling of the Court of Appeal must be quashed.[13]

[3] Appointment of Arbitrators by the Supporting Judge

The silence maintained by a party to a dispute in the mail by which the other party proposed the appointment of an arbitrator not only presumes their refusal but characterizes the disagreement of the parties on the choice of the arbitrator necessitating the referral to the supporting judge under the provisions of Article 5 of the UAA. It follows that the application for the appointment of an arbitrator before the court is admissible. With regard to the number of arbitrators, it can be inferred from the submission agreement of the parties, which stipulated that "arbitration chaired by a jurist under Congolese law will be used" that the parties have opted for a single arbitrator. This is so because the word "chaired" alone cannot suffice to infer that the parties have thought of a collegial formation of the arbitral body, one of which would be the President, since even for a tribunal made up of a single arbitrator or a united judge's court, the verb "to chair" can always be used. The supporting judge must appoint the sole arbitrator, under article 5 above, since the parties failed to appoint it.[14]

12. CA Ouest, Jul. 13, 2011, N° 53/CIV., (Cameroon), http://www.ohada.com/jurisprudence/ohadata/J-12-64.html.
13. Commercial Bank of Cameroon v. Archidiocèse de Yaoundé, N° 242/2018, Decision, [C.C.J.A.], 2e ch., (Nov. 29, 2018).
14. T. com. Pointe-Noire, Jan. 8, 2002, Ord. réf. n° 007, (Congo), http://www.ohada.com/jurisprudence/ohadata/J-13-70.html.

[4] Irregular Appointment of Arbitrators: Nullity Without Grievance

The irregular constitution of an arbitral tribunal is a serious matter, and where it is obvious, any court to which the matter is referred must rule solely on the basis of the UAA, and any ruling on the matter on the ground of a national law contrary to the provision of the UAA must be overturned. The CCJA affirmed that rule in *Le Bistro Family v. Rosace Marbrée* in the following terms:

> It was wrong for a court of appeal to hold that "the civil procedure code in its Article 127 specifies *inter alia* that no procedural act cannot be declared null for defect of form if the nullity is not expressly provided for by law," and that "better, Article 5 [now 6] of the UAA having provided for no nullity in the event of noncompliance with the procedure for appointing an arbitrator, such argument must be rejected since the party relying upon it does not prove the damage caused to them by this irregularity raised," to dismiss the objection to admissibility based on the irregularity of the constitution of the arbitral tribunal, for failure to comply with the deadlines for the appointment of arbitrators under Article 5 [now 6] of the UAA. This is so since the national law on which the court based its decision (Article 127 of the civil procedure code of Gabon) is not applicable to the present dispute, which is governed solely by the provisions of the UAA, the irregularity of the composition of the arbitral tribunal being a ground for challenging an arbitral award under Article 27 [sic][15] of the UAA, and that no provision of the said Uniform Act subordinates the annulment of an award to proof of damage by the party raising the nullity. Thus, the challenged decision of the Court of Appeal must be quashed for violation of the rules raised in the argument.[16]

[5] Absence of an Arbitration Clause: Retraction of the Court Order Appointing an Arbitrator

As mentioned before, a court cannot appoint an arbitrator to resolve a dispute where the parties have waived any preexisting arbitration agreement by a jurisdiction clause.[17] The exclusive jurisdiction of the "competent court" in the State Party housing the seat of the arbitration for the appointment of an arbitrator in the event of difficulty has been maintained, no doubt because the OHADA Legislator has not institutionalized arbitration governed by the Uniform Act. Indeed, since the UAA does not mandate the creation of arbitration centers in States Parties and parties to a dispute are not required to use such a center before implementing an arbitration procedure governed by the Uniform Act, the appointment of an arbitrator in case of difficulty could only be by court order.

15. There seems to be a typographical error in the ruling of the Court, because Art. 26 of the UAA, and not 27, deals with the grounds of annulment of an award.
16. Le Bistro Family v. Rosace Marbrée, N° 196/2018, *supra,* Chapter 2, fn. 11.
17. TPI Yaounde-Ekounou, May 6, 2013, Ord. N° 185, *supra,* Chapter 1, fn. 12.

[B] Under the CCJA Arbitration Rules

The selection and appointment of arbitrators under the CCJA arbitration rules are, to some extent, similar to the one governed by the UAA, with exceptions relating to the specific nature of the institutional nature of the proceedings governed by the CCJA arbitration rules. Article 3 of the CCJA Regulation on arbitration covers in detail the procedure, and it is useful to reproduce it entirely. It states:

> 3.1 The dispute may be settled by an arbitral tribunal made up of a sole arbitrator or of three arbitrators.
>
> Where the parties have agreed that the dispute will be settled by a sole arbitrator, they may appoint them by mutual agreement subject to confirmation of the Court. If the parties fail to agree within thirty (30) days from the notification of the request for arbitration to the other party, the arbitrator is appointed by the Court.
>
> Where three arbitrators have been stipulated, each party, in the request for arbitration or in the answer to the request, appoints one independent arbitrator, subject to confirmation of the Court. If one of the parties fails to appoint an arbitrator, the appointment is made by the Court. The third arbitrator, who presides over the arbitral tribunal, is appointed by the Court, unless the parties have agreed that the arbitrators they have appointed would appoint the third arbitrator within a given time limit. In the latter case, it is up to the Court to confirm the third arbitrator. If at the end of the deadline set by the parties or assigned by the Court, the arbitrators appointed by the parties have failed to agree, the third arbitrator is appointed by the Court.
>
> If the parties have not agreed on the number of arbitrators, the Court appoints a sole arbitrator, unless the dispute appears to justify the appointment of three arbitrators. In the latter case, the parties have fifteen (15) days to appoint the arbitrators.
>
> Where several claimants or respondents are required to submit joint proposals to the Court for the appointment of an arbitrator and they fail to agree within the time allowed, the Court may appoint the entire arbitral tribunal.
>
> 3.2 Arbitrators may be chosen from the list of arbitrators drawn up by the Court and updated annually. The members of the Court cannot be included on the said list.
>
> 3.3 In appointing arbitrators, the Court may request the opinion of the experts referred to at Article 1.1, paragraph 6, and considers, in particular, the nationality of the parties, their place of residence and that of their counsel and arbitrators, the seat of arbitration, the language of the parties, the nature of the claims, the availability of the arbitrators and, possibly, the law applicable to the dispute.
>
> When it must appoint one or more arbitrator(s), the Court proceeds as quickly as possible, and, unless the parties otherwise agree, according to the following procedure:
>
> a) the Secretary General sends each of the parties an identical list prepared by the Court and with at least three names;
> b) within a time limit set by the Secretary General, each party return this list to the Secretary General, indicating on it the names of the arbitrators by order of preference and, if applicable, crossing out the names to which it objects;
> c) after the expiry of the deadline set by the Secretary General, the Court appoints the arbitrator or arbitrators on the basis of the names approved on the lists that

> have been sent back to him, and in accordance with the order of preference indicated by the parties.
>
> If for any reason, the appointment cannot be made under this procedure, the Court may exercise its discretion in appointing one or more arbitrators.

Some new features introduced with the revised arbitrations rules of the CCJA call for few comments, i.e., the use of experts by the President of the CCJA in the appointment process (§2.02[B][1]) and the limitation of the discretion of the CCJA in the appointment process (§2.02[B][2]).

[1] Use of Experts by the President of the Court

Article 3.3 paragraph 1 completes the procedures for the appointment of an arbitrator by now providing for the possibility for the Court to seek the opinion of experts when appointing arbitrators. The methods of implementing this innovation do not seem to have already been specified, the Arbitration Bylaws of the CCJA in matters of arbitration not having been reviewed to my knowledge. While we wait, it may be considered that the possible remuneration of the experts likely to be appointed under Article 1.1 paragraph 6 will be set by the Court, perhaps after consulting the parties as to the financial impact that these costs, which could be included in the administrative costs of the procedure, could have.

[2] Limitation of the CCJA's Discretion in the Appointment of Arbitrators

The revised version of Article 3.3 of the CCJA Regulation on arbitration (which is currently in force since February 23, 2018) provides for a procedure under which the Court preselects three or more names that are communicated to the parties. Each party must indicate within a time limit set by the Secretary-General their preferences for the list drawn up by the Court, crossing out any undesirable names and indicating, if applicable, the names of the persons they want to see appointed in order of preference. If the parties take advantage of this new possibility which they are offered, the hands of the Court may appear to be tied with the preselection, which will have been made for the final designation, and the Court will not be able to proceed otherwise than in the event of difficulty. This process, which gives more freedom to the parties and their counsel to the detriment of the Court in the choice of an arbitrator might seem restrictive of the discretion of the Court which would become, under such circumstances, a simple selector of arbitrators. Its "conservative" nature may also contribute to the limitation of the progress—if any—toward genuine diversity in the appointment of arbitrators, as highlighted by Emmanuel Gaillard:[18]

> This system is the most conservative there is. As the parties abhor the unknown, the new names likely to be proposed by [the arbitration center] will most often be

18. Emmanuel Gaillard, "Nouvelles Réflexions sur la Sociologie de l'Arbitrage," *Procédures*, N°2, February 2020, p. 36 (Gaillard, 2020).

> discarded or misclassified by either party, making this system a machine to reproduce what already exists. Without the parties being suspected of bad intentions, if the existing lacks diversity—which is the case—it will nevertheless be reproduced by the mechanical play of this mode of appointment.

In any event, any party wishing to maintain the old system of appointment by the Court (no preselection to be submitted to the parties) should ensure that this is stipulated in the arbitration agreement, within the boundaries of the rules.

It must also be noted that the OHADA Legislator added elements to be considered for the appointment of arbitrators by the Court, in particular the seat of arbitration, the availability of prospective arbitrators and the law applicable to the dispute. Taking availability into account when appointing an arbitrator can help speed up proceedings if it avoids appointing arbitrators who are already overloaded with work and or cases.

§2.03 INDEPENDENCE AND IMPARTIALITY OF ARBITRATORS

Independence and impartiality will be presented under the UAA (§2.03[A]) and the CCJA Rules (§2.03[B]).

[A] Under the UAA

Under Article 7 paragraph 3 of the UAA, "the arbitrator must enjoy full exercise of their civil rights and *remain independent and impartial* toward the parties" (emphasis added). Like any other human activity implying the act of judging, independence and impartiality of the person(s) in the position to judge is the backbone. Independence of arbitrators is so crucial that the Legislator mandates that they remain independent and impartial throughout the proceedings and must disclose "any circumstance likely to create in [the minds of the parties] a legitimate doubt about their independence and impartiality"[19] before accepting their appointment and at any stage of the procedure should such circumstances arise.[20] The requirement that arbitrators enjoy full exercise of their rights reinforces their independence toward the parties.

There is at least one case of the CCJA relating to the lack of independence of an arbitrator who seemed to have had undisclosed ties with counsel of a party. The Court ruled that the arbitral tribunal is regular only if it is composed of independent and impartial arbitrators and if the procedure for its constitution is exempt from any defect. The formal inquiry of the arbitral tribunal on the nature of the collaborative ties that the arbitrator appointed by the claimant in the arbitration proceedings had with the counsel of the claimant having received no response enabling the assessment of the impact of these undisclosed ties on their independence and impartiality, it is by a correct application of Articles 7 and 26 of the UAA that the Court of Appeal determined "that it is settled case law that the arbitrator must disclose any circumstance likely to affect their judgment and to provoke in the minds of the parties a reasonable doubt on

19. UAA, Art. 7 para. 4.
20. *Id.*, Art. 7 para. 5.

their impartiality and independence which are the essence of the arbitral function," to set aside the award.[21]

[B] Under the CCJA Arbitration Rules

The requirements of independence and impartiality from arbitrators involved in proceedings governed by the CCJA Arbitration Rules are quite similar to those of the UAA. Article 4.1 of the CCJA Regulation on arbitration states, in this regard:

> 4.1 *Any arbitrator* appointed or confirmed by the Court *must be and remain impartial and independent* to the parties.
>
> ...
>
> Before their appointment or confirmation by the Court, the prospective arbitrator *must disclose in writing* to the Secretary General *any circumstances likely to raise legitimate doubts about the arbitrator's impartiality or independence.*
>
> Upon receipt of this information, the Secretary General communicates it in writing to the parties and sets a time limit for them to present their respective comments.
>
> The arbitrator *must immediately disclose,* in writing to the Secretary General and the parties, *any similar circumstances which may occur between their appointment or confirmation by the Court and the notification of the final award.*[22]

At least in one case, *Etat du Niger v. Société Africard Co Limited*, the CCJA enforced the independence and impartiality rule, by ruling that "under Article 4.1 of [its] Regulation on arbitration, any arbitrator appointed by the [CCJA] must be and remain independent from the parties."[23]

§2.04 PROCEDURES FOR CHALLENGING AND REPLACING ARBITRATORS

The procedure for challenge and replacement will be presented under both systems as well.

[A] Under the UAA

Arbitrators can be "dismissed or replaced in accordance with the parties' agreement,"[24] and where applicable, the rules of any local arbitration center that might be organizing the proceedings, as long as no provisions of such rules are contrary to the UAA.[25] The challenge and replacement of arbitrators are governed by article 8 of the UAA; the first

21. Wanmo v. Nguessi, N° 151/2017, Decision, [C.C.J.A.], 2e ch., (Jun. 29, 2017).
22. CCJA Regulation on arbitration, Art. 4.1 (Emphasis added).
23. Etat du Niger v. Société Africard Co Limited, N° 087/2018, Decision, [C.C.J.A.], Ass. plen., (Apr. 12, 2018).
24. UAA, Art. 6 para. 1.
25. On the necessity of compliance of the rules of any local, national or regional arbitration center with the UAA, *see supra*, Introduction, fn. 10.

four paragraphs deal with the challenge (§2.04[A][1]) and the last one with the replacement of an arbitrator (§2.04[A][2]).

[1] Challenge of an Arbitrator

Article 8, paragraph 1-4 of the UAA states:

> In the event of dispute, and *if the parties have not agreed on the procedure for challenging* an arbitrator, the competent court in the State Party rules on the challenge, no later than thirty (30) days after the parties and the arbitrator have been heard or duly summoned. If the competent court fails to rule within the abovementioned time period, the challenge is removed from that court and may be brought before the CCJA by the most diligent party.
>
> The decision of the competent court dismissing the challenge may be challenged only before the Common Court of Justice and Arbitration.
>
> Any ground for challenge must be raised, no later than thirty (30) days from the discovery of the fact that led to the challenge, by the party seeking to invoke it.
>
> The challenge of an arbitrator is admissible only for a reason disclosed after their appointment.[26]

Parties have latitude in determining the procedure for challenging an arbitrator, and only if there is no agreement on that issue will "the competent court in the State Party," in other words, the supporting judge, rule on the challenge. For ad hoc cases, parties will need to have carefully provided for the situation, should it arise. In institutional arbitrations, the rules of the arbitration centers involved may have a supplemental role to play as long as their provisions are in compliance with the UAA.

The Legislator promotes speed by locking up the recusal within a time frame. Any request for recusal must be raised, within thirty days of the discovery of the cause justifying it, before the competent court of the seat of arbitration, which must rule within the same period, beyond which the challenge may be referred to the CCJA if the national court has not ruled. These provisions preserve procedural public order by allowing parties to assert their legitimate grounds for the challenge while limiting the risk of delaying tactics that may involve transforming the recusal procedure into a "judicial marathon" in itself.

[2] Replacement of an Arbitrator

On the replacement of arbitrators, the fifth and last paragraph of Article 8 of the UAA states:

> When the mission of an arbitrator is terminated, or when they resign for any other reason, a replacing arbitrator is appointed according to the applicable rules to the appointment of the replaced arbitrator, unless otherwise agreed by the parties. The same procedure is followed if the arbitrator's mission is terminated by mutual agreement of the parties and in any other case when their mission is terminated.

26. Emphasis added.

One will note, in paragraph 5 of the amended Article 8 above, the flexibility of the Legislator, allowing the parties to stipulate a different procedure for the appointment of a new arbitrator where replacement is needed. The parties may thus provide in their arbitration agreement for the possibility of having the replacing arbitrator appointed by an arbitration center of the State in which the arbitration takes place.

[B] Under the CCJA Arbitration Rules

The challenge and replacement of arbitrators are governed by Article 4 of the CCJA Regulation on arbitration. Article 4.2 deals with the challenge (§2.04[B][1]), while articles 4.3 and 4.4 handle replacement (§2.04[B][2]).

[1] Challenge of an Arbitrator

Article 4.2 of the CCJA Regulation on arbitration states:

> 4.2 The application for recusal of an arbitrator based on alleged lack of independence or any other ground is made by submission to the Secretary General of a written statement specifying the facts and circumstances on which the application is based.
>
> To be admissible, the application must be sent by a party either within thirty (30) days of the party receiving notification of the appointment or confirmation of the arbitrator by the Court, or within thirty (30) days from the date on which the party filing the application for recusal has been informed of the facts and circumstances on which the application for recusal is based if that date is after the receipt of the above notification.
>
> The Court rules on admissibility of the application at the same time as, if necessary, on the merits of the application for recusal, after the Secretary General has given an opportunity for the arbitrator concerned, the parties and other members of the arbitral tribunal, if any, to present their written submissions within an appropriate time frame. These written comments are sent to the other parties and members of the arbitral tribunal.

No case handling challenge issues has been available; the first four paragraphs of Article 4.2 deal with the challenge and the last one with the replacement of an arbitrator.

[2] Replacement of an Arbitrator

Replacement of an arbitrator under the CCJA Arbitration Rules is governed essentially by Articles 4.3 and 4.4 of the CCJA Regulation on arbitration. Here again, there is no case available yet, and the full content of those provisions will be reproduced hereafter, for the reader's attention:

> 4.3 An arbitrator *must* be replaced upon death, upon acceptance by the Court of the *application for recusal of the arbitrator*, or upon acceptance by the Court of *the* resignation *of the arbitrator*.

Where the resignation of an arbitrator is not accepted by the Court and the arbitrator nevertheless refuses to continue to perform *their mission, the arbitrator must be* replaced if *the arbitrator* is a sole arbitrator *or* the Chairman of the *arbitral tribunal.*

In *the* other *cases*, the Court assesses whether *there is a need for replacement* taking into account the *state of progress* of the proceedings and the opinion of the two arbitrators *who have not resigned. If the Court considers that there is no need for replacement,* the proceedings continue and the award *is* rendered despite the refusal *of* the arbitrator whose resignation has been refused.

The Court *makes its* decision *in light of, among other things,* the provisions of Article 28 (2) of *this Regulation.*

4.4 An arbitrator *must* also be replaced *when* the Court *finds* that *the arbitrator* is *de jure* or *de facto prevented* from *carrying out their* mission or that *the arbitrator* is not *performing their duties* in accordance with Title IV of the Treaty or with *this Regulation,* or within the prescribed time limits.

When, on the basis of information that has come to its *knowledge,* the Court considers applying the preceding paragraph, it *decides* on the replacement after the Secretary General has communicated this information in writing to the arbitrator concerned, the parties and *to the other members of the tribunal, if any,* and has given them the opportunity to comment in writing within *an appropriate time frame.*

In *the event of the* replacement of an arbitrator who *does not perform their duties* in accordance with *Title* IV of the Treaty, *this Regulation on Arbitration,* or within the *allotted* time, *a new arbitrator is appointed by the Court on the advice* of the party who had appointed the arbitrator to be replaced without the Court being bound by the said *opinion.*

Where the Court is informed that, *in a three-member tribunal,* one of the arbitrators other than the president, *does not participate* in the arbitration, *without having* resigned, the Court may, pursuant to Article 4., paragraphs 3 and 4 above, not replace the said arbitrator if the two other arbitrators *agree* to continue the arbitration despite the failure of the said arbitrator to participate.

The last three paragraphs of Article 4 of the CCJA Regulation on arbitration cover respectively the terms under which arbitration proceedings are resumed after the challenge and replacement are settled,[27] warrant fair proceedings by requiring the secretary-general to allow parties and arbitrators to submit their written comments on the challenge and replacement, if any, to all the other parties and members of the tribunal,[28] and finally indicates that the rulings of the CCJA on the appointment, confirmation, challenge and replacement of arbitrators are final.[29]

The final and binding nature of such decisions rendered by the restricted commission of the Court[30] acting in its administrative capacity has been affirmed by the Court in *Ekwa Ngalle v. Société Nationale d'Hydrocarbures*, where it ruled that under Article 4 of the CCJA Regulation on arbitration, governing institutional arbitrations

27. CCJA Regulation on Arbitration, Art. 4.5.
28. *Id.*, Art. 4.6 para. 1.
29. *Id.*, Art. 4.6 para. 2.
30. The restricted commissions of the CCJA are usually selections of three judges of the CCJA appointed by the President and Vice Presidents to serve on a rolling basis.

under the aegis of that Court, the decision confirming, removing or replacing an arbitrator rests with the Court and is final. Therefore, the arbitral tribunal, established under the aegis of the CCJA, which has declared itself incompetent to assess an application for recusal of an arbitrator and has merely taken note of the decision of the Court confirming that arbitrator has not violated the Regulation on arbitration. The petition for annulment of the award for breach of the principle of independence and impartiality of an arbitrator must, therefore, be dismissed as lacking merit.[31]

The procedures for challenging and replacing an arbitration are quite straightforward and must be followed strictly for the party relying upon them to be successful.

31. Ekwa Ngalle v. Société Nationale d'Hydrocarbures, N° 102/2015, Decision, [C.C.J.A.], Ass. plen., (Oct. 15, 2015), http://www.ohada.com/jurisprudence/ohadata/J-16-95.html.

CHAPTER 3
Rights and Duties of Arbitrators

The present chapter is important, essentially because it lays down the substantial obligations of arbitrator(s) toward the parties as well as the arbitration(s) center(s) that might be involved in the arbitral process. Those obligations will also be used at a later stage to assess whether a tribunal has diligently carried out its mission, especially where the award is challenged. The arbitrator's contract (§3.01) and the status it confers upon arbitrators (§3.02) will be presented before the rights of the appointed arbitrators (§3.03), followed by the obligations of the arbitrator(s) (§3.04), the specific role of the presiding arbitrator for panels of three ((§3.05) and choice of law governing the obligations, rights and protections of the arbitrator(s) (§3.06).

§3.01 THE ARBITRATOR'S CONTRACT

Under OHADA Rules, regardless of whether the UAA or the CCJA arbitration rules apply, the appointment and confirmation, where applicable, of arbitrator(s) entails the formation of a contract.

Where the parties have chosen ad hoc arbitration, which is possible only under the UAA, the terms of reference signed between the parties and the arbitrator(s) would generally stand for the "arbitrator's contract" because it is the document containing the terms and conditions expressing the duties and rights of the respective parties. Depending on the circumstances, those terms usually cover the details of the mission of the tribunal such as issues to be resolved, applicable law(s), whether the tribunal may rule as *amiable compositeur* or not, the acceptance of the arbitrator(s) of their mission, the duration of the proceedings if different from the one provided by the applicable law, the procedural calendar, the amount of provisions on fees and costs as well as their method of calculation. Those terms also organize the way in which the accounts will be kept and designate the person who will manage them, and some other important issues parties and arbitrators may have agreed upon.

The choice by the parties of institutional arbitration under the aegis of an arbitration center or institution considerably simplifies the task of arbitrator(s) since the commitments to which the parties, as well as arbitrators, subscribe by their acceptance of the arbitration contract, are generally found in the rules of the chosen arbitration center. Thus, the arbitrator's contract under institutional arbitration governed by the UAA will be formed of the provisions of the UAA itself, the arbitrations rules of the center chosen and any other rule(s) chosen either by the parties or the arbitral tribunal to supplement that first set of rules where necessary.[1]

Under the CCJA Rules, the arbitrator's contract is formed by the signature, by each arbitrator, of a set of documents including the formal acceptance of the mission[2] and the minutes of the case management conference.[3]

§3.02 STATUS

The status of an arbitrator, or a tribunal where three arbitrators are operating, deals with the legal regime of the arbitrator(s) with regard to the arbitrator's contract mentioned supra. Like under UK law, as highlighted in *Jivraj v. Hashwani*, the arbitrator's contract is definitively not an employment contract,[4] nor is it an agency contract, as in French law.[5] An arbitrator is neither an employee nor an agent of the party who appointed them. Therefore, that party or the parties have no control over the tribunal. The arbitrator's contract is a special contract.

§3.03 RIGHTS AND PROTECTIONS OF ARBITRATORS

The essential right of arbitrator(s) is their entitlement to compensation for their performance (§3.03[A]), and under certain arbitration Rules such as the ones of the CCJA, the arbitrators are protected by judicial immunity (§3.03[B]).

1. On the choice of applicable rules, *see* Article 10 of the UAA.
2. Translated for French: "*Déclaration d'acceptation, d'indépendance et d'impartialité de l'arbitre.*" This is a binding document in which the arbitrator undertakes to commit themselves to the rules and the legal framework of their mission during its performance. For a model, *see* in the CCJA Arbitration Guide, *Guide d'Arbitrage de la CCJA-OHADA*, 2d. ed., 2018, 142-144 (Common Court of Justice and Arbitration, 2018).
3. The case management conference is an important meeting at the end of which parties and arbitrator(s) sign a binding document containing all the main terms of the proceedings. *See* Chapter 3, §3.03, *infra*.
4. Jivraj v. Hashwani [2011] UKSC 40, https://www.supremecourt.uk/cases/docs/uksc-2010-0170-judgment.pdf [accessed Mar. 1, 2020, at 11:49], para. 40, 42: "it is in my opinion plain that *the arbitrators' role is not one of employment* under a contract personally to do work .... He is rather in the category of an independent provider of services who is *not in a relationship of subordination with the parties who receive his services .... Once an arbitrator has been appointed*, at any rate in the absence of agreement between them, *the parties effectively have no control over him.*" [Emphasis added].
5. Cour de cassation [Cass.] [supreme court for judicial matters] 2e civ., Jul. 3, 1996 n° 94-10576, RJDA 11/96 n° 1414 (Edition Francis Lefebvre, 1996).

[A] Remuneration of Arbitrators

The specifics of remuneration under the UAA (§3.03[A][1]), as well as the CCJA Rules (§3.03[A][2]), will be presented.

[1] Under the UAA

In arbitration proceedings under the UAA, governed by the AAU, fees are freely agreed between the parties and the arbitrator(s) unless, as Article 10 allows, arbitration is organized and administered by a national or local arbitration center, in which case the parties will submit to its provisions. In that case, a prospective arbitrator may agree with the parties to apply a tariff similar to or proportionate to that which takes place in other arbitration centers or even provide for ad valorem pricing unless unauthorized under the mandatory provision of applicable rules of the chosen center.

[2] Under the CCJA Arbitration Rules

Under the CCJA Arbitration Rules, a schedule setting ad valorem fees is provided for by a prescriptive decision of the CCJA,[6] which constitutes an appendix to its Regulation on Arbitration. The fees are set exclusively by the Court (in its administrative capacity handling arbitration proceedings) on the basis of this schedule, and any separate agreement between the arbitrators and the parties to this effect is null and void.[7] This mandatory rule has been enforced in *Republique de Guinee v. Getma International,*[8] where the CCJA annulled an award rendered under its Arbitration Rules between the Republic of Guinea and Getma International, a foreign corporation, for the failure of the arbitral tribunal to comply with the mission entrusted to it. A later attempt to enforce the annulled award in the United States on the ground of the New York Convention was denied by the United States District Court for the District of Columbia on June 9, 2016,[9] and the refusal was affirmed by the United States Court of Appeal for the District of Columbia Circuit on July 7, 2017.[10]

This fee schedule is often criticized because of the level of remuneration it grants to arbitrators, which seems to be below the rates applied by most international arbitration institutions and which seems to grant a disproportionate percentage of the value at stake in each dispute as costs to the CCJA Arbitration Center, compared to the

6. Prescriptive Decision of the CCJA N° 004/99/CCJA of Feb. 3, 1999 on Arbitration Costs, *supra*, introduction.
7. *Id*, Art. 9.
8. Republique de Guinee v. Getma International, N°139/2015, Decision, Cour Commune de Justice et d'Arbitrage [CCJA] [Common Court of Justice and Arbitration] [C.C.J.A.], (Nov. 19, 2015), http://www.ohada.com/jurisprudence/ohadata/J-16-132.html.
9. Getma Int'l v. The Republic of Guinea N° 14-1616, Mem Op. (D.C. Jun. 9, 2016)), http://res.cloudinary.com/lbresearch/image/upload/v1465576216/getma_v_guinea_moa_105116_1730.pdf [accessed Mar. 16, 2020, 17:44].
10. Getma International v. Republic of Guinea, No. 16-7087 (D.C. Cir. 2017), https://law.justia.com/cases/federal/appellate-courts/cadc/16-7087/16-7087-2017-07-07.html [accessed Mar. 16, 2020, 17:53].

fees awarded to arbitrators. But in any event and pending a possible revision of the fee schedule, it should be noted that "If the circumstances of the case make it exceptionally necessary, the Court may, at its own initiative or upon a reasoned request of the arbitrator, fix the fees of the arbitrator at an amount greater or lower than the one that would result from the application of the schedule of fees."[11]

[B] Immunity of Arbitrators under the CCJA Arbitration Rules

The issue of liability of arbitrators does not seem to be addressed often. The Treaty seems too protective of arbitrators as its Article 49, states:

> Under the conditions determined by a Regulation, OHADA officials and employees, judges of the Common Court of Justice and Arbitration, and *arbitrators appointed or confirmed by the CCJA enjoy diplomatic privileges and immunities in the performance of their duties.*
>
> The immunities and privileges mentioned above may, depending on the circumstances, be waived by the Council of Ministers. [Emphasis added].

Such immunity has been bestowed upon the arbitrators appointed or confirmed by the CCJA to allow them to perform their duties with no worry of being sued. However, that protective fence enjoyable by arbitrators may become a source of frustration and damages to the parties in some cases of arbitrators' misconduct, for example, where they do not deliver the award within the imparted time or do it with a delay of years as was the case in *Flock v. Beatie*,[12] a Canadian case. In that case, an arbitrator who was supposed to render an award within sixty days rendered the award 33 months later, and yet the Court held that the arbitrator "is protected by arbitral immunity from suit in tort and in the contract. There is no basis to suggest [the arbitrator] acted fraudulently or in bad faith such as to displace his arbitral immunity."[13]

In institutional arbitration governed by the CCJA Arbitration Rules, the core solution would have been the same under Article 49 of the Treaty. However, the right of the arbitrators to be protected during their service and the right of the parties should be balanced, and it should be possible to sanction an arbitrator's misconduct, as was the case with a former President of the Chartered Institute of Arbitrators who has reportedly been "expelled from the Institute and ordered to pay £3,000 in costs for failing to deliver an award for four years."[14]

---

11. CCJA Regulation on Arbitration, Art. 24.4.
12. Flock v. Beattie, 2010 ABQB 193 (CanLII), <http://canlii.ca/t/28vh3>, retrieved on 2020-03-17.
13. *Id.*, at 57.
14. *The Chartered Institute of Arbitrators v. John D Campbell QC*, Decision of the Disciplinary Tribunal of CIArb (May 5, 2011), reported by David Hacking and Sophia Berry, *Ethics in Arbitration: Party and Arbitral Misconduct, in Defining Issues in International Arbitration*, Oxford University Press, http://www.lordhacking.com/Documentation/Hacking%20&%20Berry%20-%20Ethics%20in%20Arbitration%20April%202016.pdf [accessed Apr. 12, 2017, at 04:12] (David Hacking, 2017).

Many scholars from different jurisdictions have criticized court rulings giving absolute immunity to arbitrators. Commenting on *Howard v. Drapkin*,[15] Robert M. Carroll wrote that "by giving arbitrators absolute immunity, the court has taken away part of the arbitrator's incentive to be totally impartial and has replaced it with the ability to assert one party's claim over the other's. This result has created a policy of protecting biased arbitrators while discouraging the use of arbitration as an impartial dispute resolution alternative."[16] Mark Sponseller, another author, wrote on the topic:

> As arbitration becomes more of a profession than a part-time voluntary service to an individual's trade or profession, arguments advocating professional accountability become stronger. Few would contend that potential lawyers, doctors, or accountants are deterred from entering their chosen profession because of the possibility that they may be held liable for their misconduct. Therefore, the argument that potential liability for misconduct will hamper the availability of arbitration is becoming increasingly invalid. While imposing potential liability may speed this professionalization by increasing the need for malpractice insurance, increased professionalism and accountability is not an undesirable outcome.[17]

Emmanuela Truly, another author, raised additional arguments against absolute arbitrator's immunity:

> To the arbitrators the land of no sanctions can mean that they may attract all kind of appointing parties, especially those willing to use unethical means to win their case. The danger is thus that the arbitrators willing to act unethically will receive ample appointments, while remaining free from sanctions, whereas those participants who refuse to do so, will not be appointed. It can thus be argued that absolute immunity drives all participants in the arbitration procedure to a "race to the bottom," diminishing the professional standards that ensure the quality of the awards rendered.[18]

In other legal systems, arbitrators may be punished for misconduct under certain conditions,[19] and there seems to be a trend toward a possible arbitrator liability for

15. Howard v. Drapkin, 222 Cal.App.3d 843 (Cal. Ct. App. 1990), https://casetext.com/case/howard-v-drapkin [accessed Mar. 17, 2020, at 12:17].
16. Robert M. Carroll, *Quasi-Judicial Immunity: The Arbitrator's Shield or Sword*, 1991 J. Disp. Resol. 12 (1991), available at: https://scholarship.law.missouri.edu/jdr/vol1991/iss1/10 [accessed Mar. 17, 2020] (Carroll, 1991).
17. Mark A. Sponseller, *Redefining Arbitral Immunity: A Proposed Qualified Immunity Statute for Arbitrators*, 44 Hastings L.J. 421 (1993), 438-439, available at: https://repository.uchastings.edu/hastings_law_journal/vol44/iss2/5 [accessed Mar. 17, 2020] (Sponseller, 1993).
18. Emmanuela Truli, *Liability v. Quasi-Judicial Immunity of the Arbitrator: The Case Against Absolute Arbitral Immunity*, 17 Am. Rev. Intl Arb. 16 (2006), https://www.academia.edu/13444342/Liability_V._Quasi-Judicial_Immunity_of_The_Arbitrator_The_Case_Against_Absolute_Arbitral_Immunity [accessed Mar. 17, 2020 at 17:54] (Truli, 2006).
19. Cour de cassation [Cass.] [Supreme Court for judicial matters] 1e civ., Jan. 15, 2014 n° 11-17.196. Bull. civ. I n° 1 (Fr): civil liability of arbitrators for breach of duty of impartiality and good faith, or a personal fault equivalent to fraud or constituting fraud, gross negligence or denial of justice. Cour de cassation [Cass.] [supreme court for judicial matters] 1e civ., Dec. 6, 2005 n° 1660. RJDA 6/06 n° 728 (Fr).; and, upon referral, Cour d'appel [CA] [regional court of appeal] Orléans, n° 06-806, Apr. 13 2007, RJDA 3/08 n° 345 (Fr).

deliberate wrongdoing in several jurisdictions.[20] Thus, it is regrettable that the recent revision of some of the arbitration rules of the CCJA did not include this. It would have been appropriate to amend the applicable rules to the CCJA arbitration by stating that an arbitrator is not liable for any act or omission during or linked to the performance of his arbitral duties unless it is proven that the act or omission has been done in bad faith. Some other countries, such as South Africa, have included similar provisions in their recently amended arbitration Act.[21] Liability without fault regime could also be organized and be coupled with and insurance mechanism set by a minor percentage of the fees of each proceeding; this would allow compensation to be paid to parties in some cases where there would be liability without fault.

However, it seems possible to seek the responsibility of an arbitrator in the event of gross negligence, miscarriage of justice, or fraud, like under French law[22] since the CCJA itself has already ruled, in *Djoumessap Motsebo v. The OHADA Permanent Secretary* that the immunity under Article 49 of the Treaty is relative and not absolute.[23]

§3.04 OBLIGATIONS OF AN ARBITRATOR

At least eight essential obligations emerge from the rules governing arbitration under both systems (under the UAA and under the CCJA Arbitration Rules). Because they are quite similar in nature, they will be presented together with an emphasis on differences of a regime where applicable. These are the obligation to accept the appointment in writing (§3.04[A]), to perform the mission until the end (§3.04[B]), to enjoy their civil rights (§3.04[C]), to remain independent and impartial toward the parties (§3.04[D]), to act diligently and swiftly (§3.04[E]), to inform the parties (§3.04[F]), to stay the proceedings and refer the parties to a stipulated preliminary step omitted by the parties (§3.04[G]) and the obligation to give a fair and equal treatment the parties (§3.04[H]).

[A] Obligation to Accept the Appointment in Writing

Article 7 paragraph 1 of the UAA states that "The arbitrator who accepts their mission must communicate their acceptance to the parties by any means in writing." The formulation may appear redundant since in virtually all cases, acceptance is materialized by a signed document, and that could be the reason why no such provision exists in the CCJA Arbitration Rules, even though acceptance of appointment is inevitably

20. Emmanuela Truli, *supra* Chapter 4, fn. 18, at page 5, indicating that institutional rules of the American Arbitration Association and the London Court of International Arbitration already contemplate the possibility of arbitrator liability for conscious or deliberate wrongdoing.
21. *See* the South African International Arbitration Bill of 2016, § 9(1) (available at: https://www.pretoriabar.co.za/pdf/arbitrators/international%20arbitration%20act%202016.pdf [accessed Apr. 12, 2017, 16:42].
22. Cour d'appel [CA] [regional court of appeal] Paris, n° 14/05436, Mar. 31 2015, RTD com. 2016.76 obs. Loquin (Fr).
23. Djoumessap Motsebo v. The OHADA Permanent Secretary, N° 032/2015, Decision, [C.C.J.A.], Ass. plen., (Apr. 23, 2015), http://www.ohada.com/jurisprudence/ohadata/J-16-32.html.

materialized by documents signed by the arbitrator, namely the formal acceptance of the mission which is part of the arbitrator's contract.[24]

[B] Obligation to Perform the Mission until the End

Under the UAA, an arbitrator, upon acceptance of their mission, "undertakes to continue their mission until the end, unless they justify of an impediment or legitimate reason for abstention or resignation."[25] Under the CCJA Rules, the same obligation exists and is phrased differently: "The arbitrator must perform their mission to its end with diligence and swiftness."[26]

[C] Obligation to Enjoy Their Rights

Under the UAA, an arbitrator "*must* enjoy full exercise of *their* civil rights … ."[27] Here again, there is no specific provision of the CCJA Rules requiring an arbitrator to enjoy their civil rights in order to be fit to serve as an arbitrator, but the duty is implied, and someone who does not enjoy their civil rights cannot serve as arbitrator.

[D] Obligation to Remain Independent and Impartial Toward the Parties

Under the UAA, an arbitrator must remain independent and impartial toward the parties.[28] Under the CCJA Rules, "any arbitrator appointed or confirmed by the Court must be and remain impartial and independent to the parties."[29] The assertion of the duty of impartiality of the arbitral tribunal recalls the obligation, for the tribunal, to have no bias or not to be influenced in favor of a party by extrinsic elements on the merits of the dispute as they result from adversarial hearings relating to the evidence regularly produced by the parties. Comparative case law also includes illustrations of the partiality or impartiality of arbitral tribunals likely to guide the path of litigants and the CCJA in assessing situations characterizing the impartiality of an arbitral tribunal.

It is the first time that these three concepts of impartiality, diligence and swiftness are asserted as such in the CCJA Arbitration Rules, but impartiality and swiftness are not foreign to the legal order of the OHADA Member States since they are provided for by the African Charter on Human Rights, the principles of which, asserted by case law, are required in all States parties to the Treaty. Indeed, the right to a fair trial, universally recognized in various legal systems around the world,[30] is asserted under Article 7 of

24. *See supra*, Chapter 3, §3.01.
25. UAA, Art. 7 para. 2.
26. CCJA Regulation on Arbitration, Art. 4.1. para. 2.
27. UAA, Art. 7 para. 3.
28. *Id.*
29. CCJA Regulation on Arbitration, Art. 4.1., para 1.
30. For example, Article 6 § 1 of the Convention for the Protection of Human Rights and Fundamental Freedoms states that "everyone is entitled to a fair and public hearing within a reasonable time by an independent and impartial tribunal established by law." (https://www.echr.coe.int/Documents/Convention_ENG.pdf [accessed Mar. 18, 2020, at 14:49]). The right to

the African Charter on Human and Peoples' Rights,[31] which expressly recognizes "the right to be judged within a reasonable time by an impartial court." This right has been asserted several times by the Community Court of Justice of the Economic Community of West African States, ruling in matters of Human Rights (CJ ECOWAS),[32] which preceded the African Court of Human Rights (ACHR), now competent in the matter.

[E] Obligation to Act Diligently and Swiftly

Article 4.1, paragraph 2 of the CCJA Regulation on Arbitration subjects arbitrators to an obligation of diligence and swiftness, by stating that "the arbitrator must perform their mission to its end with diligence and swiftness." Swiftness, which includes the idea of "Speed, promptness in execution," reminds the arbitrator(s) that the parties expect, above all, the arbitral tribunal to resolve the dispute submitted to it quickly, without however botching the work. Until the OHADA case law specifies the contours of the

---

be tried within a reasonable time has been affirmed on several occasions by the European Court of Human Rights (ECHR), the decisions of which have often inspired African Courts ruling in matters of Human Rights. *See* for example Piabié Jean-Baptiste Bako, "L'influence de la jurisprudence de la CJUE sur l'interprétation juridictionnelle du droit communautaire ouest-africain (CEDEAO-UEMOA)," http://www.ceje.ch/files/4114/6218/2918/Geneva_JMWP_07-Bako.pdf [accessed Aug. 20, 2018, at 09:14] (Bako)). For cases: Sory Touré v. Republic of Guinea, ECW/CCJ/JUG/03/16, Decision, [Ecowas Community Court of Justice], (Dec. 16, 2016), http://prod.courtecowas.org/wp-content/uploads/2019/01/ECW_CCJ_JUD_03_16.pdf [accessed Mar. 18, 2020, at 15:22], citing: Bodaert v. Belgium, App. N° 12919/87, Eur. Ct. H.R. Ehivet & Gbagbo v. Republic of Ivory Coast, ECW/CCJ/JUD/03/13, Decision, [Ecowas Community Court of Justice], (Feb. 22, 2013), http://www.courtecowas.org/site2012/pdf_files/decisions/judgements/2013/SIMONE_MICHEL_GBAGBO_c_COTE_D_IVOIRE.pdf [accessed Aug. 20, 2018, at 09:28], citing: Lawless v. Ireland, App. N°332/57, Eur. Ct. H.R., http://hudoc.echr.coe.int/eng?i=001-57518 [accessed Mar. 19, 2020, at 10:38]; Ireland v. United Kingdom, App. N° 5310/71, Eur. Ct. H.R., http://hudoc.echr.coe.int/eng?i=001-57506 [accessed Mar. 19, 2020, at 10:58]; Brannigan & McBride v. United Kingdom, 26.05.1993; App. N° 14553/89; 14554/89, Eur. Ct. H.R., http://hudoc.echr.coe.int/fre?i=001-57819 [accessed Mar. 19, 2020, at 11:01]; Aksov v. Turkey, App. N° 21987/93, Eur. Ct. H.R., http://hudoc.echr.coe.int/eng?i=001-58003 [accessed Mar. 19, 2020, at 11:01]; A. & others v. United Kingdom, App. N° 3455/05, Eur. Ct. H.R., http://hudoc.echr.coe.int/eng?i=001-91403 [accessed Mar. 19, 2020, at 11:07].

31. Article 7 of the African Charter on Human and Peoples' Rights states that:

    1. Every individual shall have the right to have his cause heard. This comprises:
        a. The right to an appeal to competent national organs against acts of violating his fundamental rights as recognized and guaranteed by conventions, laws, regulations and customs in force;
        b. The right to be presumed innocent until proved guilty by a competent court or tribunal;
        c. The right to defense, including the right to be defended by counsel of his choice;
        d. The *right to be tried within a reasonable time by an impartial court or tribunal.*
    2. No one may be condemned for an act or omission which did not constitute a legally punishable offence at the time it was committed. No penalty may be inflicted for an offence for which no provision was made at the time it was committed. Punishment is personal and can be imposed only on the offender, https://www.achpr.org/legalinstruments/detail?id=49 [accessed Mar. 19, 2020, at 11:21]. [Emphasis added]

32. *See* Sory Touré v. Republic of Guinea, *supra*, Chapter 3, fn. 30, holding that the right to a decision within a reasonable time is assessed in light of the circumstances of the case, including its complexity, the behavior of the applicant and that of the competent administrative and judicial authorities; Ehivet & Gbagbo v. Republic of Ivory Coast, *supra*, Chapter 3, fn. 30.

concept of "swiftness," we can learn from comparative and transposable law case law, for example, that a tribunal has the duty to resolve the dispute with reasonable speed avoiding useless measures.[33]

[F] Obligation to Inform the Parties

Under both arbitration systems, there is an obligation upon arbitrator(s) to inform the parties and, where applicable, secretary-general of arbitration centers, of any facts, circumstances, situation that may raise doubts in the mind of the parties on the independence or impartiality of an arbitrator. The duty to inform exists at the onset of the proceedings and throughout them. In other words, before accepting appointment, an arbitrator must ensure there is no reason for any party involved to have doubts about the independence of the prospective arbitrator; once appointed and confirmed, where applicable, the arbitrator is under the obligation to reveal any similar fact or circumstances that may arise or come to their knowledge during the proceedings.

Under the UAA, Article 7 paragraphs 3 and 4 states:

> Any potential arbitrator informs the parties of any circumstance likely to create in their minds a legitimate doubt about their independence and impartiality and may accept their appointment only with their unanimous and written consent.
>
> From the date of their appointment and throughout the proceedings, the arbitrator must reveal any such circumstances to the parties without delay.

The CCJA Regulation on Arbitration states, at Article 4.1., paragraphs 3 to 5:

> Before their appointment or confirmation by the Court, the prospective arbitrator must disclose in writing to the Secretary-general any circumstances likely to raise legitimate doubts about the arbitrator's impartiality or independence.
>
> Upon receipt of this information, the Secretary-general communicates it in writing to the parties and sets a time limit for them to present their respective comments.
>
> The arbitrator must immediately disclose, in writing to the Secretary-general and the parties, any similar circumstances which may occur between their appointment or confirmation by the Court and the notification of the final award.

The revised version of Article 4.1 of the Regulation on Arbitration now includes the express obligation for arbitrator(s) to disclose in writing any element or circumstance likely to raise legitimate doubts about their impartiality or independence. This obligation preexisted but was reinforced. Likewise, it is specified that written submissions from the arbitrator concerned, the parties, and the other members of the arbitral tribunal must be communicated to all other stakeholders[34] (the parties to the dispute and the other arbitrators) within an appropriate period.

---

33. Cour d'appel [CA] [regional court of appeal] Paris, 1st ch. C, n° 14/05436, Feb. 4 1999: GP 2001.som. 1907 (Fr).
34. CCJA Regulation on Arbitration, Art. 4.2, para. 3.

[G] Obligation to Stay the Proceedings and Refer the Parties to an Omitted Preliminary Step

A new Article 8-1 has been added to the UAA as part of the revision of the arbitration rules in November 2017. It states that:

> In the presence of an agreement requiring the parties to comply with a pre-arbitration dispute resolution step, the tribunal, upon request of a party, ascertains that the agreement has been complied with and if applicable, refers the parties to the completion of that preliminary step.
>
> If the preliminary step has not been initiated, the arbitral tribunal stays the proceedings for a time period it deems appropriate, to allow the most diligent party to complete that step.
>
> If the preliminary step has actually been initiated, the arbitral tribunal takes notice, If applicable, of its failure.

That new provision of Article 8-1 of the UAA has been reproduced, in quasi identical terms, in Article 21-1 of the CCJA Regulation on Arbitration.[35] It expressly allows parties to insert step clauses in their agreement(s). For an illustration of such a clause, see *Société Générale de Banques en Côte d'Ivoire v. Kobenan Tah,*[36] where the agreement of the parties stipulated, for the settlement of any dispute, the obligation of a prior attempt at conciliation before, if necessary, recourse to arbitration under the CCJA Rules. It will be up to the parties, if they choose to provide for a preliminary step such as mediation, to properly draft their step clause in order to differentiate it from a clause providing for prior conciliation. Articles 8-1 of the UAA and 21-1 of the CCJA Regulation on Arbitration remind arbitrator(s) of their obligation, in the presence of a step clause in the agreement of the parties, and if a party requests it, to ensure the clause is complied with by staying the proceedings, where necessary, in order to allow the implementation of the omitted preliminary step.

Since the Legislator has not provided for any sanction, it is not a procedural formality to be carried out sua sponte by the arbitral tribunal. However, the stay of the arbitration proceedings to allow the completion of the formality in question becomes mandatory if the parties have provided for it in their agreement, and one of them expressly requests it. If the arbitral tribunal disregards the completion of such a formality, in the presence of a clear stipulation of the parties and the request of one of them, the arbitral tribunal may be sanctioned by the annulment of its award for breach of public order (procedural in this case), and or failure to comply with its mission.

Parties are advised to ensure that any request for the prior formality omitted is made in a timely manner. This can be done by ensuring that their request is recorded in the minutes of their meetings or hearings or their exchanges with the tribunal as

35. The main difference between Art. 8-1 of the UAA and Art. 21-1 of the CCJA Regulation on Arbitration is that the three paragraphs of the latter are numbered 21-1.1, 21-1.2 and 21-1.3.
36. Société Générale de Banques en Côte d'Ivoire v. Kobenan Tah, N° 075/2016, Decision, [C.C.J.A.], 2e ch., (Apr. 21, 2016), http://www.ohada.com/jurisprudence/ohadata/J-17-24.html. *See also* Roger v. Fofana, N° 024/2010, *supra*, Chapter 1, fn. 16; Tradex Centrafrique v. Transport Madina, N° 181/2019, Decision, [C.C.J.A.], 1e ch., (Jun. 26, 2019).

appropriate. As far as they are concerned, the arbitrators will have to take note of any procedural details in writing from the start of the proceedings, to prevent late claims from a party that they have raised the issue which the tribunal has ignored.

[H] Obligation to Give a Fair and Equal Treatment to the Parties

Under Article 9 of the UAA and the first sentence of Article 16 paragraph 2 of the CCJA Regulation on Arbitration,[37] parties must be treated equally, and each party must be given full opportunity to present their case. There are cases illustrating, under both the UAA (§3.04[H][1]) and the CCJA Rules (§3.04[H][2]), what amounts to fair and equal treatment to the parties and what is not.

[1] Under the UAA

There is a breach of equal treatment of parties to the arbitration which may justify the annulment of an award when:

- parties to an arbitration file divergent copies of the arbitration rules, one stating fifteen days and the other thirty days, and the arbitrators grant different time limits for the parties to prepare and present their defense (based on the divergent rules filed by the parties);
- arbitrators discriminate in applying the contract to one party while refusing to do so for the other party to the dispute; and
- the arbitrators remain silent on the submission of a party.[38]

However, there is no breach of equal treatment, and an appellate court is wrongly criticized for violating Article 9 of the UAA by rejecting the plea alleging breach of the adversarial principle on the grounds "that the [appellant] not have been prevented from asserting their rights throughout the arbitration procedure (...)" since it is established that after having fixed the deliberations of the case on August 4, 2014, the Arbitral Tribunal on July 10, 2014, requested counsel for both parties, not just counsel for the [appellee] as claimed by [the appellant], to produce a certain number of exhibits by July 17, 2014; and the documents produced for this purpose by the [appellee] were communicated to the counsel for [the appellant] on July 21, 2014, and the latter had sufficient time to reply before the award was made on 4 August 2014. The argument is devoid of merit and must be rejected.[39] The obligation imposed on arbitrators to treat the parties equally often goes hand in hand with the obligation to allow parties to assert

37. For the first time, the OHADA Legislator affirmed in the CCJA Regulation on Arbitration the right of the parties to be treated equally by the arbitral tribunal. The first sentence of para. 2 of revised Article 16 enshrines this innovation by the complete reproduction of Art. 9 of the UAA.
38. CA Centre, Feb. 6, 2008, N° 52/Civ., (Cameroon), http://www.ohada.com/jurisprudence/ohadata/ J-10-249.html.
39. Prévoyance Assurances S.A. v. Eiffage Sénégal, N° 220/2018, Decision, [C.C.J.A.], 1e ch., (Nov. 29, 2018).

their respective rights, which is often assimilated by case law to the right to adversarial proceedings.[40]

[2] Under the CCJA Rules

Under the CCJA Rules, the obligation for arbitrators to treat parties to arbitration proceedings equally has been asserted by the CCJA in *Société Ivoirienne de Raffinage v. Bona Shipholding LTD,*[41] where the CCJA ruled that under Article 19 of the CCJA Regulation on Arbitration, it is up to the arbitral tribunal to assess the appropriate investigative measures for the resolution of the dispute submitted to it. Consequently, by deciding, in the light of "the particularly complex facts of the situation" discussed by all the parties through adversarial proceedings, "that it cannot therefore in [the case at hand], conclude that there is a case of force majeure," the arbitral tribunal which rendered the award under review did not breach the principle of equal treatment between the parties, which must be observed in arbitration.

§3.05 ROLE OF THE PRESIDING ARBITRATOR

The role of the chairman of an arbitral panel is relevant only under the CCJA Rules and is governed by Article 22.3 of the CCJA Regulation on Arbitration. It is presented *infra*, at Chapter 12, §12.04[B].

§3.06 CHOICE OF LAW GOVERNING THE ARBITRATOR'S OBLIGATIONS, RIGHTS AND PROTECTIONS

Under both sets of rules (the UAA and the CCJA Rules), there is, per se, no right for the parties to arbitration proceedings to choose the law governing the rights and obligations of arbitrator(s). However, parties are free to agree on the use of some international rules applicable to arbitration proceedings, as long as those rules do not conflict with the provisions of the UAA. Some of those rules are the *International Bar Association (IBA) Guidelines on Conflicts of Interest in International Arbitration*

40. *See* for example, CA Pointe-Noire, Mar. 4, 2005, *supra*, Chapter 2, fn. 10, where the Court of Appeal of Pointe-Noire held that it results from the combined provisions of Arts. 9 and 14 paras. 5 and 6 of the UAA [before revision] that the arbitrator's compliance with the adversarial principle, the absence of which entails annulment of the award, means, on the one hand, the obligation of the tribunal to grant each party the opportunity to make their claims, to know those of their opponent and to proceed with their discussion, and on the other hand, of the prohibition to rely on arguments raised sua sponte by the arbitrator without the parties being invited beforehand to discuss them or to carry out personal investigations on their own. In the case at hand, the arbitrator who states in their award that they conducted an investigation themselves without involving the parties or subjecting their findings of facts or law to the discussion of the parties—moreover not recorded in minutes—breached the adversarial principle, since the reasoning of their award establishes peremptorily that the arbitrator relied on the information gathered during his solitary investigation. The award was annulled.
41. Société Ivoirienne de Raffinage v. Bona Shipholding LTD, N° 029/2007, Decision, [C.C.J.A.], Ass. plen., (Jul. 19, 2007), http://www.ohada.com/jurisprudence/ohadata/J-08-241.html.

(2014), the *IBA Rules on the Taking of Evidence in International Arbitration (2014)* ("IBA Rules"),[42] as well as the *Rules on the Efficient Conduct of Proceedings in International Arbitration*, known as the *"Prague Rules."*[43] Such rules can only supplement the applicable rules, and whenever they are chosen, they might incidentally have an impact on the rights and obligations of arbitrator(s). However, there is no publicly available record of reference to any such rules in arbitration proceedings governed by either the UAA or the CCJA Arbitration Rules.

42. Available at: https://www.ibanet.org/Publications/publications_IBA_guides_and_free_materials.aspx#collapse3 [accessed Mar. 20, 2020 at 17:16].
43. Available at https://praguerules.com/prague_rules/ [accessed Mar. 20, 2020, at 17:11].

CHAPTER 4

Selection of Arbitral Seat

Chapter 4 has four sections on the importance of the selection of arbitral seats (§4.01), the selection of seat by the parties (§4.02), by the CCJA in the absence of an agreement by the parties (§4.03), and the possibility to hold meetings and hearings in a location different from the seat of the arbitration under the CCJA Rules (§4.04).

§4.01 IMPORTANCE OF SELECTION OF ARBITRAL SEAT

There is a general rule under which "jurisdiction to set aside an award belongs to the competent state courts of the country in which the award was made and only alternatively to the courts of the country under the law of which the award was made."[1] There is another general rule according to which an arbitral award is rendered at the place where it has been signed.[2] Under OHADA Arbitration Rules, the seat of arbitration is very important because it dictates the applicable law to the proceedings and determines the competent courts for annulment of the award as well as any enforcement issues where enforcement is carried out on the territory of any of the seventeen OHADA Members States.[3] As it has been stressed in the introduction,[4] the CCJA has exclusive jurisdiction of last resort on all matters relating to arbitration as far as the UAA and the CCJA Arbitration Rules are involved. Thus, the national competent

1. *See* Mauro Rubino-Sammartino, *Links amongst venue, Lex Fori and jurisdiction to set aside proceedings*, https://www.lexology.com/library/document.ashx?g=64771aad-d5b4-4800-9f1c-51085c8ccdfe [accessed 21 Mar. 2020] (Rubino-Sammartino, 2020).
2. *See* Hiscox v. Outhwaite [1991] 2 WLR 1321, http://newyorkconvention1958.org/index.php?lvl=notice_display&id=892 [accessed Mar. 21, 2020]. It must be noted however, as pointed out by Mauro Rubino-Sammartino, that the law has been amended in England and now provides that "*Unless otherwise agreed by the parties, where the seat of the arbitration is in England and Wales or Northern Ireland, any award in the proceedings shall be treated as made there, regardless of where it was signed, despatched or delivered to any of the parties.*" *See* Rubino-Sammartino, *supra*, Chapter 4, fn. 1.
3. *See* in the introduction, *supra*, for the list of those seventeen countries.
4. *Supra*, Introduction fn. 14, 15.

court of the seat of the arbitration has jurisdiction to annul an award rendered under the UAA, and the decision of that court can be appealed only before the CCJA. For institutional arbitration proceedings governed by the CCJA Rules, any request for annulment is filed directly before the CCJA, the decision of which is final and binding as well.

Under OHADA rules, there are specific reasons for which the seat of arbitration is important.

First, under Articles 10 and 14 of the Treaty, the OHADA Rules, including the UAA and the CCJA Arbitration Rules are binding and mandatory in all the States Parties after they have been enacted and become enforceable.

Second, under Article 1 of the UAA, "[the UAA] is applicable to any arbitration where the seat of the arbitral tribunal is in one of the States Parties."

Third, an arbitral award "must be signed by the arbitrator(s)"[5] and "is deemed to have been rendered at the seat of the arbitration and on the day of its signing."[6]

Fourth, the jurisdiction of the CCJA covers only the geographical territory of the OHADA Member States (for personal jurisdiction) and the matters described in Article 2 of the OHADA Treaty, which includes arbitration under the UAA and the CCJA Rules (for subject matter jurisdiction). Thus, only arbitration proceedings for which the seat has been located within the OHADA geographical territory, namely in one of the seventeen Member States, are within the purview of the CCJA. In light of this, the CCJA has constantly ruled that the UAA does not apply to arbitration proceedings where the seat was outside the geographical scope of the Treaty, namely in a country other than one of the seventeen States Parties. That was the case in *Safic Alcan Commodities v. complexe Chimique Camerounais*,[7] where the arbitration seat was in London (England), and in *Ottakringger Brauerei v. Union Camerounaise des Brasseries*,[8] where the seat was in Switzerland.

Since, as mentioned above, an arbitral award is deemed to have been rendered at the seat of the arbitration, and the UAA applies to any arbitration where the seat of the arbitral tribunal is in one of the States Parties to the Treaty, to comply with those rules, all arbitration proceedings carried out within the geographic territory of OHADA are governed either by the UAA or the CCJA Rules and must have their seat in one of the States Parties to the Treaty, except for specific matters for which another treaty has provided a different arbitration mechanism. Even though the OHADA Arbitration Rules

5. CCJA Regulation on arbitration, Art. 22.3 para. 2. UAA, Art. 21 para. 1.
6. *Id.*, Art. 22.2. This specific rule does not exist per se in the UAA, but it is implied.
7. Safic Alcan Commodities v. Complexe Chimique Camerounais, N° 020/2011, Decision, [C.C.J.A.], 3e ch., (Dec. 6, 2011), http://www.ohada.com/jurisprudence/ohadata/ J-13-164. html. The CCJA ruled that arbitration that took place outside the OHADA space (in London in this case) is not governed by the UAA and the Court of Appeal which applied the UAA to such proceedings violated Article 1 of the UAA and set out its judgment to cassation. On de novo review, the CCJA held that the Court of Appeal wrongfully considered itself competent and wrongfully applied the UAA to the proceedings. Therefore, the CCJA must decline jurisdiction.
8. Ottakringger Brauerei v. Union Camerounaise des Brasseries, N° 113/2018, Decision, [C.C.J.A.], 2e ch., (May 6, 2018). On de novo review and for the same reasons that entailed cassation of the ruling of the Court of Appeal, the CCJA held that the Douala Court of Appeal did not have jurisdiction over that arbitration, the seat of which was in a country foreign country to the OHADA space.

cover any arbitration proceedings carried out within the geographical scope of the Treaty, matters not included in the ten matters currently covered by Article 2 of the Treaty,[9] or governed by specific arbitration rules under another treaty are neither governed by OHADA Arbitration Rules nor under the purview of the CCJA's jurisdiction. An illustration of that exception can be found in *Area Assurances v. Proassur*, where the CCJA ruled that notwithstanding the fact that the headquarters of the National Arbitration and Dispute Resolution Commission is in Cameroon, a State Party to the OHADA and CIMA[10] Treaties, the arbitral award rendered under the CIMA Code, which constitutes an autonomous Community law, is subject neither to the UAA nor to a Regulation under the Treaty. Thus, the related dispute does not fall under the jurisdiction of the CCJA, which must decline jurisdiction.[11]

§4.02 SELECTION OF THE SEAT BY THE PARTIES

Under Article 13 paragraph 1 of the CCJA Regulation on Arbitration, "the seat of the arbitration is set by the arbitration agreement or by a later agreement of the parties." Thus, the choice of the seat of arbitration is primarily the prerogative of the parties.

§4.03 SELECTION OF THE SEAT BY THE CCJA IN THE ABSENCE OF AGREEMENT BY THE PARTIES

In the absence of an agreement of the parties on the seat of arbitration, the seat is set by a decision of the CCJA made before the file is sent to the arbitral tribunal.[12] Finally, where circumstances make it difficult or impossible to proceed with the arbitration at the initial seat, the CCJA may, on the request of the parties, a party or the arbitrator, choose another seat.[13] It must be noted that in any event, the arbitral tribunal cannot change the seat on its own or even upon the request of a party. Only the CCJA can make such a decision. It must be remembered that those decisions are made by the CCJA in its capacity as an arbitral institution administering arbitration proceedings and not as a Court of law.[14]

9. *Supra*, Introduction, fn. 9.
10. CIMA, is the French acronym for the "*Conférence Interafricaine des Marchés d'Assurance*," the *Inter-African Conference on Insurance Markets*. It was created by the Convention establishing the International Conference of Insurance Controls (CICA), signed on Jul. 27 1962 by thirteen African States, replaced by the Treaty establishing an Integrated Organization of the Insurance Industry in African States as community organization the Inter-African Conference on Insurance Markets, signed in Yaounde (Republic of Cameroon) on Jul. 10, 1992. So far, fourteen of the OHADA States Parties have signed the Treaty: Benin, Burkina, Cameroon, Central African Republic, Comoros, Côte d'Ivoire, Gabon, Guinea Bissau, Equatorial Guinea, Mali, Niger, Senegal, Chad and Togo. Comoros has not ratified the Treaty, which is in force only in the other thirteen States. https://cima-afrique.net/historique/?lang=en a [accessed Mar. 22, 2020].
11. Area Assurances v. Proassur, N° 195/2019, Decision, [C.C.J.A.], 2[e] ch., (Jun. 27, 2019).
12. CCJA Regulation on Arbitration, Art. 13, para. 2.
13. *Id.*, Art. 12, para. 4.
14. On this important distinction, *see infra*, Chapter 5, fn. 43-47.

§4.04 HOLDING OF HEARINGS AND OTHER MEETINGS AT A PLACE DIFFERENT FROM THE SEAT

The tribunal may not have the power to change the seat of the arbitration, but unless otherwise agreed, the tribunal may, after consultation with the parties, decide to hold hearings and meetings and deliberate in any place it considers appropriate.[15]

The old version of Article 13 allowed the tribunal, after consulting the parties, to hold hearings elsewhere than the seat of the arbitration and left it to the CCJA to settle any disagreement on this question. While maintaining the possibility to hold hearings in a different location from the seat of the arbitration, the revised version of the Regulation on arbitration currently in force eliminates the possibility of having a possible dispute decided by the CCJA but, in return, gives the parties more freedom by allowing them to object to the holding of hearings, meetings and deliberations in a place different from the seat of the arbitration. Therefore, parties are advised to ensure that a common position on these details is reached before a dispute arises.

The only important thing to remember, if the tribunal decides to hold hearings and other meetings in a place different from the seat of the arbitration, is that the award itself must be signed at the seat of arbitration to remain within the boundaries of the OHADA Arbitration Rules and the purview of the CCJA for the possible petition for annulment or any other enforcement-related issues.

Apart from its Article 1 which determines the scope of its application and its Article 20 c) which states that an arbitral award must indicate the seat of arbitration, the UAA contains no other specific reference to the seat; however, most of the rules relating with the seat under the CCJA rules present above are implied for arbitration proceedings governed by the UAA.

15. CCJA Regulation on Arbitration, Art. 13, para. 3.

CHAPTER 5
Parties' Choice of the Procedure

It will be highlighted in this chapter that when it comes to the choice of the procedure, the autonomy of the parties is also the key rule (§5.01), followed by the discretion of an arbitral tribunal if the parties fail (§5.02). There are some mandatory procedural requirements that need to be complied with (§5.03), and in all cases, judicial non-interference is highly regarded by the CCJA (§5.04).

§5.01 PARTIES' AUTONOMY TO DETERMINE ARBITRAL PROCEDURE

Parties' autonomy in the determination of the procedure will be presented under the UAA (§5.01[A]) and the CCJA Rules (§5.01[B]).

[A] Under the UAA

Under Article 14, paragraph 1 of the UAA, which states that "the parties may, directly or by reference to arbitration rules, determine the arbitral procedure. They may also subject it to a procedural law of their choice," parties theoretically have the latitude to choose procedural rules for the arbitration proceedings. However, the UAA in itself can be construed as the procedural framework of arbitration proceedings it governs. Its mandatory nature, as highlighted under Article 10 of the Treaty, leaves little room to the parties for choosing other procedural rules for arbitration proceedings the UAA governs. In line with this, the CCJA ruled, in *Société Construction métalliques Ivoiriennes v. Fraternité Saint Jean-Eudes d'Abatta*, that the UAA has replaced the preexisting laws organizing arbitration in the domestic law of the States Parties to the Treaty, leaving only the possible standards of organization of institutional arbitration which are not contrary to the UAA.[1] Indeed, Article 10, paragraph 1 of the UAA states that "where the parties have agreed to refer to an arbitration institution, they are committed to applying the arbitration rules of that institution unless they expressly waive specific provisions in agreement with this institution."

Thus, parties really can choose other procedural rules only where there is a vacuum in the UAA itself or, where applicable, in the rules of any arbitration center they refer their dispute to. It must be kept in mind that any national or local arbitration center located in any of the OHADA States Parties must operate in accordance with the provisions of the UAA, and no provision of the arbitration rules of such center cannot be enforced if it conflicts with any provision of the UAA. Likewise, where parties choose ad hoc arbitration based solely on the UAA, they can agree to choose any other procedural rules, provided such rules do not conflict with the provisions of the UAA. Finally, it must be emphasized that, in light with Article 10 paragraph 1 of the UAA quoted above, the parties cannot waive any provision of the UAA; they can only waive provisions of the rules of an arbitration center they choose, and only if the said rules allow such waiver.

[B] Under the CCJA Rules

The CCJA Regulation on Arbitration "is applicable to the proceedings before the arbitral tribunal and in its silence, the rules which the parties or, failing that, the arbitral tribunal determines, with or without reference to the law of procedure applicable to arbitration, will be applicable."[2] As it was emphasized in the introduction,[3] the CCJA Arbitration Rules are mandatory, and parties can choose additional procedural rules only "in the silence" of the CCJA Arbitration Rules. The large scope of the different rules that form the CCJA Arbitration Rules[4] seems to leave very little room for any legal vacuum justifying the use of other rules, but in any event, parties are free to supplement the CCJA Arbitration Rules with other rules on matters not specifically regulated in details, such as determination of conflicts of interest, the taking of evidence, among others. For these issues, parties could refer to the *IBA Guidelines on Conflicts of Interest in International Arbitration (2014)*, the *IBA Rules on the Taking of Evidence in International Arbitration (2014)*, or the *Prague Rules* mentioned earlier.[5]

1. Société Construction métalliques Ivoiriennes v. Fraternité Saint Jean Eudes d'Abatta, N° 062/2012, Decision, [C.C.J.A.], 3e ch., (Jun. 7, 2012), http://www.ohada.com/jurisprudence/ohadata/J-14-167.html.
2. CCJA Regulation on Arbitration, Art. 16, para. 1.
3. *Supra*, Introduction, fn. 10.
4. *Id.*, fn. 22, 23.
5. *See supra*, Chapter 5, §5.01[B].

§5.02 ARBITRAL TRIBUNAL'S DISCRETION TO DETERMINE THE PROCEDURE

The discretion of an arbitral tribunal to determine the procedure will also be presented under the two systems.

[A] Under the UAA

In the absence of an agreement of the parties on the rules to govern the procedure, the arbitral tribunal may proceed with the arbitration as it deems appropriate.[6] As noted in the introduction, *supra*, the institutional arbitration governed by the CCJA Regulation on Arbitration and Articles 21-26 of the Treaty, on the one hand, and arbitration governed by the UAA, on the other hand, are completely separate and operate independently, the CCJA having repeatedly clarified the different regimes of the two arbitration systems. It follows that, in principle, the CCJA Arbitration Rules do not apply to proceedings governed by the UAA. However, one may wonder whether the wording of Article 14, paragraph 1 of the UAA, which allows the parties to refer to arbitration rules, without precision, would not allow the use of the CCJA Arbitration Rules to govern the procedure. The wording seems to allow this, but parties are advised not to refer to the CCJA Arbitration Rules for arbitration governed by the UAA to avoid any risk of confusion, except for the parties and or the arbitrators to ensure that such reference is made only to govern the procedure. If necessary, nothing prevents the arbitral tribunal from extracting specific provisions from the said Rules in order to draw up a body of rules to govern their procedure. The aim is to avoid any risk of confusion at all costs.

[B] Under the CCJA Rules

The procedural rules set out in the CCJA Regulation on Arbitration are, in principle, intended to be sufficient for the procedure. However, it is permitted to supplement them, if necessary, with rules that the parties have chosen or, in the absence of choice by them, those that the arbitral tribunal itself will decide to use as a supplement. It is not a matter of replacing the provisions of the CCJA Arbitration Rules, which are mandatory and binding on the parties and the Court (Article 10.1 of the CCJA Regulation on Arbitration), but only of supplementing them if necessary. The old version of Article 16 of the CCJA Regulation on Arbitration allowed arbitrators when required to supplement the procedural rules, to refer to "an internal law of procedure applicable to arbitration." The revised version of Article 16 paragraph 1 of the CCJA Regulation on Arbitration allows them to refer to "the procedural law applicable to arbitration," without further details. This wording may seem vague since, apart from the CCJA Arbitration Rules, there is no other set of rules governing the procedure of institutional arbitration under the aegis of the CCJA, which is not attached to any

6. UAA, Art. 14, para. 2.

national legal order because of its supranational nature. The reference to a "domestic law" of procedure, i.e., undoubtedly a national law, for example, that of a State Party to the Treaty) seems more precise to us. But in any event, the determination of a supplementary procedural law should not be a problem if the parties take care to think about it beforehand.

§5.03 MANDATORY PROCEDURAL REQUIREMENTS

It has been written that "legislation and/or judicial decisions in most developed jurisdictions require that arbitral proceedings seated in local territory satisfy minimal standards of procedural fairness and equality. These standards are variously referred to as requiring 'due process,' 'natural justice,' 'procedural regularity' or 'fair and equitable treatment.'"[7] Likewise, under OHADA Arbitration Rules, there are several mandatory procedural requirements, the absence of which may entail or justify, depending on the circumstances, stay of the arbitration proceedings or the annulment of an arbitral award. For example, as discussed *supra*, an arbitral tribunal has to stay the proceedings where parties have agreed to submit to a pre-arbitration dispute resolution step (such as conciliation or mediation), which would not have been complied with.[8] Where it is established that mandatory procedural requirements such as due process, adversarial principle, or fair and equal treatment have been breached, then the award will inevitably be annulled.[9]

§5.04 JUDICIAL NON-INTERFERENCE

Given the deeply damaging consequences they may have on the proceedings, there is no interlocutory judicial review of procedural decisions of arbitral tribunals under the OHADA Rules.

[A] Under the UAA

Judicial non-interference can be found through Articles 11 and 13 of the UAA, which respectively embody the *competence-competence* principle (§5.04[A][1]) and the exclusive jurisdiction of an arbitral tribunal where there is a valid arbitration agreement (§5.04[A][2]).

7. *See* Born, Gary B., *The Principle of Judicial Non-Interference in International Arbitral Proceedings* (Nov. 15, 2011). University of Pennsylvania Journal of International Law, Vol. 30, No. 4, 2009, at 1020. Available at SSRN: https://ssrn.com/abstract=1959827. (Born, 2009).
8. *See supra*, Chapter 3, §3.04[G].
9. *See infra*, Chapter 14 on the grounds for the annulment of an award.

[1] The Jurisdiction of an Arbitral Tribunal to Rule on Its Own Jurisdiction

Article 11, paragraph 1 of the UAA states that "the arbitral tribunal has exclusive jurisdiction to rule on its own jurisdiction, including on all issues relating to the existence or validity of the arbitration agreement." That provision characterizes the widely recognized *competence-competence* principle in international arbitration, which is regularly enforced by the CCJA like it did in *Sow v. Aka.*[10] In a recent case, *Ousseini v. Délégation de l'Union Européenne au Niger,* the CCJA held that only an arbitral tribunal has jurisdiction to examine the validity of the arbitration clause and to rule on the case on the merits and by declining jurisdiction, upon de novo review, the Court of Appeal does not incur in any way the alleged grievances and the appeal must be dismissed.[11] The CCJA also held that the "*competence-competence*" principle is autonomous.[12]

However, there are few important points parties must keep in mind regarding the "*competence-competence*" principle.

First, "any objection to arbitral jurisdiction *must* be raised before any defense on the merits except where the facts on which it is based have been disclosed later."[13] Thus, any party who is not convinced of the jurisdiction of the tribunal for any reason whatsoever will ensure that the objection is raised clearly from the outset, thus providing a possible favorable outcome if they are to refer to the competent court for remedies. Very often, a well-formulated challenge at this stage provides additional arguments to be raised before the competent court. In other words, the parties should not wait to raise possible incompetence of the arbitral tribunal for the first time before

10. *Supra,* Chapter 1, fn. 22.
11. Ousseini v. Délégation de l'Union Européenne au Niger, N° 152/2018, Decision, [C.C.J.A.], 3e ch., (Jun. 7, 2018). The CCJA added that the judgment is wrongly criticized for having, on the basis of the arbitration clause contained in the contract, declined the jurisdiction of the Court of Appeal and for having thus failed to rule on certain claims, while para. 2 of the arbitration clause makes the Niamey labor court competent for any dispute relating to the contract; that finally, this arbitration clause is manifestly null in that it departs from Art. 6 of the Civil Code and the public policy provisions of the Labor Code and cannot, in any way, justify the incompetence of the labor court. This is so since it is established that upon the claimant's referral to the labor court, the respondent objected to jurisdiction; that the Court of Appeal, to which this count was not referred, did not find the arbitration clause manifestly void.
12. La Société Bougainvilliers v. Mochet, N° 069/2015, Decision, [C.C.J.A.], Ass. plen., (Apr. 29, 2015), http://www.ohada.com/jurisprudence/ohadata/J-16-71.html. The Court of Appeal of Dakar (Senegal) held that "the parties who claim that the arbitration agreement is void and sought its cancellation, executed it in part by participating in the pre-arbitration conference, appointing an arbitrator and filing their brief, and even wished to extend the arbitration to others who are not parties to the arbitration agreement." On appeal against that ruling, the CCJA held that Arts. 11 and 4 of the UAA establish the "*competence-competence*" principle of the arbitrators and the principle of the validity of the arbitration agreement which must be assessed, without reference necessary to a state law, thus according to the common will of the parties. The Court of Appeal which refused to set aside the arbitral awards subject to its censorship on the grounds that the arbitral tribunal had, out of its judicial discretion, deduced from the facts of the case, including the desire to "extend arbitration to others who [were] not parties to the arbitration agreement," a common will of the parties to accept the said arbitration notwithstanding the cancellation of the current account agreement, did not in any way violate the law.
13. UAA, Art. 11, para. 2.

the Court hearing an appeal; incompetence must have been raised before the arbitral tribunal, and the latter must have had the opportunity to rule on its jurisdiction. Arbitrators may be advised, even in the absence of a challenge to their jurisdiction, to take notice in their award, even as a preliminary step, of their jurisdiction to settle the dispute which was submitted to them. This would reduce the risk of a later invalidation of their award for incompetence, except in cases where the causes of incompetence appear after the commencement of the proceedings.

Second, it has been ruled that the "*competence-competence*" principle, which allows arbitrators to rule on the intrinsic validity of the arbitration agreement and thus rule on their jurisdiction, is not absolute in scope since the state courts hearing an annulment petition under Article 26 of the UAA ascertain the jurisdiction of the arbitral tribunal. It follows that the petition for annulment filed in this context is admissible.[14] The CCJA affirmed the same view in *Wanmo v. Nguessi*,[15] where it specified that the competent court for annulment judge may control the arbitral tribunal's assessment of the clause that led the tribunal to retain its jurisdiction.

Third, there is no breach of Article 11, paragraph 1 of the UAA where an award has been rendered on the basis of a valid arbitration clause, as held in *Oryx Bénin v. Société Africaine de Distribution et de Négoce*.[16]

[2] The Exclusive Jurisdiction of an Arbitral Tribunal to Rule on the Merits

The first three paragraphs of Article 13 of the UAA state:

> When a dispute subject to arbitration proceedings under an arbitration agreement is brought before a State court, the latter must, if requested by one of the parties, decline jurisdiction.
>
> If the dispute has not yet been referred to the arbitral tribunal, or if no request for arbitration has been filed, the state court must also decline jurisdiction, unless the arbitration agreement is manifestly null or manifestly inapplicable to the case. In that case, the competent court renders a final decision on its jurisdiction within a maximum of fifteen (15) days. That decision can be challenged only before the Common Court of Justice and Arbitration in accordance with its Rules of Procedure.

In any event, the State court may not decline jurisdiction on its own motion.

14. CA Centre, Sept. 30, 2009, N° 381/Civ., *supra*, Chapter 1, fn. 10.
15. Wanmo v. Nguessi, N° 151/2017, *supra*, Chapter 2, fn. 21.
16. Oryx Bénin v. Société Africaine de Distribution et de Négoce, N° 154/2016, Decision, [C.C.J.A.], 3e ch., (Oct. 27, 2016), http://www.ohada.com/jurisprudence/ohadata/J-17-94.html. The CCJA held that a Court of Appeal which upheld an arbitral award rendered did not violate Art. 11, para. 1 of the UAA where the exclusive commercial distribution agreement of the parties contained a clause under which any dispute between them would be settled by an arbitral tribunal, in the absence of an amicable agreement all the parties have each signed the said contract in their various documents, including in the mission letters issued to the ad hoc arbitral tribunal.

Ten different situations have been settled by cases and will be presented hereafter. There are the autonomy of the arbitration clause (§5.04[A][2][i]), an unproven emergency requiring conservatory measures (§5.04[A][2][ii]), urgent measures involving substantive examination of the merits (§5.04[A][2][iii]), assessment, on the merits, of the nullity of an arbitration agreement (§5.04[A][2][iv]), the existence of an outright arbitration clause (§5.04[A][2][v]), no waiver of arbitration (§5.04[A][2][vi]) an arbitration clause providing for state courts only as a last resort (§5.04[A][2][vii]), the validity of an arbitration clause not reiterated in successive agreements of the parties in the absence of novation (§5.04[A][2][viii]), disputes submitted to arbitration (§5.04[A][2][ix]) and the implementation of the objection to jurisdiction (§5.04[A][2][x]).

[i] Autonomy of the Arbitration Clause

In the presence of agreements providing for recourse to arbitration for the settlement of disputes, it is in violation of Articles 4 and 13 of the UAA that a Court of Appeal retained its jurisdiction, subjecting the validity of the arbitration clause to that of the agreement which contains it, following the termination of that agreement, to decide that the claimant could not avail themselves of the arbitration clause contained in the contract, thus exposing its judgment to cassation. On de novo review, the judgment which rejected the objection to the jurisdiction of the arbitral tribunal must be quashed.[17]

[ii] Unproven Emergency Requiring Conservatory Measures

If it is true that Article 13 of the UAA authorizes the competent judge for interim measures to rule on emergency matters, even in areas where jurisdiction has been assigned to an arbitral tribunal, it is only on the condition that the parties justify the urgency that they invoke. In the absence of evidentiary documents, the alleged disagreement between shareholders and the paralysis of the normal functioning of a company's organs are not sufficient to characterize a threat to the interests of that company and its shareholders and justify the appointment of an interim administrator to manage and administer it. The only correspondence denouncing the actions of another officer of the company is insufficient. This is all the more so since the chairman of the board of directors who requests the judicial administration of the company concerned, which is a limited company with complex management based on a multitude of governing bodies, does not justify having brought the facts complained of in his correspondence to the attention of the board of directors, whom he does not dispute that he did not meet regularly. Consequently, the conditions for the jurisdiction of the judge for interim measures of the Abidjan court to hear this dispute are not met. Therefore, that judge wrongfully declared themselves competent and ordered the

17. Canac Sénégal v. Transrail, N° 082/2014, Decision, [C.C.J.A.], 2e ch., (May 22, 2014), http://www.ohada.com/jurisprudence/ohadata/J-15-173.html.

appointment of an interim director. Their decision must be overturned, and the Court of Appeal, ruling again, must declare that judge incompetent.[18]

In the presence of a contractual clause stating that "the parties must make their best efforts to reach an amicable settlement of any dispute that may arise between them under the contract. In the absence of an amicable settlement within 60 days after the corresponding request of one of the parties for an amicable [out of court] settlement, each party will be entitled to refer the matter to arbitration under the OHADA conciliation and arbitration. The arbitration will take place in Dakar ...," it was by a violation of Article 13 of the UAA that a Court of Appeal upheld the interim order which ignored the objection to jurisdiction, terminated the agreement of the parties and ruled against one of them. This is so because the decision to terminate and rule against one party in no way constitutes a protective or provisional measure under Article 13 of the UAA. Upon de novo review, it must be the termination decision that cannot be considered as a protective or provisional measure, and the arbitration agreement, which is not manifestly void, must have its effects. The interim order must be overturned, and jurisdiction of the Court declined.[19]

[iii] Urgent Measures Involving Substantive Examination of the Merits

If under paragraph 4 of Article 13 of the UAA, the competent judge for interim measures can rule in emergency matters even in the presence of an arbitration clause, the measures they would have to order must not in any way involve an examination of the dispute on the merits. The petition seeking the release of a pledge made under a demand guarantee agreement necessarily involves an examination of the validity of the guarantee agreement concluded by both parties, which results in incompetence of the judge for interim measures. Thus, the Court of Appeal, which retained its jurisdiction, disregarded the provisions of Article 13 of the UAA and set out its decision to the cassation. On de novo review, the CCJA must overturn the interim order at hand and decline jurisdiction.[20]

[iv] Assessment, on the Merits, of the Nullity of an Arbitration Agreement

The Court of Appeal, which, in order to hold that the request for a transactional protocol to be declared void falls within the jurisdiction of the state court because the dispute had not yet been referred to the arbitral tribunal, merely stated that "it also follows from Article 13, paragraph 2 of [the UAA] that if, as in the case in which the dispute has not been referred to the arbitral tribunal, the state court must also declare

18. CA Abidjan, Jul. 8, 2011, N° 260/11, (Ivory Coast), http://www.ohada.com/jurisprudence/ohadata/J-13-192.html.
19. Liquidation Société Cim Sahel Energie v. Les Ciments du Sahel, N° 047/2015, Decision, [C.C.J.A.], Ass. plén., (Apr. 27, 2015), http://www.ohada.com/jurisprudence/ohadata/J-16-47.html.
20. United Bank for Africa v. Beneficial Life Insurance, N° 018/2015, Decision, [C.C.J.A.], 2e ch., (Apr. 2, 2015), http://www.ohada.com/jurisprudence/ohadata/J-16-18.html.

itself incompetent, it is on the condition that the arbitration agreement is manifestly void," without demonstrating how the arbitration agreement contained in the transaction protocol is manifestly void, did not give a legal basis for its decision which must be quashed. Upon de novo review, it follows from the combination of the principle of validity and that of *competence-competence* in arbitral matters that the state judge cannot carry out a substantial and in-depth examination of an arbitration agreement to rule on the nullity of the latter. The manifest nullity of an arbitration agreement must arise only from the appearance of the arbitration agreement. In the case at hand, the substantial and thorough examination falling outside the jurisdiction of the state court, the Tribunal of First Instance was wrong in retaining jurisdiction. Therefore, the CCJA must overturn the challenged judgment, declare itself incompetent by reason of the arbitration agreement and refer the case and the parties to the arbitration under their transactional protocol.[21]

[v] Outright Arbitration Clause

In the presence of a clause in the agreement of the parties stipulating that "the competent jurisdiction to hear any dispute or challenge that may arise from the application or interpretation of the Memorandum of Understanding and its annex can only be an arbitral tribunal under the aegis of the International Chamber of Commerce and its arbitration rules," and under Article 13 paragraphs 1 and 2 of the UAA, any State court to which such dispute has been referred must decline jurisdiction. It is, therefore, in violation of the provisions set out above that a Court of Appeal has declared itself competent to rule on the merits of the case notwithstanding the existence of the arbitration clause, and its decisions must be overturned.[22]

The nullity of a company's General Assembly resolutions is well governed by the stipulation of the articles of association according to which "any disputes over the application of these, either between partners or between one of them and the company, will be resolved exclusively through arbitration," without any distinction between legal acts of public order and others. As a result, the judge must declare himself incompetent.[23]

The judge who, in the presence of express contractual stipulations submitting any dispute "to arbitration under the rules of the South African Arbitration Foundation in Sandton, Gauteng, South Africa," stated that since the dispute arose of the contractual non-performance in case of force majeure, the competent judge is that of the place of performance, to retain the jurisdiction of the Malian courts has disregarded the provisions of Article 13 of the UAA since, by these stipulations, the parties have

21. Sarr v. Mutuelle d'Assurances des Taxis Compteurs d'Abidjan, N° 043/2008, Decision, [C.C.J.A.], 1e ch., (Jul. 17, 2008), http://www.ohada.com/jurisprudence/ohadata/J-09-81.html.
22. Société de Manufacture de Caoutchouc de Côte d'Ivoire v. May, N° 012/2005, Decision, [C.C.J.A.], 1e ch., (Feb. 24, 2005), http://www.ohada.com/jurisprudence/ohadata/J-05-357.html.
23. Tribunal de Grande Instance [TGI] [high court] Wouri, Jun. 3, 2011, N° 640, (Cameroon), http://www.ohada.com/jurisprudence/ohadata/J-12-212.html.

unequivocally chosen arbitration as the only way to resolve their disputes; judgment overturned. On the novo review, the appeal is admissible in form but on the merits, and for the same reasons as those which led to the cassation, the judgment must be overturned, and the objection to jurisdiction is founded.[24]

[vi] No Waiver of Arbitration

The willingness of the parties to waive the arbitration agreement contained in a contract, when it is tacit, can only be manifested once the dispute has arisen. Moreover, it must be certain, i.e., the result of acts clearly and unequivocally demonstrating the intention of the party against whom it is opposed, to waive the arbitration clause and to accept the jurisdiction of the state court. Breaking a contract cannot in itself, in the absence of an unequivocal manifestation of will in this sense, characterize a tacit waiver of that arbitration agreement. In the case at hand, for the respondent, such a will could only be manifested by the unqualified acceptance of the debate on the merits before the state judge by the claimant, on the understanding that such a procedural attitude, under paragraph 2 of Article 13 of the UAA implies a tacit waiver of the arbitration agreement and acceptance of the jurisdiction of the state judge. The state judge was therefore wrong to dismiss the objection of lack of jurisdiction raised as ill-founded and to retain their jurisdiction, holding that "the parties had voluntarily waived their right to refer the dispute to arbitration, Company [A.] for breaking the contract without implementing the arbitration procedure and the Company [B.] for taking the matter to the Commercial Court." The challenged judgment must be overturned in all its provisions and, ruling again, the Court of Appeal must declare itself incompetent.[25] The reasoning of the Court of Appeal as to the impossibility of implicitly waiving the arbitration clause before the litigation arises is justified, but in the presence, in the case at hand, of a clause providing for institutional arbitration under the CCJA Rules, it is Article 23 of the Treaty which should have been targeted to justify the rejection of the alleged implied waiver, as the UAA does not apply to institutional arbitration under the CCJA Rules.[26]

[vii] Arbitration Clause Providing for State Courts Only as a Last Resort

In the interpretation of agreements, it is necessary to seek the common will of the parties. The clause of a contract stating that all disputes relating to the contract "can be

24. Nedbank v. Grands Moulins du Mali, N° 244/2018, Decision, [C.C.J.A.], 2e ch., (Nov. 29, 2018).
25. CA Pointe-Noire, Nov. 7, 2008, N° 046, (Congo), http://www.ohada.com/jurisprudence/ohadata/J-13-76.html.
26. Société Nationale Pour la Promotion Agricole v. Société des hydrocarbures du Bénin, N° 045/2008, Decision, [C.C.J.A.], Ass. plen., (Jul. 17, 2008), http://www.ohada.com/jurisprudence/ohadata/J-09-83.html; Ekwa Ngalle v. Société Nationale d'Hydrocarbures, N° 102/2015, *supra*, Chapter 2, fn. 31; Republique de Guinee v. Getma International, N°139/2015, Decision, Cour Commune de Justice et d'Arbitrage [CCJA] [Common Court of Justice and Arbitration] [C.C.J.A.], (Nov. 19, 2015), http://www.ohada.com/jurisprudence/ohadata/J-16-132.html.

settled by arbitration" must be considered as a whole, and it must be remembered that the dispute may be referred to state courts "only as a last resort." The trial judge was, therefore, right in declining jurisdiction under Article 13 of the UAA, and the judgment must be upheld.[27] A reading of the entire clause makes it clear that the parties have not planned to settle their possible disputes only by arbitration:

> Any dispute relating to the contract must be settled amicably and by direct negotiation between the client and the contractor. If negotiations fail, these disputes may be resolved through arbitration. The arbitration panel will be composed as follows, the arbitrator appointed by the client, the arbitrator appointed by the contractor, the arbitrator jointly appointed by the client and the contractor. In the absence of settlement by arbitration, disputes will be decided as a last resort by the competent courts of Ouagadougou.

By its decision, the Court of Appeal clarified the intention of the parties, recalling that recourse to state courts was only provided, in this case, after the failure of a friendly settlement or arbitration. Therefore, the trial judge declared themselves incompetent because their jurisdiction was subsidiary. But such clause is to be avoided because the condition "in the absence of a settlement by arbitration" is ambiguous: it can only be understood in the case where arbitration, for one reason or another could not be implemented, because once an arbitral tribunal will have ruled, the dispute will have been "settled by arbitration."

[viii] Validity of the Arbitration Clause not Reiterated in Successive Agreements in the Absence of Novation

Can an arbitration clause, which has not been reiterated in successive agreements of the parties, remain valid and enforceable in the absence of novation of the contract? The Court of Appeal of Ouagadougou (Burkina Faso) answered yes. In its ruling, the Court held that the existence of a transaction does not preclude invoking the provisions of the original contract, which remains the source of relations between the parties who must execute it in good faith in accordance with the provisions of Article 1134 of the Civil Code. The appellant was, therefore, right to have availed themselves of the arbitration clause under the medium-term credit agreement to object to the jurisdiction of the higher court. In addition, the trial judge violated Article 13 of the UAA, and the judgment must be overturned. Ruling again, the commercial courts of Burkina Faso must decline jurisdiction.[28]

27. CA Ouagadougou, May 19, 2006, N° 116, (Burkina Faso), http://www.ohada.com/jurisprudence/ohadata/J-09-25.html.
28. CA Ouagadougou, Mar. 21, 2008, N° 028, (Burkina Faso), http://www.ohada.com/jurisprudence/ohadata/J-12-133.html.

[ix] Disputes Submitted to Arbitration

If the parties have agreed to submit "all disputes" to arbitration, the state court to which a party has referred a dispute involving the enforcement of a mortgage through foreclosure to must, under Article 13 of the UAA, declare itself incompetent.[29]

[x] Implementation of the Objection to Jurisdiction

In any event, the state court to which a dispute governed by an arbitration clause has been referred must decline jurisdiction even where the case has not yet been referred to an arbitral tribunal,[30] and where the dispute has already been referred to arbitration, the state court before which a petition for interim or protective measures such as an expertise order has been filed must decline jurisdiction if the requested measure will prejudice the merits of the case.[31]

The state court to which a dispute governed by an arbitration clause has been referred can decline its own jurisdiction only on the condition that one of the parties requests it,[32] and the objection to the jurisdiction of the state court must be raised *in limine litis*.[33] Where the petitioner has not complied with the provisions of Article 13 of the UAA, paragraph 1, namely they failed to have raised the objection timely before the state court, the appeal before the CCJA must be dismissed[34] because such failure can be construed as a waiver of the arbitration clause, according to the ruling of the CCJA in *Société Navale Guinéenne v. Société Africaine de Commerce*.[35]

---

29. Tribunal de Grande Instance [TGI] [high court] Mifi, Aug. 1, 2006, N° 79/civ., (Cameroon), http://www.ohada.com/jurisprudence/ohadata/J-07-70.html.
30. Tribunal de Grande Instance [TGI] [high court] Ouagadougou, Sept. 28, 2005, N° 416/2005, (Burkina Faso), http://www.ohada.com/jurisprudence/ohadata/J-07-114.html.
31. *See* Ascot Commodities v. Dieye, N° 125/2016, Decision, [C.C.J.A.], 2e ch., (Jun. 23, 2016), http://www.ohada.com/jurisprudence/ohadata/J-17-66.html, in which the CCJA ruled that under Art. 891.3 of the Senegalese Code of Civil Procedure, the State Court may take interim or provisional measures when a dispute has been referred to an arbitral tribunal, provided that these measures do not prejudice the merits. In the case at hand, the expertise ordered by the first judges tended not only to safeguard the rights of the defendant, but to rule on the quantum of the remainder of the debt owed. The arbitral tribunal having had to rule on this point, the expert opinion was wrongfully ordered; therefore, the request for an opinion order must be rejected.
32. Feby Konan v. Haidar, N° 009/2006, Decision, [C.C.J.A.], 1e ch., (Jun. 29, 2006), http://www.ohada.com/jurisprudence/ohadata/J-07-23.html.
33. TPI Douala Bonanjo, Jul. 19, 2012, N° 714/Civ., (Cameroon), http://www.ohada.com/jurisprudence/ohadata/J-14-48.html. In particular, the court held that the incompetence of a state court dealing with a dispute despite the existence of an arbitration agreement between the parties is *merely relative* and must be raised *in limine litis*. The exception of incompetence raised after the parties have submitted their arguments on the merits is inadmissible. [Emphasis added].
34. Feby Konan v. Haidar, *supra*, Chapter 5, fn. 32.
35. Société Navale Guinéenne v. Société Africaine de Commerce, N° 047/2010, Decision, [C.C.J.A.], 2e ch., (Jul. 16, 2010), http://www.ohada.com/jurisprudence/ohadata/J-12-95.html. The CCJA held that by raising, for the first time, in cassation before the CCJA, the incompetence of the CCJA based on an arbitration clause, even though it is generally accepted in arbitration matters that, in a dispute to be submitted to an arbitral tribunal under an arbitration agreement, if the claimant takes the matter to a state court in spite of this agreement and the respondent does not

However, the CCJA remains competent for an appeal against the decision of a Court of Appeal, which ruled on the existence of an arbitration clause.[36]

[B] Under the CCJA Rules

The CCJA has often been often criticized for impartiality, especially because of its "double hat" in managing arbitral proceedings and then ruling the on the merits where an award is challenged. It has been said that it would not be impartial because of its acts as judge and party.[37]

After the recent reform of the OHADA Arbitration Rules, it has been written:[38]

> The same judges who, with an "administrative hat," participate in the constitution of the arbitral tribunal (first, as regards appointments, and then with respect to challenges), opine on the prima facie existence of an arbitration agreement, scrutinize the draft award and fix the arbitrators' fees, would later also consider, wearing their "judicial hat," an annulment action against, or a request for the enforcement of, an award.
>
> The European Court of Human Rights in Strasburg, France, decided in 1995 in *Procola v. Luxembourg* that one and the same organ could not render *administrative decisions* and then render a *judicial decision* in that respect in an impartial way.[39] This reasoning applies squarely to the judges at the CCJA: there is an inherent risk and therefore a permanent doubt in the mind of users of CCJA arbitration that the judges handing down the *judicial decision* will feel bound by the previous *administrative decisions* of their colleagues at the Court. It is that

---

raise the incompetence of that jurisdiction, it is because the parties have waived their arbitration agreement, the objection to the jurisdiction of the CCJA, is a new argument which, as such, must be declared inadmissible.

36. *See* Ousseini v. Délégation de l'Union Européenne au Niger, N° 152/2018, *supra,* Chapter 5, fn. 11, where the CCJA held that The inadmissibility of an appeal, raised on the ground that since the dispute had not yet been referred to an arbitral tribunal, the referral to the CCJA, which is a cassation court and that this procedural irregularity violates the principle of double degree of jurisdiction must be dismissed, as the appeal is lodged against the decision of a Court of Appeal ruling on the interpretation of the provisions of the UAA in relation to the existence of an arbitration clause. The CCJA being the cassation court in this matter, the appeal is admissible. The principle of "double degree of jurisdiction" originates form the civil law concept "*principe du double degré de juridiction.*" *See* the glossary, *infra.*
37. *See* Frédéric Maury, *Affaire Getma-Guinée: les arbitres répondent,* http://www.jeuneafrique.com/285543/societe/affaire-getma-guinee-les-arbitres-repondent/ [accessed Dec. 22, 2016, at 11:30] (Maury F., 2015). The author reported an open letter by which the three arbitrators involved in the Getma case alleged that the CCJA, as a court of law, is judge of its own action as an arbitral institution ("*La Cour, comme juridiction, est juge de sa propre action comme institution d'arbitrage*"). I have previously published the analysis appearing under this section of the book (§5.04[B]) in Mahutodji Jimmy Vital Kodo (Dir.), *Code Pratique Francis Lefebvre OHADA. Traité, Actes Uniformes et Règlements Annotés, 20-21,* 212-213, Editions Francis Lefebvre, 2019. (Kodo, Al Dabbagh, & Boismain, 2019); reproduced with the permission of Editions Francis Lefebvre.
38. Michael W. Bühler, *Out of Africa: The 2018 OHADA Arbitration and Mediation Law Reform,* 35 J Int'l Arb. 527 (2018). [Emphasis added]. (Bühler, 2018). *See also* Michael W. Bühler, Anne-Sophie Gidoin, *Le défi de la complémentarité entre le juge et l'arbitre dans l'espace OHADA,* Penant, n° 904, 2018, p. 293-294. (Bühler Michael W., 2018).
39. Procola v. Luxembourg, App. N° 14570/89, Eur. Ct. H.R., http://hudoc.echr.coe.int/eng?i=001-57944 [accessed 27, 2020. at 12:48].

possible doubt, which is the problem for parties submitting to the jurisdiction of CCJA arbitration.

Finally, in footnote n° 43 of the publication, the author indicates that "a strict separation of functions and the instauration of 'Chinese Walls' therefore does not solve the basic problem, contrary to what is sometimes suggested."[40]

Paragraph 45 of the *Procola* judgment cited by the author reads as follows:

> 45. The Court notes that four members of the Conseil d'Etat carried out both *advisory* and *judicial functions* in the same case. In the context of an institution such as Luxembourg's Conseil d'Etat the mere fact that certain persons successively performed these two types of function in respect of the same decisions is capable of casting doubt on the institution's structural impartiality. In the instant case, Procola had legitimate grounds for fearing that the members of the Judicial Committee had felt bound by the opinion previously given. That doubt in itself, however slight its justification, is sufficient to vitiate the impartiality of the tribunal in question, and this makes it unnecessary for the Court to look into the other aspects of the complaint.[41]

The criticisms presented above call upon the following observations, in order to avoid any confusion.

First, and contrary to the "*judicial*" and "*administrative*" decisions referred to by the authors, the ECHR rather contrasted "*advisory*" functions with "*judicial*" functions in *Procola v. Luxembourg.*[42] However, it is indisputable that the advisory and administrative functions are not at all the same. The "*advisory*" functions of the CCJA (which, rightfully, are not at all exercised in arbitration proceedings under the aegis of the CCJA) must be distinguished from the "*administrative*" functions of the CCJA in matters of arbitration, within the framework of which *the restricted formations of the Court*[43] *do not act as an advisory body*. Indeed, the "advisory" function of the CCJA is always performed in the Full Court[44] and is part of the judicial activity of the Court, unlike the function of *administration* of arbitration proceedings, the purely administrative nature of which emerges from Article 1 of the CCJA Regulation on Arbitration itself which provides, on the one hand, that "The decisions that the Court makes in this regard to ensure the implementation and the successful completion of arbitration proceedings and those related to the review of the award, are *administrative in nature*,"[45] and on the other hand that "The *administrative decisions* made by the Court are *devoid of res judicata effect* and *without appeal* … ."[46] Article 2.2 of the same

40. Büehler, *supra, supra,* Chapter 5, fn. 38, referring to Kodo/Aka, The CCJA as a Regional Arbitration Institution, in The Transformation of Arbitration in Africa: The Role of Arbitral Institutions 47, 56 (E. Onyema ed., Kluwer Law International 2016). (Kodo Mahutodji Jimmy Vital, 2016).
41. Procola v. Luxembourg, *supra,* Chapter 5, fn. 39. [Emphasis added].
42. *Id.*
43. While handling arbitration matters in its capacity as an arbitral institution, the CCJA acts through restricted formations ("*formation restreintes*") usually formed of three-judge panels appointed each year. *See* the glossary, *infra.*
44. "Full Court" refers to the meeting of all the judges of the court. *See* the glossary, *infra.*
45. CCJA Regulation on Arbitration, Art. 1.1, para. 2. [Emphasis added].
46. *Id.*, Art. 1.1, para. 6. [Emphasis added].

Regulation adds that "the *Court does not settle disputes itself*. It appoints or confirms the arbitrators. It is informed of the progress of the proceedings and examines draft awards."[47]

Second, the *Procola* judgment only questioned the *concurrently holding* of the "*advisory function*" (which for the CCJA is part of its "judicial" activity in accordance with the Treaty and the Rules of Procedure of the CCJA) with the "*judicial function.*" The "*advisory function*" of the CCJA, which is totally absent in arbitration, is not akin to an "*administrative function,*" and the *Procola* judgment of the ECHR, which has castigated the *concurrently holding* of "*advisory*" and "*judicial*" functions, seems to be an irrelevant argument as used by the above authors and cannot validate the criticisms presented.

Finally, there are several precedents in comparative law that seem to be closer to the operation of the CCJA and its arbitration center. For example, the Cassation Court of France held that the judgment on the merits in which a magistrate participated who had ordered, in the same case, an interim measure not prejudicing the merits, corresponds to a judgment rendered by an independent court.[48] On March 11, 2009, the same Cassation court of France, held that the decision ruling on the motion for the annulment of an arbitral award, in which participated a magistrate who was on the date of that award secretary-general of the Court of Arbitration of the International Chamber of Commerce was not rendered by a biased court, because, in their capacity as secretary-general of the ICC Court, that magistrate had exercised only the functions of *organizing* arbitration, had *no jurisdictional powers* and *had not intervened in the judicial mission of the arbitrators.*[49]

The decision of March 11, 2009 above is very relevant insofar as the situation at issue before the Cassation Court is similar to that of the CCJA in matters of arbitration. It is interesting to note that this judgment has been widely commented on, and none of the four authors commenting on it clearly disapproved of the decision of the French Cassation Court. For one commentator, the argument that the Court, in violation of Article 6 paragraph 1 of the European Convention on Human Rights, was composed, in particular of a magistrate, former secretary-general of the ICC Court of Arbitration, under the auspices of which the award was rendered, which could raise a legitimate doubt as to the impartiality of the said magistrate, is "not serious and even somewhat improper," since the institution only assists the administration of arbitration under its aegis and does not judge cases.[50]

Similarly, another author wrote that "the argument lacks seriousness in the sense that the award is rendered by the arbitrators appointed either by the parties themselves

47. *Id.*, Art. 2.2. [Emphasis added].
48. Cour de cassation [Cass.] [supreme court for judicial matters] 2e civ., Jan. 24, 2014 n° 12-01345 (Fr).
49. Cour de cassation [Cass.] [supreme court for judicial matters] 1e civ., Mar. 11, 2009 n° 08-12149; D. 2009, Somm. 880, obs. X. Delpech (Fr.), (Xavier, 2009); Gaz. Pal. 2009, 1309 note G. Huchet (Fr.); Petites Affiches [PA] 2009 n° 144 p. 20 note C. Tse (Fr.); JCP E. 2009, 1781, chr. n° 10 obs. C. Seraglini (Fr.). [Emphasis added].
50. Christophe Seraglini, *Mauvais procès quant à l'impartialité d'un magistrat*, JCP E. 2009, 1781, chr. n° 10 at 24. (Seraglini, 2009).

or by the Court on their delegation. At no time does the secretary-general interfere in the arbitration process, disrupt it or participate in it."[51] Commenting on the same judgment, a third author wrote that "the arbitration center organizes and maintains the police while the arbitral tribunal settles the dispute between the parties."[52] Likewise, the CCJA, in performing its administrative duties in arbitration matters, only "organizes" arbitration proceedings and "maintains the police"[53] and does not "settle" the dispute of the parties, which is the sole prerogative of the arbitral tribunal.

In light of these observations, it should also be noted that the French Cassation Court has held that:

> The requirement of independence and impartiality of the arbitrator falls under the control of the judge of the regularity of the award, since the arbitration center can only contract, as to the guarantee of these essential qualities of arbitrators, an obligation of means[54] possibly sanctioned by its responsibility; that the judges of the merits noted that "the ICC's arbitration rules ensured the *distinction between the function of organization of the arbitration*, in particular through the 'International Court of Arbitration,' and the *judicial function*, left to arbitrators, the 'court' having no jurisdictional powers." In this regard, the Court of Appeal was correct in concluding that the communication of the draft award to the International Court of Arbitration did not interfere with the arbitrator's judicial mission but was only aimed at ensuring the effectiveness of arbitration. Thus, the Court of Appeal rightly deduced from its statements the lawfulness of the contract for the organization of arbitration in relation to the requirements of international public order.[55]

In any event, the CCJA arbitration system can be improved; without even waiting for a possible future reform and if this can help to blur some criticisms and further reassure the "users" of institutional arbitration under its aegis, the CCJA could, after deliberation in the General Assembly, decide that when it rules in litigation on the petition to annul an award rendered under its aegis, the three judges who have composed the restricted panel that administered the arbitration proceedings will recuse themselves. This measure, which in principle should not require the meeting of the Council of Ministers, would not hinder the functioning of the plenary session of the CCJA since there would still be ten other judges each time to rule on the cases concerned.

51. Guillaume Huchet, Gaz. Pal. 2009, 1311. (Huchet, 2009).
52. Christophe Tse, *Mais jusqu'où ira-t-on ? Après les arbitres et les centres d'arbitrage, on s'en prend au juge de l'annulation* ..., Petites Affiches [PA] 2009 n° 144 p. 21 (Fr.). (Christophe, 2009).
53. It must be emphasized that the arbitral tribunal itself has the power to "maintain the police" of the hearings and all the meetings relating to the arbitration proceedings. Such "police powers" of the tribunal can be seen through Art. 19.1, para 6 which states that "The hearing of the parties *takes* place on the day *and place set* by the arbitral tribunal," and more relevant, Art. 19.5, para. 1 which states that "the arbitral tribunal invites the parties to the *hearings*, the conduct of which *are regulated by the tribunal* ... ." [Emphasis added].
54. *See* the glossary, *infra*.
55. Cour de cassation [Cass.] [supreme court for judicial matters] 1e civ., Feb. 20, 2001 n° 99-12574 (Fr). [Emphasis added].

CHAPTER 6

Evidence and Discovery

This chapter will present the disclosure and discovery powers of an arbitral tribunal (§6.01) and the role of national courts in obtaining evidence for the arbitration proceedings (§6.02).

§6.01 DISCLOSURE AND DISCOVERY POWERS OF THE ARBITRAL TRIBUNALS

[A] Under the UAA

Before mentioning the specific powers of the arbitral tribunal under the UAA, it must be recalled that an arbitral tribunal may proceed with the arbitration as it deems appropriate if the parties have not determined applicable procedural rules[1] and that the parties bear the burden of alleging and proving the facts supporting their claims.[2] Under Article 14 of the UAA, arbitral tribunals have three main investigative prerogatives.

First, an arbitral tribunal "may invite the parties to provide it with factual explanations and to submit to it, by any legally admissible means, the evidence it deems necessary for the resolution of the dispute."[3] When the tribunal goes this route, it is under the duty to ensure due process, adversarial proceedings since it can neither retain in its ruling, the arguments, explanations or evidence submitted or relied upon by a party, only if the other party has been in a position to discuss them,[4] nor can it base its ruling on sua sponte evidence without collecting comments of the parties or at least inviting them beforehand to submit them.[5]

1. UAA, Art. 14, para. 2.
2. *Id.*, para. 3.
3. *Id.*, para. 9.
4. *Id.*, para. 10.
5. *Id.*, para. 11.

Second, the arbitral tribunal has the power, unless the parties have decided otherwise, to settle any incidental claims concerning the verification of the authenticity of documents or forgery.[6] No available case at this stage illustrates the implementation of these powers that arbitrators will have to exercise with discretion but reasonably.

Finally, the arbitral tribunal may, where necessary and after consulting the parties or upon their request, appoint one or more experts to report on specific issues it determines and hear them at the hearing.[7]

In *Oryx Bénin v. Société Africaine de Distribution et de Négoce*, the CCJA held that the party which had not cooperated with the expert whose appointment it had requested, as an interlocutory measure from the arbitral tribunal, and which has refrained from commenting on the report of the expert at the request of the tribunal as well as on the observations of the opposing party could not validly reproach the confirmatory judgment of the awards at issue for the failure to respond to the submissions in violation of Article 26 of the UAA.[8] In other words, once the tribunal orders an investigative measure, such as an expertise like in the case at hand, the parties must comply with the measure. Also, the CCJA teaches us in *Prévoyance Assurances v. Eiffage Sénégal* that, like a judge, an arbitrator is not bound by the findings of the expert they have appointed.[9]

[B] Under the CCJA Rules

Under the CCJA Rules, an arbitral tribunal also has investigative powers similar to those governed by the UAA.

---

6. *Id.*, para. 14.
7. *Id.*, para. 15.
8. Oryx Bénin v. Société Africaine de Distribution et de Négoce, *supra*, Chapter 5, fn. 16. The CCJA ruled that the party which has not cooperated with the expert whose appointment it has requested, as an interlocutory measure, from the arbitral tribunal and which has refrained from commenting on the report of the expert at the request of the tribunal as well as on the observations of the opposing party cannot validly reproach the confirmatory judgment of the awards at issue for the failure to respond to the submissions in violation of Art. 26 of the UAA. This is so since, contrary to the allegations of the plaintiff in the appeal, the defendant company, in its mission letter addressed to the ad hoc arbitral tribunal, requested, as an interlocutory measure before judgment, an accounting and financial expertise of the operations carried out by the two parties, from the signature of their contract to the occurrence of dispute; that it is on the basis of the two mission letters that the arbitration rules were proposed by the ad hoc arbitral tribunal and approved by the two parties; that under Art. 9 of the said rules of arbitration, the arbitral tribunal ad hoc ordered the expert opinion by interim Judgment No. 03/2012; that following this decision ordering the appraisal of the accounts, it is not disputed on the one hand, that the plaintiff company refrained from providing the designated expert with the documents in its possession to facilitate the work of the expert and, on the other hand, that it did not comment either on the report as requested by the ad hoc arbitral tribunal or on the observations of the defendant company relating to the report which were been communicated.
9. Prévoyance Assurances S.A. v. Eiffage Sénégal, *supra*, Chapter 3, fn. 39, ruling that in order to determine the quantum of compensation, an arbitral tribunal, like any judge on the merits, is in no way bound by the opinion that an expert would record in his report, even at the request of the arbitrator.

First, the tribunal may decide, on its own motion, to hear the parties,[10] which can be done, at the discretion of the tribunal, separately if deemed necessary and in the presence of both parties' counsel.[11] Such witness hearings take place on the date and place decided by the tribunal.[12]

Second, the tribunal uses its discretion in determining the admissibility of the evidence submitted by the parties and in assessing their probative force.[13]

Third, the tribunal "may also decide to hear witnesses, experts appointed by the parties or any other person, in the presence of the parties, or in their absence provided that they have been duly summoned."[14]

Finally, the arbitral tribunal may, unless the parties agree otherwise, appoint one or more experts to report on specific issues it will determine and invite the expert(s) to testify at the hearing. If necessary, the arbitral tribunal may require a party to provide the expert with all appropriate information or to submit or make available to the expert, for scrutiny, any exhibits or other relevant items.[15] The new version of the CCJA Regulation on Arbitration, in Article 19.4, now indirectly limits the power of an arbitral tribunal to appoint experts and define their mission and hear them at hearings. The parties can now limit or even deny this possibility by an agreement because the investigatory powers of an arbitral tribunal are not obligations imposed on the arbitrators to order specific measures. In *Pyramidion v. Agence d'Exécution des Travaux d'Infrastructure du Mali*, it was held that under Article 19 of the CCJA Regulation on Arbitration, it is the prerogative the arbitral tribunal to assess the suitability of appropriate investigative measures to resolve the dispute, such as the hearing of a witness. Neither the transcript of the witness statements nor the establishment of the minutes of the hearing constitutes an obligation imposed on the arbitral tribunal by the CCJA Regulation on Arbitration, to which the parties have agreed to submit their dispute. Therefore, the arbitrators cannot be criticized for not having carried out these formalities.[16] The discretionary nature of the power of the arbitral tribunal in using its investigatory prerogatives, such as in the appointment of an expert, has been affirmed several times, like in *Etat du Mali v. Groupe TOMOTA*,[17] and in *Benin Control v. Etat du Bénin*.[18]

10. CCJA Regulation on Arbitration, Art. 19.1, para. 2.
11. *Id.*, Art. 19.1, para. 5.
12. *Id.*, Art. 19.1, para. 6.
13. *Id.*, Art. 19.1, para. 3.
14. *Id.*, Art. 19.2.
15. *Id.*, Art. 19.4.
16. Pyramidion v. Agence d'Exécution des Travaux d'Infrastructure du Mali, N° 098/2014, Decision, [C.C.J.A.], Ass. plén., (Oct. 30, 2014), http://www.ohada.com/jurisprudence/ohadata/J-15-189.html.
17. Etat du Mali v. Groupe TOMOTA, N° 033/2015, Decision, [C.C.J.A.], Ass. plén., (Apr. 23, 2015), http://www.ohada.com/jurisprudence/ohadata/J-16-33.html.
18. Benin Control v. Etat du Bénin, N° 103/2015, Decision, [C.C.J.A.], Ass. plén., (Oct. 15, 2015), http://www.ohada.com/jurisprudence/ohadata/J-16-96.html.

§6.02 ROLE OF NATIONAL COURTS IN OBTAINING EVIDENCE FOR THE ARBITRATION PROCEEDINGS

[A] Under the UAA

Article 14, paragraph 12 of the UAA, states that "where the assistance of judicial authorities is necessary for the taking of evidence, the arbitral tribunal may, sua sponte or upon request, seek the assistance of a competent court in the State Party."

On the taking of evidence, the arbitral tribunal is entitled to seek, on its own motion or on request, the assistance of the competent court. The available cases prior to the reform, which remain transposable except in specific cases, do not seem to have already decided on the practicalities of such collaboration between the arbitral tribunal and the competent court. Nevertheless, the subject is worthy of interest, particularly with regard to referral to the competent court, since the arbitral tribunal is allowed to refer to the competent court if necessary. Thus, it is necessary to determine how the arbitral tribunal will refer the matter to the competent court. Since the arbitral tribunal does not have the possibility of asking a preliminary question to the competent court, it will have to use ordinary ways to refer to the said court, probably a motion or petition.

Also in this case, and if, as it is likely to be the case, the competent court must be referred to by means of a lawyer, it must also be determined whether the arbitral tribunal should resort to a lawyer since counsel of the parties would be conflicted and may not represent the arbitral tribunal at the same time. If the arbitral tribunal is to use its own counsel in order to be able to "interrogate" the competent court, the question of the fees and costs of this incidental procedure, which would be added to the original procedure, will also have to be resolved. What would be the methods of settlement of these costs by the parties? Who would determine them? Etc. Perhaps it would be easy to get these costs settled by the parties or the only party that raised the matter before the national judge; but the issue would be more complex if the arbitral tribunal decided on its own motion to refer the matter to the competent court, as Article 14 allows. Arbitrators will ensure as much as possible to avoid or at least limit any recourse to the court to this effect. They may also, if the difficulty is foreseeable, make arrangements upstream and in agreement with the parties during the preliminary hearing.

[B] Under the CCJA Rules

Under the CCJA Arbitration Rules, there is no specific reference to national courts in obtaining evidence, probably because of the supranational nature of the CCJA itself under the Treaty. That is probably the reason why the OHADA Legislator ensured arbitration proceedings could be carried out without the need to refer any issue to national courts. Theoretically, however, it does not seem absolutely impossible that the support of a national court becomes needed in some proceedings, and the CCJA will have to set the guidelines, should the issue be raised in the future.

CHAPTER 7
Provisional Measures

The three main sections of this chapter will focus on the provisional measures ordered by an arbitral tribunal (§7.01), the judicial enforcement of the provisional measures ordered by arbitrators (§7.02) and the provisional measures ordered by national courts in aid of arbitration (§7.03).

§7.01 PROVISIONAL MEASURES ORDERED BY THE ARBITRAL TRIBUNAL

[A] Under the UAA

Article 14 of the UAA empowers an arbitral tribunal to order some provisional measures where needed. It states in its last paragraph that "the arbitral tribunal may also, upon the request of either party, order interim or conservatory measures, with the exception of interim attachments and judicial sureties which remain within the jurisdiction of state courts." Illustrating the limitation of the power of an arbitral tribunal when ordering provisional measures, the CCJA held, in *Fowe v. Banque Internationale du Cameroun pour l'Epargne et le Crédit*, that arbitral justice, unlike state courts, does not have jurisdiction for enforcement measures such as attachment of real estate or foreclosure of a mortgage.[1]

Measures likely to be ordered by a tribunal are, among other, bailiff reports,[2] mandatory injunctions,[3] injunctive reliefs,[4] order of some advance payments, temporary authorization for some construction work. The same comments and suggestions regarding the forecast of the possible costs of provisional measures that the tribunal

1. Fowe v. Banque Internationale du Cameroun pour l'Epargne et le Crédit, N° 119/2019, Decision, [C.C.J.A.], 3e ch., (Apr. 11, 2019).
2. From the French "*constat d'huissier*"; *see* the glossary, *infra*.
3. From the French "*Injonction de faire*"; *see* the glossary, *infra*.
4. From the French "*Injonction de ne pas faire*"; *see* the glossary, *infra*.

may have to order at the request of one or more parties[5] apply here. Parties would do well in providing, at the outset of the procedure, for the mechanisms for financing and allocating the costs relating to these various measures.[6]

[B] Under the CCJA Rules

Like the UAA, Article 10-1 of the CCJA Regulation on Arbitration states, about the provisional measures, that "unless otherwise stipulated, the arbitration agreement confers jurisdiction on the arbitral tribunal to rule on any claim for provisional or conservatory measures during the arbitration proceedings, with the exception of claims relating to court-ordered securities and interim attachments." Under the CCJA Regulation on Arbitration, the limitation to the power of an arbitral tribunal to order enforcement measures, as highlighted in *Fowe v. Banque Internationale du Cameroun pour l'Epargne et le Crédit,*[7] also apply because the rules are similar on this issue.

§7.02 JUDICIAL ENFORCEMENT OF PROVISIONAL MEASURES ORDERED BY ARBITRATORS

Under the UAA, judicial enforcement of interim provisional measures ordered by an arbitral tribunal will be subject to *exequatur* by the national competent courts, under Article 30 of the UAA.[8]

Under the CCJA Regulation on Arbitration, a request for *exequatur* may be filed immediately where *exequatur* is required for the enforcement of any interim provisional measure ordered by an arbitral tribunal.[9] Also, the motion for *exequatur* is filed before the President of the CCJA,[10] and the decision on *exequatur* of the awards relating to provisional or conservatory measures must be made within three (03) days of the filing of the motion to the Court.

5. *See supra,* Chapter 6, §6.02[A].
6. *See,* for the enumeration of some of these measures in French law, which is quite similar, Cécile Chainais, "*Les mesures provisoires dans le nouveau droit français de l'arbitrage: à la recherche d'une complémentarité vertueuse entre arbitre et juge étatique,*" in J. van Compernolle, J.-F. van Drooghenbroeck et A. Saletti (dir.), *L'arbitre et le juge étatique,* éd. Bruylant, 2014, p. 303 at 44. (Cécile, 2014).
7. Fowe v. Banque Internationale du Cameroun pour l'Epargne et le Crédit, N° 119/2019, *supra,* Chapter 7, fn. 1.
8. Article 30 of the UAA states that "the arbitral award is enforceable only by virtue of an *exequatur* decision issued by the competent court in the State Party."
9. CCJA Regulation on Arbitration, Art. 10-1, para. 2.
10. CCJA Regulation on Arbitration, Art. 30.4 which states that "the decision of the president granting *exequatur* cannot be appealed."

§7.03 PROVISIONAL MEASURES ORDERED BY NATIONAL COURTS IN AID OF ARBITRATION

As it was already highlighted,[11] "the existence of an arbitration agreement does not preclude a State court, at the request of a party and in the event of a recognized and reasoned emergency, from ordering provisional or conservatory measures so long as such measures do not imply a review of the merits of the case, for which only the arbitral tribunal has jurisdiction."

Under the CCJA Rules, provisional measures may be ordered by state courts, upon request by parties, only "before the file is handed over to the arbitral tribunal and, exceptionally thereafter, if the urgency of the provisional or conservatory measures requested does not allow the arbitral tribunal to rule promptly ... ."[12] the parties may apply to the competent state court for such measures. In all cases, the applications and measures taken by the competent state court must be immediately notified to the secretary-general, who informs the arbitral tribunal.[13]

11. UAA, Art. 13, para. 4.
12. CCJA Regulation on Arbitration, Art. 10-1, para. 3.
13. *Id.*, para. 4.

CHAPTER 8

Consolidation, Joinder and Intervention

During the reform of the arbitration Rules in 2017, some new features have been added to the different rules on multiparty issues (§8.01), multi contract issues (§8.02), as well as joinder and intervention (§8.03) under both sets of rules.

§8.01 MULTIPARTY ISSUES

Article 8-3 of the CCJA Regulation on Arbitration states:

> 8-3.1 Arbitration administered by the Court may take place between more than two parties if they have agreed to arbitration in accordance with this Regulation. In the event of a multiparty arbitration, any party may file claims against any other party.
> 8-3.2 Any party making a claim under Article 8-3.1, must produce the information required under Article 5 of this Regulation.
> 8-3.3 Once the matter has been referred to the arbitral tribunal, it determines the procedure to be followed for any new claim.

While it is true that Article 8-3 allows the arbitral tribunal to determine the procedure to be followed for each new request, nothing prevents the parties from providing for the terms for implementing the procedure. For example, when several parties are bound by the same contract, for example, several sellers and/or several purchasers of the shares of a company, it is recommended that they provide in the arbitration clause how the procedure will be implemented and the arbitration tribunal will be set up. In particular, it is necessary to specify whether the request must come from all the parties or whether one of them will represent them, in which case the power of attorney will be given in the contract, and how the arbitrator appointed by the plaintiff will be chosen, for example by unanimous agreement between them or, failing that, by the judge. It must also be stipulated whether all the parties dragged into the proceedings must be so personally or through one of them empowered by the contract, and the mode of appointment of the arbitrator by the respondent(s) must be modeled on the one for the claimant(s). To facilitate procedural acts, it is also advisable to provide for all the parties to the contract an election of domicile, in order to avoid the impossibility, if any, of contacting one of them at the address indicated in the contract.

§8.02 MULTI CONTRACT ISSUES

Article 8-4 deals with multiple contract issues. It states:

> 8.4.1 Claims arising out of or in connection with several contracts may be made in a single arbitration.
>
> 8.4.2 Where these claims are made under several arbitration agreements, the arbitral tribunal must ascertain that:
> a) the parties have agreed to arbitration under this Regulation and that these arbitration agreements are compatible with one another, and
> b) all parties to the arbitration have agreed to have their claims settled within a single procedure.

§8.03 JOINDER AND INTERVENTION

Forced joinder (§8.03[A]) and intervention (§8.03[B]) will be presented separately.

[A] Forced Joinder

On forced joinder, Article 8-1 states:

> 8-1.1 A party wishing to join an additional party bound by the arbitration agreement but foreign to the arbitration proceedings, submits a request for arbitration against the additional party to the Secretary General.
>
> Before the arbitral tribunal is constituted, the Court may set a deadline for submission of requests for joinder.
>
> If, at the time of the request for joinder, the Tribunal has already been constituted or one of its members has already been appointed or, if applicable, confirmed, the joinder is declared inadmissible unless the parties and the intervening party agree otherwise and the arbitral tribunal accepts it, taking into account the state of progress of the arbitration proceedings.
>
> The date of receipt of the request for joinder by the Secretary General is considered, for all purposes, at that of the introduction of the arbitration proceedings against the additional party.
>
> 8-1.2 The request for joinder must contain the following elements:
> a) the file reference of the existing proceedings,
> b) the full name and corporate name, capacity, postal address and email address of each of the parties, including the intervening party, and
> c) the information required under Article 5, paragraphs 2.b, c and d of this Regulation.
>
> 8-1.3 The request for joinder is sent by the Secretary General only if it is accompanied by the number of copies required under Article 12.1 of this Regulation and the payment of the filing fee required for initiation of the proceedings under the Schedule of fees of Annex II.

> 8-1.4 The additional party submits a response in accordance with, and subject to the necessary changes, the provisions of Article 6 of this Regulation or, if the arbitral tribunal has already been constituted, according to the instructions of the latter. The intervening party may file claims against any other party in accordance with the provisions of Article 7 above.

By creating this new provision, the OHADA Legislator expressly allows forced joinder, the practical and procedural details of which are indicated in particular by:

- setting a time limit for submitting the request for forced joinder before the tribunal is constituted or, if the tribunal is constituted (or one of its member is already confirmed) before the application, inadmissibility of the request for joinder unless the parties and the joining party agreed otherwise and that the tribunal admit it, taking into account the state of progress (Article 8-1.1);
- content of the request for forced joinder which must include the reference to the existing procedure and reference to Articles 5, 6 and 12 of the CCJA Regulation on Arbitration for the other procedural details (Articles 8-1.2 to 8-1.4).

As to the substance, Article 8-1 essentially calls for the determination of persons likely to be the subject of forced joinder in arbitration. As the legislator did not detail the criteria for identifying these persons, which it will doubtless be for the courts to specify over time, it seems useful to refer to comparative case law likely to inspire practitioners in the solutions to be suggested to jurisdictions that will decide disputes which will inevitably arise through forced joinder. Three main categories emerge from the comparative case law but will not be presented in detail here. In the case of persons who may be subject to forced joinder, there are those who are bound by an arbitration agreement and those who, without being directly linked, may be subject to arbitration under certain conditions. The disputes covered by the arbitration agreement (s) constitute a separate category.

[B] Voluntary Intervention

Article 8-2 governs voluntary intervention. It states:

> 8-2—Voluntary intervention
>
> No voluntary intervention is admissible before the constitution of the arbitral tribunal.
>
> After the constitution of the arbitral tribunal, any voluntary intervention in arbitration proceedings is subject to the prior approval of the parties and the arbitral tribunal.

There is not much to be said about voluntary intervention at this stage.

CHAPTER 9
Confidentiality

After some general comments on the confidentiality of arbitration under both systems (§9.01), a brief comment will be made on the confidentiality of investor-state arbitration (§9.02).

§9.01 GENERALITY

Article 18 of the UAA states that "the deliberations of the arbitral tribunal are confidential." Apart from that Article, there is no other specific provision about the confidentiality of the arbitration proceedings per se. However, confidentiality is implied under the UAA and generally enforceable through the arbitration rules of the vast majority of national or regional arbitration centers,[1] which all operate under the UAA.

Under the CCJA Regulation on Arbitration, there is a specific provision on the confidentiality of proceedings, at Article 14. It states:

> Arbitration proceedings are confidential. The work of the Court relating to the conduct of arbitration proceedings is subject to this confidentiality, as well as all meetings of the Court held for the administration of the arbitration. Confidentiality also covers documents submitted to the Court or drafted by it in the proceedings it administers.
>
> Unless otherwise agreed by the parties, the latter and their counsel, arbitrators, experts and all persons associated with the arbitration proceedings are bound by the duty of confidentiality of the information and documents produced during the said proceedings. Confidentiality extends, under the same conditions, to arbitral awards.

1. For a list of some of these, *see* International Trade Center (ITC), "La Médiation et l'Arbitrage dans l'Espace UEMOA. Recueil des Lois et Pratiques," http://www.intracen.org/uploadedFiles/intracenorg/Content/Publications/Receuil_arbitrage_final_Low-res.pdf [accessed May 8, 2020, at 21:11] (International Trade Center, 2018).

> The Secretary General is authorized to publish extracts from arbitral awards without mentioning elements enabling the identification of the parties.

Article 14 of the revised CCJA Regulation on Arbitration, currently in force, contains two essential changes. The last sentence of the former paragraph 1 provided for the confidentiality, *inter alia*, of the arbitral proceedings which the CCJA "expedites." The revised version refers to the procedures that the CCJA "administers." This terminology clarification is more in line with reality since the CCJA only administers the arbitration procedures carried out by the parties. The second amendment to Article 14 is innovative because the secretary-general is now allowed to publish extracts from awards after taking care to make them anonymous. It must also be noted that Article 12.1, paragraph 2 of the CCJA Regulation on Arbitration mandates that after referral of the case to the arbitral tribunal, the tribunal and the parties must send an electronic copy of all correspondence exchanged in connection with the proceedings to the secretary-general. In light of that, the secretary-general must be viewed as part and parcel of the arbitration proceedings, and a practical way of complying with that requirement is to copy the secretary-general in all communications between the parties and the tribunal. The only exception to this rule is that any deliberation of the arbitral tribunal is internal to the tribunal and must remain between its members only. The secretary-general, no more than the parties or anybody else, is entitled to have access to such deliberation at that stage. If parties and the tribunal agree, persons not involved in the arbitration proceedings may be allowed to attend the hearings.[2]

§9.02 CONFIDENTIALITY OF INVESTOR-STATE ARBITRATION

There is no specific provision relating to confidentiality for investor-state arbitration under OHADA Rules, since from the beginning, there has never been a special or different treatment for investor-state arbitration. Thus, confidentiality applies to any arbitration proceedings governed by OHADA Rules. The peculiarity of investor-state arbitration in terms of arbitration, if there is any, will be found in the specific investment instrument(s) at hand in each case.

Following the example of South Africa,[3] it would be appropriate to be able to hold public hearings in arbitration cases involving States or governmental entities and investment disputes, for transparency purposes. Even though it does not expressly exist in the current state of the applicable rules, it would be an appropriate measure to consider by the OHADA Legislator for the future.

2. CCJA Regulation on Arbitration, Art. 19.5, para. 2.
3. *See* the South African Protection of Investment Act N° 22 of 2015, § 6-4 and 13-5 (available at: https://www.thedti.gov.za/gazzettes/39514.pdf) [accessed Apr. 11, 2017, at 17:01].

CHAPTER 10

Legal Representation and Professional Conduct

The first two sections of this chapter will be dedicated to the right of the parties to legal representation (§10.01) and how it is exercised (§10.02), followed by some comments on professional conduct of legal representation (§10.03) under both arbitration systems.

§10.01 THE PARTIES' RIGHT TO REPRESENTATION

The right to representation in arbitration under OHADA Rules is implied, even though it is not expressly stated in those rules. There is no obligation for a party to an arbitration to have counsel, like it is for litigation before the CCJA.[1] Several provisions of the CCJA Regulation on Arbitration acknowledge the right to representation throughout various stages of the proceedings.

Thus, upon receipt of an arbitration request, "the Secretary General may require proof of the power of attorney of *any representative of a party* acting on behalf of the claimant(s)."[2] The "representative" here may refer to counsel or any other person representing a party.

At the stage of the appointment of arbitrators, the CCJA may consider, among other things, the place of residence "of their counsel."[3]

After it has been duly formed and has received the file of the case, the arbitral tribunal may "may *require* proof of the *power of attorney* of any representative of a party *if it deems it* necessary"[4] during the case management conference.

1. CCJA Regulation on Procedure, Art. 23.1.
2. CCJA Regulation on Arbitration, Art. 5, para. 9. [Emphasis added].
3. *Id.*, Art. 3.3, para. 1.
4. *Id.*, Art. 15.1, para. 1. [Emphasis added].

During the proceedings and at the stage of hearings, parties may be assisted by their counsel; they may also abstain from attending hearings and be represented instead by duly authorized persons.[5] The arbitral tribunal may decide to hear the parties separately if deemed necessary, in which case the hearing of each party must take place in the presence of both parties' counsel.[6]

Finally, the arbitral award must contain "e) if applicable, the first and last *names of counsel* or *any person who has represented or assisted* the parties."[7]

The ruling of the CCJA in *Kiendrebeogo v. Banque Internationale du Burkina*[8] illustrates the fact that representation by counsel is implied, as the CCJA has ruled that the notification of an arbitral award to counsel of a party is valid for the purpose of determining whether the statute of limitation has run for filing an appeal for annulment against the award.

§10.02 THE PARTIES' EXERCISE OF THEIR RIGHT TO REPRESENTATION

It must be noted, from the wording of Articles 5, paragraph 9, Article 15.1, paragraph 1, Article 19.1, paragraph 4 and Article 22.1, paragraph e) mentioned in the preceding section of this Chapter (§10.01) that a person representing a party to arbitration proceedings does not have to be an attorney or a licensed lawyer. In *Société Générale d'Electricité Ferroviaire du Congo v. Airtel Congo*, a licensed attorney represented a corporation in arbitration under the CCJA Rules. Before the award was rendered, that attorney was sentenced for imprisonment for a criminal offense. After the award has been rendered, the opposing party challenged the award on the ground of breach to international public policy, in that the arbitral tribunal has received the writings of a Lawyer sentenced to imprisonment and who, as a result, was unable to act on behalf of the corporation in the arbitration proceedings. The CCJA rejected the challenge, holding that "it follows from Article 19.1 paragraph 3 of the CCJA Regulation on Arbitration that *representation by a lawyer is not mandatory in arbitration proceedings*. Consequently, the presence of a lawyer whose conviction is alleged in no way renders the arbitral award contrary to international public policy and the appeal against the validity of the award for such award must be dismissed."[9]

5. *Id.*, Art. 19.1, para. 4.
6. *Id.*, Art. 19.1, para. 5.
7. *Id.*, Art. 22.1, para. e). [Emphasis added].
8. Kiendrebeogo v. Banque Internationale du Burkina, N° 031/2009, Decision, [C.C.J.A.], Ass. plén., (Apr. 30, 2009), http://www.ohada.com/jurisprudence/ohadata/J-10-54.html. The CCJA ruled that when the challenged arbitral award was rendered on Jan. 15, 2007 and notified on Jan. 31, 2007 to the Appellant's counsel, the latter had, under Art. 29.3 of the CCJA Regulation on Arbitration, and taking into account the fourteen-day distance period prescribed by Decision 002/99/CCJA, until Apr. 16, 2007, the first working day after Sunday April 15, to exercise its appeal in cassation. The appeal in cassation, which was not received and registered at the CCJA Registry until May 7, 2007, is inadmissible.
9. Société Générale d'Electricité Ferroviaire du Congo v. Airtel Congo, N° 099/2009, Decision, [C.C.J.A.], Ass. plén., (Oct. 30, 2014), http://www.ohada.com/jurisprudence/ohadata/J-15-190.html. [Emphasis added].

§10.03 PROFESSIONAL CONDUCT OF LEGAL REPRESENTATIVES

Since there is no elaborated and detailed set of rules on representation in the OHADA Rules, professional conduct of legal representatives is governed by the rules applicable to the bar association or professional bodies to which each party's representative belongs. Thus, any lawyer acting on behalf of a party to arbitration proceedings must abide by the professional and ethical rules of the professional body they are a member of, in addition to the procedural rules applicable to the arbitration proceedings at hand.

PART III The Arbitral Award

The existence of a valid arbitration agreement, in conjunction with the birth of a dispute to which the appropriate procedure is applied logically, leads to an arbitral award. The three chapters of this part will present the legal framework (Chapter 11), the form and content (Chapter 12), and finally, correction, interpretation, and supplementation (Chapter 13) of arbitral awards under both sets of rules.

CHAPTER 11
Legal Framework for the Award

The applicable laws (§11.01), as well as the power of an arbitral tribunal to decide a case *ex aequo et bono* (§11.02), and by referring to international trade practices (§11.03), will be presented in this chapter.

§11.01 APPLICABLE LAWS

[A] Under the UAA

The UAA states at Article 14, paragraphs 1 and 2 about the applicable law to the merits:

> The parties may, directly or by reference to arbitration rules, determine the arbitral procedure. They may also subject it to a procedural law of their choice.
>
> In the absence of such an agreement, the arbitral tribunal may proceed with the arbitration as it deems appropriate.

The autonomy of the parties in choosing the applicable law to the merit is strengthened by Article 15 of the UAA, which states that:

> The arbitral tribunal rules on the merits of the dispute under the rules of law chosen by the parties. In the absence of choice by the parties, the arbitral tribunal applies the rules it deems the most appropriate, by taking into consideration, as the case may be, international trade usages.
>
> It may also rule as *amiable compositeur* when the parties have conferred such power on it.

[B] Under the CCJA Rules

On the law applicable to the merits, Article 17 of the CCJA Regulation on Arbitration states:

> The parties are free to determine the rules of law that the tribunal will have to apply to the merits of the dispute. In the absence of the choice of the parties, the arbitral tribunal applies the rules of law which it considers most appropriate in the case.
>
> In all cases, the arbitral tribunal takes into account the stipulations of the contract and international trade usages.
>
> The arbitral tribunal may also rule as *amiable compositeur* upon express agreement of the parties.

The revised Article 17 of the CCJA Regulation on Arbitration contains three essential amendments: (i) replacement of the expression "law" with "the rules of law"; (ii) deletion of the reference to the "conflict rule" for the designation, by the arbitral tribunal, of the applicable law where the parties have not indicated it. It is now indicated that the arbitral tribunal will apply the rules it deems most appropriate. It is conceivable, however, that without indicating it, the tribunal uses the rule of conflict to determine the applicable law; finally, (iii) introduction of the reference to the "uses of international trade." The reference to "use of trade" already existed in the Regulations, but the Legislator took care to specify the "uses of international trade," as was already the case in the UAA (Article 15) where the reference existed but was not mandatory upon arbitral tribunals.

Under both the UAA and the CCJA Rules, the law applicable to the merits is primarily the prerogative of the parties, arbitral tribunals being allowed to determine such rules only where parties have not stipulated them. The parties can also give tribunals the power to decide the case *ex aequo et bono*, and international trade usage are part of the applicable law to the merits, under certain conditions. For practical reasons and because of their similarity of regime, amiable composition and international trade usage will be commented on together hereafter.

§11.02 POWER OF AN ARBITRAL TRIBUNAL TO DECIDE A CASE *EX AEQUO ET BONO*

In *Nestle Sahel v. Société Commerciale d'Importation Azar et Salame*, amicable composition is defined negatively, like the power of arbitrators, not to stick to the strict application of the rules of law, which makes it possible to ignore them as well as to deviate from them, as long as their sense of fairness demands it.[1] In order to comply with their mission, the arbitrator resolving a dispute *ex aequo et bono* is under the obligation to confront legal solutions with equity, fairness.[2] However, an arbitral tribunal to which parties have conferred the power to rule *ex aequo et bono* are not bound to rule only as *amiable compositeur*, according to the CCJA which held, in *Delpech v. Sotaci*, that "arbitrators, who relied on legal solutions to settle a dispute and

1. Nestle Sahel v. Société Commerciale d'Importation Azar et Salame, N° 028/2007, Decision, [C.C.J.A.], Ass. plen., (Jul. 19, 2007), http://www.ohada.com/jurisprudence/ohadata/J-08-250.html.
2. CA Abidjan, Apr. 27, 2001, N° 45 (Ivory Coast), http://www.ohada.com/jurisprudence/ohadata/J-02-171.html.

who *were under no obligation, contrary to the contention of one party, to rule only as amiable compositeur*, remained within the scope of the mission entrusted to them and the request to annul their award must be dismissed."[3]

On the other hand, the arbitral tribunal which based its ruling on a fact disputed by one of the parties, without providing evidence based on the Ivorian law governing the proceedings at hand, has used the powers of *amiable compositeur* that the parties have not given it and its award must be annulled.[4]

§11.03 INTERNATIONAL TRADE PRACTICES

Under the UAA, international trade usages are not mandatory; an arbitral tribunal is under no obligation to refer to them in resolving the dispute submitted to them since under Article 15, the tribunal can refer to them only if "it deems [that] most appropriate ... as the case may be."[5]

The situation is different under the CCJA Regulation on Arbitration; in *Société Ivoirienne de Raffinage v. Bona Shipholding Ltd*, the CCJA held that "uses of international trade" are understood within the meaning of revised Article 17 of the CCJA Regulation on Arbitration as general principles of law since that Article states that "in all cases, the arbitral tribunal takes into account the stipulations of the contract and the uses of international trade." Those usages are thus elevated to the rank of a mandatory rule (of public policy), at least by the Regulation on Arbitration, which has been affirmed by the CCJA through a ruling that an arbitral tribunal is under the obligation to rule in referring to those international trade usages.[6] As the CCJA pointed out in its judgment mentioned above, only commercial uses, "the existence of which is not disputed," are to be taken into account. Because of their compulsory nature in

3. Delpech v. Sotaci, N° 010/2003, Decision, [C.C.J.A.], (Jun. 19, 2003), http://www.ohada.com/jurisprudence/ohadata/J-04-65.html. [Emphasis added].
4. Nestle Sahel v. Société Commerciale d'Importation Azar et Salame, N° 028/2007, *supra*, Chapter 11, fn. 1. In the present case, it appears from the challenged arbitral award, with regard to the damage caused by corporation A to corporation B, that the latter, in its written pleadings and oral argument, contemplates said damage with regard to 23 years of collaboration with Corporation N. However, the arbitral tribunal, "while considering such a vision legitimate," did not follow Corporation B, on the grounds that its jurisdiction was determined by the arbitration clause; he claims to have only taken into account the relations of almost two calendar years which, according to him, occurred between Corporation B and its contracting partner, Corporation A. Consequently, by ordering Corporation A to pay to Corporation B, all causes of loss combined, the sum of five billion CFA francs, on the grounds that "the important role played by Corporation [A], at the end of the chain of group N companies, in the brutal sidelining of the Corporation B, is taken into consideration for the assessment of the damage suffered by Corporation B," the arbitral tribunal based the said judgment on the period of twenty-three years, however disputed, resulting from the previous collaboration between Corporation B and the group N., within which Corporation A is an autonomous entity.
5. UAA, Art. 15, para. 1.
6. Société Ivoirienne de Raffinage v. Bona Shipholding Ltd, N° 029/2007, *supra*, Chapter 3, fn. 41. In particular, the court held that, under section 17 of the CCJA Regulation on Arbitration, the arbitrator must consider international trade usages in all cases, even where the parties have expressly designated the law to apply to the merits of the dispute. In the case at hand, with reference to trade usages, the existence of which is not disputed by the appellant, the Arbitral Tribunal ruled in law as it was required to.

arbitration, the uses of trade, now taken in the international context, deserve to be defined, the OHADA Legislator not having done so. In the absence of a comprehensive inventory of the international trade usages, comparative case law would be very helpful, as well as legal scholarship suggesting a possible list of such usages[7] as well as discussing the risks of a "conflict of list" and ways to avoid them.[8]

7. *See,* for example, the list of the twenty-five items the *lex mercatoria* as drawn up by Michael J. Mustill, *The New* Lex Mercatoria*: The First Twenty-five Years*, 4 Arbitration International 86 (1988) (Mustill, 1988).
8. Emmanuel Gaillard, *Transnational Law: A Legal System or a Method of Decision Making?*, 17(1) Arb. Intl. 64, https://www.arbitration-icca.org/media/4/16644703895537/media012178525391230transnational_law_eg.pdf [accessed Apr. 2, 2020, at 14:41] (Emmanuel, 2001).

CHAPTER 12
Form and Content of Arbitral Awards

This chapter is structured into eight sections. Starting with the form and content of arbitral awards (§12.01), it presents the formal requirements of arbitral awards (§12.02) as well as the requirement that awards be reasoned (§12.03), majority awards and awards by presiding arbitrators (§12.04), separate, concurrent and dissenting opinions (§12.05), time limit, service and publication of arbitral awards (§12.06) and the awards of costs of arbitration and legal representation (§12.07) as well as interests (§12.08).

§12.01 CATEGORIES OF ARBITRAL AWARDS

Apart from the final award, which generally resolves the dispute submitted to it, an arbitral tribunal may have to render at least five different types of awards, depending on the circumstances and the behavior of the parties. Those are awards by consent (§12.01[A]), partial awards (§12.01[B]), interpretive awards (§12.01[C]), corrective awards (§12.01[D) and additional awards (§12.01[E]).

[A] Awards by Consent

At any stage of the proceedings, the tribunal may render an award by consent where the parties reach an agreement and request it to be formalized.[1] Under the UAA, it is specified that "such award has the same status and effect as any other award ending the dispute."[2] Even though there is no such precision in the CCJA Regulation on this, it must be assumed that the same rule is implied and also applies to arbitration proceedings governed by the CCJA Rules.

1. UAA, Art. 19 para. 2. CCJA Regulation on Arbitration, Art. 20.
2. UAA, Art. 19 para 2.

[B] Partial Awards

Where applicable, arbitral tribunals may render "partial awards resolving some of the claims of the parties."[3] Partial awards can also be rendered under the UAA, for example, to settle an objection to the jurisdiction of the tribunal.[4] Under the UAA, as well as the CCJA Rules, an arbitral tribunal can also use a partial award to order provisional or interim measures like those within their purview, as previously mentioned.[5]

[C] Interpretive Awards

An arbitral tribunal has the power to interpret an arbitral award by an interpretive award, namely, "explain" or clarify an award it has previously rendered.[6]

[D] Corrective Awards

Under both the UAA and the CCJA Rules, an arbitral award containing some errors may be corrected through a corrective award.[7]

[E] Additional Awards

Finally, an additional award may be used by a tribunal to supplement an award where the tribunal has omitted to rule on a claim.[8]

§12.02 FORMAL REQUIREMENTS FOR AWARDS

The formality of an arbitral award requires a specific content which must be complied with (§12.02[A]). In addition to that, awards rendered under the CCJA Rules are subject to scrutiny by the CCJA (§12.02[B]).

[A] Content of an Arbitral Award

Article 20 of the UAA, which has been reproduced identically at Article 22.1 of the CCJA Regulation Arbitration, states that:

> In addition to the operative part, the arbitral award must contain:

3. CCJA Regulation on Arbitration, Art. 23.1.
4. UAA, Art. 11, para. 3. For an illustration of a challenge involving a partial award, Commercial Bank of Cameroon v. Archidiocèse de Yaoundé, N° 242/2018, *supra*, Chapter 2, fn. 13.
5. *See supra*, Chapter 7, §7.01.
6. UAA, Art. 22, para. 2. CCJA Regulation on Arbitration, Art. 26, para. 2.
7. *Id.*
8. UAA, Art. 22, para. 3. CCJA Regulation on Arbitration, Art. 26, para. 3.

a) the last and first names of the arbitrator(s) who rendered the award;
b) its date;
c) the seat of the arbitral tribunal;
d) the last, first and corporate names of the parties, as well as their domicile or registered office;
e) if applicable, the last and first names of counsel or any person who has represented or assisted the parties;
f) the statement of the respective claims and arguments of the parties, as well as the procedural history.

The arbitral award must be reasoned.

If the arbitral tribunal has been empowered by the parties to rule as *amiable compositeur*, it must be mentioned.

This is the first time that the OHADA Legislator clearly requires an arbitral tribunal under Article 20 of the UAA, to mention in its award the power given to the arbitral tribunal to rule as *amiable compositeur*, where applicable. It is also the first time that the OHADA Legislator clearly indicated the content of an arbitration award in the CCJA Regulation on Arbitration. The content was expressly provided for in the UAA (before its reform) and implicitly for the Regulation, no ruling of the CCJA, having suggested a difficulty that would have arisen as a result of the absence of one of the mentions required. The wording of the revised paragraph 1 of Article 22, according to which "In addition to the operative part, the award must contain the indication ..." suggests that the operative part of the award must now stand out clearly and be identifiable as such. For an award to be complete, it will be necessary to add, in addition to the information required under Article 22.1 of the CCJA Regulation on Arbitration, the tribunal's ruling on the costs of the arbitration in accordance with Article 24 of the Regulation, which must contain the fees of the tribunal and the administrative costs as set by the CCJA.

In addition to the formal requirements presented above, an award must be signed to be enforceable.[9]

[B] Scrutiny of an Arbitral Award

Unlike the CCJA Regulation on Arbitration, there is no provision of the UAA requiring scrutiny of an arbitral award prior to its notification to the parties. However, such scrutiny might be required under the arbitration rules of local or national arbitration centers operating under the UAA. That is the case for the majority of the States Parties to the Treaty, namely in West Africa with Benin,[10] Burkina Faso,[11] Ivory Coast,[12]

9. UAA, Art. 21, para. 1; CCJA Regulation on Arbitration, Art. 22.3, para. 2.
10. *See* Art. 21 of the arbitration rules of the CAMEC (Benin). *See supra*, Abbreviations. (International Trade Center, 2018), *supra*, Chapter 9, fn. 1.
11. *See* Art. 31 of the arbitration rules of CAMC-O (Burkina Faso). *See supra*, Abbreviations. (International Trade Center, 2018). (International Trade Center, 2018), *supra*, Chapter 9, fn. 1.
12. *See* Art. 28 of the arbitration rules of the CACI (Ivory Coast). *See supra*, Abbreviations. (International Trade Center, 2018), *supra*, Chapter 9, fn. 1.

Mali,[13] Niger,[14] Senegal,[15] Togo,[16]; and in Central Africa, with Cameroon[17] and Congo.[18] For more insight, readers are encouraged to refer to specific arbitration rules that may apply to their proceedings in addition to the UAA, where applicable.

Scrutiny of arbitral awards under the CCJA Regulation on Arbitration requires more attention, for the following obvious reasons. Article 23 of the Regulation states:

> 23.1 The arbitral tribunal sends the drafts of the awards on jurisdiction, partial awards resolving some of the claims of the parties and its final awards to the Secretary General for a preliminary examination by the Court before those awards are signed.
>
> The other awards are not subject to the preliminary examination but are only sent to the Court for information.
>
> 23.2 The *Court may* suggest purely editorial changes, *draw the attention of the arbitral tribunal to claims which do not appear to have been processed or mandatory information which do not appear in the draft award, in the event of lack of reason, or if there is an apparent contradiction in the reasoning,* without however having the power to suggest a reasoning or a substantive solution on the merits concerning the dispute.
>
> The Court examines the draft award submitted to it within a maximum period of one (1) month from its receipt.[19]

The revised Article 23 contains three main amendments: (i) clarification of a practical modality relating to the review of draft awards by the Court, in particular, that the draft award is transmitted to the CCJA by the secretary-general; (ii) framing of the preliminary examination by the CCJA within one month, for swiftness; (iii) strengthening of the preliminary examination of the award by the CCJA. This last point deserves special attention.

Article 23 of the CCJA Regulation on Arbitration Rules listed, before the reform, a number of awards which had to be submitted to the CCJA for prior examination before notification to the parties. The Court could then "only propose purely formal changes." However, the revised Article 23.2, paragraph 1 now provides that:

---

13. *See* Art. 24 of the arbitration rules of the CECAM (Mali). *See supra*, Abbreviations. (International Trade Center, 2018), *supra*, Chapter 9, fn. 1.
14. *See* Art. 28 of the arbitration rules of the CEMAN (Niger). *See supra*, Abbreviations. (International Trade Center, 2018), *supra*, Chapter 9, fn. 1.
15. *See* Art. 37 of the arbitration rules of the CEMAC-CCIAD (Senegal). *See supra*, Abbreviations. (International Trade Center, 2018), *supra*, Chapter 9, fn. 1.
16. *See* Art. 39 of the arbitration rules of CATO (Togo). *See supra*, Abbreviations. (International Trade Center, 2018), *supra*, Chapter 9, fn. 1.
17. *See* Art. 33 of the arbitration rules of the Centre de Médiation et d'Arbitrage du GICAM (Cameroon), *See supra*, Abbreviations. https://www.legicam.cm/media/upload/2019049/reglement-darbitrage-cmag-1.pdf [accessed May 8, 2020, at 21:54].
18. *See* Art. 32.4 of the arbitration rules of the CEMACO (Congo), *See supra*, Abbreviations. https://economie.gouv.cg/sites/default/files/Documentation/Doing_Business/Lexecution_des_contrats/Le_Centre_de_mediation_et_darbitrage_du_Congo-CEMACO.pdf [accessed May 8, 2020, at 21:56].
19. [Emphasis added]. The analysis appearing under this section of the book (§12.02[B]) has also been previously published in Mahutodji Jimmy Vital Kodo (Dir.), *Code Pratique Francis Lefebvre OHADA. Traité, Actes Uniformes et Règlements Annotés, supra*, Chapter 5, fn. 37, 231-233, reproduced with the permission of Editions Francis Lefebvre.

> 23.2 The Court *may* suggest purely editorial changes, *draw the attention of the arbitral tribunal to claims which do not appear to have been processed or mandatory information which do not appear in the draft award, in the event of lack of reason, or if there is an apparent contradiction in the reasoning, without however having the power to suggest a reasoning or a substantive solution on the merits concerning the dispute.*[20]

The Court is now allowed to go beyond formal suggestions, as it can "draw the attention of the arbitral tribunal to":

- *"claims which do not appear to have been processed";*
- *"mandatory information which do not appear in the draft award";*
- *"in the event of lack of reason";*
- *"or if there is an apparent contradiction in the reasoning."*

Each of the four irregularities above on which the Court is permitted to "draw the attention of the arbitral tribunal" may constitute a ground for the annulment of the award under the following conditions.

[1] Claims That Do Not Appear to Have Been Processed

A claim that does not appear to have been processed is, in fact, the refusal or failure to respond to a request, which constitutes a breach of its mission by an arbitrator[21] under Article 29.2 (c) of the CCJA Regulation on Arbitration and likely to justify the annulment of an award. It should be noted, however, that the revised Article 26, paragraph 3 allows for an additional referral to an arbitral tribunal to rule on a claim it has omitted. As a result, the possibility of obtaining the annulment of an arbitration award for failure to respond to a claim appears to be significantly reduced.

[2] Absence of Mandatory Information in the Draft Award

The absence of mandatory information in an award is not expressly established as a ground for the annulment of an award, but it seems neither impossible nor excessive to consider that the omission of certain essential mentions in an award (such as the date, the names and signature of the arbitrators) can be equated with a failure to perform their mission, with the consequences to be drawn from it, namely, annulment under Article 29.2, paragraph c) of the CCJA Regulation on Arbitration.

20. [Emphasis added].
21. Cour d'appel [CA] [regional court of appeal] Lyon, 1e ch. civ., Jan. 15, 2004, GP 2004. som.1979 (Fr), solution adopted under French law but transposable to OHADA. On the failure of the tribunal to perform its mission, *see* Art. 29 of the CCJA Regulation on Arbitration and *infra*, Chapter 14, §14.04[B].

[3] Failure to State Reasons for the Award and Apparent Contradictions in the Reasoning

As it will be demonstrated *infra*,[22] the existence of an objectionable or erroneous reason for the award must be distinguished from the absence of a reason for the award, to which the existence of conflicting grounds or contradictory reasons[23] can be equated. However, the presence of contradictions in the reasoning constitutes no more or less the existence of contradictory reasons, the consequences of which must be drawn. Thus, at least the failure to state reasons constitutes a certain cause for the annulment of an award for the failure of the tribunal to perform its mission. It is indisputable that the purpose of this increasingly thorough review or scrutiny the CCJA is now allowed to perform is indirectly intended to reduce or limit the risks of the annulment of arbitral awards, which is commendable.

However, if the CCJA is not careful, the use of this faculty could transform it during arbitration proceedings into a "teleprompter" or "solution whisperer" indicating to tribunals grounds of potential annulment, which could amount to an inappropriate and unjustified limitation of the defense rights of the party with interest in seeking the annulment of the tainted award on the ground that the CCJA would have "whispered" to the arbitral tribunal.

Because of the "elitist" nature of arbitration, which manifests itself through a very high selectivity, on the one hand, of the persons likely to be appointed as arbitrators and, on the other hand, of those who are actually appointed by the parties and arbitral institutions, arbitrators are the subject of very high esteem which, in return, should require a very high level of competence, knowledge and professionalism. Thus, it can hardly be admitted, even conceivable, that a person who wants to be an arbitrator abstains, (by omission?) from ruling on a request submitted to them, omits mandatory information, does not know how to state the reasons of their award or write a clear, intelligible one without contradiction. This is, therefore, the case since arbitrators, rare elected officials who are sometimes credited with a myth of exceptional experience and competence setting them apart, should not need to be taken by the hand and guided in the exercise of this exceptional office reserved for an "elite" and for which, it must be remembered, the parties will have sometimes paid significant amounts in terms of fees.

Just as, while handling a case, a lower court of law does not receive such assistance from a Court of Appeal which, in turn, receives none from the cassation court (the CCJA), an arbitral tribunal should not receive such assistance. It would not come to mind imagining a commercial court submitting the draft of its judgment to an appellate court, hoping that the Court would indicate to it the elements of the draft judgment likely to entail to the reversal of the subsequent decision by the Court of Appeal. Likewise, an appellate court would not submit to the Court of Cassation (the CCJA again) its draft judgment and wait for the highest court to pinpoint the potential means of overturning the judgment if it were the subject of an appeal. The fact that

22. *See infra*, Chapter 14, §14.07[B].
23. *See* the glossary, *infra*.

arbitration and ordinary court proceedings are different has no bearing here as long as the result is the same.

In fact, the scrutiny now provided for by Article 23 of the CCJA Regulation on Arbitration seems to go beyond the scope of the administration of arbitration proceedings under Article 1 of the Regulation; it would even amount to violation of Article 24, paragraph 2 of the Treaty, according to which the CCJA *"can only suggest editorial changes"* (emphasis added) during the scrutiny of an arbitral award. The changes that the CCJA is now allowed to implement may entail the merits, something that is more than the "editorial changes permitted by the Treaty" and in these circumstances, the CCJA could hardly escape the criticism of interference, even involuntary, in the arbitration procedure, which certain business circles were already accusing it of doing, although the reproaches were largely unfounded. In other words, it is very likely that by wanting to do better, the OHADA Legislator actually exposed the CCJA to more criticism of its impartiality by pushing it more toward the edge of possible undue interference in the arbitration process, and litigants at the risk of being deprived of necessary remedies against an award, which may be an indirect violation of the right of defense. It is, therefore, highly desirable that the CCJA significantly limits the use of this option left to its discretion if it does not refrain from using it, which, however, seems preferable because of the reasons presented above.

§12.03 REQUIREMENT THAT THE AWARD BE REASONED

As highlighted in the preceding section, under both the UAA[24] and the CCJA Regulation on Arbitration,[25] an arbitral award must be reasoned, that is, state the reasons upon which the award is based. Also, the requirement that an award be reasoned has been emptied of its substance since, as indicated in Chapter 14 *infra* (§14.07[B]), Article 23.2, paragraph 2 of the CCJA Regulation on Arbitration provides for the possibility of the CCJA to draw the attention of a tribunal on a failure of their draft award to state the reasons upon which it is made, at the end of the preliminary examination of the draft award.

§12.04 MAJORITY AWARD AND AWARD BY THE PRESIDING ARBITRATOR

[A] Under the UAA

The first two paragraphs of Article 19 of the UAA state:

> The arbitral award *is* rendered in accordance with the procedure and the forms agreed by the parties.
>
> Absent any such agreement, the award *is* rendered by a majority vote when the tribunal is composed of three arbitrators.

24. UAA, Art. 20, para. 8.
25. CCJA Regulation on Arbitration, Art. 22.1, para. 8.

There is a clear requirement of a majority of the votes for panels of three arbitrators unless parties have stipulated something different.

[B] Under the CCJA Rules

The role of the chairman of an arbitral panel is relevant only under the CCJA Rules. Article 22.3 of the CCJA Regulation on Arbitration states that:

> 22.3 The arbitral award is rendered under the procedure and in the form agreed by the parties. In the absence of such an agreement, the award is rendered by a majority of votes when the tribunal is composed of three arbitrators.
>
> The arbitral award must be signed by the arbitrator(s).
>
> However, if one or two[26] arbitrators refuse to sign the award, it must be mentioned, and the award has the same effect as if it had been signed by all the arbitrators.

Although it complies with the spirit of the older Article 22 paragraph 4 of the CCJA Regulation on Arbitration and is similar to Article 32 of the International Chamber of Commerce (ICC) Arbitration Rules currently in force, the wording of the last paragraph of Article 23.3, namely that "However, if one or two arbitrators refuse to sign the award, it must be mentioned and the award has the same effect as if it had been signed by all the arbitrators" seems regrettable, for the following reasons.

First, for a panel of *three arbitrators*, the "majority of votes" under Article 22.3, paragraph 3 is, inevitably, at least *two arbitrators*.

Second, it results from Article 22.2 that and the arbitral award is deemed to have been rendered only *after it has been signed* by the arbitrator(s).

Third, it does not seem conceivable that two arbitrators would refuse to sign an award which will have been made by a majority of votes because an arbitrator cannot in principle refuse to sign the award embodying a solution that arbitrator would have chosen, namely, a solution agreed upon and voted for.

Fourth, to direct, as does Article 22.3, paragraph 3 above, that "if one or two arbitrators refuse to sign the award, it must be mentioned and the award has the same effect as if it had been signed by all the arbitrators," amounts to considering that the only arbitrator who will have signed (presumably the President of the Court, as is the case for the ICC and in the former CCJA Regulation on Arbitration), alone constitutes

26. In the English version of the CCJA Regulation on Arbitration published on the OHADA Official website (https://www.ohada.org/attachments/article/2490/Reglement-Arbitrage_CCJA-English.pdf [accessed Mar. 18, 2020, at 15:04]), there is a translation mistake at Art. 22.3 para. 3 of the Regulation as it reads "a minority," while the French original and official version reads "one or two arbitrators" ("*si un arbitre ou deux arbitres refusent de la signer*"). Thus, the proper translation has been restored by replacing "A minority of them refuses" with "one or two arbitrators refuse"; otherwise, the rule stated at that paragraph would be misleading and confusing since two arbitrators out of three are simply not a minority. *See* Appendix II, *infra*. The analysis appearing under this section of the book (§12.04[B]) has also been previously published in Mahutodji Jimmy Vital Kodo (Dir.), *Code Pratique Francis Lefebvre OHADA. Traité, Actes Uniformes et Règlements Annotés*, *supra*, Chapter 5, fn. 37, 230-231, reproduced with the permission of Editions Francis Lefebvre.

a majority over the two other arbitrators. In other words, if the two Co-arbitrators supported a different opinion from that of the President of the tribunal, the latter could, on his own, impose his vision of the solution on the whole tribunal although he was in the minority (one out of a panel of three), and this, simply because of his position as President.

Under such conditions, paragraph 3 of Article 22.3 empties the first paragraph of the same article, which states that an "award is rendered by a majority of votes when the tribunal is composed of three arbitrators," of its substance. This is because of two things, one: either there is a panel of three arbitrators ruling by the majority of two arbitrators out of three, regardless of whether the presiding arbitrator is part of that majority or the award is purely and simply made by a single judge, and no problem majority would arise. But allowing a minority arbitrator to impose his vision on the other members of the panel, maybe because he is the presiding arbitrator, does not seem to be in accordance with the wishes of the parties who would have wanted a panel of three arbitrators to whom they would have paid substantial fees. It doesn't seem fair to get the parties to pay fees for a panel of three arbitrators if, at the end of the process, the award ends up being rendered by an all-powerful President who could possibly have held the minority view.

The grammatical structure of Article 22.3 does not seem to suggest the possibility, for the parties, to require by an agreement, a tribunal ruling by a majority of two arbitrators in the absence of unanimity[27] since paragraph 3 has been separated from paragraph 1 which provides for it. Therefore, it seems very regrettable that the OHADA Legislator did not clearly subordinate the validity of an award rendered by a panel to the signature by at least two arbitrators forming the majority of the panel, notwithstanding the position of the President of the tribunal. Indeed, one could have imagined a system requiring the President of the arbitral tribunal, even if in a minority, to sign the award resulting from the majority of the two other arbitrators, allowing the President to join their dissenting opinion to the award as Article 23.4 permits it.[28] It is possible that this is due to an error,[29] but in any event, and if it is an error, the fact remains that it is the version currently in force, which seems problematic.

27. For example, Art. 20 of the United Kingdom Arbitration Act of 1996 states:

    Chairman.
    (1) Where the parties have agreed that there is to be a chairman, they are free to agree what the functions of the chairman are to be in relation to the making of decisions, orders and awards.
    (2) If or to the extent that there is no such agreement, the following provisions apply.
    (3) Decisions, orders and awards shall be made by all or a majority of the arbitrators (including the chairman).
    (4) The view of the chairman shall prevail in relation to a decision, order or award in respect of which there is neither unanimity nor a majority under subsection (3). Accessible at http://www.legislation.gov.uk/ukpga/1996/23/section/20 [accessed Mar. 20, 2020 at 16:53].

28. Article 22.4 of the CCJA Regulation on Arbitration states that "Any member of the arbitral tribunal may give their personal opinion to the president, to be attached to the award."
29. *See*, for a comparison, Articles 19 and 21 of the UAA.

§12.05 SEPARATE, CONCURRING AND DISSENTING OPINIONS

Separate, concurring and dissenting opinions have been given little room under the OHADA Arbitration Rules. There is no such reference in the UAA, and parties will have to refer to applicable institutional rules where applicable.

In the CCJA Regulation on Arbitration, a brief reference is made to dissenting opinion at Article 22.4, which states that "Any member of the arbitral tribunal may give their personal opinion to the president, to be attached to the award."

§12.06 TIME LIMIT, SERVICE AND PUBLICATION OF ARBITRAL AWARDS

Time limits (§12.06[A]), service (§12.06[B]) and publication (§12.06[C]) of arbitral awards under both sets of rules will be presented under this section.

[A] Time Limit

[1] Under the UAA

Article 12 of the UAA states that:

> If the arbitration agreement does not set a deadline, the mission of the arbitral tribunal cannot exceed six (06) months from the date on which the last appointed arbitrator accepted their appointment.
>
> The legal or contractual time limit for the arbitration may be extended, either by agreement of the parties, or at the request of one of the parties or of the arbitral tribunal, by the competent court in the State Party.

Generally speaking, from the date of the acceptance of their appointment by the last arbitrator for a panel of three or the sole arbitrator, the tribunal must render the award within six months, unless parties have agreed otherwise. Where, as it does happen often, the tribunal cannot issue the award within the allotted time, an extension of the time limit must be requested, either by the parties or by the tribunal. As highlighted by available cases, the procedural timetable set at the onset of an arbitral procedure is provisional and may be extended where necessary under the conditions set by Article 12 of the UAA. In *Prévoyance Assurances S.A. v. Eiffage Sénégal*, the CCJA ruled that:

Under paragraph 1 of Article 12 of the UAA, which states that "if the arbitration agreement does not set a deadline, the arbitrators' duties may not exceed six months from the day the last of them accepted it," when the date of acceptance by the last arbitrator of his mission is not established, as is the case, the arbitration deadline runs from the first meeting between the parties and the arbitrators. In this case, that first meeting took place on February 6, 2014, when the parties agreed with the arbitrators to "a period of four (04) to six (06) months for the end of the proceedings"; the end of the arbitration proceedings was thus set between 6 June 2014 at the earliest and 6 August

2014 at the latest, in handing down its award on 4 August 2014, the Court of Arbitration did not rule on an expired arbitration agreement, as the extension of the criticized deliberation proved to be a simple change in the timetable without affecting the validity of the arbitration agreement and the delay of the arbitration proceeding. It cannot support the annulment of the arbitration award undertaken. Furthermore, it is in vain that the claimant avails themselves of the lack of a decision of the supporting judge, then, on the one hand, that the Court of Appeal based its decision on an extension agreed by the parties and, on the other hand, that the deliberation was repeatedly extended without the parties and the arbitral tribunal seeking the office of the State judge. Therefore, by ruling as they did, the appellate judges did not violate Article 12 of the UAA referred to in the plea, which will be dismissed as unfounded.[30]

In the same ruling, the CCJA validated the extension of deliberations to which a party has not objected.[31] The new wording of Article 12 of the UAA clarifies the terms of time extensions. It should be remembered that compliance with the deadline by the arbitral tribunal is essential, because of the risk of a possible annulment of the award or all procedural acts performed after the expiration of the said deadline if no extension has been previously granted. The formulation and grammatical structure of Article 12 paragraph 2, in particular the positioning of the commas, seems to lend itself to the following two interpretations. The first hypothesis is that the extension of the period may be validly granted by the parties if they agree and without the need for recourse to the competent court in the State Party housing the seat of the Court. Second hypothesis: in all cases and even if the parties agree, only the competent court can authorize the extension of the deadline. Both positions seem good, but while waiting for case law to

30. Prévoyance Assurances S.A. v. Eiffage Sénégal, *supra*, Chapter 3, fn. 39.
31. *Id.*, ruling that it is wrong to criticize a judgment for stating that "by acknowledging receipt of the said email by email from their counsel on 07/10/2014, worded as follows: "Dear all, well received," without having objected to the modification of the deadline thus proposed (...), the [claimant] tacitly accepted the continuation of the arbitral proceedings," while the date of the deliberations decided by the parties and the Arbitral Tribunal on Jul. 17, 2014 was extended by the latter by decision of Jul. 9, 2014; that it was not a simple proposal to extend the date that the parties could have challenged; that in ruling in that way, the Court of Appeal, according to the argument, distorted the facts of the case and exposed its ruling to cassation. This is so since the extension of the deliberation made on Jul. 9, 2014 was not concurrent with the rendering of the award and preceded Jul. 17, 2014, the date on which the award was expected by the claimant; it follows that the latter had all the latitude to challenge this measure, qualified by the Arbitral Tribunal as a readiness decision, and to demand that the deliberations be continued on Jul. 17, 2014. In these circumstances, the fact for the Court of Appeal to use the term "proposed" to evoke this change of date, cannot constitute a distortion of the facts of the case of such a nature as to justify the annulment of an award. Moreover, the claimant does not specify how the alleged fact would have affected the mission of the Arbitral Tribunal; the plea is therefore devoid of all relevance and will be rejected. It is also wrong to criticize a judgment for refusing to set aside an award on the grounds that by acknowledging receipt of the decision of the arbitral tribunal extending the deliberations without making the slightest dispute, and by appearing before tribunal on the new date of deliberation, the claimant tacitly accepted the continuation of the arbitration proceedings until Aug. 4, 2014 while, according to the plea, that Art. 12 of the UAA does not allow the arbitrators to extend on their own initiative the time limit for arbitration; that the award having been rendered outside the contractual period of arbitration accepted by the parties, the Arbitral Tribunal exceeded its mission and ruled on an expired agreement; that thus, the Court of Appeal broke the law and exposed its decision to the cassation.

eventually determine the interpretation to be adopted of this provision, the first hypothesis seems to be the best to retain, for the following reasons.

Arbitration being the business of the parties, its choice enshrines the expression of their autonomy that everything should be done to promote. If for any reason, the arbitration is not completed at the end of the time period and the parties are in favor of the extension, there is nothing reprehensible or contrary to public policy to allow them to continue the proceedings as long as they lend themselves to the game, as the CCJA held in *Société Camerounaise d'Opérations Maritimes v. Express Transport Khalifa.*[32] Similarly, there is no point in lengthening the procedure by a few weeks and increasing the legal fees and fees of counsel to seek and obtain permission from a judge when the parties already agree. To this end, it would be wise for the parties to provide in advance for the interpretation to be adopted in the event that the need arises since there is no provision in the UAA expressly prohibiting it and what the law itself does not require cannot be demanded.[33] Arbitrators could also stimulate debate on the issue at the outset of the proceedings and decide on a course of action should the need arise. In any event, it is obvious that if only one party wishes the extension, or if the arbitral tribunal wishes to do so and the parties together or one of them disagree, only the competent court will have to decide.

[2] Under the CCJA Rules

Time limit is governed essentially by Article 15, paragraph 1, f) and 15.4. Article 15.1, paragraph 1 states that:

> 15.1 After it has received the file, the arbitral tribunal convenes the parties or their duly qualified representatives and counsel, to a case management conference which must be held as soon as possible and not later than forty-five (45) days from the date of referral of the case to the tribunal. During this case management conference, the arbitral tribunal may require proof of the power of attorney of any representative of a party if it deems it necessary. The arbitral tribunal may, with the agreement of the parties, hold this meeting in the form of a telephone conference or videoconference.

If a hearing is held, it must not take place more than six months at the maximum after the date of the case management conference unless parties have agreed otherwise.[34] Finally, the award must be written and signed within ninety days of the

32. Société Camerounaise d'Opérations Maritimes v. Express Transport Khalifa, N° 060/2017, Decision, [C.C.J.A.], 1e ch., (Mar. 30, 2017). The CCJA held that there is no reason to set aside an arbitral award when the party requesting the setting aside has produced documents before the arbitral tribunal after the expiry of the time limit and has collaborated in the pursuit of the arbitration until the rendering of the award without ever raising the irregularity linked to the expiration of the deadline.
33. Thales Security Systems v. Kattie, N° 30/2010, Decision, CCJA, 1e ch., (Apr. 29, 2010), http://www.ohada.com/jurisprudence/ohadata/J-11-74.html.
34. CCJA Regulation on Arbitration, Art. 15.1, para. f).

procedural order of the tribunal closing the debates unless the time limit has been extended by the Court, at its own initiative or upon request of the arbitral tribunal.[35]

The provisional nature of the procedural timetable of arbitration proceedings under the CCJA Regulation has also been asserted on multiple occasions by the CCJA. First, it ruled in *Société Nationale Pour la Promotion Agricole v. Société des hydrocarbures du Bénin,*[36] and *Ekwa Ngalle v. Société Nationale d'Hydrocarbures*[37] that the change in the procedural timetable does not systematically characterize a violation of its mission by an arbitral tribunal since the timetable is provisional. Second, an arbitral tribunal cannot be faulted for failing to render its award at the due date if, during the deliberations, while the award was being drafted, the tribunal was faced with the need to request additional information from the claimant to support its decision and was led to overturning of the said deliberation in order to request and obtain from the CCJA the extension of the period within which it was to render the challenged award.[38] Third, it was ruled in *Etat du Mali v. Seaquest-Infotel Mali,* that failure of an arbitral tribunal to notify to the parties the extension granted to the tribunal by the CCJA does not invalidate the award and the challenge on that ground cannot prosper.[39] Fourth, there is no need for an arbitral tribunal to hold a meeting with the parties before extending

35. CCJA Regulation on Arbitration, Art. 15.4. The CCJA was already allowed to extend the time period for signing the award (90 days from the procedural order closing the hearings) at the request of the arbitral tribunal. The Court itself can now extend the time limit sua sponte (revised Art. 15.4) if the circumstances make it necessary. One may wonder under what conditions the Court can use such power to extend the time period and the future will no doubt provide us with illustrations.
36. Société Nationale Pour la Promotion Agricole v. Société des hydrocarbures du Bénin, N° 045/2008, *supra,* Chapter 5, fn. 26. The CCJA held that the timetable of the proceedings, established by the arbitral tribunal during the case management conference at which, among other things, the subject of the dispute is defined, is provisional. As that date is a forecast, it is subject to change; consequently, the amendment of such a timetable, which had only a provisional or indicative character, cannot be validly regarded as a violation by an arbitral tribunal of the terms of its mission. That plea, which lacks relevance, must be rejected.
37. Ekwa Ngalle v. Société Nationale d'Hydrocarbures, *supra,* Chapter 2, fn. 31, holding that the violation of Art. 15.4 of the CCJA Regulation on Arbitration does not constitute ground for annulment of an award and it is settled case law that the timing of the proceedings is provisional, subject to change. Consequently, the modification of such a calendar made in accordance with Art. 15.4 of the aforementioned Regulation cannot be validly considered as a violation by the tribunal of the terms of its mission.
38. Société Nationale Pour la Promotion Agricole v. Société des hydrocarbures du Bénin, N° 045/2008, *supra,* Chapter 5, fn. 26. The CCJA added that in the present case, and contrary to the claimant's contention, the tribunal had made known to the parties, prior to Aug. 2, 2006, the reasons why it could not render its award on that date of Aug. 2, 2006. For instance, the arbitral tribunal asked the claimant to produce a number of exhibits and granted her a period of 30 days from the receipt of that letter, and a period of fifteen days from the receipt of the above documents to the respondent for their comments. It follows from all of the above that the plea is unfounded and must be rejected.
39. Etat du Mali v. Seaquest-Infotel Mali, N° 027/2017, Decision, [C.C.J.A.], Ass. plen., (Mar. 2, 2017), http://www.ohada.com/jurisprudence/ohadata/J-17-161.html. For the CCJA, it follows from Art. 15.4 of the CCJA Regulation on Arbitration that the arbitrator may request from the CCJA, an extension of the statutory period of 90 days prescribed for them to render their award. In the case at hand, the failure to notify the parties, by the arbitral tribunal, of the extensions obtained by decisions of the Court, is not a cause of nullity of the award. It is therefore wrong to criticize a tribunal for having rendered the award under challenge after the arbitral proceedings have been terminated, on the ground that the arbitration award was drafted outside the legal

the procedural timetable,[40] which must not, however, be construed by arbitrators as an authorization to impose modification of the procedural calendar upon the parties.

[B] Service of Arbitral Awards

Under the UAA, the reader is encouraged to check the applicable local rules.

Under the CCJA Rules, service of an award is governed, under the CCJA Regulation, by Articles 12 and 25. Titled "notification, communication and time limits," Article 12 of the CCJA Regulation on Arbitration states:

> 12.1 The memorials and all written communications submitted by any party, as well as additional documents, are filed in as many copies as there are parties plus one for each arbitrator and one electronic copy is sent to the Secretary General.
>
> Once the case has been referred to the arbitral tribunal, the latter and the parties send the Secretary General an electronic copy of all correspondence exchanged in connection with the proceedings.
>
> 12.2 All notifications or communications from the Secretary General and the arbitral tribunal are served at the address or the last known address of the party to which it is addressed, or their representative, as notified by the latter or by the other party, is applicable. The notification or communication may be made by delivery against receipt, registered letter, transport service, email, or any other electronic method enabling the proof of sending to be provided.
>
> 12.3 The notification or communication validly made is deemed established when it has been received by the interested party or, if it has been validly made in accordance with paragraph 12.2 above, should have been received by the interested party or their representative.
>
> 12.4 The time limits set by this Regulation or by the Court begin to run the day after the notification or communication is deemed to have been made under paragraph 12.3 above.
>
> When, in the country where the notification or communication was deemed to have been made on a certain date, the day after it is a public holiday or non-working day, the time limit begins to run on the first following working day.
>
> Public holidays and non-working days are included in the calculation of time limits and do not extend them. If the last day of the allotted time is a public holiday or non-working day in the country where the notification or communication is deemed to have been made, the time limit expires at the end of the first following working day.

---

time limit of 90 days, and because the decisions to extend this time limit were not notified to the appellant, thus violating Art. 15.4.

40. Société Nationale Pour la Promotion Agricole v. Société des Hydrocarbures du Bénin, N° 045/2008, *supra*, Chapter 5, fn. 26. The plea alleging that the challenged award violates Art. 15.5 of the CCJA Regulation on Arbitration, in that, "after rendering the partial award (...), the arbitrators did not believe they should convene a meeting before imposing on the parties an expertise as well as a new timetable for the enforcement of this measure" whereas, according to the plea, "this process is clearly in contradiction with the provisions of Art. 15.5 of the Regulation on Arbitration, which imposes a mandatory prerequisite for the meeting of the parties before establishing a new calendar," is not among the grounds for challenging an award rendered under the aegis of the CCJA and cannot succeed.

> After the arbitral tribunal has been constituted and with its agreement, the parties may agree to reduce the different time limits provided for in this Regulation. If circumstances warrant, the Court may, after consultation with the parties, extend, at the request of the tribunal, such a time limit or any other period resulting from this Regulation, to allow the arbitral tribunal to perform its functions.

In addition to the possibility now available to the secretary-general to have any evidence or element of the proceedings communicated by the tribunal or the parties, Article 12.2 specifies the terms of communication of the secretary-general and the arbitral tribunal with the parties or their representatives, communications that can now be made by email or any other electronic means to justify the sending. Also, procedural deadlines can be modulated since it is now permitted to reduce or extend them in the context of arbitration proceedings. Thus, the last paragraph of Article 12 allows the parties to reduce the time of proceedings in agreement with the tribunal, after the constitution of the latter. At the request of the tribunal, the CCJA is also permitted to extend any time period under the Regulation after consultation with the parties.[41]

On the notification of arbitral awards, Article 25 of the Regulation states:

> 25.1 Once the award has been rendered and after the arbitration costs have been fully paid to the Court by the parties or one of them, the Secretary General notifies the signed award to the parties.
> 25.2 Additional copies certified by the Secretary General are issued at any time to the parties requesting them.
> 25.3 By virtue of such notification, the parties waive the right to any other notification or communication incumbent upon the arbitral tribunal.

The current version of the CCJA Regulation on Arbitration requires that arbitration costs be paid to the CCJA rather than the secretary-general, as previously was the case. This payment of the full arbitration costs, which may be made by one of the parties with interest in having the award promptly notified for enforcement, is the last essential step before notification of the award to the parties, which marks the end of the arbitration process by discharging the tribunal, subject to an application for interpretation or possible supplementation of the award.

[C] Publication of Arbitral Awards

Here also, the reader is encouraged to check the situation under each national arbitration center according to the rules that may apply locally.

On the publication of arbitral awards rendered under the CCJA Rules, Article 14, paragraph 3 of the CCJA Regulation on Arbitration states that "the Secretary General is authorized to publish extracts from arbitral awards without mentioning elements enabling the identification of the parties."

---

41. For some illustration of this, *see* Ekwa Ngalle v. Société Nationale d'Hydrocarbures, *supra*, Chapter 2, fn. 31, and Société Nationale Pour la Promotion Agricole v. Société des hydrocarbures du Bénin, N° 045/2008, *supra*, Chapter 5, fn. 26.

§12.07 AWARD OF COSTS OF ARBITRATION AND LEGAL REPRESENTATION

There is not much to say on the costs and legal representation under the UAA since it is left to the parties to organize in most cases except where local or national arbitrations centers are referred to, and the rules of these apply. This situation must be handled on a case-by-case basis, and parties are referred to any specific rules that may apply if a center is involved.

On the Costs, under the CCJA Rules, Article 24 of the CCJA Regulation on Arbitration states:

> 24.1 The arbitral tribunal fixes the costs of arbitration in the arbitral award and decides which of the parties is responsible for the payment or in what proportion the costs are to be shared between the parties.
>
> 24.2 In fixing the costs, the arbitral tribunal takes into account the relevant circumstances, including the extent to which each party has conducted the arbitration proceedings swiftly and efficiently in terms of costs.
>
> 24.3 Arbitration costs include:
>
> a) the fees of the arbitrator and the administrative costs fixed by the Court, possible expenses of the arbitrator, operating costs of the arbitral tribunal, expert fees and expenses in the event of an expertise. The arbitrators' fees and the Court's administrative fees are fixed in accordance with a schedule drawn up by the General Assembly of the Court and approved by the OHADA Council of Ministers under Article 4 of the Treaty;
>
> b) the normal costs incurred by the parties for their defense, according to the assessment made by the arbitral tribunal of the related claims of the parties.
>
> 24.4 If the circumstances of the case make it exceptionally necessary, the Court may, at its own initiative or upon a reasoned request of the arbitrator, fix the fees of the arbitrator at an amount greater or lower than the one that would result from the application of the schedule of fees.
>
> Any arbitrators' fee-setting without the approval of the Court is null and void, without it being a cause for the annulment of the award.
>
> 24.5 In the event that all claims are withdrawn or the arbitration is terminated before a final award is rendered, the Court fixes the fees, the costs of the arbitrators and the administrative costs. If the parties have not agreed on sharing the costs of the arbitration or other relevant costs issues, these issues are settled by the Court.

Article 24 calls for comments in five points: supplementation of the content of an arbitral award (§12.07[A]), taking into account the behavior of the parties in setting the costs (§12.07[B]), the faculty offered to the Court to directly adjust fees (§12.07[C]), the limitation of the effects of setting fees outside the Court (§12.07[D]) and Jurisdiction of the Court for any challenge on costs(§12.07[E]).

[A] Supplementation of the Content of an Arbitral Award

It appears from the first two paragraphs of the revised Article 24 (24.1 and 24.2) that an arbitral award must contain the settlement of the costs of the proceedings and the indication of the terms of payment by the parties. This is, therefore, an essential element of the award, which supplements the information required by Article 22 of the Regulation. The arbitrators will ensure this in their award.

[B] Taking into Account the Behavior of the Parties in the Settlement of Costs

An arbitral tribunal is now allowed to adjust the settlement and allocation of the costs to be borne by the parties depending, among other things, on their general behavior during the proceedings. Thus, the tribunal may, at its discretion, indirectly sanction the delaying behavior of a party in ruling on the costs and fees.

[C] Faculty of the CCJA to Directly Adjust Fees

The CCJA was already allowed to adjust, up or down, the amount of the fees of the arbitrator(s). Under Article 24.4, paragraph 1 of the CCJA Regulation on Arbitration, the CCJA can now do so on its own motion, if circumstances so require.

[D] Limitation of the Effects of Setting Fees Outside the Court

Another substantial amendment to Article 24 consists of limiting the effects of an increase in fees made between the parties and the tribunal outside the Court. It is now expressly provided that such a situation cannot result in the annulment of the award. This express provision now renders obsolete, for the future, the ruling of the Court in *Republique de Guinee v. Getma International,*[42] where the CCJA annulled an award for noncompliance with its mission by obtaining from the parties an increase in fees outside the Court and despite its express refusal.[43]

This new provision is undoubtedly a source of relief for a part of the arbitration community that has felt that the annulment of an award under these circumstances was unjustified, but the OHADA Legislator does not seem to have taken any specific measures to prevent regrettable behavior in the future, since any separate agreement between an arbitral tribunal and the parties on fees was already prohibited and deemed null and void by Article 9 of the Prescriptive Decision N° 004/99/CCJA of February 3, 1999 Relating to Arbitration Costs,[44] a public policy provision.

In other words, the OHADA Legislator appears to have maintained the status quo, as arbitrators are now exempted in advance of any sanction in the event of an

42. *Supra,* Chapter 3, fn. 8.
43. It must be stressed however, that the new provision at Art. 24 of the CCJA Regulation on Arbitration only suppresses the annulment of an arbitral award as a sanction for setting fees outside the Court. It does not change the fact that such practice constitutes misconduct, even breach of public policy under the rules.
44. *Supra,* Introduction, fn. 24.

unauthorized increase of their fees, which is a breach of their mission[45] constituting a ground for annulment of their award, under Article 29.2 c) of the CCJA Regulation on Arbitration. In any event, the ultimate solution for the parties in the event of difficulty would be to firmly oppose any unauthorized increase, to refer it, if necessary, to the Court by requesting the challenge of the arbitrator(s), which would still seem ineffective if the deviant behavior occurred at the end of the proceedings when the award has already been drafted.

[E] Jurisdiction of the Court for Any Challenge on Costs

The last paragraph of Article 24 reminds everyone that disputes relating to fees are decided by the Court. These disputes fall under the "administrative decisions" of the CCJA in matters of arbitration under Article 1 paragraph 7 of the Regulation on Arbitration and, as such are without appeal.

§12.08 AWARD OF INTERESTS

Under both arbitration systems, there are no specific provisions on the interests, and a tribunal can award interests in addition to any monetary relief(s) decided (generally against the losing party) unless parties have stipulated otherwise.

45. It is indeed established that in arbitration proceedings governed by a Regulation, the violation by a tribunal of any provision of the applicable Regulation constitutes a breach of its mission: *see* Pawelec v. Pernod Ricard, Cour d'appel [CA] [regional court of appeal] Paris, 1e ch. C, Oct. 5 2000, GP 2001.som.1909 (Fr)., about the failure of an arbitral tribunal to state the reasons of its award, as required by the applicable regulation, but transposable to a regulation expressly deeming any unauthorized fee increase null and void—a detail often evaded or ignored by critics of the *Getma* case.

CHAPTER 13

Correction, Interpretation, and Supplementation of an Arbitral Award

As a general rule, once the award is rendered and notified to the parties, an arbitral tribunal is discharged of the case, which is known as the *fuctus officio* doctrine (§13.01). Under certain circumstances, however, an arbitral tribunal may be required to interpret (§13.02), to correct (§13.03), to supplement (§13.04) the award it has rendered. The specific procedure for those will be presented (§13.05), and some comments will be made on the revocation of fraudulently obtained awards (§13.06) and institutional appeals (§13.07).

§13.01 FUCTUS OFFICIO DOCTRINE

Fuctus officio has been defined as "having fulfilled the function, discharged the office, or accomplished the purpose, and therefore of no further force or authority. Applied to an officer whose term has expired, and who has consequently no further official authority; and also to an instrument, power, agency, etc. which has fulfilled the purpose of its creation, and is therefore of no further virtue or effect."[1]

The fuctus officio doctrine is enshrined in Article 22, paragraph 1 of the UAA and Article 26, paragraph 1 of the CCJA Regulation on Arbitration, which states that "The award *discharges*[2] the arbitral tribunal of the dispute." Unlike in some jurisdictions such as Canada where there seems to be no recognized exception to the fuctus officio doctrine,[3] the OHADA Legislator has recognized, like many other

1. *Black's Law Dictionary* Free Online Edition, https://thelawdictionary.org [accessed May 6, 2020] (Black, s.d.). *See* the glossary, *infra*.
2. [Emphasis added].
3. *See* for example the dissenting opinion (but concurring on the issue of *fuctus officio* doctrine) of Justice L'Heureux-Dubé in Chandler v. Assn. of Architects (Alberta), [1989] 2 S.C.R. 848, at 867, https://scc-csc.lexum.com/scc-csc/scc-csc/en/524/1/document.do [accessed Apr. 10, 2020, at 15:17]: "The doctrine of *functus officio* states that an adjudicator, be it an arbitrator, an

jurisdictions,[4] some exceptions to the doctrine as presented in the following paragraphs on correction, interpretation and supplementation of an award.

§13.02 INTERPRETATION OF AN AWARD

Under Article 22, paragraph 2 of the UAA and Article 26, paragraph 2 of the CCJA Regulation on Arbitration, an arbitral tribunal "has the power to interpret the award."

§13.03 CORRECTION OF AN AWARD

An arbitral tribunal also has the power to "correct any material errors or omission affecting [an arbitral award]."[5]

§13.04 SUPPLEMENTATION OF AN AWARD

Article 22 paragraph 3 of the UAA and Article 26 paragraph 3 of the CCJA Regulation on Arbitration state that "Where the Tribunal has omitted to rule on a claim, it may remedy the situation by rendering an additional award."

§13.05 PROCEDURE FOR INTERPRETATION, CORRECTION OR SUPPLEMENTATION OF AN AWARD

The request for interpretation, correction or supplementation of an award under the UAA, "must be made within thirty (30) days from the notification of the award. The tribunal has forty-five (45) days to rule. If the arbitral tribunal cannot be reconvened it falls upon the competent court in the State Party to rule."[6]

There is a slight difference under the CCJA Regulation on Arbitration as highlighted in Article 26, paragraphs 4 to 8 of the CCJA Regulation on Arbitration which state:

---

administrative tribunal or a court, once it has reached its decision cannot afterwards alter its award except to correct clerical mistakes or errors arising from an accidental slip or omission ... 'To allow the adjudicator to again deal with the matter of its own volition without hearing the entire matter "afresh" is contrary to this doctrine ... .'"

4. In General Re Life Corp. v. Lincoln National Life Insurance, N°. 17-2496 (2d Cir. 2018), https://cases.justia.com/federal/appellate-courts/ca2/17-2496/17-2496-2018-11-28.pdf?ts=154 3419007 [accessed Apr. 10, 2020, at 15:48], the U.S. Second Circuit Court of Appeals joined the Third, Fifth, Sixth, Seventh, and Ninth Circuits in recognizing, on Nov. 28, 2018, "an exception to *functus officio* where an arbitral award 'fails to address a contingency that later arises or when the award is susceptible to more than one interpretation,'" if the following three conditions are met: "(1) the final award is ambiguous; (2) the clarification merely clarifies the award rather than substantively modifying it; and (3) the clarification comports with the parties' intent as set forth in the agreement that gave rise to arbitration."
5. UAA, Art. 22, para. 2; CCJA Regulation on Arbitration, Art. 26, para. 2.
6. UAA, Art. 22, para. 4 and 5.

In either of the above cases, the request must be sent to the Secretary General within thirty (30) days of notification of the award.

The Secretary General communicates, upon receipt, the request to the arbitral tribunal and the opposing party, granting the opposing party a period of thirty (30) days to send its observations to the requesting party and the arbitral tribunal.

If the arbitral tribunal is unable to reconvene, and absent any agreement between the parties to appoint a new arbitral tribunal, the Court will appoint a sole arbitrator to rule on the petition for interpretation, rectification or supplementation of the award.

After adversarial assessment of the arguments of the parties and any documents they may have submitted, the draft of the rectifying or additional award must be sent to the Court for the preliminary examination under Article 23 of this Regulation within forty-five (45) days of referral to the arbitral tribunal.

The foregoing procedure entails no arbitrator's fees except in the case under paragraph 6 of this Article. As for the costs, if any, they are borne by the party who filed the application if it is dismissed entirely. Otherwise, they are shared between the parties in the proportion set for arbitration costs in the award subject of the motion.

The possibility now offered to an arbitral tribunal which has failed to rule on a claim to "catch up" with an additional award also undoubtedly constitutes another means of limiting the risks of the annulment of an award (for the failure of the tribunal to fulfill its mission). While it is unquestionably advantageous for an arbitral tribunal, a party may deplore having, in the best of cases, to waste time waiting for a tribunal to rule on a claim initially omitted and in the worst case, to waste time and pay a new arbitrator (when the initial tribunal can no longer be convened) to perform the mission to which the first tribunal failed after being paid. Under such conditions, arbitration could become unnecessarily too onerous for the parties, who would be the big losers.

A party wishing to file a request for interpretation, correction or supplementation of an award must do so within thirty days of notification of the award; otherwise, the request will be inadmissible.

§13.06 REVOCATION OF FRAUDULENTLY OBTAINED AWARDS

A fraudulently obtained award can be annulled if it is established before the competent court that the fraud leading to the challenged award characterizes one of the grounds for annulment under the applicable rules.[7]

§13.07 INSTITUTIONAL APPEAL

No institutional appeal mechanism is available under the OHADA rules.[8]

7. *See infra*, Chapter 14 grounds for annulment of arbitral awards.
8. *See infra*, Chapter 15 on the procedure for annulment of arbitral awards.

PART IV Annulment, Third-Party Opposition and Revision of Arbitral Awards

Once the arbitral process has reached the stage of an award, the prevailing party must, in many cases, overcome one last hurdle before being able to enforce their award, i.e., the challenge of the arbitral which, under OHADA rules, is made via a motion for annulment. Given the heavy load of information that needs to be presented on the challenge of an award, the grounds (Chapter 14) and procedure for annulment (Chapter 15) will be presented separately, followed with the other less frequently used remedies which are third-party opposition and revision of arbitral awards (Chapter 16).

CHAPTER 14

Grounds for the Annulment of Arbitral Awards

Initially, there were six grounds for the annulment of an arbitral award under the UAA and four grounds under the CCJA Regulation on Arbitration. Article 26 of the UAA states that the motion for annulment is admissible only:

(a) if the arbitral tribunal has ruled without an arbitration agreement or on a null or expired agreement;
(b) if the arbitral tribunal has been improperly composed, or the sole arbitrator was improperly appointed;
(c) if the arbitral tribunal has ruled without complying with the mission entrusted to it;
(d) if the adversarial principle has been breached;
(e) if the arbitral award is contrary to international public policy; or
(f) if the award is devoid of any reason.

Under Article 30.6 of the CCJA Regulation on Arbitration prior to the reform of November 2017, *exequatur* could be denied, or an arbitral award could be annulled on the four following grounds:

(1) if the arbitral tribunal has ruled without an arbitration agreement or on a null or expired agreement;
(2) if the arbitral tribunal has ruled without complying with the mission entrusted to it;
(3) if the adversarial principle has been breached; or
(4) if the arbitral award is contrary to international public policy.

As a result of the amendment of the Rules in November 2017, the grounds have been harmonized in the two sets of rules by incorporating under the CCJA Regulation on Arbitration, at Article 29.2, paragraph 2, the two other grounds of the UAA, namely the improper composition of an arbitral tribunal[1] and the failure to state the reasons of an award.[2] Thus, there are now six identical grounds for annulment of an arbitral award under the two sets of rules: absence of a valid arbitration agreement (§14.02), irregular composition of an arbitral tribunal (§14.03), failure of the tribunal to comply with the mission entrusted to it (§14.04), breach of the adversarial principle (§14.05) and international public policy (§14.06) and finally the failure to state the reasons of an award (§14.07). Those grounds will be presented after highlighting an important limitation of the annulment proceedings to the grounds under the applicable rules (§14.01). While there are now six grounds for the annulment of an arbitral award under the CCJA Regulation on Arbitration, it will also be demonstrated, hereafter, that the addition of those two annulment grounds under Article 29.2 of the CCJA Regulation on Arbitration is of little relevance if any at all.

§14.01 LIMITATION OF THE ANNULMENT PROCEEDINGS TO THE GROUNDS UNDER THE APPLICABLE RULES

Under both the UAA (§14.01[A]) and the CCJA Regulation on Arbitration (§14.01[B]), national courts, as well as the CCJA, have constantly ruled that only the grounds mentioned by the Legislator for each arbitration system can be considered for the annulment of arbitral awards and any ground other than those cannot lead to annulment.

[A] Under the UAA

An arbitral award governed by Article 26 of the UAA may be annulled only on the grounds described above. National arbitration law may provide no legal basis for an action for annulment for an arbitral award governed by the UAA.[3] The available case law highlights the inadmissibility of motions for annulment of arbitral awards based on national legislation (§14.01[A][1]), on other provisions of the UAA (§14.01[A][2]) or on an alleged wrongful application of the law (§14.01[A][3]).

[1] Inadmissibility of a Ground Based on National Legislation

An application for the annulment of an arbitral award *on the ground of a national legal provision on arbitration* is inadmissible. [Since the UAA is now the law governing arbitration in the OHADA Member States,[4] and has replaced preexisting domestic

1. "If the arbitral tribunal has been improperly composed, or the sole arbitrator was improperly appointed."
2. "If the award is devoid of any reason."
3. Constructions Metalliques Ivoiriennes v. Fraternite Saint Jean Eudes d'Abatta, N° 062/2012, *supra*, Chapter 5, fn. 1.
4. Under Art. 35 of the UAA and Art. 10 of the OHADA Treaty.

arbitration laws, leaving only possible organizational standards of institutional arbitration which are not contrary to it.] This is the case since an action for annulment is open only for the limited grounds listed in Article 26 of the UAA and no national provision can validly serve as a basis for the annulment of an award.[5] The plea alleging that an appellate court had violated Articles 11, 13 paragraphs 1 and 26 of the UAA by requiring pre-arbitration proceedings leading to the annulment of the arbitration agreement before the arbitral award itself may be challenged for annulment must be dismissed, notwithstanding the determinations of the Court of Appeal which have no effect on the merits regarding the grounds for annulment limited by Article 26 of the UAA since the pleaded nullity of the arbitration agreement itself was dismissed.[6]

[2] Inadmissibility of the Alleged Violation of Other Provisions of the UAA

The argument alleging that an appellate court violated Articles 11, 13 paragraphs 1 and 26 of the UAA in that it required a pre-arbitration procedure in which the arbitration agreement should first be set aside, in order for the arbitral award itself to be challenged must be dismissed, notwithstanding the assertions of the Court of Appeal which have no effect on the merits of the limited grounds for annulment set out in Article 26 of the UAA, since the ground for annulment of the award based on the nullity of the arbitration agreement has itself been rejected.[7]

[3] Inadmissibility of the Alleged Wrongful Application of the Law

The incorrect application of a law by the arbitrator, even proven, cannot, by itself, constitute a failure by the arbitrator to comply with their mission under Article 26 of the UAA. A challenge of an award on that ground lacks merits and must be dismissed.[8]

5. *See* Constructions Metalliques Ivoiriennes v. Fraternite Saint Jean Eudes d'Abatta, *supra*, Chapter 5, fn. 1.
6. La société Bougainvilliers v. Mochet, N° 069/2015, *supra*, Chapter 5, fn. 12. [Emphasis added]. In George Forrest Belgium v. Les Ciments du Sahel, N° 094/2020, Decision, [C.C.J.A.], 2e ch., (Apr. 9, 2020), it was held that the Court of Appeal which dismissed the motion for annulment of an arbitral award rendered after the six-month time limit set by the applicable rules of the arbitration center, on the ground that noncompliance with the time limit is not among the annulment grounds under Art. 26 of the UAA and also does not result from any provision of public policy of the UAA, did not violate the said Art. 26 by misinterpretation and the appeal in cassation against the judgment of the Court of Appeal must be dismissed. Likewise, under Art. 26 of the UAA, the regularity of the composition of an arbitral tribunal is assessed only in the light of the procedure of its constitution, which must comply with Articles 5 and 8 of the UAA, the impartiality and independence of the arbitrators who compose it, and not in consideration of the provisions of a national law. Therefore, the judgment of the Court of Appeal which states that the party who was aware of the composition of the arbitral tribunal and continued the arbitration without any objection, "is deemed to have acquiesced to this composition and therefore waived their right to object," did not violate any rule justifying annulment of the award; appeal in cassation dismissed.
7. *Id.*
8. Kouassi v. Armajaro, N° 037/2017, Decision, [C.C.J.A.], 3e ch., (Mar. 9, 2017), http://www.ohada.com/jurisprudence/ohadata/J-17-171.html.

[B] Under the CCJA Rules

Under the CCJA Rules also, the available case law of the CCJA highlights the inadmissibility of motions for annulment based on the alleged violation of other provision of the CCJA Arbitration Rules (§14.01[B][1]), trouble to public policy (§14.01[B][2]), violation of law and contradictions in the reasoning (§14.01[B][3]), the alleged violation of French *lex arbitri* (§14.01[B][4]), the unfounded failure to state the reasons of the award (§14.01[B][5]) and the alleged failure to comply with the procedure agreed upon (§14.01[B][6]).

[1] Inadmissibility of the Alleged Violation of Other Provisions of the CCJA Rules

The challenge of an arbitral award on the ground of violation of Article 15.5 of the CCJA Regulation on Arbitration Rules, in that, "after making the partial award (...), the arbitrators did not believe they should convene a meeting before imposing on the parties the appointment of an expert as well as a new timetable for the enforcement of this measure," whereas, according to the argument, "this process is in sharp contradiction with the provisions of Article 15.5 of the CCJA Regulation on Arbitration, which imposes a mandatory meeting of the parties before a new timetable is established," must be dismissed because such ground does not fall under the grounds for annulment under Articles 25 of the Treaty and 30.6 [which became 30.5] of the CCJA Regulation on Arbitration.[9]

Likewise, the challenge based on an argument alleging the violation, by an arbitral award, of Article 22.1 [which became 22.1 paragraph 8] of the CCJA Regulation on Arbitration, on the grounds that the challenged award insufficiently states the reasons upon which it is based must be dismissed since, under Article 29.2 of the CCJA Arbitration Rules, the challenge of an award can only be based on one of the grounds listed under Article 30.6 [which became 29.2] of the same Regulation, under which the insufficiency of the reasons for the award does not appear.[10]

[2] Inadmissibility of the Alleged Trouble to Public Policy

The challenge of an arbitral award on the ground that the arbitral tribunal has "disturbed public order in the course of the proceedings" is inadmissible.[11]

9. Societe Nationale pour la Promotion Agricole v. Societe des Huileries du Benin, N° 045/2008, *supra*, Chapter 5, fn. 26.
10. Etat du Niger v. Société Africard Co Limited, N° 141/2016, Decision, [C.C.J.A.], Ass. plen., (Jul. 14, 2016).
11. Pyramidion v. Agence d'Exécution des Travaux d'Infrastructure du Mali, N° 098/2014, *supra*, Chapter 6, fn. 16.

[3] *Inadmissibility of the Alleged Violation of Law and Contradictions in the Reasoning*

The request for annulment of an arbitral award on the grounds of violation of the law and contradictions in the reasons of the award lacks merits and must be dismissed.[12]

[4] *Inadmissibility of the Alleged Violation of French* Lex Arbitri

The request for annulment of an arbitral award on the grounds of the violation of "French *lex arbitri,*" namely French procedural law on arbitration, must be dismissed because as far as the arbitration at hand was under the aegis of the CCJA, it is governed as such, only by the CCJA Regulation on Arbitration.[13]

[5] *Inadmissibility of the Unfounded Failure to State the Reasons of an Award*

The challenge of an award on the ground that the award does not state the reasons upon which it is based, ground not provided for in Article 30.6 of the CCJA Regulation on Arbitration of March 11, 1999, must be dismissed. Thus, a party is therefore wrong to reproach an arbitral tribunal of not having "dealt with their claims in an autonomous and thorough manner," while the tribunal devoted several pages to the claims of the opposing party and maintained that they deduced from that behavior that the arbitral tribunal stated no reason for its award with regard to the claims of the party which filed the petition for annulment.[14] However, it must be noted that the ruling in *Société Nestle Cameroun v. Groupe Abbassi* is no more valid because the failure to state the reasons of an award has now been included in the grounds for annulment of an award under Article 29 of the CCJA Regulation Arbitration since the reform of 2017.

[6] *Inadmissibility of the Alleged Failure to Comply with the Procedure Agreed Upon*

The request for annulment of an arbitral award based on a failure to comply with the prior conciliation procedure, notwithstanding the fact that the arbitral tribunal did not expressly reply to this argument, is unfounded since it results from the documents in the proceedings, in particular, from the request for arbitration and a letter served by a bailiff, that the respondent has satisfied the requirements of preliminary conciliation by notifying the claimant of the existence of the dispute, requesting the preliminary

12. Ekwa Ngalle v. Société Nationale d'Hydrocarbures, *supra*, Chapter 2, fn. 31.
13. *Id.*
14. Société Nestle Cameroon v. Groupe Abbassi, N° 081/2019, Decision, [C.C.J.A.], Ass. plen., (Mar. 28, 2019), http://www.ohada.com/jurisprudence/ohadata/J-16-71.html.

conciliation and even taking care to propose a conciliator. Therefore, the request for annulment must be dismissed.[15]

On the contrary, however, the inadmissibility of a request for annulment has been wrongfully raised on the grounds that an appeal is opened only in the limited cases under Article 30.6 of the CCJA Regulation on Arbitration since one of the grounds raised is based on the noncompliance of an award with the mission of the arbitral tribunal.[16]

§14.02 ABSENCE OF A VALID ARBITRATION AGREEMENT

[A] Under the UAA

As a general rule under Article 26 of the UAA, an award rendered in the absence of an arbitration agreement is void, and the Court may suspend its provisional enforcement.[17] Enforcement of an arbitration clause negotiated by a third party is permitted when the third party acted on behalf of the plaintiff. Therefore, a ruling by an arbitrator based on the theory of appearance may not be annulled.[18]

Before presenting some cases illustrating how the absence of a valid agreement is determined by courts (§14.02[A][2]), it is important to highlight the key role they play, as the frontline of the annulment process,[19] in the assessment of the existence of a valid agreement by arbitral tribunals (§14.02[A][1]).

[1] Review, by the Competent Court for Annulment, of the Assessment of the Agreement Which Led an Arbitral Tribunal to Retain Jurisdiction

Under Article 26 paragraph 1 of the UAA, the Annulment Judge[20] has the power to review the arbitral tribunal's assessment of the arbitration clause or agreement that has determined the tribunal to retain its jurisdiction under Article 11 of the UAA. In proceeding with the arbitral tribunal's interpretation of the ambiguous clause of the articles of association of the corporation involved, the Court ruling on the annulment did not violate Article 12 of the Uniform Act on Corporations.[21] The judgment is, therefore, wrongfully criticized for having held that the clause stipulated in Article 45 of the articles of association which led to arbitration is not an arbitration clause but

15. Benin Control v. Etat du Bénin, N° 103/2015, *supra*, Chapter 6, fn. 18.
16. Etat du Niger v. Société Africard Co Limited, N° 141/2016, *supra*, Chapter 14, fn. 10.
17. Cour d'appel [CA] [regional court of appeal] de L'Ouest, Apr. 8, 2009, N° 44/Civ., (Cameroon), http://www.ohada.com/jurisprudence/ohadata/J-12-219.html.
18. CA Abidjan, Apr. 20, 2001, 1ere esp., note P. Boulanger (Côte d'Ivoire), http://www.ohada.com/jurisprudence/ohadata/J-02-127.html.
19. *See*, Chapter 15, §15.02, *infra*.
20. Namely, the competent court or judge in any State Party to the OHADA Treaty having jurisdiction to rule on the challenge of an arbitral award under Art. 25 of the UAA.
21. Uniform Act on Commercial Companies and the Economic Interest Group, https://www.ohada.org/attachments/article/537/AUSCGIE-EN_Unofficial_Translation.pdf [accessed Apr. 11, 2020, at 17:58].

rather organizing a mere pre-conciliation procedure, whereas, according to the argument, the aforementioned Article 11, establishes the priority of the arbitral tribunal to rule on the existence or the validity of an arbitration agreement, the intervention of the annulment judge being only incidental and residual; that by characterizing the clause as pathologically non-open to arbitration, the Court of Appeal has misrepresented the facts determined by the arbitrators through their judicial discretion and reviewed the merits of the arbitral award, all things which are not within the office of the annulment judge. The argument and the subsequent appeal must be dismissed.[22]

[2] Cases Where Absence of a Valid Agreement Was Not Determined

Under the available case law, three situations can be presented: non-expired arbitration agreement (§14.02[A][2][i]), illiteracy of a party which has not hindered their ability to negotiate (§14.02[A][2][ii]) and the validity of the arbitration agreement signed by the agent of a party (§14.02[A][2][iii]).

[i] Agreement Not Expired

A claimant was wrong to maintain that the Arbitration Center of GICAM having appointed, by letter of February 8, 2011, a sole arbitrator who accepted their assignment by letter of the same day, the arbitral tribunal was constituted since that same date from which they had a period of sixty days to issue their award so that on that date indicated in the award as that of its issuance, that is, on February 3, 2012, the arbitration agreement had expired. That is the case because the arbitral tribunal was formed following the decision of the Arbitration Center dated December 13, 2011, by which the Arbitration Center confirmed the arbitrators appointed by the parties and appointed the sole arbitrator initially appointed as President of the Arbitral Tribunal. Since there have been less than six months between this last date and that of the award, the argument must be rejected as lacking merits.[23]

[ii] Illiteracy of a Party That Has Not Hindered Their Ability to Negotiate

The annulment of an award is wrongfully requested on the grounds of the non-existence of an arbitration agreement since it is established in the file that by agreements of December 2006 and March 2007, the parties have stipulated an arbitration clause by which they intended to settle disputes relating thereto by arbitration. By retaining its jurisdiction, the arbitral tribunal, therefore, did not rule without an arbitration agreement. Finally, it has not been demonstrated that the supposed illiteracy of one of the parties was likely to influence their ability to negotiate

22. Wanmo v. Nguessi, N° 151/2017, *supra*, Chapter 2, fn. 21.
23. Commercial Bank of Cameroon v. Archidiocèse de Yaoundé, N° 242/2018, *supra*, Chapter 2, fn. 13.

the transactions from which they benefited, as well as their awareness of the guarantees provided by the parties in relation to the settlement of disputes likely to arise from the implementation of those agreements. It follows that the petition for annulment of the award is unfounded and must be rejected.[24]

[iii] Validity of the Arbitration Agreement Concluded by an Agent

An arbitrator cannot be criticized for having ruled without an agreement containing the arbitration clause on the ground that the agreement containing the arbitration clause had been concluded by a third party since that person, in their capacity as manager of the shop of the author of the annulment appeal, could only act in the name and on behalf of the latter. Therefore, the trial judge was right in ruling against the plaintiff on the basis of the theory of appearance.[25]

[B] Under the CCJA Rules

The proven absence (§14.02[B][1]) and the unproven absence (§14.02[B][2]) of a valid arbitration agreement will be presented.

[1] Proven Absence of a Valid Arbitration Agreement

The consent of a party to refer a dispute to institutional arbitration under the CCJA Rules cannot be presumed and no provision, neither of the Treaty nor of the CCJA Regulation on Arbitration or the Rules of procedure of the CCJA, allows to imply consent to arbitration and a waiver of objections to the arbitration from the lack of response to a letter requesting it. Also, the defendant having provided no evidence of the verbal consent they alleged, the arbitration tribunal that has ruled under such circumstances has ruled without a valid arbitration agreement, and its award must be annulled with no need to rule on the merits.[26]

[2] Unproven Absence of a Valid Arbitration Agreement

Three different situations can be presented: arbitration proceedings decided after state courts have declined jurisdiction (§14.02[B][2][i]), implied arbitration offer accepted (§14.02[B][2][ii]) and the clause providing for arbitration "in accordance with OHADA Arbitration Rules" refers to arbitration under the CCJA Rules (§14.02[B][2][iii]).

24. Société Générale Burkina Faso v. Nare, N° 012/2019, Decision, [C.C.J.A.], 1e ch., (Janv. 24, 2019).
25. CA Abidjan, Apr. 20, 2001, 1ere esp., *supra*, Chapter 14, fn. 18.
26. Etat du Mali v. CFAO, N° 039/2014, *supra*, Chapter 1, fn. 13.

[i] *CCJA Arbitration Proceedings Decided after State Courts Declined Jurisdiction and Agreed upon by Parties*

To avoid denial of justice and subsequent legal uncertainty, equity and proper administration of justice require that an arbitral tribunal necessarily hears and settles a dispute that can be heard by no state court. It is so where state courts have ruled, by a final and binding decision[27] based on the arbitration agreement of the parties, that the case falls within the jurisdiction of an arbitral tribunal and not a state court. Although the arbitration agreement does not expressly designate the Arbitration Centre of the CCJA, the arbitral tribunal appointed by the CCJA has jurisdiction, since, on one part, no other arbitration center has been chosen and on the other part, all parties have signed the minutes of the case management conference (stating the subject matter of arbitration and determining the course of the arbitral proceedings) and agreed on the application of the CCJA Arbitration Rules for the proceedings, showing their common will to submit their dispute to an arbitration panel under the aegis of the CCJA.[28]

The CCJA has also admitted the possibility of an unwritten arbitration agreement.[29]

[ii] *Implied Arbitration Offer Accepted*

The plaintiffs, who have consistently argued before the national courts that the arbitration clause contained in the financing protocol is applicable to the defendant and that the dispute between them must be submitted to arbitration, have thus made an offer of arbitration to the defendant, a thesis corroborated by a judgment of the National Supreme Court. The CCJA having, by the judgment of April 18, 2013, declared the arbitral tribunal competent, stating that the minutes of the case management conference determining the object of the arbitration and setting the arbitral proceedings have been signed by all the parties who thus agreed to the application of the CCJA Regulation on Arbitration as rules of procedure, thus demonstrating their common will to refer the dispute to an arbitral tribunal under the aegis of the CCJA, the issue of the jurisdiction of the arbitral tribunal can no longer be discussed in the same case and between the same parties since that judgment of the CCJA acquired the authority of res judicata. Thus, the contention that the award has been rendered without a valid arbitration agreement is wrong.[30]

---

27. Specifically, a decision having acquired the authority of res judicata.
28. Société Inter Africaine de Distribution v. Compagnie Malienne pour le Développement des Textiles, N° 020/2013, Decision, CCJA, Ass. plen., (Apr. 18, 2013), http://www.ohada.com/jurisprudence/ohadata/J-15-20.html.
29. *Id.*
30. Compagnie Malienne pour le Développement des Textiles v. Société Inter Africaine de Distribution, N° 160/2016, *supra*, Chapter 1, fn. 33.

[iii] The Clause Providing for Arbitration "in Accordance with OHADA Arbitration Rules" Refers to Arbitration under the CCJA Rules

The "OHADA Arbitration Rules" referred to in an arbitration clause stipulating that "any dispute arising from the interpretation of the performance of the contract will be settled by arbitration, in accordance with the OHADA Arbitration Rules; in the event of failure, the parties will refer to the national courts of the country hosting the bank's headquarters" indisputably refer to the provisions of Title IV of the Treaty devoted to institutional arbitration under the CCJA Rules and to which the parties must submit. It is, therefore, right that the arbitral tribunal has declared itself competent to hear the dispute referred to it and the argument contending that while the parties' willingness to go to arbitration can be inferred from the aforementioned arbitration clause, its terms do not allow to say that it refers to the institutional arbitration under the CCJA Rules, as stated by the arbitral tribunal and that the arbitrators, in handling the dispute, have ruled without agreement is unfounded and must be rejected.[31]

It is true that there are two arbitration systems under OHADA Rules and this ruling in *National Financial Credit Bank v. N'Diaye* that the clause referring to arbitration "under OHADA Arbitration Rules" refers to the institutional arbitration under the CCJA Rules may seem arbitrary. However, it seems justified because it has the greatest benefit to the parties by allowing them to control the cost of arbitration by the existence of a schedule of fees known in advance, to save time by allowing a single appeal against the award before the CCJA, and which gives rise to a judgment not subject to *exequatur* proceedings in the States parties to the Treaty, unlike an award which would have been rendered under the UAA and for which *exequatur* proceedings would have required before the state court in the State Party in which the arbitration seat was located, as well as the Court of any other State Party in which enforcement of the award would be sought. The only exception, in this case, would potentially be where the CCJA would have overturned, upon referral, the judgment of the state court having annulled the award or denied *exequatur* was handling the annulment and *exequatur* and determined that the award is valid, in which case, *exequatur* granted by the CCJA would be enforceable in any of the OHADA States Parties.

§14.03 IRREGULAR COMPOSITION OF AN ARBITRAL TRIBUNAL

[A] Under the UAA

As a general rule, the irregularity of the composition of an arbitral tribunal was erected on a ground for the annulment of an arbitral award by Article 27 [sic][32] of the UAA, and no provision of the said Uniform Act subordinates the annulment of an award to the evidence of damage by the party invoking the nullity; the judgment which held

31. National Financial Credit Bank v. N'Diaye, N° 111/2017, Decision, [C.C.J.A.], Ass. plen., (May 11, 2017), http://www.ohada.com/jurisprudence/ohadata/J-16-71.html.
32. An error seems to have crept into the text of the judgment, which mentioned Art. 27 of the UAA instead of Art. 26.

otherwise must be quashed for [Article 26 of the UAA].[33] There are cases where an irregular composition was found (§14.03[A][1]) and others where it was not found (§14.03[A][2]).

[1] Cases Where an Irregular Composition Was Found

There are situations where an arbitrator has been appointed by an institution different from the one stipulated by the parties (§14.03[A][1][i]) and where an arbitrator is having ties with counsel of the party who appointed them (§14.03[A][1][ii]).

[i] Appointment of the Arbitrator by an Institution Different from the One Stipulated

The irregular designation of the sole arbitrator by an arbitration institution other than the one stipulated in the arbitration clause of the binding contract of the parties is inadmissible, and the Court of Appeal which held that "it was in violation of the law that the sole arbitrator was appointed by that institution" to set aside the disputed arbitral award had complied with one of the conditions of admissibility under Article 26 of the UAA. Consequently, the plea is unfounded and must be dismissed.[34]

[ii] Arbitrator Having Ties with Counsel of the Party Who Appointed Them

The arbitral tribunal is only regular if it is composed of independent and impartial arbitrators, and if the procedure for its constitution is exempt from any defect. The formal inquiry of the arbitral tribunal on the nature of the collaborative ties that the arbitrator appointed by the claimant had with the counsel for the said claimant having received no response to assess the impact of these undisclosed ties on the independence and impartiality of the said arbitrator, it was through a fair application of Articles 7 and 26 of the UAA that the Court of Appeal retained "that it is settled case law that the arbitrator must reveal any circumstance likely to affect their judgment and to provoke in the minds of the parties a reasonable doubt on their impartiality and independence, which are the essence of the arbitral function," to annul the award.[35]

33. Le Bistro Family v. Rosace Marbrée, N° 196/2018, *supra*, Chapter 2, fn. 11. However, in George Forrest Belgium v. Les Ciments du Sahel, N° 094/2020, *supra*, Chapter 14, fn. 6, it was held that the regularity of the composition of an arbitral tribunal is assessed only in the light of the procedure of its constitution, which must comply with Articles 5 and 8 of the UAA, the impartiality and independence of the arbitrators who compose it, and *not in consideration of the provisions of a national law*. [Emphasis added].
34. ARNO c/ Libya Oil Cameroun, N° 006/2014, Decision, [C.C.J.A.], Ass. Plen., (Feb. 4, 2014), http://www.ohada.com/jurisprudence/ohadata/J-15-97.html.
35. Wanmo v. Nguessi, N° 151/2017, *supra*, Chapter 2, fn. 21.

[2] Cases Where an Irregular Composition Was Not Found

There is a situation where a magistrate in office was appointed in violation of inoperative national law (§14.03[A][2][i]), a situation in which the members of a tribunal have been appointed under the rules of the center chosen by the parties (§14.03[A][2][ii]) and the situation in which an untimely objection to the irregular composition of a tribunal was raised (§14.03[A][2][iii]).

[i] Magistrate in Office Appointed Arbitrator in Violation of Inoperative National Legislation

The annulment of an arbitral award has wrongfully been requested for the irregular composition of an arbitral tribunal, due to the appointment of a magistrate in the office at the General Prosecutor's Office at the Cassation Court as co-arbitrator, without the consent of their hierarchy, whereas, according to the argument, national legislation[36] prohibits Magistrates from "the exercise of any professional or wage-earning activity," as long as the regularity of the composition of an arbitral tribunal, within the meaning of Article 26 of the UAA, is assessed only in the light of the procedure of its constitution which must comply with Articles 5 and 8 of the UAA, impartiality and independence of the arbitrator(s) who compose it. In the case at hand, there is no evidence of any violation of the above provisions in the appointment of the challenged arbitrator, and neither its independence nor impartiality vis-à-vis the parties is called into question; the argument must be rejected.[37]

[ii] Appointment of Tribunal Members under the Rules of the Center Chosen by the Parties

It is wrong for a party to invoke the improper constitution of an arbitral tribunal, on the grounds that the GICAM Arbitration Centre has appointed a President of the tribunal, even before the litigants name their respective arbitrators, whereas the applicable legislation on arbitration legislation provides otherwise, and that the subsequent decision by which the arbitration center has confirmed the arbitrators and formalized that appointment, cannot cover the alleged irregularity. This is the case, therefore, since Article 9.4 of the GICAM Arbitration Regulations applicable to the dispute states that "If the parties have not agreed to the number of arbitrators, the Center appoints a single arbitrator, unless the dispute appears to justify the appointment of three arbitrators. In the latter case, the parties have 15 days to appoint the arbitrators"; that under Article 15.2 of the same Rules, "If one of the parties refuses or abstains from participating in the arbitration, it takes place notwithstanding that refusal or abstention"; that it is established that it was at the request of the plaintiff, and following the failure to respond to the defendant's request for arbitration, that the GICAM Arbitration

36. Namely, Art. 13 of Law n° 12/94 on the Statute of the Magistrates in Gabon.
37. Airtel Gabon v. 2JTH-Gabon, N° 203/2018, Decision, [C.C.J.A.], 3e ch., (Nov. 22, 2018).

Centre, applying the above provisions, proceeded to appoint a sole arbitrator; that it was at the request of the defendant, to which the plaintiff did not object, that the composition of the tribunal was changed, by the addition of two co-arbitrators, when the sole arbitrator had already been appointed and had already convened case management conferences, in which the defendant actually participated. If in its correspondence of July 14, 2011 bringing to the attention of the sole arbitrator the recomposition of the tribunal, the Center informed the sole arbitration of its willingness to appoint him as President of the recomposed tribunal, it is by subsequent decision, after each of the parties has appointed their arbitrator, that this appointment has been formalized. The irregularity on which the defendant relies has, therefore, not been demonstrated, as the principle of equal treatment of the parties in the composition of the tribunal has been complied with, and the argument will be rejected.[38]

[iii] Untimely Objection Relating to the Irregular Composition of a Tribunal

Relying upon Article 14, paragraph 13 of the UAA, the CCJA ruled, in *Connexion Marketing v. Synergie Gabon*, that an untimely objection to the irregular composition of an arbitral tribunal must be rejected.[39]

[B] Under the CCJA Rules

As mentioned earlier,[40] the irregular composition of an arbitral tribunal was not among the four annulment grounds of an award under Article 30.6 before the reform of 2017, which reproduced the exact same six annulment grounds under Article 26 of the UAA at Article 29.2 of the CCJA Regulation on Arbitration. Thus, there is no case or ruling of the CCJA on this issue.

§14.04 FAILURE OF THE ARBITRAL TRIBUNAL TO COMPLY WITH THE MISSION ENTRUSTED TO IT

[A] Under the UAA

The obligation of national judges handling motions for annulment of arbitral awards for noncompliance of a tribunal with its mission to state the reasons of their decision will be presented (§14.04[A][1]), followed by decisions that did not find a breach of their mission by arbitral tribunals (§14.04[A][2]).

38. Commercial Bank of Cameroon v. Archidiocèse de Yaoundé, N° 242/2018, *supra*, Chapter 2, fn. 13.
39. Connexion Marketing v. Synergie Gabon, N° 027/2010, Decision, [C.C.J.A.], 1e ch., (Apr. 29, 2010).
40. *See supra*, in the introduction to Chapter 14.

[1] Obligation of Judges to Provide Grounds for their Judgment

To validly assert that arbitrators have not complied with their mission and set aside their award under Article 26 of the UAA, a Court of Appeal must not only determine the scope of the mission of the arbitrators, considering the arbitration agreement but also specify in what way they have not complied with their mission, before drawing the consequences. By failing to do so, the Court of Appeal made a misapplication of Article 26 of the UAA, and its ruling must be reversed.[41]

[2] Decisions That Did Not Find a Breach of Its Mission by an Arbitral Tribunal

The cases that will be presented are relating to the wrongful application of the law by a tribunal (§14.04[A][2][i]), the ruling on a claim for damages set out in the terms of reference (§14.04[A][2][ii]), amiable composition not prohibiting application of legal standards leading to a fair solution (§14.04[A][2][iii]), the absence of violation of the provision of the rules of an arbitration center not chosen by the parties (§14.04[A][2][iv]), an alleged fraud relating the date of rendering an award (§14.04[A][2][v]) and the untimely objection to the expiry of the deadline for rendering an award (§14.04[A][2][vi]).

[i] Wrongful Application of the Law by an Arbitral Tribunal

On a judgment which held that the incorrect application of a law by an arbitrator, even proven, cannot, by itself, constitute a violation of its mission by the arbitrator, under Article 26 of the UAA, *see Kouassi v. Armajaro.*[42]

[ii] Tribunal Having Ruled on a Claim for Damages Set Out in the Terms of Reference

It is wrong to blame a:

- judgment ruling on the request for the annulment of an award for having violated Article 26 paragraph 4 of the UAA, by not applying in the case at hand Article 143 of the Civil, Commercial, Administrative and Financial Procedure Code [of Congo] under which "the judge is bound to rule within the limits of the dispute, as determined by the parties," on the ground, according to the plea, that even if the UAA does not have a provision to that effect, the fact remains that "certain provisions of existing national laws on arbitration may also remain applicable, ..." and that it follows that the rule of Article 143

41. Delpech v. Sotaci, N° 010/2003, Decision, [C.C.J.A.], (Jun. 19, 2003), http://www.ohada.com/jurisprudence/ohadata/J-04-65.html.
42. Kouassi v. Armajaro, N° 037/2017, Decision, [C.C.J.A.], 3^{e} ch., (Mar. 9, 2017), http://www.ohada.com/jurisprudence/ohadata/J-17-171.html.

referred to could remedy the shortcomings of [the UAA]. This is so since, contrary to the statements in the plea, the arbitral tribunal has full latitude to rule on damages which, in the case at hand, were expressly mentioned among the initial requests in the terms of reference of the arbitral tribunal. The challenged judgment did not violate Article 26, paragraphs 3 and 4, and the plea must be rejected.[43]

- tribunal for having not complied with its mission by ordering a party to pay damages and other costs of the proceedings, while the arbitration agreement limited the mission of the tribunal to "interpretation, enforcement of these or obligations that may arise from the contract" because the arbitrator's mission is framed by the object of the dispute, which on its turn is determined by the submissions and claims of the parties as set out in the minutes of the case management conference setting out the proceedings; and that, under Article 15 of the agreement of the parties, "the arbitral tribunal must rule in accordance with applicable law in the Republic of Gabon ... . " By awarding damages to a party, as a result of the dispute before it, on the basis of Articles 1147 and 1153 of the Gabonese Civil Code, the arbitral tribunal ruled in law and therefore did not overstep its mission. The plea must be rejected.[44]

[iii] Amicable Composition Does Not Prohibit the Application of Legal Standards Leading to a Fair Solution

It is wrong to reproach an arbitral tribunal for having failed to comply with its mission by ruling in law and not in equity as prescribed by the parties in their arbitration clause, in particular, by confining itself to applying texts of law where fairness and trade usages dictated a more conciliatory and measured solution, to take into account the interests of the parties. This is the case even in the presence of a stipulation by the parties that, in the absence of amicable settlement of disputes arising during the application thereof, "exclusive jurisdiction is given to an arbitral tribunal which must rule in equity and as a last resort," since the mission of *amiable compositeur* does not prohibit the application of legal standards, subject to the arbitrator verifying that they lead to a fair solution of the dispute. In the case at hand, the plea will be rejected because the appellant has not demonstrated in what way the challenged award is unfair as they claim.[45]

43. ENI-Congo v. Etablissements MIC-Vidéo, N° 093/2017, Decision, [C.C.J.A.], 2e ch., (Apr. 27, 2017).
44. Airtel Gabon v. 2JTH-Gabon, N° 203/2018, *supra*, Chapter 14, fn. 37.
45. Le Bistro Family v. Rosace Marbrée, N° 196/2018, *supra*, Chapter 2, fn. 11.

[iv] No Violation of the Provisions of the Rules of an Arbitration Center Not Chosen by the Parties

In *Prévoyance Assurances S.A. v. Eiffage Sénégal*,[46] it has been held that no violation of the rules of an arbitration center not chosen by the parties can be found. Thus, the tribunal cannot have failed to comply with its mission, and the petition for the annulment of the award must be rejected.

[v] Allegation of Fraud Relating to the Date of Rendering of an Award

The claim that a tribunal did not comply with its mission because the challenged award stated it was rendered on February 3, 2012 at 12 noon, which was an inaccurate date highlighting the fraud in the award, with the intended effect of anticipating the decision to tie it to the deadline for rendering the award, and thus circumventing the argument raised by the respondent, is wrong. This is so since this allegation is not supported by any evidence from the file or the proceedings. The request for annulment must be rejected.[47]

[vi] Untimely Objection Relating to the Expiry of the Deadline for Rendering an Award

Under Article 14, paragraph 13 of the UAA, "The party who, knowingly, fails to timely object to irregularity and proceeds with the arbitration is deemed to have waived their right to object." Applying this provision in *Société Camerounaise d'Opérations Maritimes v. Express Transport Khalifa*,[48] the CCJA held that there is no reason to annul an arbitral award for the failure of the tribunal to comply with its mission when the party requesting the setting aside has produced documents before the arbitral tribunal after the expiry of the time limit and has collaborated in the pursuit of the arbitration until the rendering of the award without ever raising the irregularity linked to the expiration of the deadline. In other words, an untimely objection is inadmissible.[49]

46. Prévoyance Assurances S.A. v. Eiffage Sénégal, N° 220/2018, *supra*, Chapter 3, fn. 39.
47. Commercial Bank of Cameroon v. Archidiocèse de Yaoundé, N° 242/2018, *supra*, Chapter 2, fn. 13.
48. *See* Société Camerounaise d'Opérations Maritimes v. Express Transport Khalifa, N° 060/2017, *supra*, Chapter 12, fn. 32.
49. It is good to mention the recent decision of the CCJA in George Forrest Belgium v. Les Ciments du Sahel, N° 094/2020, *supra*, Chapter 14, fn. 6, where the CCJA dismissed a challenge to an arbitral award rendered after the expiry of the deadline on the ground that the petition did not meet any condition of Art. 26 of the UAA. It must be noted that the Court did not say in this ruling that it is acceptable to disregard the deadline for rendering an award; it only answered the petition on the specific point, which was raised, as most cassation courts do. Thus, any party seeking the annulment of an arbitral award rendered after the expiry of the allotted time should file their petition on the ground of failure by the tribunal to comply with its mission.

[B] Under the CCJA Rules

Before illustrating how the failure of an arbitral tribunal to comply with its mission is assessed by the CCJA, which leads it to determine whether a tribunal has complied with its mission (§14.04[B][2]) or failed to do so (§14.04[B][3]), some general rules must be highlighted (§14.04[B][1]).

[1] General Rules Relating to the Mission of Arbitrators

The first rule is about the determination of the scope of the mission of an arbitral tribunal (§14.04[B][1][i]), followed by an important precision on the role of the judge assessing whether an arbitrator has complied with their mission or not, in this that it is not a mandate given by the judge to review the merit of the challenged award (§14.04[B][1][ii]).

[i] Delineation of the Mission of an Arbitral Tribunal

It is very important to always keep in mind that is it settled case law of the CCJA that the scope of the mission of an arbitral tribunal is delineated by the object of the dispute, which is determined by the claims and requests of the parties as set out in the minutes of the case management conference setting out the subject of the arbitration and the procedure.[50]

[ii] Prohibition of the Review of an Award on the Merits While Assessing Whether a Tribunal Has Complied with Its Mission

The assessment of whether an arbitral tribunal has complied with its mission or not, cannot be used as a pretext for the review of the merits of the award, but must only allow the judge to ascertain whether or not the arbitrator(s) have, on the points where their decision is criticized, complied with their mission, without having to assess the merits of their decision. Any petition requesting for the contrary must be rejected.[51]

50. Pyramidion v. Agence d'Exécution des Travaux d'Infrastructure du Mali, N° 098/2014, *supra*, Chapter 6, fn. 16; Etat du Mali v. Groupe TOMOTA, N° 033/2015, *supra*, Chapter 6, fn. 17; Société Nestle Cameroon v. Groupe Abbassi, N° 081/2019, *supra*, Chapter 14, fn. 14. In Kabamba Mulangi v. DHL Global Forwarding DR Congo, N° 127/2020, Decision, [C.C.J.A.], Ass. plen., (Apr. 30, 2020), the CCJA ruled that it is settled case law that without having to examine the merits of a challenged award, the Court may ascertain whether the arbitrators have complied with their mission defined by the arbitration agreement and delineated primarily by the purpose of the dispute as determined by the claims and requests of the parties. And where it appears from the analysis of the arbitration agreement and the challenged award, on the one hand, that the arbitrators ruled on all of the parties' respective claims and requests and, on the other hand, that they applied the appropriate rules to the merit of the case, it cannot be found that they failed to comply with their mission.
51. Etat du Mali v. ABS International Corporate, CCJA, N° 011/2011, Decision, [C.C.J.A.], Ass. plen., (Nov. 29, 2011).

Likewise, the Court ruled in *Etat du Mali v. Groupe TOMOTA* that the argument alleging noncompliance by an arbitrator with their mission cannot be for the purpose of reviewing the merits of the award. It only allows the CCJA to ascertain whether or not the arbitrators have complied with their mission, on the points where their decision is criticized, without having to assess the merits of their decision. Under Article 15 of the CCJA Regulation on Arbitration, the arbitrator's mission is delineated primarily by the parties' claims, as they arise from the minutes of the case management conference setting out the proceedings. In the case at hand, the arbitral tribunal, which found, under the Malian Law No. 87-31 of August 29, 1987 on the general regime of obligations, and in accordance with its mission, after analyzing the various elements produced and discussed by the parties, that the State of Mali has breached its contractual obligations and, using its judicial discretion, has set the compensation for the resulting damages for the co-contractor, therefore, has not decided the case as *amiable compositeur*; it follows that the argument contending that the arbitral tribunal has not complied with its mission must be rejected.[52]

[2] Cases Having Not Found Failure by Tribunals to Comply with Their Mission

There are at least ten cases illustrating various situations where the CCJA has determined that arbitrator(s) have not failed to comply with their mission. They relate to the tort liability retained without distortion (§14.04[B][2][i]), the award of damages by an arbitral tribunal (§14.04[B][2][ii]), the modification of the procedural calendar (§14.04[B][2][iii]), the preliminary search for an amicable settlement (§14.04[B][2][iv]), the reliance upon an expert report as requested by a party (§14.04[B][2][v]) or upon relevant case law applicable to the dispute at hand (§14.04[B][2][vi]), arbitration based on the minutes of a case management conference not signed by all parties but approved by the CCJA (§14.04[B][2][vii]), an arbitral tribunal wrongfully accused of having ruled as *amiable compositeur* (§14.04[B][2][viii]), ruling against a party under an agreement covered by the arbitration clause at hand (§14.04[B][2][ix]) and a tribunal accused of failing to apply, sua sponte, a limitation of liability clause, and having become counsel of a party (§14.04[B][2][x]).

[i] Tort Liability Retained Without Distortion

It is settled case law that the mission of arbitrators, defined by the arbitration agreement, is delineated primarily by the subject matter of the dispute, as determined by the parties' claims without focusing solely on the statement of the issues in the terms of reference. Thus, the arbitral tribunal, finding by interpretation exclusive of any distortion of the facts of the case, that the tort liability of the State of Mali "constantly

52. Etat du Mali v. Groupe TOMOTA, N° 033/2015, *supra*, Chapter 6, fn. 17; *see also* Société Nestle Cameroon v. Groupe Abbassi, N° 081/2019, *supra*, Chapter 14, fn. 14.

invoked by the State of Mali" is in the debate, has legally allowed itself, in respect of its mission and without violating the adversarial principle, to retain the tort liability of the State of Mali. In addition to the fact that the mission of arbitrator(s) is delineated primarily by the object of the dispute as a result from the claims of the parties without focusing solely on the statement of the points specified in the terms of reference, the arbitral tribunal which retained tort liability and subsequently the remedy of the damage by equivalent, in the form of damages in accordance with Article 123 of the Malian Law applicable to the case, took into account all the elements allowing the damage to be assessed, including the cost of acquiring the buses concerned in the case. The request for annulment was dismissed.[53]

[ii] Award of Damages by an Arbitral Tribunal

The fact that an arbitral tribunal ruling on a claim for damages orders payment of damages by breaking down the amount to be paid does not constitute a violation of its mission.[54] Likewise, the arbitrators' assertions on the facts referred to them and the determination, by their judicial discretion, of the amount of damages to be awarded on the basis of the facts submitted to their assessment do not justify the annulment of their award.[55]

[iii] Modification of the Procedural Calendar

On the various rulings by which the CCJA ruled that because of its provisional nature, the modification of the procedural timetable does not entail failure of the tribunal to comply with its mission serving as a ground for annulment of the challenged award, *see Ekwa Ngalle v. Société Nationale d'Hydrocarbures.*[56]

[iv] Preliminary Search for an Amicable Settlement

In *Etat du Bénin v. Société Commune de Participation*, the CCJA ruled that an arbitral tribunal did not rule without complying with its mission with regard to seeking an amicable settlement before deciding the case since it resulted from the award that one party sought an amicable settlement of the dispute by letters and, conversely, the other party unilaterally suspended the agreement, thus making its enforcement impossible.[57]

53. Etat du Mali v. ABS International Corporate, CCJA, N° 011/2011, *supra*, Chapter 14, fn. 51.
54. Ekwa Ngalle v. Société Nationale d'hydrocarbures, CCJA, N° 102/2015, *supra*, Chapter 2, fn. 31.
55. Benin Control v. Etat du Benin, CCJA, N° 103/2015, *supra*, Chapter 6, fn. 18.
56. Ekwa Ngalle v. Société Nationale d'Hydrocarbures, CCJA, N° 102/2015, *supra*, Chapter 2, fn. 31.
57. Etat du Bénin v. Société Commune de Participation, N° 104/2015, Decision, [C.C.J.A.], Ass. plen., (Oct. 15, 2015), http://www.ohada.com/jurisprudence/ohadata/J-16-97.html.

[v] Reliance upon an Expert Report as Requested by a Party

The agreement, which is the basis of the contract between the parties and the related legal texts, prevents any of them from being able to modify or terminate it during the performance of the contract. It follows that the use of the expert's report to determine the amount of damages and loss of profit does not divert the arbitral tribunal from its mission since it emerges from the proceedings that during the hearing, the Director of Legal Affairs of the Requesting State declared that "(...) the Tribunal must only, in assessing the damage which has been caused [to the Defendant], with documents or evidence which do not suffer from any ambiguity (...). This is why, I insist on this, it takes real expert work to determine exactly the harm which will have been caused [to the Defendant] ... ."[58]

[vi] Reliance upon Relevant Case Law Applicable to the Dispute at Hand

An arbitral tribunal cannot be reproached for having failed in its mission by excluding provisions of the Public Procurement Code which have been declared unenforceable to the case at hand by a Court of law of the Requesting State, on the ground that the provisions excluded were enacted after the agreement of the parties. The agreement of the parties provided that "In the event of termination by the Requesting State, and without breach of the contracting party, the Requesting State undertakes to pay the other party the sums corresponding to the shortfalls resulting from this termination ...," and that it follows from the minutes of the case management conference that "the tribunal may, on its own initiative or at the request of one of the parties, after hearing the parties, appoint under Article 19.3 of the CCJA Regulation on Arbitration, one or more experts... ." Consequently, the arbitral tribunal ruled in accordance with its mission and did not violate Article 30.6-2 [which became] 30.5 b)] of the CCJA Regulation on Arbitration. The petition for annulment must be rejected.[59] This ruling implicitly indicates that an arbitral tribunal can validly rely upon relevant case law or jurisprudence in the performance of its mission and cannot be accused of having failed to comply with its mission on that sole basis.

[vii] Arbitration Based on the Minutes of a Case Management Conference Not Signed by All Parties but Approved by the CCJA

It is wrong to blame an arbitral tribunal for failing in its mission since it resulted from a decision of the CCJA (in its administrative capacity supervising arbitration proceedings) that following the refusal of the appellants to participate in the case management conference, the President of the Court, at the request of the arbitral tribunal, approved the minutes of the meeting. The arbitral tribunal, in finding it had jurisdiction to settle the dispute, on the basis of the aforementioned CCJA decision, has in no way breached

58. Etat du Niger v. Société Africard Co Limited, N° 141/2016, *supra*, Chapter 14, fn. 10.
59. *Id.*

the minutes of the case management conference and subsequently has not failed to comply with its mission since it does not result from the award that the arbitral tribunal has ruled *ex aequo et bono*. Thus, the petition for annulment must be dismissed.[60]

[viii] Arbitral Tribunal Wrongfully Accused of Having Ruled as Amiable Compositeur

It is wrong to blame an arbitral tribunal for having ruled without complying with its mission, in that it ruled as *amiable compositeur* because it was mistaken in the counting of days; that "distorting the *dies ad quem*,"[61] the tribunal, therefore, considered that the partnership agreement of July 13, 2006 had been continued, matching the expiry date of the agreement with the date of the signing of the ninety-day extension, conditions precedent, justifying the unilateral and abnormal nature of the termination which occurred on May 2, 2007 at the initiative of the appellant. This is the case since the error in the calculation of the deadlines, which could have been related to the absence of an arbitration agreement, is not demonstrated, and the signature of the endorsement by the parties on September 12, 2006, fell well within the scope of the partnership agreement, on the other hand.[62]

[ix] Ruling Against a Party Under an Agreement Covered by the Arbitration Clause at Hand

It is wrong to reproach an arbitral tribunal for having exceeded its mission by awarding the defendant compensations for their losses on the basis of a 2005 contract which is not the subject of arbitration since the arbitral tribunal had previously indicated in the award that the "2005 contract" was outside its jurisdiction and that "the agreement" referred to by the tribunal in its award is the one signed by the parties and which was the subject of the arbitration proceedings.[63]

[x] Tribunal Accused of Failing to Apply, Sua Sponte, a Limitation of Liability Clause and Having Become Counsel of a Party

An arbitral tribunal is wrongfully accused of failing to comply with its mission, including by failing to apply, on its motion, the "limitation of liability clause" and by "helping and defending of one of the parties ... ." in a correspondence, which, in the view of the party challenging the award, was intended to induce a party to reconsider their claim which would have been unfounded because the grievance of the arbitrator's failure to comply with their mission allows the Court to ascertain whether or not the

60. Compagnie Malienne pour le Développement des Textiles v. Société Inter Africaine de Distribution, N° 160/2016, *supra*, Chapter 1, fn. 33.
61. *Dies ad quem* is the date from which a time period is counted. *See* the glossary, *infra*.
62. Etat du Mali v. Seaquest-Infotel Mali, N° 027/2017, *supra*, Chapter 12, fn. 39.
63. *Id*.

arbitrator complied with their mission, which is determined by the parties' claims and requests, without having to consider the merits of his decision. In the case at hand, the reason for the annulment must be rejected, on the one hand, because the issue of the application of the "limitation clause of liability" falls within the merits of the award which cannot be reviewed by the CCJA; on the other hand, because, using its investigative power, the arbitral tribunal has requested, by letter, clarifications of the parties on specific points directly related to the facts submitted to it. This act, which falls within the normal course of the arbitration proceedings, under Articles 19.1 and 15 of the CCJA Regulation on Arbitration, cannot justify the annulment of the arbitral award and the petition for annulment must be rejected.[64]

[3] Case Having Found Failure by Tribunal to Comply with Their Mission

As of date, the CCJA has found a failure to comply with its mission by arbitrators in only one case. In the *Getma* case mentioned earlier,[65] the CCJA ruled that the increase of fees directly negotiated by the arbitrators with the parties without the agreement of the Court constitutes failure of the arbitral panel to comply with their mission.[66] Given the high media coverage of this case and the criticisms which the CCJA was subjected to following its ruling, it is useful to provide the full factual background of this sensitive case.

In October 2011, the State of Guinea[67] and Getma International[68] agreed to resolve their dispute concerning the termination of a Concession Agreement before an arbitral panel of three arbitrators under the CCJA Rules. The CCJA ordered, under its arbitration rules, that the parties pay for certain fees and costs in advance of the arbitration, which amounted to about EUR 154,000, including approximately EUR 62,000 in arbitrators' fees. After the tribunal was constituted in early 2012, the tribunal sought permission from the secretary-general of the CCJA ("secretary-general") on or about April 11, 2013, to contact the parties' counsel about an increase in the arbitrators' fees. The secretary-general permitted the tribunal to do so on April 15, 2013. On April 22, 2013, the arbitral tribunal contacted the parties about increasing the arbitrators' fees from approximately EUR 62,000 to approximately EUR 450,000. By May 10, 2013, the parties had responded to the arbitral tribunal, informing it that they had "no comments" regarding the request for increased arbitrators' fees.

The tribunal interpreted the parties' silence on the fee issue as "hav[ing] no objection to [the] fee revision," and sought the parties' confirmation of this interpretation. The parties eventually agreed to the tribunal's solicitation for increased arbitrators' fees in June 2013. The tribunal then immediately notified the secretary-general of the parties' consent to increased arbitrators' fees, and the secretary-general

64. Société Nestle Cameroon v. Groupe Abbassi, N° 081/2019, *supra*, Chapter 14, fn. 14.
65. *See supra*, Chapter 3, fn. 8.
66. *Id.*
67. Guinea is a Western African country, the capital city of which is Conakry. It is different from Guinea Bissau (Portuguese-speaking and Bissau as capital city) and Equatorial Guinea (Spanish-speaking and Malabo as capital city); all those are African countries.
68. Getma International SAS is a French company registered in Paris, France.

informed the tribunal that he would "contact the [CCJA] soon to adjust the fees of the ... [tribunal]." However, on August 1, 2013, the CCJA denied the arbitral tribunal's attempt to revise and increase the arbitrators' fees that the CCJA initially ordered, citing a 1999 CCJA precedent.[69] In pertinent part, the 1999 CCJA precedent states:

> The [CCJA] shall determine the arbitrator's fees pursuant to [a fixed schedule], or at its discretion where the amount in controversy has not been stated.
>
> If the circumstances of the case render it necessary on an exceptional basis, the [CCJA] may set the arbitrator's fees at an amount that is greater or less than the amount that would result from application of the scale ... .
>
> When it sets the arbitrator's fees, the [CCJA] shall take into consideration the work done by arbitrator, the time spent, the speed of proceedings[,] and the complexity of the dispute, so as to reach a figure within the limits provided for, or above or below such limits under ... exceptional circumstances ... .
>
> Where a matter is submitted to more than one arbitrator, the [CCJA] may, at its discretion, increase the amount set aside for payment of fees, generally up to a limit of three times that provided for a single arbitrator ... .
>
> *The arbitrator's fees and expenses are set exclusively by the Court, in accordance with the provisions of the Rules of Arbitration. Any separate arrangement between the parties and the arbitrators concerning their fees is null and void.*[70]

Despite the CCJA's August 2013 order, *Getma* lobbied the CCJA on September 19, 2013, to reconsider its decision to deny the arbitral tribunal's demand for increased fees. Shortly thereafter, on October 3, 2013, the CCJA again declined to increase the initial arbitrators' fees relying on the same 1999 CCJA precedent that it cited in its August 2013 order.

On April 30, 2014, the arbitral tribunal informed the parties that it had resolved the parties' dispute and would issue an award that included a demand for EUR 450,000 in arbitrators' fees. On or about May 19, 2014, the secretary-general contacted the tribunal, notifying it that the secretary-general was in receipt of the tribunal's April 30, 2014 communication to the parties.

After recognizing that the award would include a demand for increased arbitrators' fees, and notwithstanding the CCJA's previous orders rejecting such a demand, the secretary-general "formally prohibited"[71] the tribunal from seeking any increased arbitrators' fees.

The tribunal ultimately issued an award in favor of *Getma* (EUR 39 million), which did not include an increase in the arbitrators' fees. After the arbitral tribunal issued the award, the tribunal continued to express its frustration with the CCJA over

69. Rather than a precedent, as mentioned in the records of the proceedings before the U.S. Courts, the CCJA referred to a prescriptive decision it made in 1999 on the fees and costs in arbitration under its Rules. *See supra*, Introduction, fn. 24.

70. [Emphasis added]. The facts presented here are taken from the ruling of the DC Court, *infra*, Chapter 14, fn 73.

71. May 20, 2014 Letter From Secretary General to *Getma* at 6 ("I call your attention to the fact that, if the final award includes the payment of the amount of €450,000 to the arbitrators, in accordance with the invalid arrangement, the award will potentially be subject to invalidation by . . . [the CCJA].").

the CCJA's repeated refusal to allow the tribunal to seek increased arbitrators' fees from the parties. And somehow, the tribunal eventually collected half of the increased arbitrators' fees from *Getma* (approximately EUR 225,000) in September 2014. But Guinea declined to follow suit and pay any increased arbitrators' fees, reneging on its promise to do so earlier.

On July 25, 2014, the *Republic of Guinea* filed an annulment petition with the CCJA, seeking to have the CCJA set aside the arbitral award. On November 19, 2015, the CCJA, sitting en banc,[72] annulled the arbitral award on the ground that the arbitral tribunal violated the CCJA Arbitration Rules, and thus, the tribunal's "mission" to conduct the arbitration proceeding in accordance with those rules, in seeking increased arbitrators' fees from the parties, which only the CCJA had the authority to order the parties to do.

Afterward, *Getma* petitioned the United States District Court for the District of Columbia to confirm and enforce the annulled award. Eventually, this Court also declined to confirm and enforce the *Getma* award, which "has been lawfully 'set aside' by [the CCJA], a competent authority [under the jurisdiction of which] the award was made."[73]

The decision of the CCJA annulling the award in the *Getma* case has been highly criticized by many reports that *"did not examine the extent to which the tribunal's conduct was contrary to CCJA's rules and express rulings."*[74] On December 9, 2015, the arbitrators published an "open letter" to the arbitration community in the press,[75] in which they "criticized the annulment decision as a 'legal heresy,' but based [their] analysis, in part, on somewhat puzzling assertions, like 'arbitrators' compensation has nothing to do with their task' and '[t]he role of an international arbitration institution is to protect the arbitrators that work under its aegis [.]'"[76]

It is appropriate to dwell on some of the main criticisms of the decision annulling the arbitral award, namely:

- the CCJA, in its capacity of manager of the arbitral proceedings, intervened on several occasions on the question of fees by taking positions contrary to those of the parties, its secretary-general (who "encouraged" the tribunal to proceed and request the increase by parties) and its President;
- since the parties agreed to pay the increased fees, the CCJA should not have annulled the award, and by doing so, it exceeded its power;

72. The Court sitting as a plenary, with all its judges. *See* the glossary, *infra*.
73. Getma Int'l v. The Republic of Guinea N° 14-1616, Mem Op. (D.C. Jun. 9, 2016)), *supra*, Chapter 3, fn. 9. The decision of the District court has been affirmed by the United States Court of Appeals for the District of Columbia Circuit on Jul. 7, 2017: Getma International v. Republic of Guinea, No. 16-7087 (D.C. Cir. 2017), *supra*, Chapter 3, fn. 10.
74. Catherine Rogers, When Arbitrators and Institutions Clash, or The Strange Case of Getma v. Guinea, http://kluwerarbitrationblog.com/2016/05/12/when-arbitrators-and-institutions-clash-or-the-strange-case-of-getma-v-guinea/ [accessed Dec. 22, 2016, at 11:21] (Rogers, 2016). [Emphasis added].
75. Frédéric Maury, Affaire Getma-Guinée: les arbitres répondent, http://www.jeuneafrique.com/285543/societe/affaire-getma-guinee-les-arbitres-repondent/ [accessed Dec. 22, 2016, at 11:30] (Maury F., 2016).
76. Catherine Rogers, *supra*, Chapter 14, fn. 74.

- in managing arbitral proceeding and then ruling the on the merit where an award is challenged, the CCJA would not be impartial because its acts as judge and party.

On the first issue, it is important to remember that, under the current state of the applicable rules, the secretary-general of the Arbitration Center of the CCJA performs purely administrative duties regarding arbitral proceedings. He is not a judge. Panels of designated Judges of the CCJA overseeing arbitral proceedings in their capacity of the administrative body under Article 1 of the CCJA Regulation on Arbitration are not bound by the assessments of the secretary-general; neither is the CCJA itself while sitting en banc to rule on challenges to arbitral awards. The same applies to arbitrators who, in their capacity as "judges," are not bound by statements of the secretary-general. It is assumed that the arbitrators know the arbitration rules, and it was incumbent upon them to assess the alleged statement of the secretary-general under the law applicable to their mission, the limits of which they could not ignore *before* accepting it.[77]

As the United States District Court Judge correctly pointed out:

> First, only the Secretary General permitted the tribunal to contact parties about increasing the arbitrators' fees (...). *Getma* cannot dispute that, the CCJA, and not the Secretary General, has the ultimate authority and discretion to increase the arbitrators' fees. Second, to characterize the Secretary General's communication with the tribunal as "encouragement" is not entirely accurate. The Secretary General permitted the tribunal to open discussions with the parties about increasing the arbitrators' fees and asked to be kept informed of the "outcome" of those discussions (...). The Secretary general never affirmatively represented that the CCJA would eventually approve any agreement that the tribunal solicited—he merely informed the tribunal that he would contact the CCJA about revising the arbitrators' fees (...). Third, even under the assumption that the Secretary General's communication with the tribunal served as a proxy for the CCJA's tacit consent to solicit additional arbitrators' fees from the parties, the CCJA's later rescission of that approval was entirely consistent with CCJA precedent. And such conduct is not repugnant to United States public policy, especially where courts in this country are free to reconsider and change their rulings when the circumstances demand that result, such as when controlling precedent has been overlooked.[78]

In any event, after the CCJA expressly rejected twice the fee increase that it did not decide and amount which it did not set, the arbitrators could no longer disregard the authority of the Court without breaching the applicable rules. An author expressed the same view by saying that "even faced with a terrible, horrible, no-good, very bad decision on an issue that is within an arbitral institution's exclusive competence and discretion, a tribunal has only two choices: comply or resign."[79]

77. It is important to remember that upon their appointment and before their appointment is confirmed by the CCJA, each arbitrator receives a full set of the applicable CCJA Arbitration Rules and commits to abiding by those rules by signing a document that is part of their "arbitrator agreement." *See supra*, Chapter 3, §3.01.
78. *See supra* Getma Int'l v. The Republic of Guinea N° 14-1616, Mem Op. (D.C. Jun. 9, 2016)), p. 1-11.
79. *See* Catherine Rogers, *supra*, Chapter 14, fn. 74.

The second issue on whether the annulment of the award constitutes an abuse of power of the CCJA calls for some remarks.

First, it is important to always remember that the arbitration system under the current rules of OHADA is twofold, as mentioned in the introduction: a general arbitration governed almost exclusively[80] by the UAA and an institutional arbitration under the aegis of the CCJA. On the legal regime of the latter, the CCJA has clearly established, at least since July 17, 2008, that it is governed exclusively by the provisions of Title IV of the Treaty,[81] the CCJA Regulation on Arbitration, the Arbitration Bylaws of the CCJA, their appendixes and the fee schedule of arbitration in their drafting in force at the date of the introduction of the arbitration proceedings.[82] In a ruling on November 29, 2011, the CCJA referred to Article 23 of the UAA in an institutional arbitration case to underline the authority of res judicata, which is also governed by Article 25 of the Treaty, only applicable to that institutional arbitration case. Nonetheless, that was an isolated ruling after which the CCJA has repeatedly reiterated its initial precedent on the inapplicability of the UAA to institutional arbitration,[83] and the fact that the CCJA sometimes relies upon Article 23 of the Treaty to overturn decisions of national courts which retained jurisdiction despite the presence of an arbitration clause governed by the UAA and the objection to their jurisdiction raised by a party like in *Accor Afrique v. L'Etat Togolais*[84] should only be regarded as an exception to the rule according to which provisions of the Treaty do not apply to arbitration proceedings under the UAA laid down in the introduction, *supra*, and repeated in the present section.

In its petition to the CCJA for annulment of the award, *Guinea* contended that by letter dated April 30, 2014 addressed directly to the parties, the President of the arbitral tribunal informed the parties that the final award had been signed the day before and that "it would be appropriate for arbitrators to be paid their fees prior to their transmission of the award to the CCJA [for official notice to the parties by the Secretary General of the CCJA]." Then, the President of the Court has retained the award for 23 days after signing it, in order to obtain from the parties the actual payment of the amount claimed. It was not until May 22, 2014 that the award was transmitted to the CCJA. In the meantime, the President of the arbitral tribunal sent the electronic version of the award directly to the parties before any formal notification thereof by the secretary-general of the Court, the only one authorized to carry out that formality. *Guinea* finally contended that this violation of the Rules of Arbitration has undermined the confidentiality of the arbitral proceedings provided for by Article 14 of the said Rules since the content of the award was published by the press in *Jeune Afrique* even before its formal notification to the parties by the secretary-general of the Court.[85]

80. UAA, Art. 15.
81. OHADA Treaty, Art. 21 to 26.
82. Ekwa Ngalle v. Société Nationale d'Hydrocarbures, N° 102/2015, *supra*, Chapter 2, fn. 31.
83. Etat du Mali v. ABS International Corporate, CCJA, N° 011/2011, *supra*, Chapter 14, fn. 51.
84. Accor Afrique v. L'Etat Togolais, N° 064/2020, Decision, [C.C.J.A.], 3ᵉ ch., (Feb. 27, 2020). *See also* Gomes v. Banque de l'Afrique Occidentale, N° 035/2010, *supra*, Chapter 1, fn. 23.
85. Republique de Guinee v. Getma International, N°139/2015, *supra*, Chapter 3, fn. 8, p. 3-4.

In its response, *Getma* petitioned the CCJA to grant exequatur and allow the enforcement of the challenged award, relying on three arguments.

First, Article 10 of the UAA, provides that "The fact that the parties submit their dispute to an arbitral institution requires them to apply the rules of that institution, *except for the parties to expressly disregard certain provisions of those rules.*"[86]

Second, *Getma* contented that the parties signed an arbitration clause per which "each party shall bear the cost of the arbitrator it appoints. Other costs incurred by the arbitration shall be borne equally by the parties"; therefore, by agreeing to pay the increased fees proposed by the chairman of the arbitral tribunal, the parties had expressly rejected the provisions of Articles 24.1 and 24.2 of the CCJA Regulation on Arbitration, under Article 10 of the UAA aforementioned.

Third, the violation by the arbitrators of the provisions of the CCJA Arbitration Rules relating to the costs of the arbitration could not lead to the annulment of the award.[87]

The reasoning leading to the annulment of the award by the CCJA is full of lessons:

> It follows from the combined provisions of the rules referred to in the plea[88] that, under the CCJA Arbitration Rules, *the arbitrators' fees are fixed exclusively by the [CCJA]* in accordance with the scale annexed to Decision No 004/99/CCJA Of 3 February 1999; if the circumstances of the case make it exceptionally necessary, the [CCJA] may set the fees of arbitrators to a higher or smaller amount than that which would result from the application of that scale; *any separate agreement between the parties and the arbitrator(s) over their fees is null and void.*
>
> The aim of these provisions is to ensure that the parties who have decided to submit their dispute to arbitration by the [CCJA] pay a foreseeable fee proportionate to the actual value of the dispute and determined per a scale known in advance.
>
> The provisions of Article 10 of the [UAA] relied on by *Getma* are not applicable in this arbitration case governed exclusively by the CCJA Arbitration Rules.[89]
>
> Under Article 10.1 of the CCJA Regulation on Arbitration, the arbitral tribunal which *deliberately disregarded* the essential provisions of the CCJA Arbitration Rules to which the parties have willfully agreed to submit the settlement of their dispute by the arbitration clause in their contract did not comply with its mission, setting out its award for annulment. This is so since, on one hand, the chairman of the arbitral tribunal has negotiated directly with counsel of the parties in dispute and obtained their agreement for raising the amount of the arbitrators' fees after the Court has set it. On the other hand, the chairman of the tribunal applied to the CCJA for the regularization of this increase, and the Court rejected the request twice; notwithstanding those decisions of refusal, the President of the arbitral tribunal obtained *from the party who finally prevailed,* the payment of its share of

86. [Emphasis added].
87. Republique de Guinee v. Getma International, N°139/2015, *supra,* Chapter 3, fn. 8, p. 5.
88. CCJA Regulation on Arbitration, Arts. 24.2, 24.3 and 25.1; Art. 9 of the prescriptive Decision N° 004/99/CCJA of Feb. 3, 1999 on arbitration costs.
89. It must be noted that while sometimes Art. 23 of the OHADA Treaty is relied upon in isolated cases by the CCJA in arbitration proceedings governed by the UAA, as it dit in Accor Afrique v. L'Etat Togolais, *supra,* Chapter 14, fn. 84, the UAA is never applied to proceedings governed by the CCJA Regulation on Arbitration.

the sum claimed, in addition to the latter's being ordered to pay the share of the party having been unsuccessful in the arbitration.[90]

The ruling of the CCJA above can be summed in two points:

- institutional arbitration under CCJA's rules is governed exclusively by a set of rules not including any provision of the UAA;
- arbitration fees are set exclusively by the CCJA per its arbitration fees scale, but where necessary, the fees can be raised *exclusively by the CCJA itself* upon application of the arbitrators; any direct arrangement between the parties and arbitrators is null and void.[91]

As a matter of fact, reliance upon the wrong rule (Article 10 of the UAA, inapplicable to the case) led to the misfortune of the annulment of the award. The wording of Article 9 of the *Prescriptive Decision N° 004/99/CCJA of February 3, 1999 on arbitration costs*, used by the CCJA in its ruling, makes it a mandatory rule:

> The fees and expenses of the arbitrator shall be *determined exclusively by the Court* [CCJA], in accordance with the provisions of the Arbitration Rules. Any separate agreement between the parties and arbitrators on their fees shall be *null and void.*

Therefore, it can explain why the CCJA concluded the arbitrators did not comply with their mission.

One could still argue, as *Getma* did in its petition before the CCJA, that the violation by the arbitrators of the provisions of the CCJA Arbitration Rules relating to the costs of the arbitration could not lead to the annulment of the award and by doing so, the CCJA abused its power.[92]

However, there are some recurrent universal issues in international arbitration, regardless of the legal system involved. When dealing with those issues, it is often useful to delve into comparative law, especially precedents, because converging solutions emerge from such comparison. Bias is one of those recurrent issues of international arbitration relevant to the *Getma* case. As Justice Gzell J put it in *Ict Pty Ltd v. Sea Containers Ltd*, "the test is an objective one: would a fair-minded lay observer reasonably apprehend that the arbitrators might not bring an impartial and unprejudiced mind to a resolution of the reference[?]"[93]

In the arena of international arbitration, "it is important that the arbitrators are seen by the parties to be acting impartially, even-handedly and with rectitude."[94] Some facts from the published records of the *Getma* case need to be remembered here. After

90. Republique de Guinee v. Getma International, N°139/2015, *supra*, Chapter 3, fn. 8, p 5-6. [Emphasis added].
91. This second point is based on Art. 9 of the prescriptive *Decision N° 004/99/CCJA of February 3, 1999 on arbitration costs*, according to which "The fees and expenses of the arbitrator shall be determined exclusively by the Court, in accordance with the provisions of the Arbitration Rules. Any separate agreement between the parties and arbitrators on their fees shall be null and void."
92. Republique de Guinee v. Getma International, N°139/2015, *supra*, Chapter 3, fn. 8, p. 5.
93. Ict Pty Ltd v. Sea Containers Ltd [2002] NSWSC 77 (Feb. 15, 2002) (Austl.) n°44.
94. K/S Nojarl A/S v. Hyundai Heavy Industries Limited [1992] 1 QB 863, Lloyd's Rep. 260 (Eng.) 268.

the parties have filed for arbitration, the CCJA set the fees of arbitrators on October 24, 2011. The arbitral tribunal signed the award on April 29, 2014 and its President sent a letter to the parties on April 30, 2014, informing them that "it would be appropriate for arbitrators to be paid their [increased] fees prior to their transmission of the award to the CCJA [for official notice to the parties by the Secretary General of the CCJA]." Then, the President of the Court allegedly has retained the award for 23 days after signing it, to obtain from the parties the actual payment of the amount claimed. It was not until May 22, 2014 that the award was transmitted to the CCJA.

The right of an arbitrator to exercise a lien on the award until he is paid his fees by the parties is generally admitted in some jurisdictions, especially for ad hoc arbitration if there is such a clause in the arbitration agreement or the agreement between the parties and the arbitral panel.[95] However, that solution does not apply automatically to institutional arbitration, as was the case for *Getma*. For instance, under Article 11.3 [which became 11.4] of the CCJA Regulation on Arbitration, "Only claims for which the requirements of paragraph 11.2 above are fully complied with are referred to the arbitrator. If *a request for advance* is not satisfied, the Court ... may invite the arbitral tribunal to suspend its activities ... ."

Therefore, under the CCJA Arbitration Rules, arbitrators can suspend the proceedings only where the fees set or increased[96] by the CCJA itself per its fees scale have not been paid by the parties; any attempt by the arbitrators to retain the award or suspend proceedings to obtain payment of an increase not authorized and set by the CCJA could be construed as "the pitting of the power of the arbitrators against the parties,"[97] that would constitute misconduct.[98]

It can be assumed from the established facts of the case that the final award ruling against *Guinea* has been rendered on April 29, 2014 (date of its signature), six months after the second refusal by the CCJA to admit the increase of the arbitrators' fees. Therefore, one could think that since the award was already made long before the payment of the increased fees by one party to the arbitrators, no bias could reasonably

95. *See*, for example, in Hong Kong, James Bruce Humphrey v. Dua Contractors & Co Ltd [1997] CACV86/1996), available at: http://legalref.judiciary.gov.hk/lrs/common/search/search_result_detail_frame.jsp?DIS=15507&QS=%24%28Humphrey%7CDua%7CContractors%29&TP=JU [accessed Mar. 1, 2017 at 13:35]. In other jurisdictions, *see* R v. South Devon Rly Co (1850) 15 QB 1043; Re Coombs and Freshfield and Fernley (1850) 4 Exch 839 at 841 per Parke B; Roberts v. Eberhardt (1857) 3 CBNS 482, 28 LJCP 74. However, the rule seems to have been changed in the United Kingdom; for example, *see* Cubitt Building and Interiors Ltd v. Fleetglade Ltd [2006] EWHC 3413 (TCC), 110 ConLR 36, [2007] All ER (D) 268 (Jan), available at: http://www.bailii.org/ew/cases/EWHC/TCC/2006/3413.html [accessed [Mar. 1, 2017, at 13:45], where it was ruled that an adjudicator of a dispute arising under a construction contract was not entitled to exercise a lien on the decision until payment of fees, either as a matter of contract or at law.

See also St Andrew's Bay Development Ltd v. HBG Management Ltd [2003] Scot CS 103, available at: http://www.bailii.org/scot/cases/ScotCS/2003/103.html [accessed Mar. 1, 2017, at 13:49], at 19.

96. As mentioned earlier, Art. 24.3 of the CCJA Arbitration Rules provides that "Where prevailing circumstances so exceptionally require, the Court [CCJA] may fix the fees of the arbitrator at an amount inferior or superior to the one indicated on the scale of fees."

97. *See* Ict Pty Ltd v. Sea Containers Ltd [2002] NSWSC 77, *supra*, Chapter 14, fn. 93, n°39.

98. *See id.* n°42.

be attributed to arbitrators in their ruling for *Getma*, who paid its share of the increased fees. On the other hand, it does not seem impossible for others to assume that *Getma* accepted to pay, despite consistent refusal by the CCJA, because the arbitral panel ruled in its favor, even though this could seem farfetched.

One way or another, the behavior of the arbitral panel in this case regarding the increased fees does not seem appropriate to avoid any bias because:

> Once arbitrators have accepted appointment it does not accord happily with their status to become involved in negotiations with the parties about fees or any other matters in which they have a personal interest .... Once the arbitrator has accepted the appointment, it is even less desirable for him to conclude an agreement about fees or any other matter that affects him personally with one party if the other party is not prepared to join in that agreement."[99]

It could well be said that the arbitrators "assumed such importance in their minds that they allowed themselves to be swayed by [the concern of raising their fees] to the detriment of their duty to maintain the appearance of acting in the interests of bringing down a just award."[100]

The New South Wales Court of Appeal upheld the ruling in *Ict Pty Ltd v. Sea Containers* by saying that:

> Once appointed, an arbitrator is no longer an entrepreneur so far as the parties are concerned. The arbitrator accepts a quasi-judicial position governed by law. Like a judge, not only must the arbitrator be impartial, the arbitrator must not give the appearance of bias. ... Attempts by an arbitrator to renegotiate his contract after appointment can easily undermine the confidence of one or more of the parties in the arbitrator's ability to perform the task he has agreed and is being paid to perform.[101]

Having settled the question on the misconduct of the arbitrators (in violating the provisions of the CCJA Arbitration Rules regarding fees), one can wonder if the annulment of the award was not disproportionate or, in other words, if the CCJA did not abuse its power. This is a relevant question because under similar circumstances in other jurisdictions, courts would have probably limited any sanction to removing the arbitrators as they did in *Ict Pty Ltd v. Sea Containers Ltd*.[102] Since the increased fees became an issue after the award has been rendered, there was technically no possibility of removing the arbitral panel without annulling their award, given the circumstances and the bias *Guinea* assumed in challenging the award. Had the fees increase become a serious issue at an earlier stage of the proceeding, the CCJA could have used its powers to remove the arbitral panel.[103]

99. K/S Nojarl A/S v. Hyundai Heavy Industries Limited [1992] 1 QB 863, Lloyd's Rep. 260 (Eng.) 268.
100. *See* Ict Pty Ltd v. Sea Containers Ltd [2002] NSWSC 77, *supra*, Chapter 14, fn. 93, n°37.
101. Sea Containers Ltd v. Ict Pty Ltd [2002] NSWCA 84 (Apr. 18, 2002) (Austl.) n°11.
102. *See* Ict Pty Ltd v. Sea Containers Ltd [2002] NSWSC 77, *supra*, Chapter 14, fn. 93, n°50; Sea Containers Ltd v. Ict Pty Ltd [2002] NSWCA84 (Apr. 18, 2002) (Austl.) n°2, 102.
103. Under Art. 4.4 of the CCJA Arbitration Rules, "An arbitrator must also be replaced when the Court finds that the arbitrator is de jure or de facto prevented from carrying out their mission

As soon as they became aware that there would be a serious issue regarding the fees, the arbitrators could have resigned as some arbitrators have done[104] since the applicable rules allow their resignation.[105] Because the arbitrators did not resign and the CCJA found they did not comply with their mission after the award was rendered, the only possible remedy left seemed to be the annulment of the award because of the immunity bestowed upon the arbitrators by the Treaty[106] and the seat agreement between the State of Ivory Coast (where the CCJA is headquartered).[107] From that perspective, the CCJA does not seem to have abused its powers in annulling the *Getma* award, given the circumstances, since it is not the first time in international arbitration that violation of clear guidelines regarding fees led to the annulment of an award. For example, in *Y. Mondeil v. J. de Ligault*, the Court of Appeal of Paris, France ruled that by failing to comply with the clear stipulation of an arbitration agreement, which imposed a sharing of arbitration fees with no possibility to retain novation, the arbitrators have exceeded the limits of their mission and their award must be set aside

---

or that the arbitrator is not performing their duties in accordance with Title IV of the Treaty or with this Regulation, or within the prescribed time limits."

104. *See*, for example, resignation of Mr Steele in K/S Nojarl A/S v. Hyundai Heavy Industries Limited [1992] 1 QB 863, Lloyd's Rep. 260 (Eng.) at 263, 264.

105. *See* Art. 4.4 of the CCJA Regulation on Arbitration, Appendix II, *infra*.

106. Under Art. 49 of the OHADA Treaty:

> Under conditions laid down by regulation, Civil servants and employees of OHADA, Judges of the Common Court of Justice and Arbitration as well as arbitrators appointed or confirmed by the Court enjoy diplomatic privileges and immunities during their duties.
>
> The immunities and privileges referred to above may be lifted by the Council of Ministers depending on the circumstances. Furthermore, Judges shall not be prosecuted for anything done outside the scope of their duties except with the authorization of the Court.

107. Under Art. 15 of the seat agreement between Ivory Coast and the CCJA:

> "The President, the (...) Vice-Presidents, the (...) judges, the Chief Registrar, the Experts, the Arbitrators, the Consultants and the Officials of the Court shall enjoy in the territory of Côte d'Ivoire the following immunities, privileges and exemptions: a) Immunity from jurisdiction, even after the termination of their duties, for all acts, including their words and writings in the performance of their duties. This immunity shall not apply in the case of infringements of the rules governing the movement of motor vehicles committed by an official of the Court or damage caused by a motor vehicle driven by him or owned by him. However, the Court is required to take out an insurance policy which, in case of liability, will cover any damage caused by one of its agents." *See Accord entre l'Organisation pour l'Harmonisation en Afrique du Droit des Affaires (OHADA) et le Gouvernement de la République de Côte d'Ivoire relatif au siège de la Cour Commune de Justice et d'Arbitrage (CCJA)* [Agreement between the Organization for the Harmonization of Business Law in Africa (OHADA) and the Government of the Republic of Ivory Coast Concerning the Seat of the Common Court of Justice and Arbitration (CCJA)], *Journal Officiel de l'OHADA*, 3ème année, N° 9, 15 septembre 1999, p. 8 [Official Journal of OHADA, 3rd year, N°9, Sept. 15, 1999, p. 8], http://www.idc-afrique.org/sites/default/files/journaux_officiels/09%20journal_officiel_n_09.pdf.

on that specific point.[108] If an award can be set aside because the arbitrators have disregarded the agreement of the parties regarding fees, it is not abusive to set aside another one where arbitrators have disregarded mandatory rules regarding fees, as was the case for *Getma*.

Finally, about the supposed partiality of the CCJA, which would be both "judge and arbitrator," an idea which seems to be shared by several arbitration experts, it must be remembered that the administrative functions of the CCJA in matters of arbitration[109] cannot be confused with its judicial functions[110] in the event of a challenge to an award, as highlighted in Chapter 5 (*see* §5.04[B]). A careful reading of Articles 1 and 2 of the CCJA Regulation on Arbitration and Articles 2.5, 2.6, 3.1 and 3.2 of the Arbitration Bylaws of the CCJA[111] brings out that the Court:

- designates some of its judges to serve a supervising panel of arbitral proceedings;
- makes decisions of an administrative nature, devoid of any force of res judicata, without recourse and which reasons are not disclosed;
- does not itself settle disputes but merely appoints or confirms the arbitrators, is informed of the proceedings and examines drafts of arbitral awards; and
- makes arrangements to prevent the members of the Court from being directly involved in arbitration proceedings in their personal capacity.

It follows from the foregoing that the CCJA in its capacity as a judicial body is different from the CCJA as an arbitration center. As stated above, in arbitration proceedings, the CCJA does not judge, but confines itself (only judges who are members of a designated panel overseeing a given case) to administrative tasks: initiating and supervising arbitration proceedings, setting fees and Arbitrators' fees, confirming the arbitrators, arbitrating in the event of a challenge to an arbitrator by a party, etc.

The question of the supposed partiality of the Court is entirely subjective. However, the institutional arbitration system of the CCJA is not flawed because the OHADA Legislator has wisely arranged a divide between those two main functions of the Court mentioned above. The measures taken by the CCJA through the arbitration center "are administrative in nature,"[112] and in that capacity, the CCJA itself does not rule on the merit of the cases submitted to arbitration.[113] In addition to those already presented in Chapter 5 (see §5.04[B]), several other cases from international jurisdictions also comfort this view. For example, corresponds to an independent judgment:

108. Cour d'appel [CA] [regional court of appeal] Paris, 1 ch. Suppl., Mar. 20 1986, Rev. arb. 1987. 82, obs. B. Mercadal (Fr).
109. Usually, a panel of judges of the court performing administrative duties regarding specific arbitration cases each panel is appointed to oversee.
110. The whole court (thirteen judges) sitting en banc.
111. CCJA Bylaws on Arbitration.
112. CCJA Arbitration Rules, Art. 1.1.
113. *Id.*, Art. 2.2.

- the decision handed down by a court of which a judge who had ruled on the case in summary proceedings was a member since the fact that a magistrate decides on the merits of a case in which he has previously taken interim measures does not imply an infringement of the objectively assessed impartiality requirement; and[114]
- the decision rendered by a court in which sat the judge-commissioner who, during the observation period, had made orders for the day-to-day management of a company, since those orders implied no prejudice on the matter to be decided by the Court on the viability of the reorganization plan proposed by the applicant.[115]

In illustrating this point by a much easier example: assuming a corporation having in its organizational structure a Chief Executive Officer (CEO), a Chief Financial Officer (CFO) and a Chief Human Resource Officer (CHRO). One of the duties of the CHRO is to sit on panels recruiting managers for the corporation, as well as on discipline committees along with other top executives of the corporation. If a manager of the corporation later gets involved in serious wrongdoing worthy of hearings by a discipline committee and subsequent dismissal of the manager, it would not be fair to prevent the CHRO from sitting on the discipline committee just because he was involved in the recruitment of that manager. Indeed, this situation is far from arbitration proceedings, but there is a similarity: while acting as administrative body overseeing arbitral proceedings, the CCJA could be, to some extent, compared to the CHRO sitting on a recruitment panel. Its duties and limited powers in this capacity are different from the situation in which the Court, sitting en banc, will hear a challenge to an arbitral award. It could be argued that no serious concern should be raised since, as previously mentioned, the panel of the CCJA overseeing an arbitral proceeding does not get involved in the ruling by the arbitral tribunal. Therefore, it does not seem relevant to be overly concerned about the CCJA being judge and party.

§14.05 BREACH OF THE ADVERSARIAL PRINCIPLE

[A] Under the UAA

Cases finding that the adversarial principle has been breached (§14.05[A][1]), as well as those finding that it has not been breached (§14.05[A][2]), will be presented.

114. Cour de cassation [Cass.] [supreme court for judicial matters] ass. plen., Nov. 6, 1998, *JCP 1998, II, 10198, rapport P. Sargos (Fr.); D. 1999, 1. concl. J.-Fr. Burgelin (Fr.).*
115. Tierce v. San Marino, Eur. Ct. H.R., Jul. 25, 2000, D. *2001.339; D. 2001.328 chron. C. Goyet, Remarques sur l'impartialité du tribunal (Fr).*

[1] *Cases Finding the Adversarial Principle Has Been Breached*

The adversarial principle has been breached where evidence has not been displayed to a party (§14.05[A][1][i]), where all the parties have not appeared before the self-appointed arbitrator (§14.05[A][1][ii]) and where an award has been rendered on ex parte evidence (§14.05[A][1][iii]).

[i] Failure to Disclose Evidence to a Party

Due process is one of the keystones of arbitral proceedings under the Treaty. The adversarial principle implies that each of the parties has been able to assert their claims, to know those of their adversary, and discuss them. For this principle to be complied with, any document or exhibit produced during deliberation of the tribunal must first have been communicated to the other party for possible comment or discussion. In the absence of proof of communication of the exhibits produced, the arbitral tribunal must either disregard the exhibits in its decision or reopen the hearings for disclosure if the exhibit is likely to influence the ruling of the tribunal. By admitting the exhibits produced by one party during its deliberations without their prior communication to the other party and basing its ruling, even partially on these, the arbitral tribunal has violated the adversarial principle, and its award must be annulled.[116] The issue mentioned in the case seems similar to discovery proceedings under U.S. law.

[ii] Nonappearance of All Parties Before the Self-Appointed Arbitrator

The adversarial principle has also been violated where it is not established that all the parties appeared before the sole arbitrator, and the ruling was made hastily, after only a few minutes' deliberation while the hearing which commenced at the end of the morning ended at 12:30. This irregularity exposes the award to annulment, as well as the judgment granting *exequatur*.[117] Finally, the arbitrator who, in ruling against a party, did not rely on the evidence discussed in adversarial proceedings exposes their award to annulment.[118]

[iii] Award Made on the Basis of Ex Parte Evidence

The arbitrator who relied upon ex parte evidence to rule against a party exposes their award to annulment for breach of the adversarial principle.[119]

116. CA Centre, Feb. 6, 2008, N° 52/Civ., *supra*, Chapter 3, fn. 39.
117. CA Ouest, Jul. 13, 2011, N° 53/Civ., *supra*, Chapter 14, fn. 117.
118. CA Ouagadougou, ch. com., Apr. 16, 2010, N° 043, (Burk. Faso), http://www.ohada.com/jurisprudence/ohadata/J-12-182.html.
119. *Id.*

[2] Cases Finding the Adversarial Principle Has Not Been Breached

The adversarial principle has not been breached where evidence has been received by a party which abstained from discussing it (§14.05[A][2][i]) or where an objection raised by a party has been joined to the merits by a tribunal (§14.05[A][2][ii]).

[i] Evidence Received by a Party but Not Discussed

The party which does not dispute having received the written evidence and observations of the counsel of the opposing party and which has refrained from producing their own evidence, thereby acquiescing to the expert report in question, cannot validly invoke the breach of adversarial principle.[120]

[ii] Objection Raised by a Party and Joined to the Merits by the Tribunal

An arbitral tribunal is wrongly accused of having violated the principle of adversarial procedure for having, while the debate was limited to the question of whether or not the arbitration period had expired, rendered its final award, whereas it was necessary either to make a partial award on the exception discussed or to join it to the merits and invite the claimant to present their defense on the merit of the claim since the requests and the arguments developed in support, on which the arbitral tribunal ruled in its award, are contained in the request for arbitration of which the claimant does not deny having received regular communication; that the plaintiff does not invoke any document or writing which has not been communicated to them; that during the case management conference fixing the course of the procedure, the same requests were made, the plaintiff having declared to stick to their request for rearrangement of the arbitral tribunal. It follows from the references to the award that during the hearings, the claimant maintained their objection relating to the expiry of the period of arbitration "... asking the arbitral tribunal to stick to this exception"; that the tribunal, which joined the objection of the claimant to the merits, and did not base its decision on any argument raised by the tribunal on its own motion, did not have to invite the claimant, to whom it was free to do so, to present their defense on the merits. As the irregularity complained of has not been demonstrated, the plea must be rejected as unfounded.[121]

[B] Compliance with the Adversarial Principle Under the CCJA Rules

To date, there is no known case in which an arbitral award has been annulled for breach of the adversarial principle under the CCJA Rules. Thus, all the available cases

120. Oryx Bénin v. Société Africaine de Distribution et de Négoce, N° 154/2016, *supra*, Chapter 5, fn. 16.
121. Commercial Bank of Cameroon v. Archidiocèse de Yaoundé, N° 242/2018, *supra*, Chapter 2, fn. 13.

illustrate various situations in which the CCJA determined that there has been no breach of the principle. The seven different categories that will be presented relate to parties put in a position to discuss the evidence and arguments submitted to the arbitral tribunal (§14.05[B][1]); the absence of an obligation to allocate the same time limits to the parties (§14.05[B][2]); the optional nature of the use of an expert (§14.05[B][3]); a majority award signed by all the arbitrators (§14.05[B][4]); an imprecise and vague argument (§14.05[B][5]); the inoperative nature of a party's deliberate refusal to participate in the proceedings (§14.05[B][6]) and the absence of the alleged unequal treatment and discussion of the applicable law (§14.05[B][7]).

[1] Parties Put in a Position to Discuss the Evidence and Arguments Submitted to the Arbitral Tribunal

In similarity to UAA Article 26, the adversarial principle or due process is to be strictly complied with under the CCJA Arbitration Rules. It has been held in *Etat du Bénin v. Société Commune de Participation* that the adversarial principle complied with vis-à-vis a party which became aware of the arbitration proceedings and filed a response in reply.[122] The adversarial principle has also been complied with where each party has had the opportunity to examine and discuss the exhibits and the pleas submitted to the arbitral tribunal. Especially when it is stated in the award that "all the exhibits have been well received and none of them were concealed; that the parties have had all the necessary and useful time to debate … ."[123]

The adversarial principle presupposes that each of the parties has been able to discuss the statement of the facts and the legal arguments which their opponents have opposed. It was complied with when it appeared from the evidence of the proceedings that the exhibit in the present case, the letter from a notary, was communicated during the proceedings to the petitioners and that they even spoke freely on the said document; that contrary to the assertions of the petitioners, it does not appear from the evidence in the proceedings that the exhibits were removed or that the parties were not put in a position to make known all that is necessary for the success of their request or their defense, or that the challenged award was made exclusively on the basis of the notary's letter. Finally, there is no contradiction in the arbitral tribunal: (i) having rejected the counterclaims of a party seeking to have the petitioners bear the costs incurred by them in the arbitration proceedings as being new; and (ii) having ruled on those same claims because it had the legal obligation under Article 24 of the CCJA Regulation on Arbitration to liquidate the costs of the arbitration and to decide which party is responsible for the payment, or in which proportion they are shared between the parties. The petition for annulment must be dismissed.[124]

122. Etat du Bénin v. Société Commune de Participation, N° 104/2015, *supra*, Chapter 14, fn. 57.
123. Societe Ivoirienne de raffinage v. Bona Shipholding, N° 029/2007, *supra*, Chapter 3, fn. 41.
124. Ekwa Ngalle v. Société Nationale d'Hydrocarbures, N° 102/2015, *supra*, Chapter 2, fn. 31.

[2] No Obligation to Allocate the Same Time Limits to the Parties

If compliance with the adversarial principle requires that each party has been able to make their case and discuss the arguments of their opponent so that nothing that served as a ground to the arbitral award has escaped the debate, there is, however, no obligation on the arbitrator to allocate strictly the same time limit for each claim. In the case at hand, the petitioner who, on the one hand, signed the minutes of the case management conference without any reservation and thus gave their agreement on the provisional calendar contained therein and, on the other hand, effectively communicated and filed their submissions within the time limits set out in the said minutes, cannot validly invoke any violation of their rights.[125]

[3] Optional Nature of the Use of an Expert

Compliance with the adversarial principle presupposes that each of the parties has been able to discuss the statement of the facts and the legal arguments which their adversaries have opposed. Under Article 19.3 [which became 19.4] of the CCJA Regulation on Arbitration, the issue of whether or not to appoint an expert is at the discretion of the arbitrator and cannot constitute a reason for breaching the adversarial principle in proceedings. That principle has not been breached where it results from the challenged award that the parties have been put in condition, not only to make their case but also to examine and discuss the exhibits as well as the arguments submitted to the arbitral tribunal; rejection of the petition for annulment.[126]

[4] Majority Award Signed by All the Arbitrators

No violation of the adversarial principle may be held against the arbitrators as long as it is not disputed that the arbitral award was made by a majority, was signed by the two arbitrators and the dissenting opinion of the third arbitrator was attached, in accordance with Article 22.4 of the CCJA Regulation on Arbitration.[127]

[5] Imprecise and Vague Argument

The argument alleging that an arbitral tribunal breached the adversarial principle in awarding damages to the claimants in the arbitration proceedings to which they were not parties, whereas the adversarial principle implies that even in the absence of a party, the judge or the arbitrator must ensure that the request made by the appearing

125. Pyramidion v. Agence d'Exécution des Travaux d'Infrastructure du Mali, N° 098/2014, *supra*, Chapter 6, fn. 16.
126. Etat du Mali v. Groupe TOMOTA, N° 033/2015, *supra*, Chapter 6, fn. 17. On the discretion of an arbitral tribunal for the appointment of an expert, *see also* Benin Control v. Etat du Bénin, N° 103/2015, *supra*, Chapter 6, fn. 18.
127. Pyramidion v. Agence d'Exécution des Travaux d'Infrastructure du Mali, N° 098/2014, *supra*, Chapter 6, fn. 16.

party is justified, is vague, imprecise and must be rejected. That is the case because that argument specifies neither the "claim made by the appearing party," nor "the harm which is foreign to them" and which would have benefited the claimants.[128] Likewise, when it results from the challenged award that the parties have exchanged the pleadings and produced their exhibits before the hearing, the CCJA is unable to hold that the principle of adversarial proceedings has not been complied with since the argument does not specify the exhibit which would not have been communicated to the petitioner.[129]

[6] Inoperative Nature of a Party's Deliberate Refusal to Participate in the Proceedings

The deliberate refusal of a person to participate in arbitration proceedings does not infringe the principle of adversarial proceedings since default arbitration is admitted by Article 10.2 of the CCJA Regulation on Arbitration, according to which if one of the parties refuses to participate in the arbitration, this takes place notwithstanding this refusal or this abstention. Thus, the prong of an argument based on that contention lacks merit and must be rejected.[130]

[7] Absence of the Alleged Unequal Treatment and Discussion of the Applicable Law

A challenged arbitral award is wrongly criticized for breaching the adversarial principle based on the unequal treatment of the parties, the manner in which they have treated within the award and the lack of discussion on applicable law as presented in the post-hearing submissions, in that, on one the hand, the correspondence of the tribunal on April 24, 2016 had the sole purpose of allowing the defendant to find a more solid basis for their claims and, on the other hand, the law applied was not discussed; that thus, according to the petitioner, the arbitral tribunal "upset the balance of the trial (...) and introduced the breach of equal treatment of the parties," which should lead to the nullity of the award. This is so because the fact for an arbitral tribunal to invite the litigants to shed light on precise points of their dispute is part of the investigative powers of the tribunal under Article 19.1 of the CCJA Regulation on Arbitration. It does not constitute an unequal treatment of said parties characterizing the breach of the adversarial principle. In the case at hand, the plea must be rejected since it follows from the challenged award that the parties have validly made their case, including on the applicable law; that they have examined and discussed the evidence and arguments submitted to the arbitral tribunal.[131]

---

128. Etat du Bénin v. Société Commune de Participation, N° 104/2015, *supra*, Chapter 14, fn. 57.
129. Compagnie Malienne pour le Développement des Textiles v. Société Inter Africaine de Distribution, N° 160/2016, *supra*, Chapter 1, fn. 33.
130. *Id.*
131. Société Nestle Cameroon v. Groupe Abbassi, N° 081/2019, *supra*, Chapter 14, fn. 14.

§14.06 BREACH OF INTERNATIONAL PUBLIC POLICY

The OHADA Legislator has not specified the content of the international public policy under OHADA Rules, which needs to be "deciphered"[132] by case law. Consequently, "the content of this public policy depends on the general interest of the geographic territory under the Treaty and of the particular interests whose violation cannot be supported by the OHADA legal order."[133] The CCJA has taken the lead in the determination of the international public policy of OHADA, through some decisions that will be presented hereafter, both applying the UAA (§14.06[A]) and the CCJA Arbitration Rules (§14.06[B]).

[A] Under the UAA

Unlike *exequatur* granted under the CCJA Arbitration Rules, *exequatur* granted by a national judge of a State Party to the Treaty is enforceable only in their country because the public order is specific to each state and the one of a specific state could be different from the one of another state. Thus, the judge who grants *exequatur* can only make a decision having an effect in their own jurisdiction. So far, there are few cases dealing with breach of public policy.

In *Oryx Bénin v. Société Africaine de Distribution et de Négoce*, the CCJA ruled that it is wrong to reproach an arbitral award for being contrary to internal and international public policy for having violated Article 76 paragraph 3 of the Bylaws of the Bar Association of Benin by holding that the retainment of a lawyer has been duly authorized by the President of the Bar Association whereas, according to the argument, this lawyer obtained court decisions before being authorized by the President of the Bar Association since it is established that by letter dated December 31, 2012, addressed to ad hoc arbitral tribunal, the President of the Bar Association of Benin had given his consent to the retainment of the lawyer concerned as counsel for the defendant.[134]

---

132. *See* Barthélemy Mercadal, Modèle Universel de Contrat d'Affaires, Editions Francis Lefebvre, 2019, 176 at 441. (Mercadal, Modèle Universel de Contrat d'Affaires, 2019).
133. *Id.*
134. Oryx Bénin v. Société Africaine de Distribution et de Négoce, N° 154/2016, *supra*, Chapter 5, fn. 16. There are little details in the summary of the facts, but it can be taken from this ruling that a mere allegation of violation of some national rules is not sufficient to characterize breach of public policy entailing annulment of an arbitral award. For a case where breach of international public policy has been found, *see* République du Benin v. Société Générale de Surveillance, N° 068/2020, Decision, [C.C.J.A.], 3ᵉ ch., (Feb. 27, 2020), in which the CCJA ruled that res judicata, which constitutes a fundamental principle of justice, in that it ensures judicial security, is part of the international public policy under Art. 26 e) of the UAA. As such, it prevents an arbitrator from ruling again in the same case between the same parties and having the same object, where a court of law before which no jurisdictional objection was raised had already ruled. Consequently, the partial arbitral award which declares the arbitral tribunal competent to rule again on a request inviting it to "note that the contract concluded on Dec. 5, 2014 [between the parties] is and remains valid, effectively binds the [parties] and that the [Republic of Benin] has not complied with its terms," while the said contract was already annulled by the state court, constitutes a breach of international public policy and must be annulled.

[B] Under the CCJA Rules

There is a majority of cases where the CCJA determined public policy has not been breached (§14.06[B][2]) and few cases where there was a breach (§14.06[B][1]).

[1] Cases Where Breach of International Public Policy Have Been Found

Two examples will be presented, on res judicata (§14.06[B][1][i]) and the annulment of a national decree by an arbitral tribunal (§14.06[B][1][ii]).

[i] Res Judicata

In order to properly discuss public policy violation issue under the CCJA, one must look at the concept of res judicata. While it is a common law principle, such an issue is totally applicable here because the CCJA operates as the final judge, similar to the French Cassation Court, or even the Supreme Court of the United States, as mentioned in the introduction.[135] This means that no decision of the CCJA can be challenged before any other court in any of the seventeen States Parties to the Treaty. Even if it has been challenged before a cassation Court, the judgment rendered by a Court of Appeal between parties nevertheless remains a final decision having the force of res judicata as long as it is not annulled. When a challenge to an arbitral award has been dismissed, the award becomes irrevocable. The authority of res judicata, a fundamental principle of justice ensuring the legal certainty of a situation acquired, cannot be violated without violating the international public policy under Articles 29.2 and 30.6-4 [which became 30.5] of the CCJA Regulation on Arbitration. Therefore, the arbitrator who has ruled again in the same case opposing the same parties has violated the international public, and their award must be annulled.[136]

[ii] Annulment of a Decree by an Arbitral Tribunal

While it is common ground that an arbitral tribunal has jurisdiction to hear disputes arising from the exercise by a State of its prerogatives as a public authority, as far as that State may resort to arbitration in respect of its rights, that judicial power must be limited to the question of redress owed to a private natural or legal person resulting from damage due to the exercise of those prerogatives as a public authority, without having to judge the validity of the acts taken by the State in exercising its prerogatives. It follows that the award, which, instead of being limited to pecuniary penalties, declared that a decree had no effect on the agreement of the parties and consequently

135. *Supra*, Introduction, fn. 13, 14.
136. Planor Afrique v. Atlantique Telecom, N° 03/2011, Decision, CCJA, Ass. plen., (Jan. 31, 2011), http://www.ohada.com/jurisprudence/ohadata/J-12-136.html.

decided that the said agreement was not suspended as a result of that decree has violated international public policy and must be annulled.[137]

[2] Cases Where Breach of International Public Policy Have Not Been Found

So far, at least nine situations have been identified relating to a dispute relating to internal arbitration (§14.06[B][2][i]), an unclear argument (§14.06[B][2][ii]), the contractual liability of a party determined by an arbitral tribunal (§14.06[B][2][iii]), a state enjoined to stay its decision to suspend the enforcement of a contract (§14.06[B][2][iv]), the jurisdiction of an arbitral tribunal retained on the basis of a judgment of the CCJA (§14.06[B][2][v]), the extension of an arbitration clause to a non-signatory after incompetence of state courts has been raised by petitioners (§14.06[B][2][vi]), the extension of their agreement by the parties (§14.06[B][2][vii]), the inapplicability of the Labor Code to the revocation of a corporate office (§14.06[B][2][viii]) and the application of harmonized OHADA law and the French law on a supplementary basis (§14.06[B][2][ix]).

[i] Dispute Relating to Internal Arbitration

The dispute between two corporations under Beninese law relating to internal trade is a matter of internal arbitration. And when it results from the arbitration clause under which the dispute was submitted to arbitration, that the law applicable to the merits of the dispute is Beninese law, it is wrong to invoke the violation of the international public policy as an argument for an annulment the award made in such arbitration proceedings. The petition must be rejected.[138]

[ii] Unclear Argument

The argument alleging breach of international public policy without specifying how the challenged award would be contrary to international public policy cannot prosper since the petition for the annulment of an arbitral award can only be based on one or many of the grounds under Article 30.6 [which became 30.5] of the CCJA Regulation on Arbitration.[139]

137. Etat du Bénin v. Société Commune de Participation, N° 104/2015, *supra*, Chapter 14, fn. 57.
138. Societe Nationale pour la Promotion Agricole v. Societe des Huileries du Benin, N° 045/2008, *supra*, Chapter 5, fn. 26.
139. Societe Nationale pour la Promotion Agricole v. Societe des Huileries du Benin, CCJA, N° 04/2011, Decision, CCJA, 1e ch., (Jun. 30, 2011), http://www.ohada.com/jurisprudence/ohadata/J-12-137.html.

[iii] Contractual Liability of a Party Determined by an Arbitral Tribunal

The arbitral tribunal which analyzed the elements about the disputed agreement of the parties, produced and debated *inter partes*,[140] to retain the petitioner's liability, deduced from it, on the basis of Malian Law applicable to the case, that the claimant breached their contractual obligations and ordered them to pay compensation for the damage suffered, did in no way breach international public policy and the petition for annulment must be dismissed.[141]

[iv] State Enjoined to Stay its Decision to Suspend the Enforcement of a Contract

The arbitral tribunal which ordered a state to stay the enforcement of the decision of the state to suspend a contract which it has freely signed or to have to repair the effects of its act [through compensation], has not infringed the sovereign prerogatives of that state and did not violate in any way international public order. Therefore, the challenge must be dismissed.[142]

[v] Jurisdiction of an Arbitral Tribunal Retained on the Basis of a Judgment of the CCJA

An arbitral tribunal which declared itself competent by virtue of a judgment of the CCJA has ruled on its jurisdiction under Article 11 of the UAA and 10.3 of the Arbitration Rules and has, therefore, not violated the said Articles. Regarding the regularity or not of the second arbitral tribunal established by the court, it should be recalled that when the proceedings were resumed, the respondent proposed the appointment of an arbitrator, unlike the claimants who proposed three. The parties were not agreeing on the number of arbitrators, and under Article 3 of the CCJA Regulation on Arbitration, according to which "If the parties have not agreed on the number of arbitrators, the Court appoints a sole arbitrator, unless the dispute seems to justify the appointment of three arbitrators ...," the CCJA, by an administrative decision not subject to appeal under Article 1.1 of its Regulation on Arbitration, appointed a sole arbitrator. Consequently, the award is in no way contrary to international public policy.[143]

---

140. *Inter partes* suggests the adversarial principle has been complied with. *See* the glossary, *infra*.
141. Etat du Mali v. Tomota SA, CCJA, N° 033/2015, *supra*, Chapter 6, fn. 17.
142. Benin Control v. Etat du Bénin, N° 103/2015, *supra*, Chapter 6, fn. 18.
143. Compagnie Malienne pour le Développement des Textiles v. Société Inter Africaine de Distribution, N° 160/2016, *supra*, Chapter 1, fn. 33. This is one of the rare cases of the CCJA that seem confusing in that the CCJA did not follow its own precedents according to which the UAA and the CCJA Arbitration Rules are two separate set of rules applying to two different types of arbitration. But in any event, this isolated ruling must not be construed as having changed the rule and parties will do well in ensuring that they do not mix the UAA and the CCJA Arbitration Rules in the same proceedings.

[vi] Arbitration Clause Extended to a Non-Signatory After Incompetence of State Courts has Been Raised by Petitioners

The claimants, who on their own have deduced that the contract binding them must be extended to the respondent and that for this reason, the dispute must be settled through arbitration, thus objecting to the jurisdiction of the state judges, cannot validly reproach the award for being contrary to international public order in that the arbitral tribunal extended the arbitration clause to the respondent who was not a signatory of the said clause. This is the case because the objection has been sanctioned by final and binding decisions having res judicata effect. Thus, the petition for annulment must be dismissed.[144]

[vii] Extension of Their Agreement by the Parties

A claimant is wrong to criticize an award for being contrary to international public policy for a poor calculation of the time limits which prevented them from raising the lapse of the agreement between the parties which led to the dispute, since the parties have waived their right to avail themselves of the non-fulfillment of one of the conditions precedent of their agreement within the initial period, thus wishing to continue the performance of the agreement under the new conditions adopted by them. This is so since the parties have agreed in their agreement of July 13, 2006 that "The fulfillment of the above conditions must be established by the two Parties in a common document, which will thereby formalize the date of entry into force of the agreement. The conditions precedent to the entry into force of the agreement above must have been fulfilled at the latest sixty (60) days after the signature of the said agreement, unless the parties mutually agree, before the end of this period, on a later date. The concession agreement will automatically be terminated in the event that the conditions specified above are not fulfilled by the deadline thus fixed;" that on September 12, 2006, the parties, represented by the same persons, signed an amendment stipulating that "In order to finalize the formalization for the entry into force of the Partnership Agreement signed on July 13, 2006 between [them], the two parties agree to postpone ninety (90) days from the signing of this document (...). Thus, the deadline for entry into force of the agreement is fixed by mutual agreement and for an additional period of ninety (90) days from September 12, 2006; during this period, the Tripartite Agreement for the management of the special account (between the parties) will be signed as well as the finalization of the specifications." Since the agreement of the parties has been extended, the claimant was wrong in claiming it has lapsed. It follows that the challenged arbitral award is not contrary to international public policy, and the petition of its annulment must be dismissed.[145]

144. *Id.*
145. Etat du Mali v. Seaquest-Infotel Mali, N° 027/2017, *supra*, Chapter 12, fn. 39.

[viii] The Labor Code Does Not Apply to the Revocation of a Corporate Office

It is wrong to blame an award for breach of international public order in that it had flagrantly violated the Cameroonian Labor Code that the parties are supposed to apply and which gives exclusive jurisdiction to Cameroonian jurisdictions, while compliance with international public order postulates the taking into account and compliance with national laws of the States, insofar as these laws do not violate the international commitments of the State since, on the one hand, the dispute before the arbitral tribunal arose from the revocation of the mandate of a managing director of a public limited company by its board of directors falling under the provisions of the Uniform Act on Corporations; and on the other hand, it does not appear from the file that this director occupied, by the employment contract, another effective job in addition to his social mandate. It follows that the exclusive jurisdiction of the Cameroon labor courts invoked is not justified. Therefore, the award is not contrary to international public policy because the dispute has been referred to the arbitral tribunal in accordance with the will of the parties, and the petition for annulment must be dismissed.[146]

[ix] Application of Harmonized OHADA Law and French Law on a Supplementary Basis

An arbitral award has been wrongfully criticized for having violated international public order, in that the arbitral tribunal has dismissed the arbitration clause without the knowledge of the parties, has made a unilateral interpretation of the order of referral without questioning the parties and ruling out the law of the parties, thereby failing to comply with the will of the parties under Article 21 of the Treaty. So is the case where the arbitral tribunal which, after assessing the case, determines that "since the [minutes of the case management conference] is a consensual document requiring the signature of the Parties alongside those of the members of the arbitral tribunal, under Article 15.2 of the CCJA Regulation on Arbitration, it is ineffective for the petitioner to maintain that the wording found cannot be considered to expressly modify Article 20.1 of the contract due to the fact that the arbitral tribunal did not question the Parties on their intentions" and "considers that the autonomy of the Parties, pivotal principle in international arbitration in particular with regard to the determination by the Parties of the law applicable to the merits of the dispute, commands to give full effect to the choice of the Parties freely expressed in the minutes of the case management conference specifying unequivocally the rules the parties wish to see applied to the resolution of their dispute," to deduce that it will apply "Harmonized law (Uniform Acts) applicable in the OHADA States Parties and French law in a supplementary manner, according to the first item of their agreement in the minutes of the case management conference," did not breach international public policy and the petition for annulment lack merits.[147]

---

146. National Financial Credit Bank v. N'Diaye, N° 111/2017, *supra*, Chapter 14, fn. 31.
147. Société Nestle Cameroon v. Groupe Abbassi, N° 081/2019, *supra*, Chapter 14, fn. 14.

§14.07 FAILURE TO STATE THE REASONS OF AN AWARD

[A] Under the UAA

The majority of the available cases presented hereafter demonstrates that it may be difficult to get an arbitral award annulled for failure to state the reasons of the award because it is sufficient for the arbitrator(s) to answer each claim or contention of the parties (§14.07[A][1]). Once that is established, usually, the test is met, whether the reasoning in law is right or not. None of the cases below has found a failure of a tribunal to state the reasons of their award (§14.07[A][2]).

[1] Reasons Sufficiently Stated in the Award

The merits of each arbitration award must be clearly stated in the award. In a case handled by a Court of Appeal in Cameroon, it has been ruled that an arbitral tribunal, that ruled that "the termination by [Corporation A] of its various contracts with [Corporation B] not only failed to comply with the forms prescribed in Article 7 of the agreement, namely a formal notice by a registered letter which remained unsuccessful but was not accompanied by a prior acknowledgment of the failure of the service provider justifying the said termination, as provided for in Article 14 of the agreement; that such violations of the law of the parties fall within the manifest bad faith of [Corporation A] and constitute an abusive termination of the contracts made with its above-mentioned agent (...)," had sufficiently justified its decision as to the liability of the plaintiff in a breach of its contractual relationship with the defendant before it ordered the plaintiff to pay compensation for the civil damage. Since no new evidence has been provided to the court to justify the annulment of that award, it must be confirmed in all respects.[148]

[2] Arbitral Award Containing a Response to All the Claims of the Parties

An arbitral award is wrongfully criticized for failure to state the reasons upon which it is based, by not responding to the claims of the appellant and the contradiction between the reasons of the award since the annulment judge found, using their judicial discretion assessing the facts submitted to them, that the challenged award answered all the claims of the parties.[149]

Likewise, an arbitral award is wrongfully criticized for having not stated the reasons upon which it is based, in breach of Article 26-6 of the UAA whereas, on one hand, the tribunal did not explain why it awarded the sum of 1,373,638,000 FCFA to the claimant instead of the 1,901,531.060 FCFA claimed and, on the other hand,

148. CA Centre, Apr. 28, 2010, N° 199/Civ., (Cameroon), http://www.ohada.com/jurisprudence/ohadata/J-12-73.html.
149. Trois N v. Sicim, N° 110/2018, Decision, [C.C.J.A.], 2ᵉ ch., (May 17, 2018). [Emphasis added].

ordered the respondent to the arbitration proceedings to pay damages to the amounting to FCFA 185,000,000, without determining or under the law the fault committed by the respondent, since the argument relating to the failure to state the reasons of the award, under Article 26 of the UAA, is a formal requirement aimed at verifying that the content of the award responds to the claims and arguments of the parties. It is not intended to serve as a ground for reviewing the merits of the award or for assessing its merits by the Court handling the annulment request. In the case at hand, the plea is unfounded and must be rejected, as long as it appears from the reading of the award that it does contain the reasons in its wording.[150]

[B] Under the CCJA Rules

As it was already highlighted in the chapter on form and content of awards,[151] the newly imported sixth annulment ground of an arbitral award under Article 29.2 f) of the CCJA Regulation on Arbitration, namely, an award "devoid of any reason," seems theoretical because Article 23.2 of the same Regulation has emptied Article 29.2 f) of its substance since it allows the CCJA, during the preliminary examination of a draft award under Article 23 of the Regulation on Arbitration, to draw the attention of the tribunal on any "lack of reason" affecting the draft of their award. Each time the CCJA would choose to use that prerogative on an award lacking the reasons on which it is made, an annulment ground would inevitably be removed.

The absence of reasons for an arbitral award must be distinguished from the existence of objectionable or erroneous reasons. Once the reasons for the award are stated in it, it does not matter whether they are convincing or not[152] or objectionable,[153] which are not grounds for annulment of the award. However, the reasons are lacking when the award consists of a single operative part if no document or exhibit of the procedure makes up for the absence of reasons.[154]

---

150. Airtel Gabon v. 2JTH-Gabon, N° 203/2018, *supra*, Chapter 14, fn. 37 [Emphasis added]. *See also* George Forrest Belgium v. Les Ciments du Sahel, N° 094/2020, *supra*, Chapter 14, fn. 6, emphasizing that failure to state the reasons of an arbitral award is not intended to serve as a ground for reviewing the merits of the award or for assessing its merits by the court handling the annulment request.
151. *See supra*, Chapter 12, §12.02[B][3].
152. Centre de Cablages Electroniques de Laval v. Comeca, Cour d'appel [CA] [regional court of appeal] Paris, 1e ch. C, Nov. 8 2001, Rev. arb. 2001.som.925 (Fr).
153. Fontan Tessaur v. ISS Abilis France, Cour d'appel [CA] [regional court of appeal] Paris, 1e ch. C, Mar. 25 2004, Rev. arb. 2004.671 Note J. Ortscheidt (Fr). *See also* Ihs Ci v. Projex Ci, N° 128/2020, Decision, [C.C.J.A.], Ass. plen., (Apr. 30, 2020), in which the CCJA held that Under Art. 29.2 of the CCJA Regulation on Arbitration, failure to state the reasons of an arbitral award, as a ground for the annulment of said award, sanctions a total lack of reasons and does not confer on the annulment judge the power to assess the relevance of the reasons stated by the arbitrators. In the case at hand, since the challenged award contains many reasons in its wording, the alleged grievance (failure to state the reasons of the award) lacks merits and the petition for annulment must be dismissed.
154. Cour d'appel [CA] [regional court of appeal] Paris, n° n°13/17699, Dec. 9 2014: GP 2015.1063.som.s note D. Bensaude (Fr).

While it is true, as the CCJA has held in *Ekwa Ngalle v. Société Nationale d'Hydrocarbures*,[155] that the contradiction of reasons is not as such a ground for the annulment of an award under the CCJA Arbitration Rules, the other ruling of the CCJA in *Barou Entreprise des Travaux v. Société d'Exploitation des Mines d'Or de Sadiola*,[156] according to which the contradiction of reasons in a court judgment is equivalent to a lack of reasons, in that the contradictory reasons cancel each other and may justify the quashing of the affected judgment, seems transposable in matters of arbitration. The reason for this is that the contradiction between the reasons of an award can have the same effect of annulment and render, in some cases, the affected award unenforceable as things stand; and if an award is unenforceable because of its reasons, that may amount to an absence of those reasons, justifying, the annulment of the award under Article 29.2 f) of the CCJA Regulation on Arbitration. Under such circumstances, the arbitral tribunal may well be found to have failed to comply with its mission, which would also justify the annulment of the award, because when the reasons for an arbitral award are required under institutional arbitration rules, as is the case under the CCJA Arbitration Rules, their absence constitutes a violation of their mission by the arbitrators.[157]

In light of the above, it may not be an exaggeration to assert that, in reality, this is not a real ground for annulment. In any event, it remains to be seen in the future how those two provisions of the CCJA Regulation on Arbitration (Articles 23 and 29.2 f)) will be reconciled by the CCJA if an award is ever challenged on the ground of failure to state its reasons.

155. Ekwa Ngalle v. Société Nationale d'Hydrocarbures, N° 102/2015, *supra*, Chapter 2, fn. 31.
156. Barou Entreprise des Travaux v. Société d'Exploitation des Mines d'Or de Sadiola, N° 040/2009, Decision, [C.C.J.A.], 1e ch., (Jun. 30, 2009), http://www.ohada.com/jurisprudence/ohadata/J-10-78.html.
157. Pawelec v. Pernod Ricard, Cour d'appel [CA] [regional court of appeal] Paris, *supra*, Chapter 12, fn. 45.

CHAPTER 15

Procedure and Consequences of the Annulment of Awards

This chapter presents the annulment procedure under each set of rules, namely the UAA (§15.02) and the CCJA Arbitrations Rules (§15.03), followed by the consequences of the annulment (§15.04). In any event, the annulment procedure can take place only where the parties have not waived it (§15.01).

§15.01 WAIVER OF THE ACTION FOR ANNULMENT

The challenge of an arbitral award can be admissible only if the parties have not waived such recourse. To be effective, the waiver follows strict rules which must be presented for both arbitration systems, even though they share common traits.

[A] Waiver under the UAA

Previous case law considered that any clause waiving an action for annulment was deemed unwritten,[1] while the CCJA held, in *Delpech v. Sotaci*,[2] that an action for annulment of an arbitral award was possible under the former version of Article 25 of the UAA.[3] Then, the Court of Appeal of Abidjan held that the waiver of any remedy being a mere obligation for each party to do something, its violation does not affect the admissibility of the action for annulment exercised by one of the parties, but opens the right to damages. It follows that the action for annulment is admissible.[4]

1. CA Abidjan, Apr. 27, 2001, 2e esp., (Côte d'Ivoire), http://www.ohada.com/jurisprudence/ohadata/J-02-127.html.
2. Delpech v. Sotaci, N° 010/2003, Decision, *supra*, Chapter 14, fn. 41.
3. Under Art. 25, para. 2 of the UAA of Mar. 11, 1999, arbitral awards 'may be the subject of an appeal for annulment, which must be brought before the competent judge in the State Party.'
4. CA Abidjan, Jul. 25, 2003, N°1060, (Côte d'Ivoire), http://www.ohada.com/jurisprudence/ohadata/J-03-292.html.

The new Article 25 of the UAA currently in force expressly provides for the possibility of waiving annulment of an arbitral award. However, it is not a good idea for a party to forego in advance their potential right to challenge an arbitral award, since the effects of such a waiver clause may prove harmful to the weaker party during the negotiations, which may thus find themselves unable to seek the annulment of the award, should it get affected by one or more of the limited annulment grounds listed by the OHADA Legislator under Article 26 of the UAA.

In any event, if the parties knowingly choose to waive in advance their right to seek an annulment, they must expressly stipulate it since according to the settled case law of the CCJA relating to the waiver under the CCJA Arbitration Rules (*see* §15.01[B]) which can be transposed under the UAA in the issue, the waiver is not presumed and must clearly result from the stipulation of the parties.

[B] Waiver under the CCJA Rules

Article 29.2, paragraph 1 of the CCJA Regulation on Arbitration states that "The parties may agree to waive the action for annulment of the arbitral award, provided the award does not breach international public policy." It has been held by the CCJA in *Republique de Guinee Equatoriale v. Commercial Bank Guinea Ecuatorial* that under Article 29 (2) of the CCJA Regulation on Arbitration, even where there are grounds for annulling an award, an application for setting aside the award will be inadmissible if the parties have previously and clearly waived their right to any recourse against the award.[5]

However, the *waiver is not presumed*. In the presence of an unwritten arbitration agreement, the plaintiff is deemed not to have waived the right to challenge the validity of the award under Article 29.2 (1) of the CCJA Arbitration Rules, since it does not appear from any exhibit of the file that the parties to the said agreement intended to explicitly waive their right to challenge the award.[6]

Under well-established precedent of the CCJA, waiver by the parties of any challenge against an arbitral award must result from the clearly expressed and unequivocal will of the parties, because the terms "any award rendered by the arbitral tribunal will be final, enforceable against the parties" are only being only circumlocutions reflecting the res judicata effect which attaches to the award rendered under the aegis of the CCJA. They mean that such an award cannot be questioned and is not subject to any other remedy than that of a challenge of validity [now called request for annulment] cannot be prevented by the mere reference to the "final" character of the award contained in the arbitration clause.[7]

---

5. Republique de Guinee Equatoriale v. Commercial Bank Guinea Ecuatorial, N° 012/2011, Decision, CCJA, Ass. plen., (Nov. 29, 2011), http://www.ohada.com/jurisprudence/ohadata/J-13-142.html.
6. Societe Inter Africaine de Distribution v. Compagnie Malienne pour le Developpement des Textiles, N° 020/2013, *supra*, Chapter 14, fn. 28 [Emphasis added].
7. Etat du Mali v. Groupe TOMOTA, N° 033/2015, *supra*, Chapter 6, fn. 17.

Likewise, the mere use of the term "last resort" in an arbitration agreement between the parties is not sufficient to reflect an express waiver of the right to challenge an award.[8] The arbitration agreement containing the passage "all disputes arising from this contract or in connection with it (...) will be finally settled under the Arbitration Rules of the [CCJA] (...)," does not prohibit the application by either party for setting aside the award if any express waiver of recourse does not appear from that agreement. The word "final" does not imply the waiver of the action for annulment specially provided by the CCJA Arbitration Rules, a right which can be waived only by express stipulation in the arbitration agreement. Since it is not the case here, it is necessary to reject the objection of inadmissibility raised by the defendant.[9]

Neither the referral to the ordinary courts of a request for provisional measures nor the service of a certificate of ownership as in the case at hand, can by themselves presuppose the waiver by their author of an arbitration clause, which can only result from an unambiguous manifestation of the will of the parties.[10]

However, a party that is not formally a signatory to an agreement providing for arbitration is entitled to bring an action for annulment of the arbitral award if it infringes on their rights.[11]

§15.02 ANNULMENT PROCEDURE UNDER THE UAA

The purpose of the petition for annulment (§15.02[A]), followed with inadmissible remedies against an arbitral award (§15.02[B]), the applicable law (§15.02[C]), jurisdiction (§15.02[D]), the statute of limitations (§15.02[E]), the review of the decision of the competent court by the CCJA (§15.02[F]) and the supplementary jurisdiction of the CCJA for the motion for annulment (§15.02[G]) will be presented.

[A] Purpose of the Petition for Annulment

It is inferred from Article 25 of the UAA that the action for annulment is not aimed at reviewing the merits of the challenged award[12] and the judges ruling on the action for annulment of an award cannot replace the arbitral tribunal in its assessment of the merits.[13] It is, therefore, wrong to blame a court to which a request for annulment of an arbitral award has been referred for having drawn consequence from the fact that "only failure to respond to the claims and the absence of reasoning can justify the action for annulment, in light of the above analysis," to dismiss this prong of the argument, the annulment judge having in no way committed the alleged grievance and thus having

8. Etat du Mali v. ABS International Corporate, CCJA, N° 011/2011, *supra*, Chapter 14, fn. 51; Ekwa Ngalle v. Société Nationale d'Hydrocarbures, N° 102/2015, *supra*, Chapter 2, fn. 31.
9. Nestle Sahel v. Societe Commerciale d'Importation Azar et Salame, N° 028/2007, *supra*, Chapter 11, fn. 1.
10. Sodima v. Dramera, N° 097/2015, Decision, CCJA, 1e ch., (Jul. 23, 2015), http://www.ohada.com/jurisprudence/ohadata/J-16-194.html.
11. Planor Afrique v. Atlantique Telecom, N° 03/2011, *supra*, Chapter 14, fn. 134.
12. Trois N v. Sicim, N° 110/2018, *supra*, Chapter 14, fn. 147.
13. Prévoyance Assurances S.A. v. Eiffage Sénégal, *supra*, Chapter 3, fn. 39.

satisfied the obligation of formal verification of the answers given to the parties' claims, without looking into the relevance of the answers provided by the arbitrators to the claims of the parties, which in principle is beyond jurisdiction. Thus, the petition for overturning the decision must be dismissed.[14]

[B] Inadmissible Remedies Against an Arbitral Award

Under Article 25, paragraphs 1 and 2 of the UAA, "The award is not subject to opposition, appeal or cassation. It may be subject to a motion for annulment, which must be filed before the competent court in the State Party." Additionally, paragraph 4 of the same Article 25 states that "The decision of the competent court in the State Party on the motion for annulment may only be appealed in cassation before the Common Court of Justice and Arbitration." So far, three specific remedies have been found inadmissible against an arbitral award governed by the UAA, i.e., appeal (§15.02[B][1]), appeal in cassation (§15.02[B][2]) and a joint appeal against an award and the order ruling on the motion for annulment (§15.02[B][3]).

[1] Appeal

It follows from Article 25 of the UAA that an appeal cannot be lodged against an arbitral award, which can only be the subject of an action for annulment, a third-party opposition, or an application for review.[15]

[2] Appeal in Cassation

An arbitral award under the UAA cannot be challenged by way of an appeal in cassation, and such an appeal is inadmissible.[16]

[3] Joint Appeal Against the Award and the Order Ruling on the Motion for Annulment

It follows from Article 25 of the UAA that only the decision of the national court ruling on the action for annulment of an arbitral award subject to appeal in cassation before the CCJA. The appeal against both the arbitral award, which cannot be appealed, and the order that ruled on the request for annulment of the said award, is clearly in violation of Article 25 of the UAA and inadmissible, especially because the sole ground

14. Trois N v. Sicim, N° 110/2018, *supra*, Chapter 14, fn. 147.
15. Wassolo Ltd v. Fourniture Equipement et Divers, Cour d'appel de commerce [CA] [regional commercial court of appeal] Abidjan, 17 janvier 2019, 1e ch., N°347/2018, (Ivory Coast). Inaya v. Ciment d'Afrique, Cour d'appel de commerce [CA] [regional commercial court of appeal] Abidjan, Jun. 20, 2019, 1e ch., N° 410/2019, (Ivory Coast).
16. Emcica Congo Sarl v. Electra, N° 021/2015, Decision, [C.C.J.A.], 3e ch., (Apr. 9, 2015).

of appeal is limited to criticizing the arbitral award in lieu of the decision ruling on the request for the annulment of the said award.[17]

[C] Applicable Law

The only law applicable to the annulment of an arbitral award rendered under the UAA is the UAA, which determines the general framework of such action.[18]

[D] Jurisdiction

According to Article 25, paragraph 2 of the UAA, the action for annulment of an arbitral award "must be filed before the competent court in the State Party." Thus, the competent court for such annulment action must be determined in each of the seventeen States Parties of the Treaty. Since information pertaining to the competent court in all of those jurisdictions is not available, the general rule set by the CCJA on the determination of the competent court will be presented (§15.02[D][1]), followed by examples of countries in which courts of appeal have jurisdiction (§15.02[D][2]) and finally a special situation requiring the attention of practitioners (§15.03[D][3]).

[1] General Rule on the Determination of the Competent Court for Annulment

The general rule has been set in *Sarci v. Atlantique Telecom*,[19] and reiterated in *Delpech v. Sotaci*,[20] in which the CCJA held that since the UAA has not specified the competent judge before whom the action for annulment must be brought, it is necessary, when the seat of the arbitral tribunal was in a State Party to the Treaty, to refer to the national law of that country for this determination.[21]

[2] Jurisdiction of the Court of Appeal of the Seat of Arbitration

Legislative developments in many States Parties have established or maintained the jurisdiction of the Court of Appeal of the seat of the arbitration. In many countries where it has not been the case, courts have made their own determination, sometimes by relying upon cases from other countries and legal scholarship. This is the case, for example, in Benin (§15.02[D][2][i]), Burkina Faso (§15.02[D][2][ii]), Cameroon (§15.02[D][2][iii]), Congo (§15.02[D][2][iv]) and Ivory Coast (§15.02[D][2][v]).

17. Technifer GC v. Injelec, N° 096/2018, Decision, [C.C.J.A.], 1e ch., (Apr. 26, 2018).
18. CA Abidjan, Jul. 25, 2003, N° 1060, *supra*, Chapter 15, fn. 4.
19. Sarci v. Atlantique Telecom, N° 044/2008, *supra*, Chapter 2, fn. 5.
20. Delpech v. Sotaci, N° 010/2003, *supra*, Chapter 14, fn. 41.
21. Sarci v. Atlantique Telecom, N° 044/2008, *supra*, Chapter 2, fn. 5.

[i] Benin

Under Article 1170 of the Code of Civil Procedure of the Republic of Benin,[22] the petition for the annulment of an award rendered under the UAA must be filed before the Court of Appeal of the seat of arbitration by way of summons.

[ii] Burkina Faso

Relying upon legal scholarship, the Court of Appeal of Ouagadougou (Burkina Faso) ruled that in the absence of the designation of the competent judge by national law in Burkina Faso, it seems appropriate to recognize in the Court of Appeal the jurisdiction in which the award was rendered [namely the seat of arbitration] the competent court under Article 25 paragraph 3 [which became 4] of the UAA as second-level jurisdiction for the decisions rendered by an arbitral tribunal, and whose decisions are subject of an appeal in cassation. Moreover, States Parties, such as Ivory Coast and Senegal, whose national law on arbitration organizes such a remedy, have designated the Court of Appeal of the seat of the award as the competent court. It is, therefore, appropriate to declare the commercial chamber of the Ouagadougou Court of Appeal competent to hear this appeal.[23]

[iii] Cameroon

It is wrong to criticize a Court of Appeal for having "ruled as a last resort, in collegiality and unanimously, as the chamber of civil and commercial appeals," while, according to the argument, Article 25 of the UAA prohibits the appeal in arbitration and admits only the action for annulment, since in the case at hand the Court ruled only on the strict basis of the grounds presented to it, after having specified that it ruled "on the action for annulment presented by [one of the parties]." This is the case because the court will have ruled as an appellate court only if it had reviewed the award on the merits, the details noted by the appellant being superfluous.[24]

[iv] Congo

In the current state of the Congolese judicial organization, the Court whose decisions are, in principle, subject to appeal in cassation and which hears litigation of provisional

22. *See* Law n° 2008-07 of Feb. 28, 2011 on the Code of Civil, Commercial, Social, Administrative and Accounts Procedure in the Republic of Benin: https://sgg.gouv.bj/doc / loi-2008-07/).
23. CA Ouagadougou, Apr. 16, 2010, ch. com., n° 043 (Burkina Faso), *supra*, Chapter 14, fn. 118. Quoting professor Paul Gérard Pougoue, the court specifically held that "according to legal scholarship, 'By providing that the decision of the competent judge can only be appealed in cassation before the CCJA, Article 25 paragraph 3 [which became 4] of the UAA seems more favorable to the jurisdiction of the court of appeal. Decisions made by the judges at first level are usually subject to appeal to the second level of jurisdiction. The arbitrator constitutes the first level, and the action for annulment is filed at the second level.'"
24. Wanmo v. Nguessi, N° 151/2017, *supra*, Chapter 2, fn. 21.

enforcement, by means of the defense to provisional enforcement, is undoubtedly the appeal court, to the [exclusion] of the Supreme Court whose decisions, as a judge of cassation, cannot, in principle, be subject to censorship by a higher cassation court. It follows, under the combined provisions of Articles 25 paragraph 3 [which became 4] and 28 paragraph 2 of the UAA, that the Court of Appeal in the jurisdiction of which the arbitral award was rendered is the competent judge for the motion for annulment of such award as well as litigation of the provisional execution of the award. In the case at hand, the applicant's motion for the defense to provisional enforcement is admissible, as the applicant has previously justified having filed a motion for annulment of the arbitral award.[25]

[v] Ivory Coast

Courts had retained the jurisdiction of the Court of Appeal[26] on the basis of old laws which have since been replaced. Article 9 of Ordinance No. 2012-158 of February 9, 2012 determining the intervention of national courts in arbitration proceedings maintained the jurisdiction of the Court of Appeal by providing that "motion for annulment of an arbitral award on is brought by way of summons before the Court of Appeal of the place of the seat of the arbitral tribunal." A newer legislation enacted in 2017[27] has created a special commercial Court of Appeal, which is the competent court, at least for trade-related arbitration proceedings, as highlighted by some of its rulings on the matter.[28]

[3] The Importance of Carefulness for Practitioners Representing Parties Before the CCJA

In the Republic of Mali, there was a national decree of 1994 on Civil Procedure.[29] Article 923 of that decree designated the Court of Appeal as the only court competent to hear motions for the annulment of arbitral awards. In 1999, a new decree modifying the Civil Procedure Code was enacted in the country.[30] In 2009, another decree modifying the Civil Procedure Code of the country was enacted, without listing Article 923 of the 1994 decree among the provisions that were amended or repealed.

25. CA Pointe-Noire, Oct. 8, 2004, n° 180 (Burkina Faso), http://www.ohada.com/jurisprudence/ohadata/J-13-72.html.
26. CA Abidjan, Apr. 27, 2001, N° 45, *supra*, Chapter 11, fn. 2; Delpech v. Sotaci, N° 010/2003, *supra*, Chapter 14, fn. 41.
27. Decret n° 2017-501 du 2 août 2017 portant création de la cour d'appel de commerce d'Abidjan et fixant son siège, son ressort territorial et sa composition, https://www.ilo.org/dyn/natlex/docs/SERIAL/107295/132008/F-2047133431/CIV-107295.pdf [accessed Apr. 23, 2020 at 16:38].
28. Wassolo Ltd v. Fourniture Equipement et Divers, *supra*, Chapter 15, fn. 15; Inaya v. Ciment d'Afrique, *supra*, Chapter 15, fn. 15.
29. Décret n°94-226/P-RM du 28 juin 1994 portant ancien Code de procédure civile, commerciale et sociale.
30. Décret n°09-220/P-RM du 11 mai 2009 portant modification du Code de procédure civile, commerciale et sociale en vigueur au Mali.

By a ruling N° 035 of May 12, 2010, the Court of Appeal of Bamako (Mali) held that "in the current state of judicial practice and settled case law in Mali, motions for annulment of arbitral awards are brought before the court of first level where the award was rendered," to decline jurisdiction and to refer the parties to avail themselves before the competent court, thus basing its decision on the settled case law of the Malian courts. Ruling on the appeal in cassation against that judgment of the Court of Appeal, the CCJA approved, in *Niare v. Total Mali* in 2016, the Court of Appeal of Bamako for having declined jurisdiction. It specifically held that the ruling of the Court of Appeal in no way lacked a legal basis. Thus, the appellant having failed to prove the alleged survival of Article 923 of the 1994 decree referred to in the plea, the Bamako Court of Appeal did not in any way violate the articles referred to in the plea which will be rejected.[31] Thus, under applicable case law in Mali since the *Niare v. Total Mali* decision in 2016, the Court of First Level and not the Court of Appeal had jurisdiction to hear motions for annulment of arbitral awards rendered under the UAA.

However, in 2019, the CCJA reversed the position it took in *Niare v. Total Mali*. In *NCT Trading v. Gamby Service*, the CCJA overturned a ruling of the commercial tribunal of Bamako (first-level jurisdiction) by which the said commercial tribunal retained its jurisdiction and ruled on the motion for annulment of an arbitral award rendered under the UAA. In doing so, the CCJA held that in the Republic of Mali, State Party to the Treaty, within which the UAA applies, Article 923 of Decree No. 94-226/P-RM of June 28, 1994 on the old Code of Civil, Commercial and Social Procedure designates the Court of Appeal as the only court competent to hear motions for the annulment of an arbitral award. It is, therefore, appropriate for the CCJA to note, sua sponte, that it is in violation of Article 25 of the UAA and 923 of the 1994 Decree mentioned above that the Commercial Court of Bamako retained its jurisdiction to rule on the action for annulment brought against an arbitral award rendered under the UAA. The judgment must be quashed with no need to examine the grounds of the appeal in cassation.[32]

There is, therefore, a conflict of case law on the question, the judgment of 2016 validating the jurisdiction of the commercial court retained by the Court of Appeal of Bamako and the 2019 judgment sanctioning a commercial court for having retained its jurisdiction.[33]

31. Niare v. Total Mali, N° 163/2016, Decision, [C.C.J.A.], 3e ch., (Dec. 1, 2016). According to the CCJA, Decree No 09-220/P-RM of May 11, 2009 amending the Code of Civil, Commercial and Social Procedure in Mali, does not mention among the provisions concerned, those of Art. 923 Decree No. 94-226/P-RM of Jun. 28, 1994 of the former Code of Civil Procedure, provisions of which are also contrary to those of Art. 18 of Decree N° 99-254/P-RM dated Sept. 15, 1999 under the new Code of Civil, Commercial and Social Procedure according to which "The jurisdiction of the courts on the basis of the matter is determined by the rules relating to judicial organization and by the special provisions."
32. NCT Trading v. Gamby Service, N° 053/2019, Decision, [C.C.J.A.], 1e ch., (Mar. 14, 2019).
33. The two conflicting rulings of the CCJA on the matter are: *Niare v. Total Mali*, in 2016, by which it held that the action for annulment of an arbitral award must be brought before a court of first level, such as the commercial tribunal; and *NCT Trading v. Gamby Service*, in 2019, in which the CCJA overturned the decision by which the commercial tribunal retained jurisdiction.

Pending a possible legislative evolution on the subject in Mali, one way to resolve the issue would be to file a request for an advisory opinion before the CCJA the next time a Malian court hears an application to annul an arbitral award under the UAA. The Court to which the motion for annulment of the award would have been referred will then have to stay proceedings, transmit a copy of the file, the two conflicting judgments of the CCJA on the question and documents establishing the state of national legislation on the subject to the CCJA which would then examine the case en banc and issue an opinion that would resolve the issue and unify the case law. Any lawyer in such a case may also suggest, by reasoned and detailed submissions, to the said court to stay the proceedings and to request an advisory opinion from the CCJA.

[E] Statute of Limitations

Article 27 paragraph 1 of the UAA states that "The motion for annulment is admissible as soon as the award is rendered. It ceases to be if it has not been filed within one month from the notification of the award with exequatur." Few remarks will be made on the starting point of the running of the statute of limitations (§15.02[E][2]) as well as the consequences of noncompliance with it (§15.02[E][1]).

[1] Inadmissibility of a Late Motion for Annulment

An action for annulment exercised outside the time limit after service of the award is inadmissible. The Court of Appeal which, in order to declare admissible the appeal exercised on December 26, 2007 against an award served on November 16, held that the first request for annulment based on a national provision dated November 30, 2006 suspended the time limit for appeal by one month, violated by misinterpretation Article 27 of the UAA and exposed its judgment to cassation.[34] The motion for annulment filed on July 29, 2010 against an award with *exequatur* which was served on the applicant on July 9, 2008 is inadmissible.[35]

[2] Starting Point of the Deadline from the Service of an Award with Exequatur

The fact that the Community legislator[36] did not stop at the "service of the award" but specified "the notification of the award with exequatur" implies that if the one-month statute of limitation under Article 27 must run from the service of the award, it is on the condition that this service is related to an award with *exequatur*. It follows that, in the case at hand, the arbitral award served without *exequatur* does not comply with the requirements of Article 27 of the UAA and cannot cause the statute of limitations to run.

34. Pme Financement v. Tanko, N° 049/2012, Decision, [C.C.J.A.], 2e ch., (Jun. 7, 2012).
35. Libya Oil Chad SA v. Gamma, N° 034/2017, Decision, [C.C.J.A.], 3e ch., (Mar. 9, 2017), http://www.ohada.com/jurisprudence/ohadata/J-17-168.html.
36. Community Legislator is an expression court sometimes use to designate the OHADA Legislator.

Therefore, the motion for annulment filed before the one-month statute of limitations began to run occurred within the legal time frame and is admissible.[37]

[F] Review of the Decision of the Competent Court by the CCJA

Under Article 25, paragraph 4 of the UAA, "The decision of the competent court in the State Party on the motion for annulment may only be appealed in cassation before the Common Court of Justice and Arbitration." First, an appeal in cassation before the CCJA is the only recourse against the ruling of the national competent court ruling on a motion for annulment of an arbitral award governed by the UAA (§15.02[F][1]) [1]. It does not stay the enforcement of the judgment, which has ruled on the motion for annulment (§15.02[F][2]) and must be limited to the review of the judgment itself and not the reasons of the award (§15.02[F][3]).

[1] Appeal in Cassation

The only recourse against decisions rejecting motions for annulment and defenses against the provisional enforcement of an award is an appeal in cassation, which must be brought before the CCJA. Any appeal brought against such a decision before a National Supreme Court would constitute a dilatory and illegal procedure in that it was not provided for by any text.[38]

The inadmissibility of the appeal brought against a decision rendered on the action for the annulment of an award is wrongly raised, on the ground that because of a contractual stipulation of the parties according to which "jurisdiction is given to an arbitral tribunal which will have to rule in equity as a last resort ...," any court decision rendered as a last resort is not subject to appeal and can only be appealed in cassation and that thus, only the arbitral award and not the judgment of the Court of Appeal, was subject to an appeal in cassation since it follows from Article 25 of the UAA that the decision of the Court of a State Party ruling on the motion for annulment of an arbitral award is subject to appeal in cassation before the CCJA. The objection to admissibility lacks merits, and the appeal is admissible.[39]

[2] No Stay of Proceedings

An annulled award *ipso facto* ceases to have any effect, and the annulment judge need not expressly say so in their decision, which would be redundant. The judgment ruling on the appeal to set aside an award is enforceable in that the appeal to which it may be

37. CA Pointe-Noire, Mar. 4, 2005, (Congo), *supra*, Chapter 2, fn. 10.
38. Tribunal de commerce [T.com.] [Ordinary commercial court] Pointe-Noire, Jan. 9, 2008, N° 001, http://www.ohada.com/jurisprudence/ohadata/J-13-71.html.
39. Le Bistro Family v. Rosace Marbrée, N° 196/2018, *supra*, Chapter 2, fn. 11.

subject under Article 25 paragraph 3 [which became 4] of the UAA, namely *the appeal in cassation before the CCJA, does not stay enforcement of the challenged judgment.*[40]

[3] Limitation of the Review to the Reasons of the Judgment and not the Award

In *Hotel Eda Oba v. Xoelevator*, the CCJA ruled that the petition for review of a judgment which rejected the motion for annulment of the award at hand, based on the alleged ground that the challenged judgment does not state the reasons for which the challenge to the arbitral award itself was dismissed must be rejected, where it is established that in reality, the petitioner was criticizing the reasons of the arbitral award and not the reasons of the decision that ruled on the challenge against the arbitral award.[41] This decision is another reminder that any challenge that would lead a court to review the merit of an arbitral award will not succeed, as highlighted in Chapter 14 *supra* (*see* §14.04[B][1][ii]).

[G] Supplementary Jurisdiction of the CCJA for the Motion for Annulment

In order to ensure swiftness in the proceedings, the OHADA Legislator has given a supplementary jurisdiction to the CCJA to handle any motion for annulment if the national court to which it has been referred fails to rule within three months. Article 27, paragraph 2 of the UAA states to that effect that:

> The competent court rules within three (03) months of its referral. *If that court fails to rule within that time period, it is divested of the case and the action may be brought before the Common Court of Justice and Arbitration within the next fifteen (15) days.* The latter must rule within a maximum of six months of referral. In that case, the time limits specified in the Rules of procedure of the Common Court of Justice and Arbitration are reduced by half.[42]

The framing of the motion for annulment within a time frame is an innovation by the OHADA Legislator intended to introduce swiftness into the arbitration procedure. Thus, after three months if the national court to which the motion for annulment has been referred has not ruled, the matter can be referred to the CCJA. In this case, it is necessary to determine in what capacity the CCJA will rule under such circumstances: would that be a decision equivalent to that of the competent court to which the matter

40. CA Pointe-Noire, Mar. 4, 2005, (Congo), *supra*, Chapter 2 fn. 10. [Emphasis added].
41. Hotel Eda Oba v. Xoelevator, N° 094/2017, Decision, [C.C.J.A.], 2e ch., (Apr. 27, 2017). *See also* Agence pour la Sécurité de la Navigation Aérienne en Afrique et à Madagascar v. Snack Bags, N° 011/2015, Decision, [C.C.J.A.], 2e ch., (Apr. 2, 2015). For a recent ruling of the CCJA dismissing the petition for review of a judgment which rejected the motion for annulment of a challenged award, *see* Vivo Energy Mali v. Fasogaz, N° 037/2020, Decision, [C.C.J.A.], 1e ch., (Feb. 13, 2020). And for a decision which dismissed the appeal in cassation against a decision which annulled an arbitral award, *see* Société Africaine des Relations Commerciales et Industrielles v. Atlantique Telecom, N° 177/2020, Decision, [C.C.J.A.], 1e ch., (May 28, 2020).
42. [Emphasis added].

would have been initially referred and which would not have not ruled within the allotted time and which, therefore, would be subject to an appeal in cassation before the CCJA? Or would it be a decision of last resort? The applicable rules do not specify this, but the second hypothesis seems more appropriate because the CCJA remains a cassation court, the decision of which is subject to no further appeal[43], and it will make no sense to make an exception in this case.

The fact that the CCJA can perform de novo review of cases after cassation, (thus putting itself exceptionally in the shoes of a trial judge or Court of Appeal, depending on the circumstances) should not be an excuse to transform it into a trier of fact or a lower court, at the risk of making the procedures cumbersome and rendering the whole OHADA legal system counterproductive. Consequently, it should be considered that when it has to rule to make up for the deficiency of a national court at the end of the three-month period (regardless of the cause), the CCJA decides as a last resort on the challenge of the award.

As a result, it is possible that in some cases (delaying tactics of a party or possible difficulties affecting the functioning of the local court), things happen in such a way as to prevent the competent national courts from ruling within the three-month time limit, which would automatically make the CCJA competent if it were referred to by a party. Some parties may be tempted to take advantage of this possibility with the risk, in the long run, of a "bottleneck of the CCJA" if it were to be called upon from all sides for this purpose.

This is so because the parties always have an interest in the CCJA deciding directly and once and for all on an appeal without having to exhaust the appeal before the national court against the decision of which a possible appeal in cassation would be lodged before the CCJA. This represents a considerable saving of time and money for the parties. It would, therefore, be necessary to be able to rely on the swiftness of national courts so as to avoid indirectly burdening the CCJA and depriving the parties of a double degree of jurisdiction, even if the latter might have an interest in it.

The last part of Article 27 paragraph 2 of the UAA specifies that the CCJA "must rule within a maximum of six months of referral," in which case "*the time limits specified in the Rules of procedure of the Common Court of Justice and Arbitration are reduced by half.*"[44] A list of those time limits likely to be involved in annulment proceedings can be found in Appendix IV *infra*.

§15.03 ANNULMENT PROCEDURE UNDER THE CCJA RULES

Four items will be presented under this section, i.e., the exclusive jurisdiction of the CCJA for the annulment of an arbitral award governed the CCJA Rules (§15.03[A]), the notification for the motion for annulment to the opposing party (§15.03[B]) and the

43. For example, that is already the case when the CCJA, after overturning judgments of courts of appeal ruling on challenges to injunction to pay orders, reviews the merits of those injunctions to pay orders under Art. 14 of the OHADA Treaty and Arts 1-15 of the Uniform Act on Debt Collection and Enforcement Measures.
44. [Emphasis added].

statute of limitations (§15.03[C]) and the timeline of the proceedings before the CCJA (§15.03[D]).

[A] Exclusive Jurisdiction of the CCJA

Article 29.1 of the CCJA Regulation on Arbitration states that "The party filing a motion for annulment of an award rendered by an arbitral tribunal under this Regulation must refer to the Court by a motion that the Court notifies the opposing party." A Court of Appeal [or any other national court] has no jurisdiction to hear the motion to annul an arbitral award rendered under the CCJA Rules, only the CCJA being competent in such a case.[45] The exclusive jurisdiction of the CCJA is so established that it has retained jurisdiction in an arbitration-related dispute of which no national jurisdiction could no longer hear.[46]

[B] Notification of the Motion to the Opposing Party

The inadmissibility of a motion for annulment of an arbitral award, raised by a defendant on the ground that they have not been properly served under to Article 29.1 of the CCJA Regulation on Arbitration must be dismissed, as long as it is established that the motion has been served to the elected domicile of the defendant, namely, to the attorney of the defendant in Abidjan. Thus, the defendant is deemed to have received notification of the motion.[47]

[C] Statute of Limitations

Under Article 29.3 of the CCJA Regulation on Arbitration, "The motion for annulment can be filed as soon as the award is rendered. It becomes inadmissible if it has not been filed within two (2) months of notification of the award under Article 25 of this Regulation." The wording of that provision suggests that there is no need for a party to the arbitration proceedings to serve the award to the opposing party before filing a motion for annulment of the award since, under Article 25 of the Regulation, the award is notified to the parties by the secretary-general of the CCJA. That notification triggers

45. CA Ouagadougou, Jun. 5, 2009, N° 34, N° 001(Burkina Faso), http://www.ohada.com/jurisprudence/ohadata/J-12-168.html.
46. *See* Societe Inter Africaine de Distribution v. Compagnie Malienne pour le Developpement des Textiles, N° 020/2013, *supra*, Chapter 14, fn. 28.
47. Société Nestle Cameroon v. Groupe Abbassi, N° 081/2019, *supra*, Chapter 14, fn. 14. In Kabamba Mulangi v. DHL Global Forwarding DR Congo, N° 127/2020, *supra*, Chapter 14, fn. 50, the CCJA ruled that failure of a petitioner to notify their motion for annulment of an arbitral award to the opposing party does not incur any penalty. However, that ruling is no more relevant because under the new version of Art. 29.1 of the CCJA Regulation on Arbitration currently in force, a motion for annulment of an arbitral award must be served to the opposing party by the registrar of the CCJA and no more by the petitioner.

the running of the statute of limitations, and any motion for annulment filed after the running of the statute is inadmissible.[48]

[D] Timeline of the Proceedings Before the CCJA

Article 29.4 of the CCJA Regulation on Arbitration States that "The Court processes the case and rules under its Rules of Procedure. In this case, the procedural time limits are reduced by half. The Court must rule on the motion for annulment within six (6) months of its referral."

Once the motion for annulment of an arbitral award is filed before the CCJA, the proceedings take place like ordinary appeals in cassation, the only difference being that the Court must rule within six months of referral and all the time limits and statutes of limitations under the Rules of Procedure of the CCJA are halved. Those time limits can be seen in Appendix IV, *infra*.

§15.04 CONSEQUENCES OF THE ANNULMENT OF ARBITRAL AWARDS

[A] Under the UAA

Article 29 of the UAA states that "In the event of the annulment of the arbitral award and unless the annulment is based on the fact that the tribunal has ruled without an arbitration agreement or on a void or expired one, it rests upon the most diligent party, if they so wishes, to initiate new arbitration proceedings in accordance with this Uniform Act."

The Court of Appeal of Abidjan (Ivory Coast) held in 2001 that "Article 29 of the UAA states that, in the event of annulment of a challenged award, it is up to the most diligent party to initiate, if it wishes, a new arbitration procedure. The Court of Appeal, which has annulled an arbitral award, cannot review the merit of the award and the parties must therefore be sent back to better avail themselves."[49]

[B] Under the CCJA Rules

The consequences of the annulment of an arbitral award governed by the CCJA Rules are dictated by Article 29.5 of the said Rules, which state that:

---

48. Kiendrebeogo v. Banque Internationale du Burkina, N° 031/2009, *supra*, Chapter 10, fn. 8, ruling that when the challenged arbitration award was rendered on Jan. 15, 2007 and notified on Jan. 31, 2007 to the counsel of the applicant, the latter had, under Art. 29.3 of the CCJA Regulation on Arbitration, and taking into account the fourteen-day distance period under the prescriptive Decision 002/99/CCJA, until Apr. 16, 2007, the first working day after Sunday, Apr. 15, 2007 to file their motion for annulment. The motion, which was not filed at the Registry of the CCJA until May 7, 2007, is inadmissible.
49. CA Abidjan, Apr. 27, 2001, N° 45, *supra*, Chapter 11, fn. 2. However, it follows from Art. 33 of the UAA that the rejection of a petition for annulment reinforces the enforceability of the challenged arbitral award (Sicim Spa Succursale Cameroun v. Trois N, N° 021/2020, Decision, [C.C.J.A.], 2^{e} ch., (Jan. 30, 2020)).

> If the Court denies recognition and res judicata effect of the award referred to it, the award is annulled.
>
> The Court reviews the case de novo and rules on the merits if the parties have requested that.
>
> If the parties have not requested de novo review, the proceedings are resumed at the request of the most diligent party, starting, if necessary, from the last step of the arbitration proceedings held valid by the Court.

Over the years, the CCJA has determined the consequences of the annulment of an arbitral award governed by its Arbitration Rules, which are currently three. First, the application for *exequatur* of an arbitral award, which is to be annulled, must be dismissed.[50]

Second, to prosper, the request for de novo review of a dispute after the annulment of an award must result from the common will of all parties[51] and clearly expressed by them. Because of the opposition of a party to the dispute and based on the contract which did not provide for the review, it must be concluded that the conditions for the application of [Article 29.5 of the CCJA Regulation on Arbitration] are not met; consequently, the request for de novo review filed by the other party to the dispute must be rejected.[52]

Finally, where a challenged arbitral award has been annulled for the absence of a valid arbitration agreement, there is no reason to start new arbitration proceedings under the aegis of the CCJA again.[53]

50. Etat du Bénin v. Société Commune de Participation, N° 104/2015, *supra*, Chapter 14, fn. 57.
51. Société Inter Africaine de Distribution v. Compagnie Malienne pour le Développement des Textiles, N° 020/2013, *supra*, Chapter 14, fn. 28.
52. Nestle Sahel v. Societe Commerciale d'Importation Azar et Salame, N° 028/2007, *supra*, Chapter 11, fn. 1.
53. Etat du Mali v. CFAO, N° 039/2014, *supra*, Chapter 1, fn. 13.

CHAPTER 16

Third-Party Opposition and Revision of Arbitral Awards

This chapter presents the other two possible recourses available against arbitral awards under OHADA Rules, which are third-party opposition (§16.01) and revision (§16.02).

§16.01 THIRD-PARTY OPPOSITION OF ARBITRAL AWARDS

[A] Under the UAA

Article 27, paragraph 5 states that "The arbitral award may be the subject of third-party opposition by any person before the court of the State Party which would have had jurisdiction in the absence of arbitration and when that award prejudices his rights." There is no available record of third-party opposition cases, and it remains to be seen in the future how things will evolve.

[B] Under the CCJA Rules

Third-party opposition to arbitral awards under the CCJA Rules is governed by Article 33 of the CCJA Regulation on Arbitration. It states:

> Third-party opposition against arbitral awards is brought before the Court. The same applies to judgments of the Court, where the Court has ruled on the merits under Article 29.5, of this Regulation.
>
> Third-party opposition is filed under Article 47[1] of the Rules of procedure of the Common Court of Justice and Arbitration.

1. Article 47 of the CCJA Rules of Procedure states:

There are no available third-party opposition cases yet, and the reader is referred to available legal scholarship on the available case law on third-party opposition under Article 47 of the CCJA Rules of Procedure.[2]

§16.02 REVISION OF ARBITRAL AWARDS

[A] Under the UAA

Article 25, paragraph 6 of the UAA states that an arbitral award:

> May also be the subject of a motion for revision before the arbitral tribunal due to the discovery of a fact likely to have a decisive influence on the settlement of the dispute and which, before the rendering of the award, was unknown to both the arbitral tribunal and the party requesting the revision. Where the arbitral tribunal can no longer be convened, the motion for revision is brought before the Court in the State Party, which would have had jurisdiction in the absence of arbitration.

Here too, there is no publicly available case handling motions for revision, and it will have to be watched in the coming years.

[B] Under the CCJA Rules

The motion for revision[3] of arbitral awards rendered under the CCJA Rules is governed by Article 32 of the CCJA Regulation on Arbitration, which states:

> Upon discovery of a fact likely to exert a decisive influence and which, prior to the rendering of the award, was unknown to the arbitral tribunal or the party

---

1. Any natural person or legal entity may *file a motion* for third party objection to a judgment rendered without it being appealed, if this judgment is prejudicial *their* rights.
2. The provisions of Articles 23 and 27 of these Rules apply to the *motion* for third-party objection. It must in addition:
   a) specify the *challenged* judgment;
   b) state how this judgment is prejudicial to the rights of the opposing third party;
   c) state the reasons why the third party was unable to participate in the main dispute.
   The *motion must* be filed against all the parties to the main litigation.
3. The *challenged* judgment *must* be modified insofar as it upheld the third-party proceedings. The original of the judgment on third-party objection *must* be appended to the minutes of the *challenged* judgment. Mention of the judgment on the third-party judgment must be made in the margins of the original of the *challenged* judgment.

2. *See* for example, Mahutodji Jimmy Vital Kodo, *Code Pratique Francis Lefebvre OHADA. Traité, Actes Uniformes et Règlements Annotés, 20-21*, 195-198, Editions Francis Lefebvre, 2019 **Invalid source specified**.
3. The word 'revision' has been preferred to 'review' which was used in the translated version of the CCJA Regulation, to avoid any confusion with the 'review' of an award or a judgment. It is commonly used. *See* Nathalie Voser and Anya George, *Revision of Arbitral Awards*, In 'Post Award Issues,' ASA Bulletin Special Series N° 38, 43-74, https://www.swlegal.ch/media/filer_public/32/63/32637dcf-3c36-46a1-b8bf-98f3cdf21573/09-chapter-3.pdf [accessed on Apr. 27, 2020 at 15:32] (Voser & Anya); (Fouchard, Gaillard, & Goldman, 1999), *supra*, Chapter 1, fn. 26, p. 919.

> requesting the revision, a motion for revision may be filed against the award before the Secretary General. The Secretary General forwards the motion for revision to the arbitral tribunal.
>
> In the absence of an agreement by the parties on the appointment of a new arbitral tribunal:
>
> a) where the arbitral tribunal was made up of a sole arbitrator and cannot be reconvened, the Court appoints a sole arbitrator to rule on the application for revision;
> b) where the arbitral tribunal was made up of three arbitrators and cannot be reconvened, the Court appoints, after consultation with the parties, either a new tribunal made up of three arbitrators or a single arbitrator to rule on the motion for revision;
> c) where the arbitral tribunal was made up of three arbitrators and one or more of these arbitrators cannot be reconvened, the Court appoints, after consultation with the parties, arbitrators to complete the arbitral tribunal which rules on the motion for revision.

There are at least two cases involving the revision of an arbitral award. It has been held in *Etat du Niger v. Société Africard Co Limited* that the CCJA can stay the enforcement of an arbitral award where the opening of the revision proceedings against its judgment on the motion for annulment of the said award may, as a consequence, call into question the award itself as related to that judgment by a relationship which is not at arm's length.[4] As a rule, unless the provisional enforcement of the award has been ordered by the arbitral tribunal, the filing of the motion for annulment stays the enforcement of the arbitral awards until the CCJA has ruled. In the case at hand, since the challenged awards are not provisionally enforceable and their enforcement may have irreparable consequences, it is necessary to stay the enforcement as requested.[5]

In *Fonds Africain de Garantie et de Coopération Economique v. Banque Sénégalo-Tunisienne*,[6] the CCJA declared the petition for revision of an arbitral award inadmissible on the ground that the alleged new fact was already brought to the attention of the petitioner and was not "new fact" justifying the revision sought.

4. Referring to the French expression "*lien de dépendance necessaire.*" *See* the glossary, *infra*.
5. Etat du Niger v. Société Africard Co Limited, N° 087/2018, *supra*, Chapter 2, fn. 23.
6. Fonds Africain de Garantie et de Coopération Economique v. Banque Sénégalo-Tunisienne, N° 068/2013, Decision, [C.C.J.A.], Ass. plen., (Nov. 14, 2013).

PART V Recognition, Enforcement & Other Effects of Awards

This final part of the book presents the additional formalities that need to be accomplished before the enforcement of an award can take place (Chapter 17) and specific other effects and situations that may sometimes affect certain arbitral award, i.e., preclusions of claims, lis pendens and stare decisis (Chapter 18).

CHAPTER 17
Recognition and Enforcement of Arbitral Awards

The main step toward successful enforcement of an arbitral award is to prove the existence of said award (§17.01) and ensure none of the grounds for refusing to recognize the award is present (§17.02). Sometimes, the recognition proceedings must be suspended pending a motion to annul an award (§17.03), which is why the special regime for jurisdiction and terms of recognition and enforcement of awards must be presented (§17.04), followed with the recourse against the decision ruling on the request for *exequatur* of an award (§17.05) and finally the recognition and enforcement of or arbitral award not rendered under OHADA Rules (§17.06).

§17.01 PROOF OF ARBITRAL AWARDS

[A] Under the UAA

The first three paragraphs of Article 31 of the UAA state:

> Recognition and *exequatur* of the arbitral award assume that the party availing itself of the existence of the award establishes the existence of the arbitral award.
>
> *The existence of the arbitral award is established by the production of its original accompanied by the arbitration agreement or copies of these documents meeting the requirements for their authenticity.*[1]
>
> If those documents are not written in the official language(s) of the State Party where the *exequatur* is requested, the party must submit a certified translation by a translator registered on the list of experts established by the competent courts.

The text does not specify the conditions for assessing the authenticity of an award for the purpose of establishing its existence, and it may be necessary to refer to the local

1. [Emphasis added].

legislation of the seat of the arbitration proceedings or the place where the need to establish the existence of the award arises, which could possibly be the jurisdiction in which the enforcement of the award is sought. However, the parties are advised to request several originals from the arbitral tribunal or the arbitration center, where applicable, including certified true or legalized copies if available.

[B] Under the CCJA Rules

On the issue of proof of an arbitral award, Article 28 of the CCJA Regulation on Arbitration states that "The original of any award rendered under this Regulation is lodged with the Secretary General. In all cases not specifically covered by this Regulation, the Court and the arbitral tribunal proceed by drawing their inspiration from this Regulation and making their best efforts to ensure that the award is enforceable."

§17.02 GROUNDS FOR REFUSING TO RECOGNIZE ARBITRAL AWARDS

[A] Under the UAA

Under Article 31 paragraph 4 of the UAA, there is only one ground for refusing to recognize an award, as the text states that "Recognition and exequatur are denied *if the award is manifestly contrary to an international public policy rule.*"[2]

[B] Under the CCJA Rules

Under the CCJA Arbitration Rules, "Exequatur is not granted if a motion for annulment of the award has already been filed under Article 29 abovementioned and is pending before the Court. In such a case, both motions are joined."[3] But the real grounds for refusing to recognize an arbitral award are stated under Article 30.5, according to which "Exequatur can be denied only in the following cases:

a) if the arbitral tribunal has ruled without an arbitration agreement or on a null or expired agreement;
b) if the arbitral tribunal has ruled without complying with the mission entrusted to it;
c) if the adversarial principle has been breached;
d) if the arbitral award is contrary to international public policy."

Those grounds for refusing to recognize an award under the CCJA Regulation on Arbitration are covered in Chapter 15 dedicated to the annulment grounds of arbitral awards under Article 29 of the Regulation.

2. [Emphasis added].
3. CCJA Regulation on Arbitration, Art. 30.2, para. 2.

§17.03 SUSPENSION OF RECOGNITION PROCEEDINGS PENDING A MOTION TO ANNUL AN AWARD

[A] Under the UAA

Under Article 28, paragraph 1 of the UAA, "Except where the provisional enforcement of the award has been ordered by the arbitral tribunal, *the filing of the annulment action stays the enforcement of the award* until the competent court in the State Party or the Common Court of Justice and Arbitration, as the case may be, has ruled."[4]

[B] Under the CCJA Rules

Article 30.2, paragraph 3 of the CCJA Regulation on Arbitration states that "Unless the provisional enforcement of the award has been ordered by the arbitral tribunal, a motion for annulment suspends the enforcement of the arbitral award until the Court has ruled."

§17.04 JURISDICTION AND TERMS FOR RECOGNITION AND ENFORCEMENT OF AWARDS GOVERNED BY OHADA RULES

Under the UAA, the national competent court has jurisdiction for recognition and *exequatur* (§17.04[A]), and under the CCJA Rules, the President of the Court or a delegate judge has jurisdiction (§17.04[B]).

[A] Recognition and Exequatur by the National Competent Court under the UAA

Under Article 30 of the UAA, "The arbitral award is enforceable only by virtue of an *exequatur* decision issued by the competent court in the State Party." That "competent court" must be determined on a case-by-case basis under the Civil Procedure Code of each State Party to the Treaty or any other local legislation. It may be assumed that in many of those States, the competent court would be the same one for the annulment of arbitral awards. *Exequatur* is deemed to have been granted if the state court to which a request for recognition or *exequatur* has been referred, has not ruled within fifteen (15) days from the day of referral. If *exequatur* is granted, or if the referral court remains silent until the end of the fifteen (15) days as mentioned above, the most diligent party refers to the chief clerk or the competent authority in the State Party in order to affix the executory formula upon the origin of the award. The procedure relating to the request for *exequatur* is not adversarial.[5]

Just as the CCJA may systematically become competent for actions for annulment where national courts to which the action is referred fail to rule within the allocated

4. [Emphasis added].
5. UAA, Art. 31, para. 5-6.

time limit, any dysfunction preventing those national competent courts from a timely ruling could transform these jurisdictions into "automatic dispensers of *exequatur.*" Any party who would have an interest in requesting the annulment of an award should, therefore, file their motion for annulment as soon as the award is rendered, as permitted by Article 27 paragraph 1 of the UAA. This is particularly the case if the party concerned wishes to prevent the provisional enforcement, which may have been ordered by the Court.

[B] Recognition and Exequatur by the President of the CCJA or a Delegate Judge under the CCJA Rules

Under the CCJA Rules, *Exequatur* may be granted upon an award as soon as it has been rendered. It is requested by a *motion to the President of the Court*, with a copy to the secretary-general. The latter immediately forwards to the Court the documents allowing the establishment of the existence of the arbitral award and the arbitration agreement to be established.[6] The President of the CCJA or any other judge of the Court who has received a delegation from the President may issue *exequatur.*[7] Available case law indicates a request for *exequatur* addressed to the President of the CCJA is valid (§17.04[B][1]. The specifics of the timeline (§17.04[B][2]) and the joinder of proceedings (§17.04[B][3]) need to be presented before some decisions granting *exequatur* (§17.04[B][4]).

[1] Validity of the Request for Exequatur Addressed to the President and Not to the Court

An applicant was right to request the *exequatur* from the President of the CCJA and not from the Court itself, since, at the date of their application, the motion for annulment of the arbitral award had not yet been filed by the opposing party. Under these conditions and Articles 30.2, 30.4 and 30.5 of the Arbitration Rules of the Court, only the President of the said CCJA or the judge delegated by him to that effect is empowered to grant or deny, upon non-adversarial proceedings, *exequatur* by reasoned order. Therefore, the *exequatur* request is admissible.[8]

[2] Timeline

It is possible to grant *exequatur* as soon as the award is rendered (§17.04[B][2][i]) because there is no time limit to grant *exequatur* (§17.04[B][2][ii]).

6. CCJA Regulation on Arbitration, Art. 30.1, paras. 1-2. [Emphasis added].
7. *Id.*, Art. 30.2.
8. Benin Control v. Etat du Bénin, N° 103/2015, *supra*, Chapter 6, fn. 18; Etat du Bénin v. Société Commune de Participation, N° 104/2015, *supra*, Chapter 14, fn. 57.

[i] Possibility of Granting Exequatur as Soon as the Award Is Rendered

Since awards rendered under the aegis of the CCJA have become res judicata and are considered as final decisions because they are no longer subject to suspensive remedies, they may be subject to a motion for *exequatur* as soon as they are rendered in accordance with Article 30 of the CCJA Regulation on Arbitration, whether or not the arbitration agreement stipulated that, without this possibility being an obstacle to the filing of a motion for annulment of the award at hand.[9]

[ii] No Time Limit to Grant Exequatur

In addition to the fact that an *exequatur* order cannot have the effect of depriving a party of their right to seek annulment of the arbitral award, Article 30 of the CCJA Regulation on Arbitration provides no time frame for issuing the *exequatur* order, the only requirement relating to the connection between the *exequatur* and annulment proceedings arises from Article 30.3 [now 30.2, paragraph 2], which states that "exequatur is not granted if a motion for annulment of the award has already been filed under Article 29 abovementioned and is pending before the Court." Since in the case at hand, no motion for annulment of the award has been filed before the CCJA that could impede the issuance of the *exequatur*, on the date at which the *exequatur* order was made, the argument based on the violation of Article 29.3 of the CCJA Regulation on Arbitration in that it "deprives [the applicant] of their legitimate and fundamental right to challenge the award ... as long as [the *exequatur* order] ... is maintained" must be rejected.[10]

[3] Joinder of Proceedings

It is in the interests of the parties and of fair justice that the proceedings relating to the request for *exequatur* and the motion for annulment of the same arbitral award be joined and settled by a single decision[11] and also where the two proceedings are linked.[12]

9. Etat du Mali v. ABS International Corporate, CCJA, N° 011/2011, *supra*, Chapter 14, fn. 51.
10. Planor Afrique v. Atlantique Telecom, N° 03/2011, *supra*, Chapter 14, fn. 134.
11. République de Guinée Equatoriale v. Commercial Bank Guinea Ecuatorial, N° 02/2011, Order, [C.C.J.A.], (Sep. 30, 2011), http://www.ohada.com/jurisprudence/ohadata/J-13-142.html.
12. Societe Inter Africaine de Distribution v. Compagnie Malienne pour le Developpement des Textiles, N° 020/2013, *supra*, Chapter 14, fn. 28; Benin Control v. Etat du Bénin, N° 103/2015, *supra*, Chapter 6 fn. 18; Etat du Bénin v. Société Commune de Participation, N° 104/2015, *supra*, Chapter 14, fn. 57; Etat du Mali v. Seaquest-Infotel Mali, N° 027/2017, *supra*, Chapter 12, fn. 39; Société Nestle Cameroon v. Groupe Abbassi, N° 081/2019, *supra*, Chapter 14, fn. 14.

[4] *Decisions Granting Exequatur*

Available case law shows that *exequatur* is granted sometimes by the President of the CCJA (§17.04[B][4][i]) sometimes by the Full Court (§17.04[B][4][ii]), in the absence of a challenge to the award at hand (§17.04[B][4][iii]) or where the challenge is either inadmissible or lacking merits (§17.04[B][4][iv]).

[i] Exequatur *Granted by Order of the President of the CCJA*

In some cases, the President of the CCJA held that in accordance with Article 30.2 of the CCJA Regulation on Arbitration, *exequatur* is granted on the occasion of a non-adversarial procedure by order of the President of the CCJA or of the judge delegated for this purpose and confers enforceability on the award enforceable in all States Parties, to grant *exequatur* by order.[13]

[ii] Exequatur *Granted by a Judgment of the CCJA*

In *Société Nestle Cameroon v. Groupe Abbassi,*[14] the CCJA granted *exequatur* to an arbitral award after having joined the challenge proceedings and the application for *exequatur* and found the award was valid.

[iii] Absence of a Challenge to the Award

In the absence of a challenge of an award made under the aegis of the CCJA within the time limit set by the provisions of the CCJA Arbitration Rules, *exequatur* must be granted to the award, which becomes enforceable in all the States Parties to the Treaty afterward.[15]

[iv] Inadmissible Motion for Annulment or Lacking Merit

The enforcement of a challenged award must be ordered when the motion for annulment of the said award has been declared inadmissible[16] or rejected on the merits.[17]

---

13. Societe Inter Africaine de Distribution v. Compagnie Malienne pour le Developpement des Textiles, N° 01/2015, Order, [C.C.J.A.], http://www.ohada.com/jurisprudence/ohadata/J-16-199.html; Gillet v. Bourse Régionale des Valeurs Mobilières, N° 003/2015, Order, [C.C.J.A.], (Jun. 4, 2015), http://www.ohada.com/jurisprudence/ohadata/J-16-201.html.
14. Société Nestle Cameroon v. Groupe Abbassi, N° 081/2019, *supra*, Chapter 14, fn. 14.
15. Atlantique Télécom v. Planor Afrique, N° 016/2009, Order, [C.C.J.A.], (Aug. 19, 2009), http://www.ohada.com/jurisprudence/ohadata/J-10-187.html.
16. République de Guinée Equatoriale v. Commercial Bank Guinea Ecuatorial, N° 012/2011, *supra*, Chapter 15, fn. 5.
17. Societe des Huileries du Benin v. Societe Nationale pour la Promotion Agricole, N° 06/2011, Order, [C.C.J.A.], (Dec. 21, 2011), http://www.ohada.com/jurisprudence/ohadata/J-13-178.html. *See also* Attijari bank Senegal v. Senegal, N° 002/2009, Order, [C.C.J.A.], (Jan. 1, 2009),

§17.05 RECOURSE AGAINST THE DECISION RULING ON THE REQUEST FOR *EXEQUATUR*

There is no recourse available against the decision which has granted *exequatur* (§17.05[A]), but any decision denying *exequatur* may be challenged before the CCJA (§17.05[B]).

[A] Absence of Recourse If *Exequatur* Is Granted

The decision of the competent court of the State Party[18] as well as the one of the President of the CCJA or the Judge delegate[19] granting *exequatur* cannot be appealed.

[B] Referral of the Decision Denying *Exequatur* to the CCJA

Whether it has been rendered by the national competent court's under the UAA (§17.05[B][1]) or, under the CCJA Rules, by the President of the CCJA or the delegate judge (§17.05[B][2]), the decision denying *exequatur* of an award can be challenged before the CCJA.

[1] Referral of the National Competent Court's Decision under the UAA to the CCJA

The decision which rejects *exequatur* can be challenged only before the Common Court of Justice and Arbitration.[20] Since the UAA does not specify the regimen of such action, it must be filed and handled like an ordinary appeal in cassation against the decision of a court of a State Party under Article 14 of the Treaty.

The lis pendens objection to the jurisdiction of the CCJA, on the grounds that the order made by the judge responsible for the enforcement was appealed and that, in so doing, the CCJA must divest itself for the benefit of that Court of Appeal lacks merit, since according to Article 32 of the UAA "the decision which denies *exequatur* is only subject to appeal in cassation before the CCJA" and it follows from the appellant's reply brief dated 21 July 2014 that by the judgment of 14 May 2014, of which the extract of the Court record[21] drawn up on 20 June 2014 is produced in the file, that the Court of Appeal declared the appeal inadmissible.[22]

---

http://www.ohada.com/jurisprudence/ohadata/J-16-93.html; République de Guinée Equatoriale v. Commercial Bank Guinea Ecuatorial, N° 012/2011, Decision, [C.C.J.A.], Ass. plen., (Nov. 29, 2011), http://www.ohada.com/jurisprudence/ohadata/J-12-193.html; Etat du Mali v. Seaquest-Infotel Mali, N° 027/2017, *supra,* Chapter 12, fn. 39.

18. UAA, Art. 32, para. 2.
19. CCJA Regulation on Arbitration, Art. 30.4.
20. UAA, Art. 32, para. 1.
21. *See* the French "*extrait du plumitif*" in the glossary, *infra.*
22. Geodis Projects Cameroon v. Tenga, N° 166/2017, Decision, [C.C.J.A.], 1e ch., (Jul. 27, 2017).

It is wrong to raise an objection of inadmissibility based on "the extinction of the subject-matter of the appeal in cassation" on the basis of the order granting *exequatur* to the challenged arbitral award, and of the bailiff's report noting the enforcement of the said award in Libreville, because the enforcement of an arbitral award does not confer it any irrevocable character since under Article 32 paragraph 3 of the UAA the motion for annulment of the award automatically entails, within the limits of the referral to the competent judge of the State Party, appeal against the decision granting *exequatur*. Consequently, the author of the motion for annulment of the award, which led to the judgment under appeal, has a definite interest in the examination of their appeal, and the objection of inadmissibility must be dismissed.[23]

[2] Referral of the Decision of the President of the CCJA or the Delegate Judge to the CCJA

Article 30. paragraph 3 of the CCJA Regulation on Arbitration states that:

> If exequatur is denied, the party requesting exequatur may refer the matter to the Court within fifteen (15) days of the notification of the rejection of its motion. This time limit is reduced to three (03) days if the appeal relates to *exequatur* of an award of the arbitral tribunal on provisional or conservatory measures. The party requesting exequatur notifies the appeal to the opposing party.

§17.06 RECOGNITION AND ENFORCEMENT OF ARBITRAL AWARDS NOT RENDERED UNDER OHADA RULES

Under Article 34 of the UAA, "arbitral awards rendered on the basis of rules different from those provided for in this Uniform Act are recognized in the States Parties under the conditions provided for by international conventions possibly applicable and, in the absence thereof, under the same conditions as those provided in this Uniform Act." This provision means that the recognition and enforcement of any award rendered under a different rule than the OHADA Rules are not primarily governed by the UAA. The UAA comes into play only in the absence of specific provisions or guidelines in the laws UAA governing the award, on a supplementary basis. Despite this, it has been suggested that "awards rendered outside the OHADA zone will be recognized and executed by the local judge pursuant to Article 31 of the 2018 UAA, like any award rendered in one of the OHADA Member States."[24] On the contrary, however, the settled case law of the CCJA suggests a rather strict application of Article 34 of the UAA singling out awards rendered outside the OHADA geographical scope, as will be demonstrated by the following cases concerning an award governed by the New York Convention (§17.06[A]) and another one under the aegis of the ICC (§17.06[B]).

23. Le Bistro Family v. Rosace Marbrée, N° 196/2018, *supra*, Chapter 2, fn. 11.
24. Michael W. Bühler, '*Out of Africa: The 2018 OHADA Arbitration and Mediation Law Reform,*' *supra*, Chapter 5, fn. 38 at 522 (Bühler, 2018).

[A] Award for the Exequatur of Which the New York Convention Is Applicable

In *Vodacom International v. Congolese Wireless Network*, the CCJA held that it should be noted automatically that, in accordance with Article 34 of the UAA, the *exequatur* of arbitration awards handed down in third states to the Treaty[25] is carried out according to international conventions if the state where the award was rendered and the State Party where the award is invoked are linked in this area. In this case, Belgium (the country where the award was rendered) and the Democratic Republic of Congo (country of enforcement) being bound by international conventions (notably that of New York as of June 10, 1958), the President of a court has wrongfully relied upon the UAA to deny *exequatur* of the award. The challenged order of the President of that court must be quashed, and the parties returned to the same and similar condition they were in prior to that order.[26]

[B] Award Rendered Under the Aegis of the International Chamber of Commerce

In *Geodis Projects Cameroon v. Tenga*, the CCJA held that the enforcement of an award rendered by the International Court of the International Chamber of Commerce in Paris in a dispute between two Cameroonian corporations is governed by the United Nations Convention for the Recognition and Enforcement of Foreign Arbitral Awards, which binds France and Cameroon, and not by the provisions of Article 34 of the Agreement on cooperation in justice matters, between the United Republic of Cameroon and the French Republic, which conditions the recognition of judgment and decisions rendered in civil, social or commercial matters by the courts sitting on the territories of the two States, to the exhaustion of the remedies. This is the case since the conditions of the abovementioned Cooperation Agreement were not applicable in this case because Article 28 paragraph 6 of the Arbitration Regulation of the International Chamber of Commerce of Conciliation and Arbitration to which the parties had freely chosen to submit their dispute stipulates that "any award is binding on the parties [;] by submitting their dispute to these rules, the parties undertake to enforce the award to be

25. A third State to the OHADA Treaty refers to a State or country which has not signed and ratified the Treaty and on the territory of which the Treaty and the Uniform Acts are not enforceable. In other words, any country outside the seventeen States Parties.
26. Vodacom International v. Congolese Wireless Network, N° 003/2017, Decision, [C.C.J.A.], 2[e] ch., (Jan. 26, 2017), http://www.ohada.com/jurisprudence/ohadata/J-17-149.html. For a similar example of an award rendered in a country not Party to the Treaty and governed by the New York Convention, *see* Namemco Energy Limited v. VODACOM International Limited, N° 069/2020, Decision, [C.C.J.A.], 1[e] ch., (Mar. 12, 2020), in which the CCJA held that the UAA is not applicable in the Democratic Republic of the Congo to an award rendered in France under the ICC Rules. Thus, it is wrong that the President of the Commercial Court of Kinshasa Gombe applied Art. 1 of the UAA to such dispute which does not raise the application of either the Treaty, or a Regulation or Uniform Act and its ruling must be overturned. On de novo review, it must be noted that the case does not concern OHADA law, and the CCJA must do what the Court of Appeal should have done, *i.e.*, to decline jurisdiction.

rendered without delay, and are deemed to have waived all remedies to which they can validly renounce." By relying on Article 34 of the UAA to deny the enforcement of such an award, the competent judge of the Court of First Instance violated, by the refusal of the application, the aforementioned Article 34 and set out their decision to be overturned. It is, therefore, necessary to quash the challenged order and to say that there is no reason for de novo review.[27]

27. Geodis Projects Cameroon v. Tenga, N° 166/2017, Decision, [C.C.J.A.], 1e ch., (Jul. 27, 2017). *See also* République du Benin v. Société Générale de Surveillance, N° 068/2020, *supra*, Chapter 14, fn. 134, in which the CCJA recently relied upon Art. 26 e) of the UAA to annul a partial award rendered under the ICC rules (likely used as a supplement to the UAA by the parties), for breach of international public policy.

CHAPTER 18

Preclusions, Lis Pendens and Stare Decisis

The preclusive effect of the award will be presented first (§18.01), followed by the preclusive effect of the decisions of the CCJA (§18.02).

§18.01 PRECLUSIVE EFFECT OF THE AWARD

Article 23 of the UAA states that "As soon as it is rendered, the arbitral award has res judicata effect regarding the dispute it settles."

Under Article 27 of the CCJA Regulation on Arbitration:

> 27.1 Any arbitral award rendered under this Regulation is final and binding on the parties and has res judicata effect in the territory of each State Party, in the same way as decisions rendered by the courts of the State. It may be enforced on the territory of any of the States Parties.
>
> 27.2 By submitting their dispute to this Regulation, the parties undertake to enforce the upcoming award without delay.
>
> 27.3 The arbitral tribunal may, by a reasoned decision, order or deny the provisional enforcement of the award if such enforcement has been requested.

The binding nature of an award regularly rendered under the CCJA Arbitration Rules is emphasized for the parties. This compulsory character already existed implicitly before the 2017 reform. Article 27, paragraph 2 of the Rules reiterates the direct consequence of the choice of institutional arbitration governed by the CCJA Rules of Arbitration (under Article 10, paragraph 1 of the Rules), namely the obligation for the parties to submit to the Rules and their annexes and above all, to enforce the resulting award without delay. The binding nature of the award upon the parties embodies the preclusive effect of the award with regard to the matters resolved.

§18.02 PRECLUSIVE EFFECT OF THE DECISIONS OF THE CCJA

As it was presented in the introduction, *supra*, the decisions of the CCJA are final and binding, under Article 20 of the Treaty, which states that "The judgments of the Common Court of Justice and Arbitration have the power of res judicata and enforceability. They are enforced in the territory of each of the States Parties under the same conditions as national legal decisions. In the same case, no decision contrary to a judgment of the Common Court of Justice and Arbitration may be enforced in the territory of a State Party." Some comments on the principle will be made (§18.02[A]), followed by some cases illustrating its implementation in various situations (§18.02[B]).

[A] Principle

The principle of res judicata is violated when a court reviews a case already decided by the competent courts by a final decision.[1]

[B] Effects of Res Judicata Attached to the Decisions of the CCJA

Three main rules apply: the judgment of the CCJA always has primacy over the judgment of a national court in the event of a conflict between the two (§18.02[B][1]); it is impossible to enforce a judgment rendered in violation of the jurisdiction of the CCJA in the OHADA States Parties (§18.02[B][2]) and any new appeal in cassation against a case already decided by the CCJA is inadmissible (§18.02[B][3]).

[1] Primacy of the Judgment of the CCJA in the Event of Conflict with a Judgment of a National Court

In the event of a conflict between a decision of the CCJA judgment and another decision, the decision contrary to that of the CCJA cannot be enforced and must be annulled. This is so, for example, when it is established that it is the same Judgment No. 14 of November 12, 2008, retracted on January 25, 2012 by the Bobo-Dioulasso Court of Appeal, which had been referred to the CCJA censorship, which dismissed the appeal dated December 4, 2012. Thus, the CCJA's rejection decision which has the effect of consolidating the judicial recovery ordered by Judgment No. 14 is clearly in contradiction with that referred to who orders the liquidation; it follows that the judgment of January 25, 2012 cannot be enforced and must, therefore, be annulled.[2]

1. Maersk v. Akpa Tchotch, N° 082/2019, Decision, [C.C.J.A.], 1e ch. (Mar. 28, 2019).
2. Kabore v. Cori, N° 080/2015, Decision, [C.C.J.A.], Ass. plén. (Apr. 29, 2015), http://www.ohada.com/jurisprudence/ohadata/J-16-80.html.

[2] Impossible Enforcement of a Judgment Rendered in Violation of the Jurisdiction of the CCJA in the OHADA States Parties

In *Société Générale de Banques en Guinée v. Hann*, it has been held that since a decision rendered in defiance of Article 16 of the Treaty cannot be enforced in the territory of a State Party, in accordance with Article 20 of the said Treaty, the judgment rendered by a National Supreme Court in defiance of the jurisdiction of the CCJA when the matter was already referred to the CCJA could not have res judicata effect, because of the stay of the proceedings before the national court operated by the referral to the CCJA.[3] Likewise, the judgment rendered in violation of Articles 18 paragraph 3 and Article 20 of the Treaty relating to the harmonization of business law in Africa is null and of no effect and cannot have any influence on the judgment of the CCJA of December 17, 2015 with which it is in contradiction.[4]

[3] Inadmissibility of New Appeals in Cassation

Here too, two rules illustrate this inadmissibility: the inadmissibility of an appeal against a judgment already reviewed by the CCJA (§18.02[B][3][i]) and res judicata prevents the review of the same judgment which has been the subject of parallel appeals in cassation before the CCJA and the national Supreme Court of a State Party to the Treaty (§18.02[B][3][ii]).

[i] Inadmissibility of an Appeal Against a Judgment Already Reviewed by the CCJA

Under Articles 20 of the Treaty and 41 of the CCJA Rules of Procedure, judgments of the CCJA have res judicata effect, enforceability and binding force from the day of their rendering. It follows that an appeal in cassation brought by a person, acting by the same legal representative and assisted by the same counsel, against a judgment which has already been reviewed by the CCJA through judgment, is inadmissible.[5]

Also, a judgment of the CCJA, which has acquired res judicata effect, cannot be appealed. This was the case when the plaintiff filed a third-party appeal against Judgment No. 083 rendered on December 4, 2012 by the CCJA, which consolidated the receivership[6] of the co-defendant company ordered by Judgment No. 014/08 of November 12, 2008 by dismissing the appeal against that judgment; in addition, by Judgment No. 080/2015 rendered on April 29, 2015 in the same case, the CCJA overturned Judgment No. 006 rendered on January 25, 2012 by the Court of Appeal of

3. Société Générale de Banques en Guinée v. Hann, N° 067/2015, Decision, [C.C.J.A.], Ass. plén. (Apr. 29, 2015), http://www.ohada.com/jurisprudence/ohadata/J-16-67.html.
4. Maisons Sans Frontières v. Elco Construction, N° 188/2017, Decision, [C.C.J.A.], 2e ch. (Jul. 27, 2017).
5. Total Guinée v. Société Pétrolière de Guinée, N° 124/2015, Decision, [C.C.J.A.], 1_e ch. (Oct. 29, 2015), http://www.ohada.com/jurisprudence/ohadata/J-16-1117.html.
6. From the French 'redresement judiciaire'; *see* the glossary, *infra*.

Bobo-Dioulasso on the third-party opposition of plaintiff, which retracted Judgment No. 014/08, stating that it was in clear contradiction with Judgment No. 006 and that consequently could not be enforced and that nothing remains to be tried. It follows from the above that only Judgment No. 083 of December 4, 2012 consolidating the receivership remains valid and that the various proceedings, in this case, are connected to the same litigators. Thus, it is necessary to take notice of res judicata attached to the Judgment No. 083/2012.[7]

[ii] Res Judicata Prevents the Review of the Same Judgment Which Has Been the Subject of Parallel Appeals in Cassation

When, in parallel with the appeal before the national cassation court, the applicant has lodged a second appeal in cassation before the CCJA, which has been resolved by judgment, the request for annulment of the decision of the national court of cassation must be declared inadmissible ex officio because of res judicata effect of the decision of the CCJA.[8]

7. Compagnie d'Opérations et de Reconditionnement Industriel v. Kabore, N° 120/2018, Decision, [C.C.J.A.], 1e ch. (May 31, 2018).
8. Africof v. Banque Islamique de Guinée, N° 080/2017, Decision, [C.C.J.A.], 1e ch. (Apr. 27, 2019).

Appendices

APPENDIX I

Title IV of the OHADA Treaty on Arbitration

Title IV. ARBITRATION

Article 21. Under an arbitration clause or submission agreement, any party to a contract, whether one of the parties has his domicile or habitual residence in one of the States parties or whether the contract is performed or to be performed wholly or partially in the territory of one or many States Parties, may submit a contractual dispute to the arbitration procedure under this Article.

Article 22. The dispute may be settled by a sole arbitrator or by three arbitrators. In the following Articles, the term "arbitrator" refers equally to the arbitrator (s).

Where the parties have agreed that the dispute *will* be settled by a sole arbitrator, *they may appoint them* by mutual agreement subject to *confirmation* of the Court. If the parties fail to agree within thirty days *from* the notification of the request for arbitration to the other party, the arbitrator *will be* appointed by the Court.

Where three arbitrators *have been stipulated*, each party, *in the request for arbitration or in the answer to the request, appoints* one independent arbitrator, subject to *confirmation* of the Court. If one of the parties fails to appoint an arbitrator, the *appointment is made* by the Court. The third arbitrator, who *presides over* the arbitral tribunal, *is* appointed by the Court, unless the parties have agreed that the arbitrators they *have appointed* would appoint the third arbitrator within a given time limit.

In *the latter case, it is up to the Court to* confirm the third arbitrator. *If, at the end of the deadline set by the parties or assigned by the Court, the arbitrators appointed by the parties* have failed to agree, the third arbitrator *is* appointed by the Court.

If the parties have not agreed *on* the number of arbitrators, the Court *appoints* a sole arbitrator, unless the dispute appears to justify the appointment of three arbitrators. In *the* latter case, the parties *have fifteen days to appoint the arbitrators.*

Arbitrators may be *chosen* from the list of arbitrators drawn up by the Court and updated annually. The members of the Court *cannot* be included on the said list.

In the event of the challenge of an arbitrator by a party, the Court rules without appeal.

An arbitrator must be replaced when they are dead or unable to perform, when they have to resign as a result of a challenge or for any other reason, or when the Court, after receiving *their* observations, finds that they are not performing their mission, in accordance with the provisions of this title or the arbitration rules, or within the allotted time. In each of these cases, the procedure under the second and third paragraphs above is followed.

Article 23. Any court of a State Party to which a dispute that the parties had agreed to submit to arbitration has been referred will decline jurisdiction if one of the parties so requests, and must, if necessary, refer to the arbitration procedure under this Treaty.

Article 24. Before signing a partial or final award, the arbitrator must submit the draft to the Common Court of Justice and Arbitration.

The Court can only suggest editorial changes.

Article 25. Arbitral awards rendered under these Rules are final and binding on the parties and have res judicata effect in the territory of each State Party, in the same way as decisions rendered by the courts of the State.

They may be enforced under an *exequatur* decision.

The Common Court of Justice and Arbitration has sole jurisdiction to make such a decision.

Exequatur can be denied only in the following cases:

1. if the arbitrator has ruled without an arbitration agreement or on *a null or expired agreement*;
2. if the arbitrator tribunal *has ruled* without *complying with the mission entrusted to them*;
3. if the *adversarial principle* has been breached;
4. if the arbitral award *is contrary to* international public policy.

Article 26. The Regulation on Arbitration of the Common Court of Justice and Arbitration is set by the Council of Ministers under the conditions of Article 8. It is published in the official journal of *the Organization*. It is also published in the official journal of the States Parties or by any other appropriate means.

APPENDIX II

Regulation of the CCJA on Arbitration

Organization for the Harmonization of Business Law in Africa—Council of Ministers

The Council of Ministers of the Organization for the Harmonization of Business Law in Africa (OHADA),

- Having regard to the Treaty on the Harmonization of Business Law in Africa, signed on October 17, 1993 in Port Louis, as amended on October 17, 2008 in Quebec, in particular its Articles 2, 8, 21, 26 and 39;
- Having regard to opinion No. 04/2017/AU of October 5-6, 2017 of the Common Court of Justice and Arbitration;

After deliberating;

Adopts by unanimous vote of the States *Parties*[1] present and voting, the Rules providing the following:

Chapter One—Powers of the Common Court of Justice and Arbitration in arbitration matters

Article 1—Exercise by the Court of its powers

1.1 The Common Court of Justice and Arbitration, hereinafter referred to as "the Court," *exercises,* under the *following* conditions,[2] the power to administer *arbitration proceedings*[3] within the scope defined by Article 21 of the Treaty on the Harmonization of Business Law in Africa, hereinafter referred to as the "Treaty."

1. "Member States" has been replaced with "States Parties," to reflect the original French expression used "Etats Parties."
2. "Shall exercise under the conditions defined below" has been replaced with "exercises, under the following conditions."
3. "Arbitrations" has been replaced with "arbitration proceedings."

The decisions *that the Court makes in this regard*[4] to ensure the implementation and *the*[5] successful *completion*[6] of *arbitration*[7] proceedings and *those*[8] related to the review of the award, are administrative *in* nature.[9]

In the administration of[10] arbitration proceedings, the Court is assisted by a secretary-general.

Members of the Court *with the*[11] nationality *of*[12] a State directly involved in *arbitration* proceedings *must recuse themselves* sua sponte[13] from the formation of the Court in the case at hand.[14] The President of the Court *proceeds with*[15] their replacement, if *necessary*,[16] by order.

The Court *communicates*[17] with the arbitral tribunal and[18] the parties during the arbitration through the Secretary General. *The latter*[19] *notifies*[20] them of *their*[21] decisions, as well as those *made*[22] by the Court.

The President of the Court may *call upon*[23] experts for *advisory*[24] opinion *under the conditions defined by*[25] the *Arbitration Bylaws*[26] of the Court.

4. "Taken by the Court as such" has been replaced with "That the Court makes in this regard" because it seems better to "make" a decision, according to Collins Dictionary.
5. "The" has been inserted after "and."
6. "Outcome" has been replaced with "completion."
7. Throughout the whole CCJA Arbitration Rules, "Arbitral" has been replaced with "arbitration," so as to read "arbitration proceedings." However, "arbitral proceedings" is also correct.
8. "Of proceedings" has been replaced with "those."
9. "Of administrative nature" has been replaced with "administrative in nature."
10. "To administer" has been replaced with "in the administration of."
11. "Sharing the same" has been replaced with "with the."
12. "As" has been replaced with "of."
13. "Shall refrain" has been replaced with "must recuse themselves sua sponte." "Shall" has been replaced because of the rule in *Gutierrez de Martinez v. Lamagno* presented in the introduction, *supra*. The verb used in the original French version "*se déporter*" refers to a judge or arbitrator who withdraws themself from hearing a case. Various dictionaries use different expressions "to withdraw" (Katz, 2010), but "to recuse oneself sua sponte" has been preferred to reflect the meaning of the French expression "*se déporter.*"
14. "From participating to the Court in that case" has been replaced with "from the formation of the Court in the case at hand."
15. "Shall proceed to" has been replaced with "proceeds with."
16. "Applicable" has been replaced with "necessary," to reflect Collings Dictionary which translates the French "*le cas échéant*" as "if necessary."
17. "Shall communicate" has been replaced with "communicates."
18. "With" has been removed after "and."
19. "She shall" has been replaced with "the latter," to reflect the French version "*Celui-ci.*"
20. "Notify" has been replaced with "notifies"; also, "forwards" might seem more suitable since the verb used in the French version "*transmettre*" is generally translated as "forward" something to someone.
21. "Her" has been replaced with "their."
22. "Of those taken" has been replaced with "those made."
23. "Have recourse to" has been replaced with "call upon."
24. "An" has been replaced with "advisory."
25. "Pursuant to" has been replaced with "under the conditions defined by."
26. "Internal Rules" has been replaced with "Arbitration Bylaws," in reference to the Jun. 2, 1999 Arbitration Bylaws of the CCJA (*Règlement Intérieur de la CCJA en matière d'Arbitrage du 2 Juin 1999).*

The administrative decisions *made*[27] by the Court *are devoid of*[28] res judicata effect and without appeal.[29] The grounds for these decisions may be communicated to all parties, provided one of the parties involved in the *arbitration* proceedings *makes the request*[30] before the decision is made.

1.2 The Court *exercises*[31] the *jurisdictional*[32] powers *assigned to it*[33] by Article 25 of the Treaty in *terms*[34] of res judicata and *exequatur* of arbitral awards, in its ordinary judicial *capacity*[35] and *in accordance with*[36] the applicable procedure.[37]

1.3 The powers of the Court defined above at paragraph 1.1 regarding the administration of *arbitration* proceedings *are*[38] exercised *under*[39] chapter II of these Rules.

The *jurisdictional*[40] powers of the Court defined above at paragraph 1.2 *are*[41] exercised *under* chapter III of these Rules and the Rules of procedure of the Court.

Chapter II—Procedure before the Common Court of Justice and Arbitration

Article 2—*Mission*[42] of the *Common* Court *of Justice and Arbitration*

2.1 The *Mission of the Court is to administer,*[43] in accordance with these Rules, *arbitration* proceedings when a contractual dispute, pursuant to an arbitration agreement, is referred to it by any party to a contract, either where one of the parties has *their domicile or habitual residence*[44] in *one*[45] or more of the States *Parties*, or where the contract is performed or to be performed, in whole or in part, in the territory of one or more States *Parties*.

27. "Taken" has been replaced with "made."
28. "Shall not have a" has been replaced with "are devoid of."
29. "May not be appealed" has been replaced with "without appeal." NB: "without appeal" here means there is no recourse available."
30. "So requested" has been replaced with "makes the request."
31. "Shall exercise" has been replaced with "exercises."
32. "Judicial" has been replaced with "jurisdictional."
33. "Defined" has been replaced with "assigned to it."
34. "Respect" has been replaced with "terms," so as to read "in terms of," which is a proper way to render the French expression "*en matière de*" used in the original version according to Collins Dictionary.
35. "Composition" has been replaced with "capacity," because "the Court, in its ordinal judicial capacity" seems more suitable to translate the original French version "*La Cour, dans sa formation contentieuse ordinaire.*"
36. "Pursuant to" has been replaced with "in accordance with."
37. "The procedure provided for it" could also be used.
38. "Shall be" has been replaced with "are."
39. "Pursuant to the provisions of" has been replaced with "under."
40. "Judicial" has been replaced with "jurisdictional."
41. "Shall be" has been replaced with "are."
42. "The role" has been replaced with "mission."
43. "Role of the Court shall be the administration" has been replaced with "the mission."
44. "Is a resident or has her *or his* usual place of residence" has been replaced with "*their domicile or habitual residence.*"
45. "The territory of one" has been replaced with "one," as in the original French version.

The Court may also administer *arbitration* proceedings[46] based on an *investment instrument,*[47] *such as*[48] an Investment Code or a Bilateral or Multilateral Investment Treaty.

2.2 The Court *does*[49] not settle disputes *itself.*[50] *It appoints*[51] or *confirms* the arbitrators. It *is*[52] informed of the progress of the proceedings and *examines*[53] draft awards.

2.3 The operation of *the* Court in arbitration matters is governed by its *Arbitration Bylaws,*[54] as adopted by the general assembly. These *Arbitration Bylaws*[55] *are enforceable*[56] *after their*[57] approval by the Council of Ministers *under*[58] Article 4 of the Treaty.

Article 3—Appointment of arbitrators

3.1 The dispute may be settled by an arbitral tribunal *made up*[59] of a sole arbitrator or of three arbitrators.

Where the parties have agreed that the dispute *will*[60] be settled by a sole arbitrator, *they may appoint them*[61] by mutual agreement subject to *confirmation*[62] of the Court. If the parties fail to agree within thirty (30) days *from*[63] the notification of the request for arbitration *to the other party*, the arbitrator *is*[64] appointed by the Court.

Where three arbitrators *have been stipulated,*[65] each party, *in the request for arbitration or in the answer to the request, appoints*[66] one independent arbitrator, subject to *confirmation*[67] of the Court. If one of the parties fails to appoint an arbitrator,

---

46. "Arbitration procedures" and "arbitral proceedings" also seem correct but "arbitration proceedings" has been retained for consistency purposes.
47. "Instrument related to an investment" has been replaced with "investment instrument."
48. "In particular" has been replaced with "such as."
49. "Shall" has been replaced with "does."
50. "Itself settle disputes" has been replaced with "settle disputes itself."
51. "The Court shall appoint" has been replaced with "it appoints."
52. "Shall be" has been replaced with "is."
53. "Shall review" has been replaced with "examines," to mark the difference between the "light examination of the draft" that is conducted with the Court and the judicial review of an award when the award is challenged.
54. "Internal Rules" has been replaced with "Arbitration Bylaws."
55. "Internal Rules" has been replaced with "Arbitration Bylaws."
56. "Shall enter into force" has been replaced with "are enforceable."
57. "Upon" has been replaced with "after their."
58. "Pursuant to the provisions of" has been replaced with "under."
59. "Composed" has been replaced with "made up," which is the first on the list of synonyms of "consist of something" in the Collins Dictionary.
60. "Shall" has been replaced with "will."
61. "She may be appointed" has been replaced with "they may appoint them" for gender neutrality.
62. "Approval" has been replaced with "confirmation," which is used in the French original version.
63. "Following" has been replaced with "from."
64. "Shall be" has been replaced with "is." Nb: the present imperative has been used in the French version.
65. "The dispute is to be referred to three arbitrators" has been replaced with "three arbitrators have been stipulated."
66. "Shall in the request for arbitration or in the answer to the request appoint" has been replaced with "*in the request for arbitration or in the answer to the request, appoints.*"
67. "The approval" has been replaced with "confirmation," which is used in the French original version.

the *appointment is made*[68] by the Court. The third arbitrator, who *presides over*[69] the arbitral tribunal, *is*[70] appointed by the Court, unless the parties have agreed that the[71] arbitrators they *have appointed*[72] would appoint the third arbitrator within a given time limit. In *the latter case,*[73] *it is up to the Court to*[74] confirm the third arbitrator. *If, at the end of the deadline set by the parties or assigned by the Court, the arbitrators appointed by the parties* have failed to agree,[75] the third arbitrator *is*[76] appointed by the Court.

If[77] the parties have not agreed *on*[78] the number of arbitrators, the Court *appoints*[79] a sole arbitrator, unless the dispute appears[80] to justify the appointment of three arbitrators. In *the*[81] latter case, the parties *have fifteen (15) days to appoint the arbitrators.*[82]

Where *several claimants or respondents are required to submit joint proposals to the Court for the appointment of an arbitrator*[83] *and they fail to agree*[84] within the *time allowed,*[85] the Court may appoint *the entire*[86] arbitral tribunal.

3.2 *Arbitrators*[87] may be *chosen*[88] from the list of arbitrators drawn up by the Court and updated annually. The members of the Court *cannot*[89] be included on the said list.

68. "Latter shall be appointed" has been replaced with "the appointment is made.
69. "Will act as president of" has been replaced with "presides over."
70. "Shall be" has been replaced with "is."
71. "Two" has been removed after "the."
72. "Have designated" has been replaced with "have appointed."
73. "Such event" has been replaced with "the latter case," which also appears in European legislative content: https://eur-lex.europa.eu/LexUriServ/LexUriServ.do?uri=OJ:L:2005:201:0003:0022:EN:PDF.
74. "The Court shall" has been replaced "it is up to the Court to."
75. "If the two arbitrators fail to agree on an appointment within the time limit fixed by the parties or the Court" has been replaced with "*If, at the end of the deadline set by the parties or assigned by the Court, the arbitrators appointed by the parties* have failed to agree."
76. "Shall be" has been replaced with "is."
77. "Where" has been replaced with "if."
78. "Upon" has been replaced with "on."
79. "Shall appoint" has been replaced with "appoints."
80. "That the Court considers that the dispute is such as" has been replaced with "the dispute appears."
81. "Such" has been replaced with "the."
82. "Shall appoint an arbitrator within a period of fifteen (15) days" has been replaced with "have fifteen (15) days to appoint the arbitrators."
83. "There are more than two parties, either as claimants or respondents, who have to submit to the Court joint proposals for the appointment of an arbitrator" has been replaced with "Where several claimants or respondents are required to submit joint proposals to the Court for the appointment of an arbitrator."
84. "And where they fail to agree on such appointment" has been replaced with and they fail to agree."
85. "Fixed time limit" has been replaced with "time allowed."
86. "Each member of the" has been replaced with "the entire."
87. "The" has been removed before "arbitrators."
88. "Elected" has been replaced with "chosen."
89. "**May be**" has been replaced with "cannot" because the translated version "The members of the Court *may be included* on the said list" conveys exactly the opposite of the original French version as well as Article 3 of the Arbitration Bylaws of the CCJA of June 2, 1999 under which no member of the CCJA can be personally involved in arbitration proceedings under the CCJA Rules.

3.3 In appointing arbitrators, the Court may request the opinion of the experts *referred to*[90] at Article 1.1, paragraph 6, and *considers*,[91] in particular, the nationality of the parties, their *place of* residence *and that* of their counsel *and* arbitrators,[92] the seat of[93] arbitration, the language of the parties, the nature of the claims, the availability of the arbitrators and, *possibly*,[94] the law applicable to the *dispute*.[95]

When it must[96] appoint one or more arbitrator(s), the Court *proceeds*[97] as quickly as possible, and, *unless the parties otherwise agree*,[98] according to the following procedure:

a) the Secretary General *sends*[99] each of the parties an identical list prepared by the Court *and with*[100] at least three names;
b) within a time limit *set*[101] by the Secretary General, each party *returns*[102] this list to the Secretary General, indicating on it the names of the arbitrators by order of preference and, if applicable, *crossing out*[103] the names to which it *objects*;[104]
c) after *the*[105] expiry of the deadline *set*[106] by the Secretary General, the Court *appoints*[107] the arbitrator or arbitrators[108] on the basis of the names approved on the lists *that have been sent back*[109] to him, and *in accordance with*[110] the order of preference indicated by the parties.

90. "Mentioned" has been replaced with "referred to."
91. "Shall consider" has been replaced with "considers."
92. "Their residence, the residence of their counsel, the residence of the arbitrators" has been replaced with "their place of residence and that of their counsel and arbitrators."
93. "The" has been removed after "of."
94. "If applicable" has been replaced with "possibly," for two reasons: first, the French word used in the original version, "*éventuellement*" is translated as "possibly in English; second, the expression "if applicable, the law applicable to the dispute" would be confusing for the readers because of the repetition of "applicable."
95. "Merits" has been replaced with "dispute" because the expression used in the original French version, "*du droit applicable au différend*," refers to the Law applicable both to the merit and the procedure. Thus, "*droit applicable au différend*" encompasses the two types of law and must be translated as "the law applicable to the dispute."
96. "Where it has to" has been replaced with "when it must."
97. "Shall proceed" has been replaced with "proceeds."
98. "Unless otherwise agreed by the parties" has been replaced with "unless the parties agree otherwise," as a preference for the active voice.
99. "Shall send" has been replaced with "sends."
100. "Comprising" has been replaced with "and with."
101. "Fixed" has been replaced with "set."
102. "Shall return" has been replaced with "returns."
103. "Deleting" has been replaced with "crossing out," to reflect the original French verb used, "*rayer*."
104. "Has an objection" has been replaced with "it objects."
105. "The" has been inserted before "expiry."
106. "Fixed" has been replaced with "set."
107. "Shall appoint" has been replaced with "appoints."
108. "The" has been removed before "arbitrators."
109. "Sent" has been replaced with "that have been sent back."
110. "Following" has been replaced with "in accordance with."

If, for any reason,[111] the appointment *cannot*[112] be made *under*[113] this procedure, the Court may exercise its *discretion in appointing*[114] one or more arbitrators.

Article 4—Independence, *recusal*[115] and replacement of arbitrators

4.1 Any arbitrator appointed or confirmed by the Court *must*[116] be and remain impartial and independent *to*[117] the parties.[118]

The arbitrator[119] *must*[120] *perform*[121] *their*[122] mission *to its end with diligence and swiftness.*[123]

Before *their*[124] appointment or confirmation by the Court, the prospective arbitrator *must*[125] disclose in writing to the Secretary General any[126] circumstances likely to raise legitimate doubts about the arbitrator's impartiality or independence.

Upon receipt of this information, the Secretary General *communicates it in writing to*[127] the parties and *sets*[128] a time limit[129] for *them*[130] to present their respective comments.

111. "Whatsoever" has been removed after "reason."
112. "May not" has been replaced with "cannot."
113. "Pursuant to" has been replaced with "under."
114. "Discretionary powers to appoint" has been replaced with "discretion in appointing."
115. "Challenge" has been replaced with "recusal," to reflect the French word "*récusation*" that has been used.
116. "Shall" has been replaced with "must."
117. "Of" has been replaced with "to."
118. "Involved in the arbitration" has been removed, because although it is implied, this part does not appear in the French original version.
119. "She" has been replaced with "the arbitrator" to use a gender-neutral expression.
120. "Shall" has been replaced with "must."
121. "Pursue" has been replaced with "perform"; "carry on" could also be used.
122. "Her" has been replaced with "their" for gender neutrality.
123. "Efficiently and diligently until the end of the proceedings" has been replaced with "with diligence and swiftness."
124. "Her" has been replaced with "their" for gender neutrality.
125. ", shall" has been replaced with "must." NB: in the original French version, the present tense is used, but it has an imperative meaning; thus, "must" is more appropriate here.
126. "Facts or" does not appear in the original French version and has been removed before "circumstances."
127. "Shall inform" has been replaced with "communicates it in writing to" to reflect the original French wording and avoid possible confusion because simply "informing" the parties in writing could mean that the Secretary General will tell the parties in writing that it has received some information, while the exact information must be forwarded to the parties to ensure their appropriate decision.
128. "Shall fix" has been replaced with "sets."
129. "Deadline" could also be used here.
130. "The parties" has been replaced with "them."

The arbitrator *must*[131] immediately disclose, in writing to the Secretary General and the parties, any[132] *similar circumstances*[133] which may occur between *their*[134] appointment or confirmation by the Court and the notification of the final award.

4.2 The *application for recusal*[135] of an arbitrator based on alleged lack of independence or any other *ground*[136] *is*[137] made by submission to the Secretary General of a statement specifying the facts and circumstances on which the *application*[138] is based.

To be admissible, the *application*[139] *must*[140] be sent by a party either within thirty (30) days *of the party receiving*[141] notification of the appointment or confirmation of the arbitrator by the Court, or within thirty (30) days from the date *on which*[142] the party filing the *application for recusal*[143] *has been*[144] informed of the facts and circumstances on which the *application for recusal*[145] is based if *that*[146] date is *after*[147] the receipt of *the above*[148] notification.

The Court *rules on*[149] admissibility of the *application*[150] at the same time *as,*[151] if necessary,[152] on the merits of the *application for recusal,*[153] after the Secretary General has given an opportunity for the arbitrator concerned, the parties and other members of the arbitral tribunal, *if any,*[154] to *present their written submissions within an*

131. ", shall" has been replaced with "must." NB: in the original French version, the present tense is used, but it has an imperative meaning; thus, "must" is more appropriate here.
132. "Facts and" does not appear in the original French version and has been removed before "circumstances."
133. "Circumstances of similar nature" has been replaced with "similar circumstances."
134. "Her" has been replaced with "their" for gender neutrality.
135. "Challenge" has been replaced with "application for recusal." NB: request for recusal, petition for removal, challenge, are all acceptable but I chose "application for recusal" for consistency.
136. "Reason" has been replaced with "ground."
137. "Shall be" has been replaced with "is." NB: in the original French version, the present tense is used, but it has an imperative meaning; thus, "must" could be more appropriate here.
138. "Challenge" has been replaced with "application."
139. "Challenge" has been replaced with "application for recusal."
140. "Shall" has been replaced with "must."
141. "From the date of receipt by that party of the" has been replaced with "from the date of receipt by that party of the."
142. "When" has been replaced with "on which."
143. "Challenge request" has been replaced with "application for recusal."
144. "Was" has been replaced with "has been."
145. "Challenge request" has been replaced with "application for recusal."
146. "Such" has been replaced with "that."
147. "Subsequent to" has been replaced with "after."
148. "Such" has been replaced with "the above."
149. "Shall rule upon the" has been replaced with "rules on."
150. "Request" has been replaced with "application."
151. "And at the same time" has been replaced with "at the same time as."
152. "It deems" has been removed before "necessary."
153. "Challenge" has been replaced with "application for recusal."
154. "Any other members of the arbitral tribunal" has been replaced with "other members of the arbitral tribunal, if any."

appropriate time frame.[155] These written comments are sent to the other parties and[156] members of the arbitral tribunal.

4.3 An arbitrator *must*[157] be replaced upon death,[158] upon acceptance by the Court of the *application for recusal of the arbitrator,*[159] or upon acceptance by the Court of *their* resignation.[160]

Where the resignation of an arbitrator is not accepted by the Court and the arbitrator nevertheless refuses to continue to perform *their mission,*[161] *the arbitrator must be*[162] replaced if *the arbitrator*[163] is a sole arbitrator *or*[164] the Chairman of the *arbitral tribunal.*[165]

In *the*[166] other *cases,*[167] the Court assesses[168] whether *there is a need for replacement*[169] taking into account the *state of progress*[170] of the proceedings and the opinion of the two arbitrators *who have not resigned.*[171] *If the Court considers that there is no need for replacement,*[172] the proceedings continue[173] and the award *is*[174] rendered despite the refusal *of*[175] the arbitrator whose resignation has been refused.

The Court *makes its*[176] decision *in light of, among other things,*[177] the provisions of Article 28 paragraph 2 of these Rules.

---

155. "Comment in writing within a reasonable period of time" has been replaced with "present their written submissions within an appropriate time frame."
156. "To the" has been removed after "and."
157. "Shall" has been replaced with "must."
158. "Her" has been removed before "death" for gender neutrality, but the death of the arbitrator is implied here.
159. "Challenge against her" has been replaced with "application for recusal of the arbitrator."
160. "Upon acceptance by the Court of his resignation" has been replaced with "upon acceptance by the Court of *their* resignation" for gender neutrality.
161. "The role assigned to her" has been replaced with "their mission."
162. "She shall be" has been replaced with "the arbitrator must be."
163. "She" has been replaced with "the arbitrator" for gender neutrality.
164. "Or if she is" has been replaced with "or," for gender neutrality.
165. "Arbitration Tribunal" has been replaced with "arbitral tribunal" for consistency.
166. "Any" has been replaced with "the."
167. "Events" has been replaced with "cases."
168. "Shall consider" has been replaced with "assesses."
169. "The replacement is appropriate" has been replaced with "there is a need for replacement."
170. "Progress" has been replaced with "state of progress." *See* e.g., https://ec.europa.eu/commission/sites/beta-political/files/1_en_act_communication.pdf.
171. "Two remaining arbitrators" has been replaced with "the two arbitrators who have not resigned."
172. "Where the Court deems replacement unnecessary" has been replaced with "if the Court considers that there is no need for replacement."
173. "Shall" has been removed before "continue."
174. "Shall be" has been replaced with "is."
175. "To participate by" has been replaced with "of."
176. "Court shall make a" has been replaced with "makes its."
177. "Having regard, in particular, to" has been replaced with "in light of, among other things."

4.4 An arbitrator *must*[178] also be replaced *when*[179] the Court *finds*[180] that *the arbitrator*[181]is *de jure* or *de facto prevented*[182] from *carrying out*[183] *their*[184] mission or that *the arbitrator*[185] is not *performing their duties*[186] in accordance with Title[187] IV of the Treaty or with *these*[188] Rules, or within the prescribed time limits.

When, on the basis of information that has come to its *knowledge,*[189] the Court considers applying the preceding paragraph, it *decides*[190] on the replacement after the Secretary General has communicated this information in writing to the arbitrator concerned, the parties and *to the other members of the tribunal, if any,*[191] and has given them the opportunity to comment in writing within *an appropriate*[192] *time frame.*[193]

In *the event of the*[194] replacement of an arbitrator who *does not perform their duties*[195] in accordance with *Title*[196] IV of the Treaty, these *Arbitration Rules,*[197] or within the *allotted*[198] time, *a new arbitrator is appointed by the Court*[199] *on the advice*[200] of the party who had appointed the arbitrator to be replaced without the Court being bound by the said *opinion.*[201]

Where the Court is informed that, *in a three-member tribunal,*[202] one of the arbitrators other than the president, *does not participate* in the arbitration, *without having* resigned,[203] the Court may, *under*[204] Article 4, paragraphs 3 and 4 above, not

178. "Shall" has been replaced with "must."
179. "Where" has been replaced with "when."
180. "Decides" has been replaced with "finds."
181. "She" has been replaced with "the arbitrator" for gender neutrality. "They" is also suitable.
182. "Is prevented *de jure* or *de facto" has been replaced with "de jure or de facto prevented."*
183. "Fulfilling" has been replaced with "carrying out."
184. "Her" has been replaced with "their" for gender neutrality.
185. "She" has been replaced with "the arbitrator" for gender neutrality.
186. "Fulfilling her role" has been replaced with "performing their duties."
187. "Part" has been replaced with "Title."
188. "In accordance with the" has been replaced with "these."
189. "Attention" has been replaced with "knowledge."
190. "Shall decide" has been replaced with "decides."
191. "Any other members of the arbitral tribunal, if appropriate" has been replaced with "to the other members of the tribunal, if any."
192. "A reasonable" has been replaced with "an appropriate."
193. "Period of time" has been replaced with "time frame."
194. "Case of" has been replaced with "in the event of the."
195. "Is not fulfilling her role" has been replaced with "does not perform their duties."
196. "Part" has been replaced with "Title."
197. "Rules of Arbitration" has been replaced with "Arbitration Rules."
198. "Prescribed" has been replaced with "allotted."
199. "The appointment of a new arbitrator shall be made by the Court" has been replaced with "a new arbitrator is appointed by the Court."
200. "Upon the recommendation" has been replaced with "on the advice of."
201. "Recommendation" has been replaced with "opinion."
202. "In an arbitral tribunal composed of three arbitrators," has been replaced with ", in a three-member tribunal."
203. "Is not participating in the arbitration even though she has not resigned," has been replaced with "does not participate in the arbitration, without having resigned."
204. "Pursuant to" has been replaced with "under."

replace the said arbitrator if the two other arbitrators *agree*[205] to continue the arbitration despite the failure of the said arbitrator to participate.

4.5 Once reconstituted, and after having invited the parties to *submit*[206] their comments, the arbitral tribunal *determines*[207] *the extent to which*[208] the prior proceedings *are to be resumed.*[209]

4.6 In all cases listed above at paragraphs 4.1 to 4.4 leading to the replacement of an arbitrator, the Secretary General *allows*[210] the parties and the other arbitrators[211] to present their written comments on the replacement, and *communicates*[212] *these*[213] information to the other parties and members[214] of the arbitral[215] tribunal.

The Court's ruling on the appointment, confirmation, *recusal*[216] or replacement of an arbitrator *under paragraph 3.3 of Article 3*[217] of these Rules *cannot*[218] be appealed.

Article 5—Request for arbitration

Any party wishing to *resort*[219] to arbitration *under*[220] Article 21 of the Treaty, the *terms of*[221] which are *set out*[222] in these *Arbitration* Rules,[223] *sends its*[224] request to the Secretary General.

This Request *must*[225] contain:

a) the surnames, first names, capacity, *corporate*[226] name, postal and email addresses of the parties, with indication of the address for service for the continuation of the proceedings;

205. "Have agreed" has been replaced with "agree."
206. "Furnish" has been replaced with "submit."
207. "Shall determine" has been replaced with "determines."
208. "To what extent" has been replaced with "the extent to which."
209. "Shall be repeated" has been replaced with "are to be resumed."
210. "Shall put" has been replaced with "allows."
211. "In a position" has been removed after "arbitrators."
212. "Shall communicate" has been replaced with "communicates."
213. "This" has been replaced with "these."
214. "To the" has been removed before "members."
215. "Arb" has been removed before "arbitral."
216. "Disqualification" has been replaced with "recusal" as in the original French version.
217. "Pursuant to the provisions of Article 3, paragraph 3.3" has been replaced with "under paragraph 3.3 of Article 3."
218. "May not" has been replaced with "cannot."
219. "Have recourse" has been replaced with "resort."
220. "Pursuant to" has been replaced with "under."
221. "Arrangements for" has been replaced with "the terms of."
222. "Provided" has been replaced with "set out."
223. "Rules of arbitration" has been replaced with "arbitration rules."
224. "Shall submit her" has been replaced with "sends its." "Sends their" also is suitable.
225. "Shall" has been replaced with "must."
226. "Business" has been replaced with "corporate." *See* the glossary, *infra*.

b) the arbitration agreement *binding*[227] the parties, either based on a contract or any other instrument or, if *applicable,*[228] the *investment instrument*[229] *on*[230] which the request is based;
c) a brief statement of the dispute, the claimant's claims and arguments, as well as *the statement of the amount of his claims;*[231]
d) any useful information and proposals concerning the number and choice of arbitrators;
e) *agreements between the parties*[232] *on*[233] the seat of[234] arbitration, the language of[235] arbitration, the law applicable to the arbitration agreement, the[236] *arbitration* proceedings and the[237] merits of the dispute;[238] *in the absence of such agreements, the wishes of the claimant for arbitration on these various issues are expressed;*[239]

The Request *must be accompanied by the payment of*[240] the filing fees *required under*[241] *the Schedule of fees of Annex II to these Arbitration Rules.*[242]

The Secretary General *immediately notifies*[243] respondents of the date of receipt of the request, *attaches*[244] to this notification a copy of the request with all the supporting documents, a copy of these Rules *and acknowledges receipt of their*

227. "Entered into between" has been replaced with "binding," because the original French word used "*liant*" means "binding." Also, a party may be bound by an arbitration agreement they have not signed; therefore, it is not exact to use "entered into … ."
228. "Appropriate" has been replaced with "applicable." *See* the glossary, *infra.*
229. "Instrument related to an investment" has been replaced with "investment instrument." *See* the glossary, *infra.*
230. "Upon" has been replaced with "on."
231. "an indication of any amount(s) claimed" has been replaced with "as the statement of the amount of his claims."
232. "The agreements entered into between the parties" has been replaced with "agreements between the parties."
233. "Relating to" has been replaced with "on."
234. "The" has been removed after "of."
235. "The" has been removed after "of."
236. "To" has been removed before "the."
237. "To" has been removed before "the."
238. "Claim" has been replaced with "dispute."
239. "f) failing such agreements, the applicant for arbitration shall state his views on these issues" has been replaced with "in the absence of such agreements, the wishes of the claimant for arbitration on these various points are expressed." NB: there is no section "f" in the original French version.
240. "Shall include payment for" has been replaced with "must be accompanied by the."
241. "The proceedings pursuant" has been replaced with "required under."
242. "To the schedule of the costs" has been replaced with "the Schedule of fees of Annex II to these Arbitration Rules."
243. "Shall immediately notify all" has been replaced with "immediately notifies."
244. "And attach" has been replaced with "attaches."

request[245] to the claimant. The Secretary General may require proof of the *power of attorney*[246] of any representative of *a party*[247] acting on behalf *of the claimant(s)*.[248]

The date of receipt by the Secretary General of the request for arbitration, in accordance with this Article,[249] constitutes the date of commencement of the arbitration proceedings.

If the request for arbitration is not accompanied by the amount of *the fee referred to*[250] in paragraph 3 of this Article, or if the *Secretary General's request*[251] to send *them*[252] a sufficient number of copies of the request and all *the documents*[253] has not been *complied with*,[254] the Secretary General may *set a time limit for the claimant to comply with*[255] these requests and, if necessary, extend this *time limit*.[256] *Upon its expiry*,[257] the request for arbitration *will*[258] be dropped, without *impeding the*[259] reintroduction of the same *claims*[260] at a later date in a new request for arbitration.

Article 6—Response to the request

The *respondent(s)*[261] *must*,[262] *within thirty (30) days of the date of receipt of the notification of the request for arbitration by the Secretary General, submit their response to the Secretary General*.[263]

In the case *referred to*[264] at Article 3.1, paragraph 2 of these Rules, *the agreement of the parties must be reached within*[265] the time limit of thirty (30) days provided *for*[266] in the said article.

245. "Shall forward an acknowledgement to" has been replaced with "and acknowledges receipt of their request."
246. "Authority" has been replaced with "power of attorney."
247. "One of the parties" has been replaced with "a party."
248. "Claimant or claimants" has been replaced with "claimant(s)."
249. Commas "," have been inserted after "arbitration" and "article."
250. "Duty indicated" has been replaced with "the fee referred to."
251. "Request made by the Secretary General" has been replaced with "the Secretary General's request."
252. "Him" has been replaced with "them" for gender neutrality.
253. "Documentation" has been replaced with "the documents."
254. "Fulfilled" has been replaced with "complied with."
255. "Grant the claimant a period in which to meet" has been replaced with "set a time limit for the claimant to comply with."
256. "Deadline" has been replaced with "time limit" for consistency.
257. "When it expires" has been replaced with "upon its expiry."
258. "Shall" has been replaced with "will," used in the original French version "*sera*."
259. "This constituting an obstacle to" has been replaced with "without impeding."
260. "Requests" has been replaced with "claims."
261. "Respondent or respondents" has been replaced with "respondent(s)."
262. "Shall" has been replaced with "must."
263. "Submit their response to the notification to the Secretary General within thirty (30) days of receiving it from the Secretary General" has been replaced with "within thirty (30) days of the date of receipt of the notification of the request for arbitration by the Secretary General, submit their response to the Secretary General."
264. "Above mentioned" has been replaced with "referred to."
265. "The parties shall agree within" has been replaced with "the agreement of the parties must be reached within."
266. "For" has been inserted.

The response *must*[267] contain:

a) confirmation or not of *their*[268] surnames, first names, *corporate*[269] name and address as stated by the *claimant,*[270] with *the address for service*[271] for the proceedings;
b) confirmation or not of the existence of an *arbitration* agreement[272] resulting from a contract or any other instrument *between the parties referring to arbitration under these Rules;*[273]
c) a brief statement[274] of the dispute and the *respondent's position on*[275] the *claims against them*[276] with a statement of the *arguments*[277] and evidence upon which *their defense will be based.*[278]
d) the responses of the respondent *on all*[279] the issues raised in the request for arbitration under paragraphs (d) and (e) of Article 5 above.

Article 7—*Response to*[280] counterclaim

If[281] the respondent has filed a counterclaim in *their*[282] response, the claimant *may,*[283] within thirty (30) days *of receiving the response, respond to the counterclaim with a supplementary memorial.*[284]

267. "Shall" has been replaced with "must."
268. "The" has been replaced with "their" for gender neutrality.
269. "Business" has been replaced with "corporate." *See* the glossary, *infra.*
270. "Applicant" has been replaced with "claimant" for consistency.
271. "Election of residence" has been replaced with "the address for service."
272. "Between the parties" has been removed because that part was not specified in the French version and as explained earlier, a party may be bound by an arbitration agreement they have not signed.
273. "That refers to the arbitration provided for under these Rules" has been replaced with "between the parties referring to arbitration under these Rules."
274. "Summary" has been replaced with "statement."
275. "The response of the respondent to" has been replaced with "the respondent's position on."
276. "Brought against her" has been replaced with "claims against them."
277. "Grounds" has been replaced with "arguments."
278. "Will rely for her defence" has been replaced with "their defense will be based."
279. "As regards" has been replaced with "on all."
280. "Counterclaim" has been replaced with "response to counterclaim" as in the original French version "*Réponse à la demande reconventionnelle.*"
281. "Where" has been replaced with "if."
282. "His" has been replaced with "their" for gender neutrality.
283. "Shall" has been replaced with "may" as in the original French version.
284. "within thirty (30) days from the date of receipt of the Counterclaim in an additional submission" has been replaced with "within thirty (30) days of receiving the response, respond to the counterclaim with a supplementary memorial."

Article 8—*Provision on* costs of the arbitration[285]

After receiving[286] the request for arbitration, the response and, if applicable, the *supplementary memorial*[287] *as referred to in*[288] Articles 5, 6, and 7 above, or upon expiry of the time limit within which *they must have been received,*[289] the secretary-general *applies to*[290] the Court *for setting the provision for the costs*[291] of the arbitration, the commencement of the *arbitration* proceedings and if *necessary,*[292] the place of arbitration.

The file *is*[293] sent to the arbitrator once the arbitral tribunal is constituted and[294] the decisions made *pursuant to paragraph 11.2 of Article 11*[295] of these Rules have been *complied with.*[296]

Article 8-1—Forced joinder[297]

8-1.1 *A*[298] party wishing to *join an additional*[299] party bound by the arbitration agreement but foreign to the *arbitration* proceedings, *submits*[300] *a request for arbitration against the additional party* to the Secretary General.[301]

Before the arbitral tribunal is constituted, the Court may *set*[302] a deadline for submission of requests for *joinder.*[303]

If, *at the time of the request for joinder,* the Tribunal has already been constituted *or one of its members has already been appointed or, if applicable, confirmed,*[304] the *joinder is*[305] declared inadmissible unless *the parties and the* intervening party *agree*

285. "First advance costs of the arbitration" has been replaced with "provision on costs of the arbitration."
286. "Upon receipt of" has been replaced with "after receiving."
287. "Additional submission" has been replaced with "supplementary memorial."
288. "Pursuant to the provisions of" has been replaced with "as referred to."
289. "To file" has been replaced with "they must have been received."
290. "Shall request" has been replaced with "applies to."
291. "To fix a provisional advance to cover the costs" has been replaced with "for setting the provision for the costs."
292. "Appropriate" has been replaced with "necessary."
293. "Shall be" has been replaced with "is."
294. "Once" has been removed after "and."
295. "In accordance with Article 11.2" has been replaced with "pursuant to paragraph 11.2 of Article 11."
296. "Fulfilled" has been replaced with "complied with."
297. "Intervention" has been replaced with "joinder."
298. "The" has been replaced with "a."
299. "Involve an" has been replaced with "join an additional."
300. "Shall submit" has been replaced with "submits."
301. "To the Secretary General a request for arbitration against the latter" has been replaced with "a request for arbitration against the additional party to the Secretary General."
302. "Fix" has been replaced with "set."
303. "Intervention" has been replaced with "joinder."
304. "If the Tribunal has already been constituted when the request for intervention is made or if one of the members has already been appointed or, if appropriate, confirmed" has been replaced with "If, at the time of the request for joinder, the Tribunal has already been constituted or one of its members has already been appointed or, if necessary, confirmed."
305. "Intervention shall be" has been replaced with "joinder is."

otherwise[306] and the arbitral tribunal accepts it, *taking into account*[307] the state of progress of the *arbitration* proceedings.

The date of receipt of the request for *joinder*[308] by the Secretary General *is considered, for all purposes, at that*[309] of the introduction of the *arbitration* proceedings against the intervening party.

8-1.2 The request for *joinder must*[310] contain the following elements:

a) the file reference *of*[311] the existing proceedings,
b) the *full name and corporate name,*[312] capacity, postal address and email address of each of the parties, including the intervening party, and
c) the *information*[313] required *under*[314] Article 5, paragraphs 2.b, c and d of these Rules.

8-1.3 The request for *joinder*[315] *is*[316] sent by the Secretary General *only*[317] if it is accompanied by the number of copies *required under*[318] Article 12.1 of these Rules and *the*[319] payment of the filing fee required for initiation of the proceedings *under the Schedule of fees of Annex II.*[320]

8-1.4 The intervening party *submits*[321] a response *in accordance with,*[322] and subject to the necessary changes,[323] the provisions of Article 6 of these Rules or, if the arbitral tribunal has already been constituted, *according to*[324] the instructions of the latter. The intervening party may *file*[325] claims against any other party in accordance with the provisions of Article 7 above.

306. "Otherwise agreed by the parties and the intervening party" has been replaced with "the parties and the intervening party agree otherwise."
307. "Considering" has been replaced with "taking into account."
308. "Intervention" has been replaced with "joinder."
309. "Shall be deemed to be the date" has been replaced with "is considered, for all purposes, at that."
310. "Shall" has been replaced with "must."
311. "For" has been replaced with "of."
312. "Name and full title" have been replaced with "full name and corporate name."
313. "Elements" has been replaced with "information.
314. "In" has been replaced with "under."
315. "Intervention" has been replaced with "joinder."
316. "may only" has been replaced with "is" because "may only sent" is incorrect; it should read "may only **be** sent."
317. "Only" has been inserted after "general.
318. "Provided in" has been replaced with "required under."
319. "The" has been inserted after "and."
320. "In the schedule of costs" has been replaced with "under the Schedule of fees of Annex II."
321. "Shall submit" has been replaced with "submits."
322. "Accordingly" has been replaced with "in accordance with."
323. "Pursuant to" has been removed after "changes."
324. "Pursuant to" has been replaced with "according to."
325. "Submit" has been replaced with "file."

Article 8-2—Voluntary intervention

No voluntary intervention *is*[326] admissible before the constitution of the arbitral tribunal.

After the constitution of the arbitral tribunal, any voluntary intervention *in*[327] *arbitration* proceedings *is*[328] subject to *the prior*[329] approval *of*[330] the parties and the arbitral tribunal.

Article 8-3—Multiple parties

8.3.1 *Arbitration*[331] administered by the Court may take place between more than two parties if they have agreed to[332] arbitration in accordance with these Rules. In the event of a *multi-party arbitration*,[333] *any*[334] party may *file*[335] claims against any other party.

8.3.2 Any party *making a claim*[336] pursuant to Article 8.3.1, *must*[337] produce the *information*[338] required *under*[339] Article 5 of these Rules.

8.3.3 *Once the matter*[340] has been referred to the arbitral tribunal, it determines the procedure to be followed for any new claim.

Article 8-4—Multiple contracts

8.4.1 Claims arising out of *or in connection with several contracts*[341] may be made *in*[342] a single *arbitration*.[343]

8.4.2 Where these claims are made under several arbitration agreements, the arbitral tribunal *must ascertain*[344] that:

a) the parties have agreed *to*[345] arbitration *under*[346] these Rules and that these arbitration agreements are compatible with one another, and

326. "Shall be" has been replaced with "is."
327. "To an" has been replaced with "in."
328. "Shall be" has been replaced with "is."
329. "The prior" has been inserted before "approval" to reflect the original French version "*subordonnée à l'approbation préalable*."
330. "By" has been replaced with "of."
331. "An arbitral procedure" has been replaced with "arbitration."
332. "Have recourse to" has been removed after "to."
333. "Multipartite arbitral procedure" has been replaced with "multiparty arbitration."
334. "Each" has been replaced with "any."
335. "Submit" has been replaced with "file."
336. "Which submits claims" has been replaced with "making a claim."
337. "Shall" has been replaced with "must."
338. "Elements" has been replaced with "information."
339. "In" has been replaced with "under."
340. "As soon as the file" has been replaced with "once the matter."
341. "out of several contracts or in connection with them" has been replaced with."
342. "Within the framework of" has been replaced with "in."
343. "Arbitral procedure" has been replaced with "arbitration."
344. "Shall note" has been replaced with "must ascertain."
345. "To have recourse to" has been replaced with "to."
346. "Pursuant to" has been replaced with "under."

b) all parties to the arbitration have agreed *to have their*[347] claims *settled*[348] within a single procedure.

Article 9—Absence of an arbitration agreement

Where, *prima facie*, there is no arbitration agreement between the parties requiring the application of these *Arbitration Rules,*[349] if the respondent objects to the arbitration of the Court or does not file a *response*[350] within the[351] thirty (30) days *referred to*[352] in Article 6 above, the claimant *is*[353] informed by the Secretary General that he *intends to refer the matter to*[354] the Court *with a view to seeing it decide that arbitration cannot take place.*[355]

The Court *rules in light of*[356] the claimant's comments submitted within the *following*[357] thirty (30) days, if the latter deems *them necessary.*[358]

Article 10—Effects of the arbitration agreement

10.1 Where the parties have agreed to resort to arbitration[359] administered by the Court, they *submit*[360] ipso facto *to*[361] the provisions of *Title IV of the Treaty,*[362] *these Rules,*[363] the[364] *Arbitration Bylaws*[365] of the Court, their[366] annexes, and the schedule of fees of the Court, *in force*[367] on the date of the commencement of the *arbitration proceedings under*[368] Article 5 of these Rules.

347. "That the" has been replaced with "to have their."
348. "Will be decided" have been replaced with" "settled."
349. "Rules of arbitration" has been replaced with "arbitration rules."
350. "Reply" has been replaced with "response."
351. "Period of" has been removed after "the."
352. "Provided" has been replaced with "referred to."
353. "Shall be" has been replaced with "is."
354. "May ask" has been replaced with "intends to refer the matter to."
355. "To decide whether arbitration should take place" has been replaced with "with a view to seeing it decide that arbitration cannot take place."
356. "Decides based on" has been replaced with "rules in light of."
357. "Next" has been replaced with "following."
358. "It necessary to file such comments" has been replaced with "them necessary."
359. "An arbitration" has been replaced with "arbitration."
360. "Shall be deemed thereby to conform" has been replaced with "submit."
361. "With" has been replaced with "to."
362. "Part IV of these Rules" has been replaced with "Title IV of the Treaty," which is the first item on the list in the original French version ("*aux dispositions du titre IV du Traité*") and has been omitted. Also, the Arbitration Rules of the CCJA are split in chapters only with no main part; therefore, referring to "Part IV of these Rules" would mislead the reader.
363. "Part IV of these Rules" has been replaced with "these Rules," because, as explained in the preceding note, the Arbitration Rules of the CCJA are split in chapters only with no main part; therefore, referring to "Part IV of these Rules" would mislead the reader.
364. "Of" has been removed before "the."
365. "Internal Rules" has been replaced with "Arbitration Bylaws."
366. "Including" has been removed before "their."
367. "As effective" has been replaced with "in force."
368. "Pursuant to" has been replaced with "under."

10.2 If one of the parties refuses or *abstains from participating in*[369] the arbitration, the arbitration *takes place*[370] notwithstanding *that*[371] refusal or *abstention.*[372]

10.3 Where one party raises one or more arguments relating to the existence, validity or scope of the arbitration agreement, the Court, *having found prima facie the existence of this agreement,*[373] may decide, *without prejudging the admissibility or the merits of these arguments, that the arbitration will take place.*[374] In this case, *it will be up to the arbitral tribunal to make all decisions on its own jurisdiction.*[375]

10.4 *The*[376] arbitral tribunal *has exclusive jurisdiction to*[377] rule on its own jurisdiction and on the admissibility of the request for arbitration.

Unless otherwise *stipulated,*[378] if the arbitral tribunal *considers that*[379] the arbitration agreement *is*[380] valid *and*[381] the contract binding the parties is null or *nonexistent,*[382] the arbitral tribunal *is competent*[383] to determine the respective rights *of the parties*[384] and *rule on*[385] their claims and *submissions.*[386]

Article 10-1—Provisional measures

Unless otherwise *stipulated,*[387] the arbitration agreement *confers*[388] jurisdiction on the arbitral tribunal to *rule on*[389] any claim for provisional or conservatory measures during

369. "Fails to participate to" has been replaced with "abstains from participating in."
370. "Shall proceed" has been replaced with "takes place."
371. "Such" has been replaced with "that."
372. "Failure" has been replaced with "abstention."
373. "After having noted the prima facie existence of this agreement" has been replaced with "having found *prima facie* the existence of this agreement."
374. "May decide whether the arbitration should take place, without prejudice to" has been replaced with ", without prejudging the admissibility or the merits of these arguments, that the arbitration will take place." NB: *"peut décider, sans préjuger (...), que l'arbitrage aura lieu,"* is used. It means "may decide, (...) that the arbitration will take place." Thus, "whether the arbitration should take place" would be wrong in this context. So would be "without prejudice," which means "Without abandonment of claim, right, privilege and without implied admission of liability" (*See Black's Law Dictionary* online, https://thelawdictionary.org/without-prejudice/), and which is different from the French expression used, *"sans préjuger de,"* which means "without prejudging."
375. "The arbitral tribunal shall rule on its jurisdiction" has been replaced with "It will be up to the arbitral tribunal to make all decisions on its own jurisdiction."
376. "Only" has been removed before "the."
377. "Shall" has been replaced with "has exclusive jurisdiction to."
378. "Agreed" has been replaced with "stipulated," to comply with the expression used in the original French version *"sauf stipulation contraire."*
379. "Deems" has been replaced with "considers that."
380. "Is" has been inserted before "valid."
381. "But" has been replaced with "and."
382. "Inexistent" has been replaced with "nonexistent."
383. "Shall have jurisdiction" has been replaced with "is competent."
384. "Parties' respective rights" has been replaced with "respective rights of the parties."
385. "To decide" has been replaced with "rule on."
386. "Conclusions" has been replaced with "submissions."
387. "Unless provided otherwise" has been replaced with "unless otherwise stipulated."
388. "Shall confer" has been replaced with "confers." For an example, *see* https://www.itlos.org/jurisdiction/.
389. "Decide" has been replaced with "rule on."

the *arbitration* proceedings, *with the exception of*[390] claims relating to *court-ordered securities*[391] and *interim attachments*.[392]

Where exequatur is necessary for the enforcement of awards rendered under the paragraph above, a request for exequatur may be filed immediately.[393]

Before the file is *handed over*[394] to the arbitral tribunal and, *exceptionally thereafter*,[395] *if*[396] the *urgency*[397] of the provisional or conservatory measures requested *does not allow*[398] the *arbitral tribunal*[399] to rule promptly, the parties may apply to *the*[400] competent state court for such measures.

These applications, *as well as the*[401] measures taken by the competent state court *are immediately*[402] notified to the Secretary General *who informs*[403] the arbitral tribunal.

Article 11—*Deposit*[404] on costs of the arbitration

11.1 The Court *sets*[405] the amount of the *deposit* on costs to cover the costs of arbitration incurred by the claims which have been referred to it, *in accordance with*[406] Article 24 of these Rules, unless these claims are *filed*[407] *under*[408] Articles 8-1.2 and 8.1.3 of these Rules, in which case paragraph[409] 11.3 below applies.

This *deposit is then adjusted if*[410] the amount of the dispute is modified by at least *a*[411] quarter or if any new circumstances *make*[412] such readjustment necessary.

390. "Except" has been replaced with "with the exception of."
391. "Judicial safeties" has been replaced with "court-ordered securities."
392. "Conservatory seizures" has been replaced with "interim attachments." *See* the glossary, *infra*.
393. "Awards rendered within the framework of the above paragraph may be subject to immediate enforcement if the enforcement is necessary for implementation of these provisional or conservatory awards" has been replaced with "Where *exequatur* is necessary for the enforcement of awards rendered under the paragraph above, a request for *exequatur* may be filed immediately."
394. "Forwarded" has been replaced with "handed over."
395. "In exceptional circumstances, even" has been replaced with "exceptionally thereafter."
396. "Where" has been replaced with "if."
397. "Urgent nature" has been replaced with "urgency."
398. "May not permit" has been replaced with "does not allow."
399. "Arbitrator" has been replaced with "arbitral tribunal" as in the French original version.
400. "Any" has been replaced with "the."
401. "And any" has been replaced with ", as well as."
402. "Shall be" has been replaced with "are immediately."
403. "Without delay; the latter shall accordingly" has been replaced with "who informs."
404. "Advance" has been replaced with "deposit."
405. "Shall fix" has been replaced with "sets."
406. "Pursuant to" has been replaced with "in accordance with."
407. "Pursued" has been replaced with "filed."
408. "In accordance with" has been replaced with "under."
409. "Article" has been replaced with "paragraph" as used in the original French version.
410. "May be subject to readjustment where" has been replaced with "is then adjusted if."
411. "One" has been replaced with "a."
412. "Render" has been replaced with "make."

Where[413] counterclaims are *filed*[414] by the respondent, the Court may *set*[415] separate *deposits* on costs for the claims and the counterclaims.[416] When the Court *sets*[417] separate *deposits* on costs, each party *must*[418] pay the *deposit* on costs corresponding to *their respective*[419] claims.

11.2 The *deposits* on costs *are due*[420] in equal shares by the claimant(s) and the *respondent(s)*.[421] However, *their payment may be made in full by each of the parties for the main claim and the counterclaim, in case the other party fails to pay their share.*[422]

The *deposits* on costs *thus set*[423] *must*[424] be paid in full to the Court before the file is *handed over*[425] to the arbitrator. The payment of at most three quarters of the amount *set*[426] may be secured by *a satisfactory*[427] bank guarantee.

11.3 Where claims are *filed*[428] *under*[429] Articles 8-1, 8-2 and 8-3 of these Rules, the Court *sets*[430] one or more *deposits* and *decides*[431] which party is responsible for *the*[432] payment[433] or in what proportion this payment *must be split*[434] *among*[435] them. Where the Court *has*[436] previously *set*[437] *a deposit* in accordance with this *paragraph,*[438] the latter is replaced by the *deposit(s)*[439] *set in accordance with*[440] this paragraph. In that

413. "When" has been replaced with "where."
414. "Introduced" has been replaced with "filed."
415. "Fix" has been replaced with "set."
416. "If so requested by a party" has been removed after "counterclaims" because that conditions does not exist in the original French version, from which the translation has been made.
417. "Established" has been replaced with "sets."
418. "Shall" has been replaced with "must," to comply with the original French version "*doit,*" which makes the payment mandatory.
419. "Its" has been replaced with "their respective."
420. "Shall be payable" has been replaced with "is due."
421. "Respondents has been replaced with "respondent(s)" to encompass "*le ou les défendeurs*" used in the French original version.
422. "Any party shall be free to pay the whole of the advance on costs in respect of the principal claim and the counterclaim, should the other party fail to pay his share" has been replaced with "their payment may be made in full by each of the parties for the main claim and the counterclaim, in case the other party fails to pay their share."
423. "Fixed" has been replaced with "thus set."
424. "Shall" has been replaced with "must."
425. "Sent" has been replaced with "handed over."
426. "Fixed" has been replaced with "set."
427. "An adequate" has been replaced with "a satisfactory."
428. "Made" has been replaced with "filed."
429. "Pursuant to" has been replaced with "under."
430. "Shall fix" has been replaced with "sets."
431. "Decide" has been replaced with "decides."
432. "Their" has been replaced with "the."
433. "," has been removed after "payment."
434. "Shall be divided" has been replaced with "must be split."
435. "Between" has been replaced with "among."
436. "Had" has been replaced with "has."
437. "Fixed" has been replaced with "set."
438. "Article" has been replaced with "paragraph," which is also used in the French original version.
439. "Advance or advances" has been replaced with "deposit(s)."
440. "Pursuant to" has been preplaced with "set in accordance with."

case, the amount of any *deposit previously paid*[441] by one party *is*[442] considered *a*[443] partial payment by this party of its share of the *deposits (s) set*[444] by the Court in accordance with this paragraph.

11.4 *Only claims for which the requirements of paragraph 11.2 above are fully complied with are referred to the arbitrator.*[445]

If *a request for deposit*[446] is not satisfied, the Court, upon request of the Secretary General, may invite the arbitral tribunal to suspend its activities and *set*[447] a time limit which *cannot*[448] be less than thirty (30) days, on expiry of which the claims *to which the deposit correspond*[449] *are considered*[450] withdrawn. Such a withdrawal does not deprive the party concerned of the right to subsequently *reintroduce*[451] the same claim in other proceedings.

Article 12—Notification, communication and time limits

12.1 The memorials and all written communications submitted by any party, *as well as*[452] additional documents, *are*[453] filed *in*[454] as many copies as *there are parties*[455] plus one for each arbitrator and one electronic copy *is*[456] sent to the Secretary General.

Once the *case has been referred to the arbitral tribunal,*[457] the *latter*[458] and the parties send[459] *the Secretary General*[460] an electronic copy of all correspondence exchanged in connection with the proceedings.

12.2 All notifications or communications from the Secretary General and the arbitral tribunal *are served*[461] at the address or the last known address of the party to which it is addressed, or *their*[462] representative, as notified by the latter or by the other

441. "Paid previously" has been replaced with "previously paid."
442. "Shall be" has been replaced with "is."
443. "As" has been replaced with "a."
444. "Fixed" has been replaced with "set."
445. "The arbitrator shall only be seized with the claims for which payment has been entirely satisfied pursuant to Article 11.2 above" has been replaced with "Only claims for which the requirements of paragraph 11.2 above are fully complied with are referred to the arbitrator."
446. "The request for an advance" has been replaced with "a request for deposit."
447. "Fix" has been replaced with "set."
448. "May not" has been replaced with "cannot."
449. "Which correspond to the advance" has been replaced with "to which the deposit correspond."
450. "Shall be considered to be" has been replaced with "are considered."
451. "Pursue" has been replaced with reintroduce."
452. "And all" has been replaced with "as well as."
453. "Shall be" has been replaced with "are."
454. "With" has been replaced with "in."
455. "The number of the parties," has been replaced with "there are parties."
456. "Shall be" has been replaced with "is."
457. "Once the arbitral tribunal has been seized of the file," has been replaced with "once the case has been referred to the arbitral tribunal."
458. "Arbitral tribunal" has been replaced with "latter."
459. "Shall send" has been replaced with "send."
460. "To the Secretary General" has been removed from the end of the sentence and inserted (without "to") before "an."
461. "Shall be served" has been replaced with "are served."
462. "His" has been replaced with "their" for gender neutrality.

party, *is*[463] applicable. The notification or communication may be *made*[464] by delivery against receipt, registered letter, transport service, email or any other electronic method enabling the proof of sending to be provided.

12.3 The notification or communication validly made *is deemed established*[465] when it has been received by the interested party or, if it has been validly made in accordance with *paragraph*[466] 12.2 above, should have been received by the interested party or *their*[467] representative.

12.4 The time *limits*[468] *set*[469] by these Rules or by the Court *begin to run*[470] *the day after the*[471] notification or communication is deemed to have been made *under paragraph 12.3 above.*[472]

When, in the country where the notification or communication was deemed to have been made on a certain date, the day after it is a public holiday or non-working day, the time limit begins to run on the first following working day.[473]

Public[474] holidays and non-working days *are*[475] included in the calculation of time limits and *do not extend*[476] them. If the last day of the *allotted time*[477] is *a public*[478] holiday or[479] non-working day in the country where the notification or communication is deemed to have been made, the time limit *expires*[480] at the end of the first following working day.

After the arbitral tribunal has been constituted[481] and with *its agreement,*[482] the parties may agree to reduce the different time limits provided *for*[483] in these Rules. If circumstances *warrant,*[484] the Court may, after consultation with the parties, *extend, at*

463. "As" has been replaced with "if."
464. "Sent" has been replaced with "made."
465. "Shall be considered to be acquired" has been replaced with "is deemed established."
466. "Article" has been replaced with "paragraph" to comply with the French original version.
467. "Her" has been replaced with "their" for gender neutrality.
468. "Limit" has been replaced with "limits" for the plural.
469. "Provided" has been replaced with "set."
470. "Shall start running" has been replaced with "begin to run."
471. "From the day following the date a" has been replaced with "the day after the."
472. "In accordance with the preceding paragraph" has been replaced with "under paragraph 12.3 above."
473. "When the next day following such date is an official holiday, or a non-working day in the country where the notification or communication is deemed to have been made, the time limit shall start to run on the first following working day" has been replaced with "When, in the country where the notification or communication was deemed to have been made on a certain date, the day after it is a public holiday or non-working day, the time limit begins to run on the first following working day."
474. "Official" has been replaced with "public."
475. "Shall be" has been replaced with "are."
476. "Shall not prolong" has been replaced with "do not extend."
477. "Relevant time limit granted" has been replaced with "allotted time."
478. "An official" has been replaced with "a public."
479. "A" has been removed after "or."
480. "Shall expire" has been replaced with "expires."
481. "," has been removed after "constituted."
482. "the agreement of the latter" has been replaced with "its agreement."
483. "Provided" has been replaced with "provided for."
484. "So justify" has been replaced with "warrant."

the request of the tribunal,[485] such a time limit or any other period resulting from these Rules, to *allow*[486] the arbitral tribunal to *perform*[487] its functions.

Article 13—Seat of the arbitration

The seat of the arbitration *is set*[488] by the arbitration agreement or by *a later agreement of*[489] the parties.

Failing such agreement, it *is set*[490] by a decision of the Court made before the file is sent to the arbitral tribunal.

Unless otherwise agreed[491] and after consultation with the parties, the arbitral tribunal may decide to *hold hearings and meetings*[492] and deliberate in any place it *considers appropriate.*[493]

Where circumstances make *it difficult or impossible to proceed with the arbitration at the place that had been set,*[494] the Court *may, at the request of the parties, a party or the arbitrator, choose another seat.*[495]

Article 14—Confidentiality of *arbitration* proceedings

Arbitration proceedings *are*[496] confidential. The work of the Court relating to *the*[497] conduct of *arbitration* proceedings *is*[498] subject to this confidentiality,[499] as well as *all meetings*[500] of the Court held for the *administration of*[501] the arbitration. Confidentiality *also covers*[502] documents submitted to the *Court*[503] or drafted by it in the *proceedings it administers.*[504]

485. "At the request of the tribunal extend" has been replaced with "extend, at the request of the tribunal."
486. "Enable" has been replaced with "allow."
487. "Fulfil" has been replaced with "perform."
488. "Shall be determined" has been replaced with "is set."
489. "Later agreement between" has been replaced with "a later agreement of."
490. "Shall be determined" has been replaced with "is set."
491. "," has been removed after "agreed."
492. "Conduct the hearing and hold meetings" has been replaced with "hold hearings and meetings."
493. "Sees fit" has been replaced with "considers appropriate."
494. "Conducting the arbitration proceedings impossible or difficult in the place which had been fixed," has been replaced with "it difficult or impossible to proceed with the arbitration at the place that had been set."
495. "May choose another seat, at the request of the parties, or of one party, or of the arbitrator" has been replaced with "may, at the request of the parties, a party or the arbitrator, choose another seat."
496. "Shall be" has been replaced with "are."
497. "The" has been inserted after "to."
498. "Shall be" has been replaced with "is."
499. "To this rule of confidentiality" has been replaced with "this confidentiality."
500. "Any meeting" has been replaced with "all meetings."
501. "Purpose of administering" has been replaced with "administration of."
502. "Shall also apply to" has been replaced with "also covers."
503. "Latter" has been replaced with "Court."
504. "Course of the administered proceedings" has been replaced with "proceedings it administers."

Unless otherwise agreed by *the*[505] parties, the latter and their counsel, *arbitrators, experts*[506] and *all persons associated with the arbitration*[507] proceedings *are*[508] bound by the duty *of*[509] confidentiality of the information and[510] documents produced during the said proceedings. Confidentiality *extends,*[511] under the same conditions,[512] to arbitral awards.

The Secretary General *is authorized to*[513] publish extracts from arbitral awards without mentioning elements *enabling the identification of* the parties.[514]

Article 15—Minutes of the *case management conference*[515]

15.1 After it has received the file, the arbitral tribunal *convenes*[516] the parties or their duly qualified *representatives*[517] and counsel, to a *case management conference* which *must*[518] be held as soon as possible and not later than forty five (45) days from the date of *referral of the case to the tribunal.*[519] During this *case management conference*, the arbitral tribunal may *require*[520] proof of the *power of attorney*[521] of any representative of a party *if it deems it*[522] necessary. *The arbitral tribunal may, with the agreement of the parties, hold this meeting in the form of a telephone conference or videoconference.*[523]

505. "All" has been replaced with "the."
506. "The" has been removed before "arbitrators" and "experts."
507. "Any person involved in arbitral" has been replaced with "all persons associated with the arbitration," for many reasons. First, "any" has been replaced to comply with the French original version in which "*toutes,*" meaning "all" has been used. Second, "person involved in arbitral proceedings" has been replaced with "persons associated with the proceedings" to comply with the expression used in the original French version, "*les personnes associées à la procédure d'arbitrage,*" because there may be a difference between "being [directly] involved" in proceedings, as a party, or a direct actor of the proceedings, and being only "associated with" the proceedings, like a staff member of the administrative formation of the Court or the Secretary General handling the proceedings. As an illustration, the OHADA Legislator has referred to the involvement of a State in arbitration proceedings ("*Etat impliqué directement dans une procédure arbitrale*"—"State directly involved in arbitral proceedings") at paragraph 4 of Article 1.1 and "*parties impliquées dans la procédure d'arbitrage*" ("the parties involved in the arbitral proceedings") at paragraph 7 of Article 1.1.
508. "Shall be" has been replaced with "are."
509. "Duty to respect the" has been replaced with "duty of."
510. "Of the" has been removed after "and."
511. "Shall extend" has been replaced with "extends."
512. "," has been added after "conditions."
513. "May" has been replaced with "is authorized to."
514. "Which would enable the parties to be identified" has been replaced with "which would enable the parties to be identified."
515. "Scoping meeting" has been replaced with "case management conference."
516. "Shall summon" has been replaced with "convenes."
517. "Representatives" has been put in plural form like in the original French version.
518. "Shall" has been replaced with "must" to comply with the original French version.
519. "Receipt of the file" has been replaced with "referral of the case to the tribunal."
520. "Request" has been replaced with "require."
521. "Authority" has been replaced with "power of attorney."
522. "As deemed" has been replaced with "if it deems it."
523. "Upon request of the parties, the arbitral tribunal may decide that this meeting shall be held in the form of a telephone conference or video conference" has been replaced with "The arbitral tribunal may, with the agreement of the parties, hold this meeting in the form of a telephone conference or videoconference."

The purpose of the *case management conference is:*[524]

a) to *take notice of*[525] the *referral*[526] to the arbitral tribunal and determine the claims *it must settle.*[527] *These claims are listed as they result from the memorials respectively*[528] filed by the parties on that date, with a summary of the reasons for these claims and the *arguments*[529] raised *on the merit;*[530]
b) to *determine*[531] whether an agreement exists between the parties on the issues listed in Articles 5(e) and 6 (b) and (d) above. In the absence of such an agreement, the arbitral tribunal *determines*[532] that the award *will have to settle*[533] this issue;
c) to *take notice of*[534] the agreement *of*[535] the parties on the language of the *arbitration* proceedings or *allow*[536] the arbitral tribunal to decide *on it*[537] during the meeting;[538]
d) *to allow, if necessary,*[539] the arbitral tribunal to ask the parties if they intend to *give*[540] it the powers of *amiable compositeur under*[541] Article 17 of these Rules;
e) to *make*[542] appropriate *arrangements*[543] for the conduct of the *arbitration procedure*[544] *that*[545] the arbitral tribunal intends to apply and the *terms of its application;*[546]
f) to *set a provisional calendar for the arbitration proceedings specifying*[547] the dates for filing the respective *memorials*[548] deemed necessary *and, if*

524. "Shall be" has been replaced with "is."
525. "Establish" has been replaced with "take notice of."
526. "Fact that the matter has been referred" has been replaced with "the referral."
527. "To determine the claims to be decided" has been replaced with "determine the claims it must settle."
528. "It shall proceed to list the claims as contained in the submissions" has been replaced with "These claims are listed as they result from the memorials respectively."
529. "Grounds" has been replaced with "arguments."
530. "In support thereof" has been replaced with "on the merit."
531. "State" has been replaced with "determine."
532. "Shall declare" has been replaced with "determines."
533. "Shall decide" has been replaced with "will have to settle."
534. "Note" has been replaced with "take notice of."
535. "Between" has been replaced with "of."
536. "To enable" has been replaced with "allow."
537. "This issue" has been replaced with "on it."
538. "Pursuant to Article 13-1" has been removed because there is no counterpart in the original French version.
539. "If necessary, to allow" has been replaced with "to allow, if necessary."
540. "Confer on" has been replaced with "give."
541. "Pursuant to" has been replaced with "under."
542. "Take" has been replaced with "make."
543. "Measures" has been replaced with "arrangements."
544. "Arbitral proceedings" has been replaced with "arbitration procedure."
545. "Which" has been replaced with "that."
546. ", and the methods to apply them" has been replaced with "and the terms of its application."
547. "Draft a provisional timetable, fixing" has been replaced with "set a provisional calendar for the arbitration proceedings specifying."
548. "Submissions" has been replaced with "memorials."

necessary,[549] the date for hearing arguments, after which the *hearings will be*[550] declared closed. The date of the hearing *must not be set*[551] later than six (06) months from the date of the *case management conference*[552] unless agreed otherwise by the parties.

15.2 The arbitral tribunal *drafts*[553] minutes of the *case management conference*[554] which it *signs*[555] after collecting any comments *from the parties.*[556]

The parties or their representatives *are also*[557] invited to sign *the*[558] minutes. *If*[559] one of the parties refuses to sign *the*[560] minutes or expresses reservations *against them,*[561] *the minutes are*[562] submitted to the Court for approval.

A copy of *the minutes of the case management conference is*[563] sent to the parties and their counsel, as well as to the Secretary General.

15.3 *If necessary,*[564] the provisional *calendar*[565] for arbitration referred to in the minutes of the *case management conference*[566] *may*[567] be amended by the arbitral tribunal, on its own initiative after comments from the parties or at their request.

This modified calendar is sent to the Secretary General for transmission to the Court.[568]

15.4 The arbitral tribunal *must write*[569] and sign the award within ninety (90) days after its order closing the debate, *unless extended by the Court,*[570] at its own initiative or upon request of the arbitral tribunal.

549. ", as well as" has been replaced with "and, if necessary."
550. "Hearing shall be" has been replaced with "hearings will be."
551. "Fixed by the arbitration tribunal shall not be" has been replaced with "must."
552. "Meeting" has been replaced with "case management conference."
553. "Shall draft" has been replaced with "drafts."
554. "Scoping meeting" has been replaced with "case management conference."
555. "Shall sign" has been replaced with "signs."
556. "Which the parties may have" has been replaced with "from the parties."
557. "Shall also be" has been replaced with "are also."
558. "These" has been replaced with "the."
559. "Where" has been replaced with "if."
560. "These" has been replaced with "the."
561. "About these minutes" has been replaced with "against them."
562. "It shall be" has been replaced with "the minutes are."
563. "These minutes shall be" has been replaced with "the minutes of the case management conference is."
564. "If necessary" has been removed after "tribunal."
565. "Timetable" has been replaced with "calendar."
566. "Scoping meeting" has been replaced with "case management conference."
567. "Shall" has been replaced with "may."
568. "This amended timetable shall be sent to the Court" has been replaced with "This modified calendar is sent to the Secretary General for transmission to the Court."
569. "Shall issue" has been replaced with "must write."
570. "This is extended by an order of the Court" has been replaced with."

15.5 *Where*[571] the award does not *put an end to*[572] the *arbitration* proceedings, a meeting is *immediately*[573] organized *to set,*[574] under the same conditions, a new timetable *for the award that will completely resolve the dispute.*[575]

Article 16—Rules governing the proceedings

The present rules are applicable to the proceedings before the arbitral tribunal and, where silent, the rules agreed-upon by the parties or, failing those, the rules determined by the arbitral tribunal, with or without reference to the law applicable to the arbitration, will apply.[576]

Parties must[577] be treated *equally*[578] and each party *must*[579] have every opportunity to *assert their*[580] rights. The parties *must*[581] act *swiftly and loyally*[582] in conducting the proceedings and[583] refrain from any dilatory tactics.

The party which, knowingly, refrains from raising[584] an irregularity *without delay and proceeds with the arbitration is*[585] deemed to have waived *its claim.*[586]

571. "When" has been replaced with "where."
572. "Finally terminate" has been replaced with "put an end to."
573. "Instantly" has been replaced with "immediately."
574. "In order to draft" has been replaced with "to set."
575. "Governing the final award" has been replaced with "for the award that will completely resolve the dispute."
576. "The rules applicable to the arbitral proceedings, shall be the present rules and, in the event of an omission from these, any rules which the parties or failing them, the arbitral tribunal, establish, whether by referring to rules of procedure of the national law applicable to the arbitration or not" has been replaced with "*The present rules are applicable to the proceedings before the arbitral tribunal and, where silent, the rules agreed-upon by the parties or, failing those, the rules determined by the arbitral tribunal, with or without reference to the law applicable to the arbitration, will apply.*" There is no reference to "the national law applicable to the arbitration" in the original French version and even though it might be assumed, it is preferable to wait until the CCJA itself determines such interpretation.
577. "The parties shall" has been replaced with "parties must."
578. "On an equal footing" has been replaced with "equally."
579. "Shall" has been replaced with "must."
580. "Pursue her" has been replaced with "assert their." "Assert" has been used because the French expression used, "*faire valoir ses droits,*" translates into "assert one's rights." "Their" has been used for gender neutrality.
581. "Shall" has been replaced with "must."
582. "Efficiently and with loyalty" has been replaced with "swiftly and loyally."
583. "Shall" has been removed after "and."
584. "Any party who knowingly fails to raise" has been replaced with "The party which, knowingly, refrains from raising."
585. "Promptly and pursues the arbitral proceedings, shall be" has been replaced with "without delay and proceeds with the arbitration is deemed."
586. "The right to claim this irregularity" has been replaced with "its claim."

Article 17—Law applicable to the merits[587]

The parties *are free to determine*[588] the rules of law *that the tribunal will have to apply*[589] to the merits of the dispute. In the absence of *the choice of the parties,*[590] the arbitral tribunal *applies*[591] the *rules of law which it considers most appropriate in the case.*[592]

In *all cases,*[593] the arbitral tribunal *takes*[594] into account the *stipulations*[595] of the contract and international trade *usages.*[596]

The arbitral tribunal may also rule as *amiable compositeur* upon express agreement of the parties.

Article 18—New claims

After the arbitral tribunal has signed the minutes of the *case management conference,*[597] the parties may not file new claims outside the scope of these minutes, unless authorized[598] by the arbitral tribunal which *considers*[599] the nature of these new claims, the state of progress of the proceedings and any other relevant circumstances.

Article 19—*Processing*[600] the case

19.1 The arbitral tribunal *must*[601] proceed as *soon*[602] as possible to establish the facts of the case by all appropriate means.

After *scrutiny of*[603] the written submissions of the parties and the underlying evidence filed by them,[604] the arbitral tribunal *hears*[605] the parties in an *adversarial*[606]

---

587. "Of the dispute" has been removed after "merits."
588. "Shall agree upon" has been replaced with "are free to determine."
589. "To be applied by the arbitral tribunal" has been replaced with "that the tribunal will have to apply."
590. "Any such agreement" has been replaced with "the choice of the parties."
591. "Shall apply" has been replaced with "applies."
592. "Law determined by the conflict of law rules which it deems appropriate in the circumstances" has been replaced with "rules of law which it considers most appropriate in the case," because there is no mention of "conflict of law rules" in the original French version and some arbitration proceedings may not require no conflict of law rule at all.
593. "In any event" has been replaced with "in all cases," which is used in the French original version. "In any event" translates the French expression "*en tout état de cause,*" which was not used in Article 19 of the Rules.
594. "Shall take" has been replaced with "takes."
595. "Terms" has been replaced with "stipulations," which is used in the original French version.
596. "Practices" has been replaced with "usages."
597. "Scoping meeting" has been replaced with "case management conference."
598. "To do so" has been removed after "authorized."
599. "Shall consider" has been replaced with "considers."
600. "Establishing the facts of" has been replaced with "processing." *See* the glossary, *infra*.
601. "Shall" has been replaced with "must."
602. "Promptly" has been replaced with "soon."
603. "Having reviewed" has been replaced with "scrutiny."
604. "The parties" has been replaced with "them."
605. "Shall hear" has been replaced with "hears."
606. "An contradictory" has been replaced with "an adversarial," to read "an adversarial setting."

setting *if one of them so requests.*[607] In the absence of such a request, the arbitral tribunal may, *on its own motion, decide to hear the parties.*[608]

The arbitral tribunal may invite the parties to provide factual explanations and to *present before it,*[609] by any legally admissible means, the evidence *it*[610] deems necessary to settle the dispute. It *decides*[611] on the admissibility of the evidence and freely assess their probative force.

The parties *appear either in person or*[612] by duly *authorized*[613] persons. They may be assisted by their counsel.

The arbitral tribunal may decide to hear the parties separately if deemed necessary. In that case, the hearing of each party *must*[614] take place in the presence of both parties' counsel.

The hearing of the parties *takes*[615] place on the day *and place set*[616] by the arbitral tribunal.

If one of the parties, although *duly*[617] summoned, does not attend the hearing, the arbitral tribunal, after *ensuring*[618] that the notice has reached the party, may proceed with its mission *in the absence of a valid excuse from the missing party and,*[619] the debate *will*[620] be deemed *adversarial.*[621]

The minutes of the parties' hearing, duly signed, *are sent in copy to the Secretary General of the Court.*[622]

19.2 The arbitral tribunal may also decide to hear witnesses, experts *appointed*[623] by the parties or any other person, in the presence of the parties, or in their absence provided that *they*[624] have been duly summoned.

19.3 The arbitral tribunal may decide *the case*[625] on the sole basis of documentary evidence,[626] upon request or agreement of the parties.

607. "Upon request of any of them" has been replaced with "if one of them so requests."
608. "Automatically decide to hear them" has been replaced with "on its own motion, decide to hear the parties."
609. ", and to produce" has been replaced with "present before it."
610. "Which it" has been replaced with "it."
611. "Shall decide" has been replaced with "decides."
612. "Shall appear in person or be represented" has been replaced with "appear either in person or."
613. "Authorised" has been replaced with "authorized."
614. "Shall" has been replaced with "must."
615. "Shall take" has been replaced with "takes."
616. "And at the place fixed" has been replaced with "and place set."
617. "She has been properly" has been replaced with "duly."
618. "Making sure" has been replaced with "ensuring."
619. "Unless the party provides a valid reason" has been replaced with "in the absence of a valid excuse from the missing party and."
620. "Shall" has been replaced with "will."
621. "Contradictory" has been replaced with "adversarial."
622. "Shall be addressed to the Secretary General of the Court" has been replaced with "are sent in copy to the Secretary General of the Court."
623. "Commissioned" has been replaced with "appointed." *See* the glossary, *infra.*
624. "The latter" has been replaced with "they."
625. "Decide" has been replaced with "decide the case."
626. "," has been inserted after "evidence."

19.4 Unless *the parties agree otherwise,*[627] the arbitral tribunal may appoint one or more experts *to report on specific issues it will*[628] determine and invite the *expert(s)*[629] to testify at the hearing. If *necessary,*[630] the arbitral tribunal may require *a*[631] party to *provide the expert with*[632] all appropriate information or to submit *or make available to the expert, for scrutiny, any exhibits or other relevant items.*[633]

19.5 The arbitral tribunal *invites*[634] the parties to the hearings, the conduct of which are regulated by the tribunal. These hearings *must*[635] be *adversarial.*[636]

Unless *the arbitral tribunal and the parties agree,*[637] the hearings *are not*[638] open to persons *not involved in*[639] the proceedings.

Article 19-1—Closing of the *arbitration* proceedings

19-1.1 The arbitral tribunal *orders*[640] the closing of the *arbitration* proceedings:

a) as soon as possible after the *final*[641] stage of submissions on the merits by the parties *under the procedural calendar;*[642]
b) if the claimant withdraws *their*[643] claim, unless the respondent objects[644] and the arbitral tribunal acknowledges that *the respondent*[645] has a legitimate interest in *having the dispute finally resolved;*[646]

627. "Otherwise agreed by the parties" has been replaced with "the parties agree otherwise" to limit the use of the passive voice.
628. "To provide it with a report on precise points which it shall" has been replaced with "to report on specific issues it will."
629. "Latter" has been replaced with "expert(s)."
630. "Applicable" has been replaced with "necessary." NB: the two expressions are quite equivalent but "necessary" has been preferred for consistency.
631. "One" has been replaced with "a."
632. "Communicate to the expert" has been replaced with "provide the expert with."
633. "To the expert any exhibits or other relevant items, or to make these accessible for the purpose of examination" has been replaced with "or make available to the expert, for scrutiny, any exhibits or other relevant items."
634. "Shall invite" has been replaced with "invites."
635. "Shall" has been replaced with "must."
636. "Contradictory" has been replaced with "adversarial."
637. "agreed by the arbitral tribunal and the parties" has been replaced with "the arbitral tribunal and the parties agree."
638. "Shall not be" has been replaced with "are not."
639. "Foreign to" has been replaced with "not involved in."
640. "Shall order" has been replaced with "orders."
641. "Last" has been replaced with "final."
642. ", according to the timetable for the proceedings" has been replaced with "under the procedural calendar."
643. "His" has been replaced with "their" for gender neutrality.
644. "To this" has been removed after "objects."
645. "She" has been replaced with the "respondent."
646. "Obtaining a definitive ruling on the dispute" has been replaced with "having the dispute finally resolved."

c) if the arbitral tribunal finds that *the continuation of the proceedings has, for any other reason, become superfluous or impossible.*[647]

19-1.2 After *the proceedings have been closed,*[648] the parties *cannot*[649] submit any claim or raise any *argument.*[650] *Nor can they make submissions or produce exhibits, unless upon the express and written request of the Arbitral Tribunal.*[651]

Article 20—Consent award

If the parties agree during the *arbitration* proceedings, they may *ask*[652] the arbitral tribunal to record this settlement in the form of an arbitral award made by consent of the parties.

Article 21—Jurisdictional objection

21.1 If *a party*[653] intends to challenge the jurisdiction of the arbitral tribunal to hear all or part of the dispute for any reason,[654] *it*[655] must raise this objection in the *memorials under*[656] Articles 6 and 7 of these Rules and, at the latest, during the *case management conference.*[657]

21.2 At any time in the proceedings, the arbitral tribunal *may assess,* sua sponte,[658] its own jurisdiction on *public policy grounds on which the parties are then invited to make their submissions.*[659]

21.3 The arbitral tribunal may rule on a jurisdictional objection either by rendering an interim procedural award or in a final or partial award on the merits, which may all be subject to a motion for annulment.

647. "Pursuing the proceedings has become superfluous or impossible for any other reason" has been replaced with "the continuation of the proceedings has, for any other reason, become superfluous or impossible."
648. "Closing of the proceedings" has been replaced with "the proceedings have been closed."
649. "May not" has been replaced with "cannot."
650. "Plea" has been replaced with "argument."
651. "They similarly may not submit any comments or exhibits unless the arbitral tribunal so requests expressly and in writing" has been replaced with "Nor can they make submissions or produce exhibits, unless upon the express and written request of the Arbitral Tribunal."
652. "Request" has been replaced with "ask."
653. "Any of the parties" has been replaced with "a party."
654. "Reason whatsoever" has been replaced with "reason."
655. "She" has been replaced with "it."
656. "Submissions as provided in" has been replaced with "memorials under."
657. "Scoping meeting" has been replaced with "case management conference."
658. "Automatically examine" has been replaced with "assess, sua sponte."
659. "Grounds of public policy. In such cases, the parties shall be invited to present their own comments" has been replaced with "public policy grounds on which the parties are then invited to make their submissions."

When *a motion for annulment is filed*[660] against an interim award *by which*[661] the arbitral tribunal upheld its jurisdiction, the *arbitration* proceedings *are not*[662] suspended.

Article 21-1—Preliminary step to settle the dispute before the arbitration

21-1-1. *In the presence of an agreement requiring the parties to comply with a pre-arbitration dispute resolution step, the tribunal, upon request of a party, ascertains that the agreement has been complied with and, if applicable, refers the parties to the completion of that preliminary step.*[663]

21-1-2. If *the*[664] preliminary step has not been initiated, the arbitral tribunal *suspends*[665] the *proceedings*[666] for a time period *it*[667] deems appropriate, to allow the most diligent party to complete *that*[668] step.

21-1-3. If *the*[669] preliminary step has *actually*[670] been initiated, the arbitral tribunal *takes notice,*[671] if *applicable,*[672] of its failure.

Article 22—Arbitral award

22.1 *In addition to the operative part, the arbitral award must contain:*[673]

a) the first and last names of the *arbitrator(s) who*[674] rendered the award;
b) the date of the award;
c) the seat of the arbitral tribunal;
d) the *first, last and corporate names*[675] of the parties, as well as their *domicile*[676] or registered office location;

660. "a party files a motion for annulment" has been replaced with "a motion for annulment is filed."
661. "Where" has been replaced with "by which."
662. "Shall not be" has been replaced with "are not."
663. "In case the parties agreed to follow a preliminary step to settle the dispute before the arbitration, upon request of one of the parties, the tribunal shall examine if this condition has been met and shall refer, if applicable, to the completion of this preliminary step" has been replaced with "In the presence of an agreement requiring the parties to comply with a pre-arbitration dispute resolution step, the tribunal, upon request of a party, ascertains that the agreement has been complied with and, if applicable, refers the parties to the completion of that preliminary step."
664. "This" has been replaced with "the."
665. "Shall suspend" has been replaced with "suspends."
666. "Procedure" has been replaced with "proceedings."
667. "Which it" has been replaced with "it."
668. "This" has been replaced with "that."
669. "This" has been replaced with "the."
670. "Effectively" has been replaced with "actually."
671. "Shall take note" has been replaced with "takes notice."
672. "Appropriate" has been replaced with "applicable."
673. "Apart from the terms of the decision, the arbitral award shall contain" has been replaced with "In addition to the operative part, the arbitral award must contain."
674. "Arbitrators having" has replaced with "arbitrator(s) who."
675. "First and last names and trade name" has been replaced with "first, last and corporate names."
676. "Residence" has been replaced with "domicile."

e) *if applicable,*[677] the first and last names of counsel or any person *who has*[678] represented or assisted the parties; and
f) the[679] statement of the respective claims[680] and arguments of the parties, as well as the procedural history.

The arbitral award must *be reasoned.*[681]

If the arbitral tribunal has been empowered by the parties to *rule*[682] as *amiable compositeur, it must*[683] be mentioned.

22.2 The *arbitral award is deemed to have been*[684] rendered at the seat of the *arbitration and on the day of its signing after examination by the Court.*[685]

22.3 The *arbitral award is*[686] rendered *under*[687] the procedure and in the form agreed by the parties. *In the absence of such an agreement,*[688] the award *is*[689] rendered by a majority of votes when the tribunal is composed of three arbitrators.

The arbitral award *must*[690] be signed by the *arbitrator(s).*[691]

However, if *one or two arbitrators refuse*[692] to sign the award, *it must be mentioned and the award has the same effect as if it had been signed by all the arbitrators.*[693]

22.4 Any member of the *arbitral* tribunal[694] may *give*[695] *their*[696] personal opinion to the president, to be attached to the award.

---

677. "When appropriate" has been replaced with "if applicable."
678. "Having" has been replaced with "who has."
679. "Of" has been replaced before "the."
680. ", pleas" has been removed after "claims."
681. "State the reasons on which it is based" has been replaced with "state the reasons on which it is based."
682. "Decide" has been replaced with "rule."
683. "This shall" has been replaced with "it must."
684. "Award shall be deemed to be" has been replaced with "arbitral award is deemed to have been."
685. "Arbitral proceedings on the date on which it is signed after scrutiny by the Court" has been replaced with "arbitration and on the day of its signing after examination by the Court."
686. "Award shall" has been replaced with "arbitral award is."
687. "In accordance with" has been replaced with "under."
688. Failing such agreement" has been replaced with "in the absence of such an agreement."
689. "Shall be" has been replaced with "is."
690. "Shall" has been replaced with "must."
691. "Arbitrator or arbitrators" has been replaced with "arbitrator(s)."
692. "A minority of them refuses" has been replaced with "one or two arbitrators refuse." It is important to note that the French original version specifically refers to the refusal of "one or two arbitrators ("*si un arbitre ou deux arbitres refusent de la signer*"). Therefore, this passage cannot be translated by "a minority," since two arbitrators out of three are simply not a minority.
693. "Mention shall be made of such refusal, and the award shall have the same effect as if all the arbitrators had signed it" has been replaced with "it must be mentioned and the award has the same effect as if it had been signed by all the arbitrators."
694. "Tribunal" has been replaced with "arbitral tribunal."
695. "Communicate" has been replaced with "give."
696. "Her" has been replaced with "their" for gender neutrality.

Article 23—*Preliminary examination by the Court*[697]

23.1 The arbitral tribunal *sends the drafts of the awards on jurisdiction, partial awards resolving some of the claims of the parties*[698] and its final awards to the Secretary General for *a preliminary examination by the Court before those awards are signed.*[699]

The other awards *are not subject to the preliminary examination* but *are only sent to the Court for information.*[700]

23.2 The Court may *suggest*[701] purely *editorial changes,*[702] draw the attention of the arbitral tribunal to claims which do not *appear*[703] to have been *processed*[704] or mandatory *information*[705] which do not appear in the draft award, in the event *of lack of reason*[706], or if there is an apparent contradiction in the reasoning, without however[707] having the power to suggest a reasoning or a *substantive*[708] solution on the merits *concerning*[709] the dispute.

The Court *examines*[710] the draft award submitted to it within a maximum period of one (1) month *from its*[711] receipt.

Article 24—Decision *on*[712] the costs of the arbitration

24.1 The arbitral tribunal *fixes*[713] the costs of arbitration in the *arbitral*[714] award and *decides*[715] which of the parties is responsible *for the payment*[716] or in what proportion *the costs*[717] are to be shared between the parties.

697. "Court scrutiny of the award" has been replaced with "preliminary examination by the Court."
698. "Shall address its draft jurisdictional and partial awards which decide some of the parties' claims," has been replaced with "sends the drafts of the awards on jurisdiction, partial awards resolving some of the claims of the parties."
699. "Court scrutiny before these awards are signed" has been replaced with "a preliminary examination by the Court before those awards are signed."
700. "Shall not be submitted for prior scrutiny, they shall only be forwarded to the Court for information purposes" has been replaced with "are not subject to the preliminary examination but are only sent to the Court for information."
701. "Propose" has been replaced with "suggest."
702. "Formal amendments" has been replaced with "editorial changes."
703. "Seem" has been replaced with "appear."
704. "Addressed" has been replaced with "processed."
705. "Statements" has been replaced with "information."
706. "That the award does not properly state the reasons in which it is based" has been replaced with "of lack of reason," because there is a difference between "not properly stating the reasons" of an award and a "lack of reason" of the award, which is mentioned in the original French version ("*en cas de défaut de motivation*").
707. "," has been removed after "without" and "however."
708. "Substantive" has been inserted before "solution."
709. "In respect of" has been replaced with "concerning."
710. "Shall examine" has been replaced with "examines."
711. "After the" has been replaced with "from its."
712. "As to" has been replaced with "on."
713. "Shall fix" has been replaced with "fixes."
714. "Arbitration" has been replaced with "arbitral."
715. "Decide" has been replaced with "decides."
716. "Payment of these costs" has been replaced with "for the payment."
717. "Those" has been replaced with "the costs."

24.2 *In fixing the*[718] costs, the arbitral tribunal *takes into account the*[719] relevant circumstances, including the extent to which each party has conducted the arbitration proceedings *swiftly*[720] and efficiently in terms of *costs.*[721]

24.3 Arbitration costs[722] include:

a) the fees of the arbitrator and the administrative costs fixed by the Court, possible expenses of the arbitrator, *operating costs*[723] of the arbitral tribunal, expert fees and expenses in *the event*[724] of an expertise. The arbitrators' fees and the Court's administrative fees *are*[725] fixed *in accordance with*[726] a schedule *drawn up*[727] by the General Assembly of the Court and approved by the OHADA Council of Ministers *under*[728] Article 4 of the Treaty;

b) the normal *costs*[729] incurred by the parties for their *defense,*[730] *according to the assessment made by the arbitral tribunal of the related claims of the parties.*[731]

24.4 If the circumstances of the case *make it exceptionally necessary,* the Court may, at its own initiative or upon *a reasoned* request of the arbitrator, fix the fees of the arbitrator at *an amount greater or lower than the one that would result from the application of the* schedule of fees.[732]

Any arbitrators' fee-setting without the approval of the Court is null and void, without it being a cause for the annulment of the award.[733]

24.5 *In the event that all claims are withdrawn or the arbitration is terminated before a final award is rendered, the Court fixes the fees, the costs of the arbitrators and*

718. "Where it decides on" has been replaced with "in fixing the."
719. "May take into account any" has been replaced with "takes into account the."
720. "Quickly" has been replaced with "swiftly."
721. "Cost" has been replaced with "costs."
722. "Shall" has been removed after "costs."
723. "Functioning fees" has been replaced with "operating costs."
724. "In case" has been replaced with "the event."
725. "Shall be" has been replaced with "are."
726. "Pursuant to" has been replaced with "in accordance with."
727. "Defined" has been replaced with "drawn up."
728. "Pursuant the provisions of" has been replaced with "under."
729. "Fees" has been replaced with "costs."
730. "Defence" has been replaced with "defense."
731. "In accordance with the related claims of the parties as interpreted by the arbitral tribunal" has been replaced with "according to the assessment made by the arbitral tribunal of the related claims of the parties."
732. "If the circumstances of the case exceptionally so require, the Court may fix, at its own initiative or upon motivated request of the arbitrator, the fees of the arbitrator at a higher or lower rate than would apply pursuant to the schedule of fees" has been replaced with "If the circumstances of the case make it exceptionally necessary, the Court may, at its own initiative or upon a reasoned request of the arbitrator, fix the fees of the arbitrator at an amount greater or lower than the one that would result from the application of the schedule of fees."
733. "Any decision on the fees made without the approval of the Court is null and void, and shall not be used a ground for annulment of the award" has been replaced with "Any arbitrators' fee-setting without the approval of the Court is null and void, without it being a cause for the annulment of the award."

the administrative costs. If the parties have not agreed on sharing the costs of the arbitration or other relevant costs issues, these issues are settled by the Court.[734]

Article 25—Notification of the award

25.1 *Once the award has been rendered and after the arbitration costs have been fully paid to the Court by the parties or one of them, the Secretary General notifies the signed award to the parties.*[735]

25.2 Additional copies certified[736] by the Secretary General *are*[737] issued at any time[738] to the parties requesting them.

25.3 *By virtue of*[739] such notification, the parties waive the right to any other notification or communication *incumbent upon*[740] the arbitral tribunal.

Article 26—Interpretation, correction *and additional*[741] award

The award *discharges*[742] the arbitral tribunal of the dispute.

Nevertheless, the arbitral tribunal has the power to interpret the award or to correct any material errors or omissions affecting it.[743]

Where the Tribunal has omitted to rule on[744] a claim, it may *remedy the situation*[745] by rendering an additional award.

734. "If all claims are withdrawn, or if the arbitral proceedings are terminated before a final award has been rendered, the Court shall fix the fees, expenses of the arbitrators and the administrative costs. If the parties have not agreed on sharing the costs of arbitration, or other relevant questions concerning costs, the Court shall decide these issues" has been replaced with "In the event that all claims are withdrawn or the arbitration is terminated before a final award is rendered, the Court fixes the fees, the costs of the arbitrators and the administrative costs. If the parties have not agreed on sharing the costs of the arbitration or other relevant costs issues, these issues are settled by the Court."
735. "When the award is made, the Secretary General shall notify the parties of the text signed by the arbitral tribunal, after the arbitration costs have been fully paid to the Court by the parties or one of the parties" has been replaced with "Once the award has been rendered and after the arbitration costs have been fully paid to the Court by the parties or one of them, the Secretary General notifies the signed award to the parties."
736. "True" has been removed because the original French expression used "*copies certifiées conformes*" translates as "certified copies."
737. ", may be" has been replaced with "are."
738. "Exclusively" has been removed after "time" because the original French version does not specify the exclusivity, although it is implied because of the confidentiality of the proceedings.
739. "Pursuant to" has been replaced with "by virtue of."
740. "To be made by" has been replaced with" incumbent upon."
741. "To or addition of the" has been replaced with "and additional."
742. "Shall discharge" has been replaced with "discharges."
743. "The arbitral tribunal shall nevertheless have the power to interpret the award or to rectify material errors and omissions affecting the award" has been replaced with "Nevertheless, the arbitral tribunal has the power to interpret the award or to correct any material errors or omissions affecting it."
744. "Part of" has been removed after "on," because no mention to partial ruling is made at this article in the French original version.
745. "Do so" has been replaced with "remedy the situation."

In either of the above cases, the request must be sent to the Secretary General within thirty (30) days of notification of the award.[746]

The Secretary General communicates, upon receipt, the request to the arbitral tribunal and the opposing party, granting the opposing party a period of thirty (30) days to send its observations to the requesting party and the arbitral tribunal.[747]

If the arbitral tribunal is unable to reconvene, and absent any agreement between the parties to appoint a new arbitral tribunal, the Court *will*[748] appoint a sole arbitrator to *rule on the petition*[749] for interpretation, *rectification or supplementation*[750] of the award.

After *adversarial assessment of*[751] the arguments of *the*[752] parties and any documents[753] they may have submitted, the *draft of the rectifying or additional*[754] award must be *sent to the Court for the preliminary examination under* Article 23 of these Rules within forty five (45) days of referral to the arbitral tribunal.

The foregoing procedure entails no arbitrator's fees except in the case under paragraph 6 of this Article. As for the costs, if any, they are borne by the party who filed the application if it is dismissed entirely. Otherwise, they are shared between the parties in the proportion set for arbitration costs in the award subject of the motion.[755]

Article 27—*Res judicata*[756] and provisional enforcement

27.1 Any arbitral award rendered *under* these Rules *is final and binding*[757] on the parties and *has*[758] res judicata effect in the territory of each State *Party,*[759] *in the same*

746. "In one or the other events mentioned above, a request must be made within thirty (30) days from the date of the notification of the award Upon receipt of the request, the Secretary General communicates it to the arbitration tribunal and the opposing party, granting the latter a period of thirty (30) days to send his comments to the requesting party and to the arbitration tribunal" has been replaced with "In either of the above cases, the request must be sent to the Secretary General within thirty (30) days of notification of the award," because the paragraphs are separated in the original French version.
747. The current paragraph has been detached from the preceding one to comply with the original French version.
748. "Shall" has been replaced with "will."
749. "Decide the request" has been replaced with "rule on the petition." *See* the glossary, *infra*.
750. "Correction to or addition" has been replaced with "rectification or supplementation."
751. "Examining" has been replaced with "adversarial assessment."
752. "Both" has been replaced with "the" because the original French version did not specify "both parties" since there might be more than two parties.
753. "Which" has been removed after "documents."
754. "The rectifying or additional draft" has been replaced with "draft of the rectifying or additional."
755. This paragraph has been omitted from the translated version published on the official Website and I have added it.
756. "Effect" has been removed after "judicata."
757. "Shall have mandatory effect on the parties" has been replaced with "is final and binding."
758. "Final" has been replaced with "has."
759. "Member States" has been replaced with "States Parties," to reflect the original French expression used "Etats Parties."

way as decisions rendered by the courts of the State.[760] It may be *enforced*[761] on the territory of any of the States *Parties.*

27.2 By submitting their dispute to these Rules, the parties *undertake*[762] to enforce the *upcoming*[763] award without delay.

27.3 *The arbitral tribunal may, by a reasoned decision, order or deny the provisional enforcement of the award if such enforcement has been requested.*[764]

Article 28—Lodging and legal validity of the award

The original of any award *rendered under*[765] these Rules *is*[766] lodged with the Secretary General.

In all *cases not specifically covered*[767] by these Rules, the Court and the arbitral tribunal *proceed*[768] *by drawing their inspiration from these rules*[769] and *making their best efforts*[770] to ensure that the award is enforceable.[771]

Chapter III—Motion for annulment, recognition and enforcement of arbitral awards

Article 29—Motion for annulment

29.1 *The*[772] party *filing*[773] a motion for annulment of an award rendered by an arbitral tribunal *under these Rules must refer to the Court by a motion that the Court notifies*[774] the opposing party.

760. "To the same extent as judgments made by domestic courts" has been replaced with "in the same way as decisions rendered by the courts of the State."
761. "Subject to forced enforcement" has been replaced with "enforced," because "enforcement" already entails coerced execution of the award. Thus, "forced enforcement" would be redundant.
762. "Shall undertake" has been replaced with "undertake."
763. "Future" has been replaced with "upcoming."
764. "The arbitral tribunal may order provisional enforcement of the arbitral award upon request of such enforcement" has been replaced with "The arbitral tribunal may, by a reasoned decision, order or deny the provisional enforcement of the award if such enforcement has been requested." NB: The precision about a "reasoned decision" has been omitted in the translated version and I have added it.
765. "Made in accordance with" has been replaced with "rendered under."
766. "Shall be" has been replaced with "is."
767. "Other instances not expressly provided" has been replaced with "cases not specifically covered."
768. "Shall act" has been replaced with "proceed."
769. "In accordance with the spirit of" has been replaced with "by drawing their inspiration from these rules."
770. "Shall make every effort" has been replaced with "making their best efforts."
771. "At law" has been removed after "enforceable."
772. "Any" has been replaced with "the."
773. "Which submits" has been replaced with "filing."
774. "Pursuant to the Rules of the a Court shall address a request to the Court; the Court shall accordingly notify" has been replaced with "under these Rules must refer to the Court by a motion that the Court notifies."

29.2 *The*[775] parties may agree to waive the action for annulment of the arbitral award,[776] provided the award does not breach international public policy.

The *motion for annulment is admissible only:*[777]

a) if the arbitral tribunal has ruled without an arbitration agreement or on *a null or expired agreement;*[778]
b) if the arbitral tribunal *has been*[779] *improperly*[780] composed, or the sole arbitrator was *improperly*[781] appointed;
c) if the arbitral tribunal *has ruled*[782] without *complying with the mission entrusted to it;*[783]
d) if the *adversarial principle*[784] has been breached;
e) if the arbitral award *is contrary to*[785] international public policy;[786]
f) if the award *is devoid of any reason.*[787]

29.3 The *motion*[788] for annulment *can be filed*[789] as soon as the award is *rendered.*[790] It *becomes inadmissible*[791] if it has not been *filed*[792] within two (2) months *of*[793] notification of the award *under*[794] Article 25 of these Rules.

29.4 The Court *processes the case and rules under*[795] its Rules of procedure.

In this case, the procedural time limits are reduced by half.[796]

The Court *must rule on the motion for*[797] annulment within six (6) months of its *referral.*[798]

---

775. "the" has been replaced with "The."
776. ")" has been replaced with ",".
777. "Annulment request shall only be permitted" has been replaced with "motion for annulment is admissible only."
778. "An agreement that is void or expired" has been replaced with "a null or expired agreement."
779. "Was" has been replaced with "has been."
780. "Irregularly" has been replaced with "improperly."
781. "Irregularly" has been replaced with "improperly."
782. "Ruled" has been replaced with "has ruled."
783. "Conforming to the mandate with which it has been entrusted" has been replaced with "complying with the mission entrusted to it."
784. "Principle of adversarial procedure" has been replaced with "adversarial principle." *See* the glossary, *infra.*
785. "Breaches" has been replaced with "is contrary to."
786. "Or" has been removed because there is no equivalent in the original French version.
787. "Fails to state the reasons on which it is based" has been replaced with "is devoid of any reason."
788. "Request" has been replaced with "motion."
789. "Shall be permitted" has been replaced with "can be filed."
790. "Made." has been replaced with "rendered."
791. "Shall cease to be admissible" has been replaced with "becomes inadmissible."
792. "Made" has been replaced with "filed."
793. "From" has been replaced with "of."
794. "Pursuant to" has been replaced with "under."
795. "Shall hear and decide this issue pursuant to the provisions of" has been replaced with "processes the case and rules under."
796. "In such event, the deadlines shall be halved" has been replaced with "In this case, the procedural time limits are reduced by half."
797. "Shall render a decision on" has been replaced with "must rule on the motion for."
798. "Seizure" has been replaced with "referral."

29.5 If the Court denies recognition and res judicata effect of the award referred to it, the award *is*[799] annulled.

The Court reviews the case de novo[800] and *rules*[801] on the merits if the parties have requested *that.*[802]

If the parties have not requested *de novo review,*[803] the proceedings are resumed at the request of the most diligent party, starting, *if necessary, from the last step of the arbitration proceedings held valid by the Court.*[804]

Article 30—Exequatur

30.1 *Exequatur may be granted upon an award as soon as it has been rendered.*[805]

Exequatur is[806] requested by *a motion*[807] to the President of the Court, *with a copy to*[808] the Secretary General. The latter *immediately forwards*[809] to the Court the documents allowing *the existence of the arbitral award and the arbitration agreement to be established.*[810]

30.2 *Exequatur is*[811] granted,[812] within fifteen (15) days of the filing of the request, by order of the *president of*[813] the Court or the judge *delegate,*[814] and *makes*[815] the award enforceable in all States *Parties. Exequatur* proceedings *are not adversarial.*[816]

799. "Shall be" has been replaced with "is."
800. "It shall re-hear the case" has been replaced with "The Court reviews the case de novo."
801. "Rule" has been replaced with "rules."
802. "It to do so" has been replaced with "that."
803. "For the Court to re-hear the case and rule on the merits" has been replaced with "*de novo review.*"
804. "From the last step in the arbitral proceedings recognized as valid by the Court, as applicable" has been replaced with ", if necessary, from the last step *of* the arbitration proceedings held valid by the Court."
805. "The award may be enforced as soon as it is rendered" has been replaced with "*Exequatur* may be granted upon an award as soon as it has been rendered" because the original French version, "*La sentence est susceptible d'exequatur dès son prononcé,*" does not waive the *exequatur* requirement, which is mandatory; it rather suggests that the prevailing party can apply for *exequatur* as soon as the award has been rendered. But in any event, *exequatur* must be granted before an arbitral award becomes enforceable, except where there is voluntary enforcement by the losing party.
806. "Shall be" has been replaced with "is."
807. "Application" has been replaced with "a motion."
808. "And a copy addressed to" has been replaced with "with a copy to."
809. "Shall immediately communicate" has been replaced with "immediately forwards."
810. "The Court to establish the existence of the arbitral award and of the arbitration agreement" has been replaced with "the existence of the arbitral award and the arbitration agreement to be established."
811. "Shall be" has been replaced with "is."
812. "," has been inserted after "granted."
813. "Presiding judge at" has been replaced with "president of."
814. "Appointed for this purpose" has been replaced with "judge delegate." *See* the glossary, *infra*.
815. "Shall make" has been replaced with "makes."
816. "These proceedings shall not be contradictory" has been replaced with "*exequatur* proceedings are not adversarial."

Exequatur is not granted if a motion for annulment of the award has already been filed under Article 29 abovementioned and is pending before the Court.[817] In such a case, both *motions are*[818] joined.

Unless *the*[819] provisional enforcement of the award has been ordered by the arbitral tribunal, a motion for annulment *suspends*[820] the enforcement of the arbitral award until the Court has ruled.

The Court *also has*[821] jurisdiction to rule on any dispute related to provisional enforcement.

The decision on *exequatur* of the awards *relating to provisional or conservatory*[822] measures *must*[823] be made within three (03) days of the[824] filing of the *motion*[825] to the Court.

30.3 *If exequatur is denied,*[826] the party requesting *exequatur* may *refer the matter*[827] to the Court within fifteen (15) days of the notification of the rejection *of its motion.*[828] This time limit *is*[829] reduced to three (03) days if the appeal relates to[830] *exequatur* of an award of the arbitral tribunal on provisional or conservatory measures. The *party requesting exequatur notifies*[831] the *appeal to the opposing party.*[832]

30.4 The decision of the *president*[833] granting *exequatur cannot*[834] be appealed.

30.5 *Exequatur can be denied only*[835] in the following cases:

a) if the arbitral tribunal has ruled without an arbitration agreement or on *a null or expired agreement;*[836]

---

817. "*Exequatur* shall not be granted if the Court has already been seized for the same award of a request pursuant to Article 29 abovementioned" has been replaced with "*Exequatur* is not granted if a motion for annulment of the award has already been filed under Article 29 abovementioned and is pending before the Court."
818. "Requests shall be" has been replaced with "motions are."
819. "The" has been inserted after "unless."
820. "Shall suspend" has been replaced with "suspends."
821. "Shall have" has been replaced with "also has."
822. "On interim or provisional" has been replaced with "relating to provisional or conservatory."
823. "Shall" has been replaced with "must."
824. "Date of the" has been removed after "the."
825. "Request" has been replaced with "motion."
826. "When enforcement is rejected" has been replaced with "if *exequatur* is denied" because there is a difference between *exequatur*, which is mandatory for the enforcement to take place, and the enforcement itself. In the French original version, *exequatur* is mentioned ("*Si l'exequatur est refusé*").
827. "Only appeal" has been replaced with "refer the matter."
828. "Of its motion" has been inserted after "rejection."
829. "Shall be" has been replaced with "is."
830. "The" has been removed after "to."
831. "Court shall notify" has been replaced with "party requesting *exequatur* notifies." The wording of the original French version does not suggest that the Court has to notify the appeal to the opposing party, but rather the party requesting *exequatur*.
832. "The opposing party of the appeal" has been replaced with "appeal to the opposing party."
833. "Presiding judge of the Court" has been replaced with "president."
834. "May not" has been replaced with "cannot."
835. "May only be refused" has been replaced with "can be denied only."
836. "An agreement that is void or expired" has been replaced with "a null or expired agreement."

b) if the arbitral tribunal *has ruled*[837] without *complying with the mission entrusted to it*;[838]
c) if the *adversarial principle*[839] has been breached;
d) if the arbitral award *is contrary to*[840] international public policy.

Article 31—Executory formula[841]

31.1 The Secretary General *issues*[842] to the requesting party a certified true copy of the original of the award filed *under*[843] Article 28 of these Rules, including the *exequatur*[844] certificate. This certificate *states*[845] that *exequatur was granted to the award,*[846] *as the case may be, either by an order of the President of the Court duly notified, or by a judgment of the Court dismissing a motion for annulment, or by a judgment of the Court overturning a denial of exequatur.*[847]

31.2 In view of the certified copy of the award *bearing*[848] the certificate *of*[849] the Secretary General of the Court, the national authority appointed by the State *Party*[850] *for which exequatur has been requested*[851] *affixes the executory formula on the award as it is in force in that State.*[852]

---

837. "Ruled" has been replaced with "has ruled."
838. "Conforming to the mandate with which it has been entrusted" has been replaced with "complying with the mission entrusted to it."
839. "Principle of adversarial procedure" has been replaced with "adversarial principle." *See* the glossary, *infra.*
840. "Breaches" has been replaced with "is contrary to."
841. "Enforcement certificate" has been replaced with "executory formula." *See* the Lexicon.
842. "Shall deliver" has been replaced with "issues."
843. "In conformity with the provisions of" has been replaced with "under."
844. "Enforcement" has been replaced with "*exequatur.*" *See* the glossary, *infra.*
845. "Shall state" has been replaced with "states."
846. "Enforcement of the arbitration award has been granted" has been replaced with "*exequatur* was granted to the award," because there is a difference between *exequatur*, which enables enforcement, and the enforcement itself.
847. "Either by a ruling of the presiding judge of the Court, which has been duly served and has become final, in the absence of any motion for annulment filed within 15 days as provided herein above, or by a ruling of the Court annulling a decision to reject *exequatur*" has been replaced with ", as the case may be, either by an order of the President of the Court duly notified, or by a judgment of the Court dismissing a motion for annulment, or by a judgment of the Court overturning a denial of *exequatur.*"
848. "With" has been replaced with "bearing."
849. "From" has been replaced with "of."
850. "Member States" has been replaced with "States Parties," to reflect the original French expression used "Etats Parties."
851. "In which enforcement has been solicited" has been replaced with "for which *exequatur* has been requested" because the French original version specifies the State for which *exequatur* has been requested ("*l'Etat Partie pour lequel l'exequatur a été demandé*"). Therefore, "in which enforcement has been solicited" would be wrong, since enforcement may happen in any of the 17 States Parties to the Treaty.
852. "*Exequatur* to the award pursuant to the rules applicable in the above mentioned State" has been replaced with "affixes the executory formula on the award as it is in force in that State" because there is only one *exequatur*, which is granted by the President of the Court and the national authority appointed by the State Party can only affix the executory formula, like a stamp certifying that *exequatur* has already been granted and the award is now fully

Article 32—Motion[853] for review

Upon discovery of a fact likely to exert a decisive influence and which, prior to the rendering of the award, was unknown to the arbitral tribunal or the party requesting the review, a motion for review may be filed against the award before the Secretary General. The Secretary General forwards the motion for review to the arbitral tribunal.[854] In the absence of an agreement by the parties on the appointment of a new arbitral tribunal:

a) *where*[855] the arbitral tribunal *was made up*[856] of a sole arbitrator and *cannot*[857] be reconvened, the Court *appoints*[858] a sole arbitrator to *rule on the application for*[859] review;
b) *where*[860] the arbitral tribunal *was made up*[861] of three arbitrators and *cannot*[862] be reconvened, *the Court appoints, after consultation with the parties, either a new tribunal made up of three arbitrators or a single arbitrator to rule on the motion for review;*[863]
c) *where*[864] the arbitral tribunal *was made up*[865] of three arbitrators[866] and one or more of these arbitrators *cannot be*[867] reconvened, *the Court appoints, after consultation with the parties, arbitrators to complete the arbitral tribunal which rules on the motion for review.*[868]

---

enforceable in that State Party. Thus, saying "*exequatur* to the award ..." would be confusing in suggesting *exequatur* has been granted by the national authority appointed, which is not the case.

853. "Application" has been replaced with "motion."
854. "The arbitration award may be the subject of an application for review lodged with the Secretary General, who shall notify the arbitral tribunal, pursuant to the discovery of a fact likely to exert a decisive influence and which was unknown to the arbitral tribunal or the party applying for a review before the award was rendered" has been replaced with "Upon discovery of a fact likely to exert a decisive influence and which, prior to the rendering of the award, was unknown to the arbitral tribunal or the party requesting the review, a motion for review may be filed against the award before the Secretary General. The Secretary General forwards the motion for review to the arbitral tribunal."
855. "When" has been replaced with "where."
856. "Is composed" has been replaced with "made up."
857. "May" has been replaced with "cannot."
858. "Shall appoint" has been replaced with "appoints."
859. "Decide the application for a" has been replaced with "rule on the application for."
860. "When" has been replaced with "where."
861. "Is composed has been replaced with "made up."
862. "May" has been replaced with "cannot."
863. "After consultation with the parties, the Court shall appoint either a new tribunal composed of three arbitrators, or a sole arbitrator to decide the application for a review" has been replaced with "the Court appoints, after consultation with the parties, either a new tribunal made up of three arbitrators or a single arbitrator to rule on the motion for review."
864. "When" has been replaced with "where."
865. "Is composed has been replaced with "made up."
866. "," has been removed after "arbitrators."
867. "May" has been replaced with "cannot be."
868. "after consultation with the parties, the Court shall appoint arbitrators to complete the arbitral tribunal to decide the application for a review" has been replaced with "the Court appoints, after consultation with the parties, arbitrators to complete the arbitral tribunal which rules on the motion for review."

Article 33—Third party opposition

Third party opposition against arbitral awards is brought before the Court. The same applies to judgments of the Court, where the Court has ruled on the merits under Article 29.5, of these Rules.[869]

Third party opposition *is*[870] filed *under*[871] Article 47 of the *Rules of procedure of the Common Court of Justice and Arbitration.*[872]

Article 33—Final provisions

These Rules, which *repeal*[873] the *Arbitration Rules of March 11*[874] 1999, *will*[875] be published in the OHADA Official Gazette within sixty (60) days *of their adoption.*[876] They will[877] also be published in the Official Gazette of the States *Parties.*

Conakry, November 23, 2017.

869. "Opposition against arbitral awards filed by a third party shall be addressed to the Court. The same shall apply to decisions of the Court where the Court has ruled on the merits of the dispute in accordance with Article 29.5, paragraph 2 above" has been replaced with "Third party opposition against arbitral awards is brought before the Court. The same applies to judgments of the Court, where the Court has ruled on the merits under Article 29.5, of these Rules."
870. "Shall be" has been replaced with "is."
871. "Pursuant to the provisions of" has been replaced with "under."
872. "Rules of procedure" has been replaced with "Rules of procedure of the Common Court of Justice and Arbitration."
873. "Abrogate" has been replaced with "repeal."
874. "Rules of Arbitration of the Common Court of Justice and Arbitration dated 11 March" has been replaced with "Arbitration Rules of March 11."
875. "Shall" has been replaced with "will."
876. "From its approval" has been replaced with "of their adoption." *See* the glossary, *infra.*
877. "It shall" has been replaced with "they will."

APPENDIX III

Uniform Act on Arbitration

The Council of Ministers of the Organization for the Harmonization of Business Law in Africa (OHADA),

- Having regard to the Treaty for the Harmonization of Business Law in Africa, signed on October 17, 1993 in Port Louis, as amended on October 17, 2008 in Quebec, in particular its Articles 8, 21, 26 and 39;
- Having regard to opinion No. 04/2017/AU dated October 5, 6, 2017 of the Common Court of Justice and Arbitration;
- After deliberation,

  Adopts by unanimous vote of the States *Parties*[1] present, the Uniform Act set out below:

CHAPTER 1: SCOPE

Article 1. This Uniform Act *is*[2] applicable to any arbitration *where*[3] the seat of the arbitral tribunal is[4] in one of the *States Parties.*

Article 2. Any natural or legal person may resort to arbitration with respect to any rights on which *they have*[5] the free disposal.

States, other public territorial *authorities,*[6] public entities and any other legal person under public law may also be *parties*[7] to[8] arbitration, regardless of the legal

1. "Member States" has been replaced with "States Parties," to reflect the original French expression used "Etats Parties."
2. "Shall be" has been replaced with "is."
3. "When" has been replaced with "where."
4. "Is located" has been replaced with "is"; "located," which is unnecessary, has been removed.
5. "She has" has been replaced with "they have."
6. "Bodies" has been replaced with "authorities" as the latter, which is used in the French version of the UAA, is more accurate.
7. The plural form is used in the original French version.
8. "An" has been replaced after "to."

nature of the contact, without being able to invoke their own *law*[9] to object to the arbitrability of *a*[10] dispute, to their capacity to submit to arbitration[11] or to the validity of the arbitration agreement.

Article 3. *Arbitration*[12] may be based on an arbitration agreement or an *investment instrument,*[13] *such as an*[14] investment code or a bilateral or multilateral investment treaty.

Article 3-1. The arbitration agreement may be in the form of an arbitration clause or of a submission agreement.

The arbitration clause is *the*[15] agreement whereby the parties *undertake*[16] to submit to arbitration disputes which may arise[17] or result from a contractual relationship.

The submission agreement is *the*[18] agreement whereby the parties to an existing dispute agree to settle it through arbitration.

The arbitration agreement must be[19] in writing, or in any other form evidencing its existence, in particular by reference to a document *stipulating it.*[20]

Article 4. The arbitration agreement *is*[21] independent *of*[22] the main contract.

Its validity *is*[23] not affected by the nullity of *that*[24] contract, and it *is assessed*[25] in accordance with the common *will*[26] of the parties, without reference to a national law.

---

9. In the French version, "Droit" is used without the plural form; it has the meaning of "applicable law" or legislation as a whole in the State Party under consideration. Therefore, "law" as a general concept has been chosen.
10. "The" has been replaced with "a," to reflect the original French version.
11. In the French language the expression used has the idea of "ability to compromise" to arbitration.
12. "An arbitration" has been replaced with "Arbitration," used in the original French version, construed as an arbitral procedure.
13. "An instrument regarding an investment" has been replaced with "an investment instrument."
14. "In particular an" has been replaced with "such as an."
15. "An" has been replaced with "the."
16. "Agree," which is not wrong per se in the context, has been replaced with "undertake," which better emphasizes the idea of commitment of the parties to arbitration when a dispute arises.
17. To simplify the style, "out of" has been deleted after "arise."
18. "An" has been replaced with "the."
19. To simplify the style, "made" has been removed after "be."
20. The comma "," after "particular" has been deleted and "containing the agreement" has been replaced with "stipulating it," which was used in the original French version. It must be understood that "it" refers to the arbitration agreement in this context.
21. "Shall be" has been replaced with "is," used in the original French language, even though the meaning of the sentence must be construed as "shall be."
22. "From" has been replaced with "of" for clarity of the style, because "independent of" is, in the context as explained in the Collins Dictionary, the most appropriate way to express the difference between the arbitration contract and the main contract which has no bearing on each other.
23. "Shall" has been replaced with "is," used in the original French language, even though the meaning of the sentence must be construed as "shall be"; then "be" has been deleted.
24. "The" has been replaced with "that."
25. "Shall be interpreted" has been replaced with "is assessed."
26. "Intention" has been replaced with "will."

The parties may *always,*[27] by mutual agreement, resort to arbitration, even when proceedings are already pending before a state *court.*[28]

CHAPTER 2: CONSTITUTION OF THE ARBITRAL TRIBUNAL

Article 5 The *assignment*[29] of an arbitrator *can*[30] be performed only[31] by a natural person.

The arbitral tribunal *is*[32] *made up*[33] of *either* a sole arbitrator or three arbitrators. *In the absence of* agreement *between* the parties,[34] the arbitral tribunal *is*[35] *made up*[36] of a sole arbitrator.

Article 6 Arbitrators *are*[37] appointed, *dismissed*[38] or replaced *in accordance with*[39] the parties' agreement.

Where[40] the parties have agreed to appoint two arbitrators despite the provisions of Article 5, paragraph 2 of this Uniform Act, the arbitral tribunal *is*[41] *supplemented*[42] by a third arbitrator mutually chosen by the parties.

In the absence of[43] any such agreement, the arbitral tribunal *is*[44] *supplemented* by the appointed arbitrators, or, *in the absence of*[45] any agreement between them, the competent *court*[46] in the *State Party.*[47] The same *applies*[48] *in the case of an appointment*

27. "In any case, the parties may" has been replaced with "the parties may always."
28. "Jurisdiction" has been replaced with "court." It must be noted that "court" has a broad meaning, including even a single judge, depending on each jurisdiction.
29. "Duties" in the plural form has been replaced with "assignment" (non plural), which is a synonym to "mission" used in the original French version (non plural form).
30. "May" has been replaced with "can."
31. "May only be performed" has been replaced with "may be performed only," to emphasize the type of person that is allowed to serve as arbitrator: no legal entity can do it and only natural persons can sit as arbitrators.
32. "Shall be" has been replaced with "is."
33. "Composed" has been replaced with "made up," which is the first on the list of synonyms of "consist of something" in the Collins Dictionary.
34. "Absent agreement of the parties" has been replaced with "in the absence of agreement between the parties."
35. "Shall be" has been replaced with "is."
36. "Composed" has been replaced with "made up," which is the first on the list of synonyms of "consist of something" in the Collins Dictionary.
37. "Shall be" has been replaced with "are."
38. "Revoked" has been replaced with "dismissed."
39. "Pursuant to" has been replaced with "in accordance with."
40. "When" has been replaced with "where," to ensure consistency with the CCJA Arbitration Rules.
41. "Shall be" has been replaced with "is."
42. "Completed" has been replaced with "supplemented," which has the meaning of "adding to something" to make it complete (HarperCollins Publishers, s.d.).
43. "Absent" has been replaced with "in the absence of."
44. "Shall be" has been replaced with "is."
45. "Absent" has been replaced with "in the absence of."
46. "Jurisdiction" has been replaced with "court" because "jurisdiction," used in the original French version, does not mean "jurisdiction" in English.
47. "Member State" has been replaced with "State Party."
48. "Shall apply" has been replaced with "applies."

made necessary by reason of recusal, incapacity, death, resignation or dismissal of an arbitrator.[49]

In the absence of[50] agreement between the parties on the appointment procedure, or *if their stipulations are*[51] insufficient:

a) in case of an arbitration *with* three arbitrators, each party *appoints*[52] one arbitrator, and the two arbitrators so appointed *choose*[53] the third arbitrator; if *a*[54] party *does not*[55] appoint an arbitrator within thirty (30) days of *receiving a*[56] request for arbitration from the other party, or if the two arbitrators fail to agree on the *choice of the*[57] third arbitrator within thirty days (30) of their appointment, the appointment *is*[58] made, upon the request of *a*[59] party, by the competent *court*[60] in the State *Party;*[61]
b) in case of an arbitration with a sole arbitrator, if the parties *cannot*[62] agree on the choice of the arbitrator, the latter *is*[63] appointed, upon the request of *a*[64] party, by the competent *court*[65] in the State *Party.*[66]

---

49. "If an arbitrator is challenged, becomes incapacitated, dies, resigns or is revoked" has been replaced with "in the case of an appointment made necessary by reason of recusal, incapacity, death, resignation or dismissal of an arbitrator." For instance, the challenge of an arbitrator does not automatically result in his removal from a panel; thus, it seems more appropriate to refer to the "recusal" of an arbitrator instead of the expression "if an arbitrator is challenged" as used in the published text.
50. "Absent" has been replaced with "in the absence of."
51. "In the event that their agreement is" has been replaced with "if their stipulations are insufficient."
52. "Shall" has been removed after "party."
53. "Shall" has been removed after "appointed." "Appoint" has been replaced with "choose" used in the original French version.
54. "One" has been replaced with "a."
55. "Fails to" has been replaced with "does not."
56. "The receipt of the" has been replaced with "receiving a."
57. This has been inserted.
58. "Shall be" has been replaced with "is" to reflect the original French version.
59. "One" has been replaced with "a."
60. "Jurisdiction" has been replaced with "competent."
61. "Member State" has been replaced with "State Party."
62. "Are unable to" has been replaced with "cannot."
63. "Shall be" has been replaced with "is" to reflect the original French version.
64. "One" has been replaced with "a."
65. "Jurisdiction" has been replaced with "competent."
66. "Member State" has been replaced with "State Party."

The decision to appoint an arbitrator by the competent *court*[67] *is*[68] made within fifteen (15) days *of referral to the court,*[69] unless the laws of a State *Party*[70] *provides for*[71] a shorter time period. This decision *is*[72] subject to no appeal.

Article 7 The arbitrator who accepts *their*[73] *mission*[74] *must*[75] communicate *their*[76] acceptance to the parties by any means in writing.

The arbitrator undertakes to *continue*[77] *their*[78] *mission*[79] until the end, unless *they justify*[80] of an impediment or legitimate reason for abstention or resignation.

The arbitrator *must*[81] enjoy full exercise of *their*[82] civil rights and[83] remain independent and impartial *toward*[84] the parties.

Any potential arbitrator *informs* the parties of any circumstance likely to create in their minds a legitimate doubt about *their*[85] independence and impartiality[86] and may accept *their*[87] appointment only[88] with their unanimous and written consent.

From the date of *their*[89] appointment and *throughout*[90] the proceedings, the arbitrator *must*[91] reveal any such circumstances to the parties *without delay.*[92]

---

67. "Jurisdiction" has been replaced with "competent."
68. "Shall be" has been replaced with "is" to reflect the original French version.
69. "From when it was seized" has been replaced with "of referral to the court."
70. "Member State" has been replaced with "State Party."
71. "Foresee" has been replaced with "provides for," because the French verb used here, "prévoir," means "to provide for" or "make arrangements for"; while "foresee" has a meaning closer to "forecast," "envisage," "predict," etc. Therefore, the appropriate and accurate expression should be "provide for."
72. "Shall be" has been replaced with "is" to reflect the original French version.
73. "His" has been replaced with "their."
74. "Mandate" has been replaced with "mission," used in the original French language.
75. "Shall" has been replaced with "must," for consistency and clarity purposes, because of the *Gutierrez de Martinez v. Lamagno rule* presented in the introduction, *supra.*
76. "His" has been replaced with "their."
77. "Complete" has been replaced with "continue" because as used, "complete" already means to fulfill, to accomplish, or to conclude. Therefore, if "complete" is used, the following part "until the end" would be useless.
78. "His" has been replaced with "their."
79. "Mandate" has been replaced with "mission," used in the original French language.
80. "He justifies" has been replaced with "they justify."
81. "Shall" has been replaced with "must," for consistency and clarity purposes, because of the *Gutierrez de Martinez v. Lamagno* rule.
82. "His" has been replaced with "their."
83. "Shall" has been removed after "and," to maintain the imperative induced by "must" at the beginning of the sentence.
84. "Vis-à-vis," inexistent in American English according to Collins Dictionary, has been replaced with "toward."
85. "His" has been replaced with "their."
86. "," has been removed after "impartiality."
87. "His" has been replaced with "their."
88. "Only" has been removed after "may" and inserted after "appointment."
89. "His" has been replaced with "their."
90. "During the course of" has been replaced with "throughout."
91. "Shall" has been replaced with "must."
92. "Without delay" has been added to reflect the promptness or swiftness of the information that must be given to the parties by the arbitrator, as expressed in the original French version "sans délai."

Article 8 In *the event*[93] of *dispute,*[94] and if the parties have not agreed on the *procedure for challenging an arbitrator,*[95] the competent *court*[96] in the *State Party*[97] *rules*[98] *on the challenge,* no later than thirty (30) days after the parties and the arbitrator have been heard or duly summoned. If the competent *court*[99] fails to *rule*[100] within the[101] above-mentioned time period, the challenge *is*[102] *removed from that court* and may be brought before the Common Court of Justice and Arbitration by the most diligent party.

The decision of the competent *court*[103] dismissing the challenge[104] may be challenged[105] only[106] before the Common Court of Justice and Arbitration.

Any ground *for*[107] challenge must be raised, no later than thirty (30) days *from the discovery of the fact that led to*[108] the challenge, by the party seeking to invoke it.

The challenge of an arbitrator *is*[109] admissible[110] only for *a* reason *disclosed* after *their*[111] appointment.

When the *mission*[112] of an arbitrator is terminated, or when *they resign*[113] for any other reason, a replacing[114] arbitrator is appointed according to the applicable rules to the *appointment*[115] of the replaced arbitrator, unless otherwise agreed by the parties. The same procedure *is*[116] followed if the arbitrator's *mission*[117] is *terminated*[118] by

93. "In case of" has been replaced with "in the event of."
94. "Disagreement" has been replaced with "dispute."
95. The "challenge procedure," which is vague, has been replaced with "the procedure for challenging an arbitrator," to make the difference between the challenge of an arbitrator ("récusation" in French) and the challenge of an arbitral award.
96. "Jurisdiction" has been replaced with "court."
97. "Member State" has been replaced with "State Party."
98. "Shall decide the challenge" has been replaced with "rules," to reflect the meaning of the original French word "statuer." *See* the glossary, *infra.*
99. "Jurisdiction" has been replaced with "court."
100. "Render a decision" has been replaced with "rule."
101. "This" has been replaced with "the" to avoid unnecessary repetition because "this" already refers to the time period mentioned above.
102. "Shall be" has been replaced with "is" to reflect the original French version.
103. "Jurisdiction" has been replaced with "court."
104. "Application" has been removed after "challenge."
105. The specific challenge provided for by Article 8 here refers to a "petition for cassation" or "appeal in cassation," known in French as "pourvoi en cassation."
106. "Only" has been removed after "may."
107. "Of" has been replaced with "for."
108. "After the fact having motivated" has been replaced with "from the discovery of the fact that led to."
109. "Shall be" has been replaced with "is."
110. "Allowed" might be more appropriate; or "admitted."
111. "His" has been replaced with "their."
112. "Mandate" has been replaced with "mission," used in the original French language.
113. "He resigns" has been replaced with "they resign."
114. Or "substitute?"
115. "Nomination" has been replaced with "appointment."
116. "Shall be" has been replaced with "is."
117. "Mandate" has been replaced with "mission," used in the original French language.
118. "Revoked" has been replaced with "terminated."

mutual agreement of the parties *and in*[119] any other case when *their*[120] *mission*[121] is terminated.

CHAPTER 3: ARBITRAL PROCEEDINGS[122]

Article 8.1 In *the presence*[123] of an agreement *requiring*[124] the parties to *comply with*[125] a *pre-arbitration dispute resolution step,*[126] the tribunal, upon[127] request of *a party,*[128] *ascertains that*[129] *the agreement has been complied with*[130] and *if applicable,*[131] *refers the parties to*[132] the completion of *that*[133] preliminary *step.*[134]

If *the*[135] preliminary *step*[136] has not been initiated, the arbitral tribunal *stays*[137] the *proceedings*[138] for a time period it deems appropriate, to allow the most diligent party to *complete that step.*[139]

If *the*[140] preliminary *step*[141] has *actually*[142] been initiated, the arbitral tribunal *takes notice,*[143] If applicable,[144] of its failure.

Article 9 The parties *must* be treated equally and each party *must* be given full opportunity to present *their*[145] case.

119. "Or" has been replaced with "and in."
120. "His" has been replaced with "their."
121. "Mandate" has been replaced with "mission," used in the original French language.
122. The original French title is "L'instance arbitrale."
123. "Case" has been replaced with "the presence."
124. "Imposing upon" has been replaced with "requiring."
125. "Follow" has been replaced with "comply with."
126. "Preliminary phase for the settlement of the dispute prior to any arbitration" has been replaced with "pre-arbitration dispute resolution step."
127. "The" has been removed after "upon."
128. "One of the parties" has been replaced with "a party."
129. "Examine" has been replaced with "ascertains that."
130. "This condition has been met" has been replaced with "the agreement has been complied with."
131. "As the case may be" has been replaced with "if applicable."
132. "Shall mandate" has been replaced with "refers the parties to."
133. "This" has been replaced with "that."
134. "Phase" has been replaced with "step."
135. "This" has been replaced with "the."
136. "Phase" has been replaced with "step."
137. "Shall suspend" has been replaced with "stays."
138. "Procedure" has been replaced with "proceedings."
139. "Initiate this phase" has been replaced with "complete that step."
140. "This" has been replaced with "the."
141. "Phase" has been replaced with "step."
142. "Effectively" has been replaced with "actually."
143. "Shall take note" has been replaced with "takes notice."
144. "As the case may be" has been replaced with "if applicable."
145. "Its" has been replaced with "their."

Article 10 Where the parties have agreed to refer to an arbitration institution, *they are committed to applying*[146] the arbitration rules of *that*[147] institution unless they expressly *waive*[148] specific provisions in agreement with this institution.

The arbitral proceedings *start on*[149] the date on *which*[150] one of the parties initiates the procedure of the constitution of the arbitral tribunal.

Article 11 The arbitral tribunal *has exclusive jurisdiction*[151] to rule on its own jurisdiction, *including on all issues relating to*[152] the existence or validity of the arbitration agreement.

Any objection to arbitral jurisdiction *must*[153] be raised before any defense on the merits except where the facts on which it is based have been disclosed later.

The arbitral tribunal may rule on its own jurisdiction in the award dealing with the merits or in a partial award subject to the annulment action.

Article 12 *If*[154] the arbitration agreement does not set a *deadline,*[155] the *mission*[156] of the arbitral tribunal *cannot*[157] exceed six (06) months from the date on which the last appointed arbitrator accepted *their*[158] appointment.

The legal or contractual time limit for the arbitration may be extended, either *by*[159] agreement of the parties, or *at the*[160] request of one of the parties or of the arbitral tribunal, by[161] the competent *court*[162] in the *State Party.*[163]

Article 13 When a dispute *subject to arbitration proceedings under*[164] an arbitration agreement is brought before a State court, the latter must, if *requested by one of the parties,*[165] *decline*[166] jurisdiction.

146. "Shall be deemed to have agreed on the application of" has been replaced with "they are committed to applying."
147. "This" has been replaced with "that."
148. "Agreed to exclude" has been replaced with "waive."
149. "Shall start at" has been replaced with "starts on."
150. "When" has been replaced with "on which."
151. "Alone is competent" has been replaced with "has exclusive jurisdiction."
152. "As well as on any issues concerning" has been replaced with "including on all issues relating to."
153. "Shall" has been replaced with "must," to comply with the original French version.
154. "Where" has been replaced with "if."
155. "A time limit" has been replaced with "deadline."
156. "Mandate" has been replaced with "mission," used in the original French language.
157. "May not" has been replaced with "cannot."
158. "His" has been replaced with "their."
159. "Upon" has been replaced with "by."
160. "Upon" has been replaced with "at the."
161. "Or" has been removed before "by" because if not removed, the sentence would mean that the competent court in the State Party can also request the extension of the time limit, which it not what the French version of the Uniform Act provides for.
162. "Jurisdiction" has been replaced with "court."
163. "Member State" has been replaced with "State Party."
164. ", for which an arbitral tribunal is seized pursuant to" has been replaced with "under."
165. "If one of the parties so requests" has been replaced with "if requested by one of the parties."
166. "Declare that it lacks" has been replaced with "decline."

If[167] the *dispute has not yet been referred to the arbitral tribunal,*[168] or if no *request for arbitration*[169]has been filed, the state court *must* also *decline jurisdiction,*[170] unless the arbitration agreement is manifestly null or manifestly inapplicable to the case. In that case, the competent *court*[171] *renders a final decision*[172] on its jurisdiction within a maximum of fifteen (15) days. *That*[173] decision *can be challenged only before*[174] the Common Court of Justice and Arbitration in accordance with its Rules of Procedure.

In any *event,*[175] the *State court*[176] may not *decline jurisdiction*[177] on its own motion.

However, the existence of an arbitration agreement *does*[178] not preclude a State court, at the request of a party and in the event of a recognized and reasoned emergency, *from ordering*[179] provisional or conservatory measures so long as such measures do not imply *a review*[180] of the merits of the case, for which only the arbitral tribunal *has jurisdiction.*[181]

Article 14 The parties may, directly or by reference to arbitration rules, determine the arbitral procedure. They may also *subject it*[182] to a procedural law of their choice.

In the absence of such an agreement,[183] the arbitral tribunal may *proceed with*[184] the arbitration as it deems appropriate.

In support of their claims, the parties bear the burden of alleging and *proving*[185] the facts.

The parties *must*[186] act *with swiftness and loyalty*[187] in the conduct of the proceedings and[188] refrain from any *dilatory tactics.*[189]

If, without *relying on a*[190] legitimate reason:

167. "Where" has been replaced with "if."
168. "The arbitral tribunal is not yet seized" has been replaced with "the dispute has not yet been referred to the arbitral tribunal."
169. "Arbitral request" has been replaced with "request for arbitration."
170. "Declare itself incompetent" has been replaced with "decline jurisdiction."
171. "Jurisdiction" has been replaced with "court."
172. "Shall issue a final decision" has been replaced with "renders a final decision."
173. "Its" has been replaced with "that."
174. "Only be appealed before" has been replaced with "can be challenged only before."
175. "Case" has been replaced with "event" because the French expression used "en tout état de cause" is commonly translated "in any event."
176. "Competent Jurisdiction" has been replaced with "State court," used in the French version.
177. "declare itself incompetent" has been replaced with "decline jurisdiction" and the position changed in the sentence for clarity purposes.
178. "Shall" has been replaced with "does."
179. "To order" has been replaced with "from ordering."
180. "An examination" has been replaced with a "review."
181. "Is competent" has been replaced with "has jurisdiction."
182. "Make it subject" has been replaced with "subject it."
183. "Absent such agreement" has been replaced with "in the absence of such an agreement."
184. "Conduct" has been replaced with "proceed with."
185. "Adducing evidence to prove" has been replaced with "proving."
186. "Shall" has been replaced with "must."
187. "Quickly and with loyalty" has been replaced with "with swiftness and loyalty."
188. "Shall" has been removed after "and."
189. "Actions" has been replaced with "tactics."
190. "Invoking" has been replaced with "relying on a."

a) the claimant does not submit *their*[191] claim, the arbitral tribunal *terminates*[192] the arbitral proceedings;
b) the respondent does not *present*[193] *their*[194] defense, the arbitral tribunal *continues*[195] the arbitral proceedings without, however, considering this failure *per se* as an acceptance of the claimant's allegations;
c) one of the parties fails to appear at the hearing or to produce documents, the arbitral tribunal may continue the proceedings and *rule*[196] on the basis of the evidence before it.

The arbitral tribunal may invite the parties to provide it with factual explanations and to submit to it, by any legally admissible means, the evidence it *deems*[197] necessary for the *resolution of*[198] the dispute.

It *may*[199] retain in its ruling, the arguments, explanations or documents submitted *or relied upon* by the parties, *only if the latter*[200] have been in a position to discuss them.

It *cannot*[201] base its ruling on sua sponte *arguments*[202] without *inviting the parties beforehand*[203] to submit *their*[204] comments.

Where the assistance of judicial authorities is necessary for the taking of evidence, the arbitral tribunal may, sua sponte[205] or upon request, seek the assistance of a competent *court*[206] in the *State Party.*[207]

The[208] party who, knowingly, *fails to timely object to*[209] irregularity and proceeds with the arbitration is deemed to have waived *their*[210] right to object.

The arbitral tribunal,[211] unless *the parties agree otherwise,*[212] *also has the power*[213] to *settle*[214] any incidental claims concerning the verification of the authenticity of documents or forgery.

191. "Its" has been replaced with "their."
192. "Shall terminate" has been replaced with "terminates."
193. "Submit" has been replaced with "present."
194. "Its" has been replaced with "their."
195. "Shall continue" has been replaced with "continues."
196. "Decide" has been replaced with "rule."
197. "Believes will be" has been replaced with "deems."
198. "Solution to" has been replaced with "resolution of."
199. "May not" has been replaced with "may ... only if" because the imperative has been conveyed in the original French language.
200. "Unless both parties" has been replaced with "only if the latter."
201. "Shall not" has been replaced with "cannot" because the imperative has been conveyed in the original French language.
202. "Evidence established on its own motion" has been replaced with "sua sponte arguments," because the French word "moyen" means "argument," not evidence, which is "preuve" in French. However, there is the expression "moyen de preuve" in French, which is not evidence established on its own motion.
203. "Previously inviting each of the parties" has been replaced with "inviting the parties beforehand."
204. "Its" has been replaced with "their."
205. "On its own motion" does mean "sua sponte" as well; but has been replaced for consistency.
206. "Jurisdiction" has been replaced with "court."
207. "Member State" has been replaced with "State Party."
208. "A" has been replaced with "the," which is used in the original French language.

If necessary, the arbitral tribunal may, after consulting the parties or upon their request, appoint one or more experts to report on specific issues it determines and hear them at the hearing.

The arbitral tribunal may also, upon the request of either party, order interim or conservatory measures, with the exception of *interim attachments*[215] and *court-ordered securities*[216] which remain within the jurisdiction of state courts.

Article 15 The arbitral tribunal *rules*[217] on the merits of the dispute *under*[218] the rules of law chosen by the parties. *In the absence of*[219] choice by the parties, the arbitral tribunal *applies*[220] the rules it deems the most appropriate, by taking into consideration, as the case may be, international trade *usages*.[221]

It may also *rule*[222] as *amiable compositeur* when the parties have *conferred such power on it*.[223]

Article 16 The arbitral *proceedings*[224] end with the rendering of a final award.

They[225] may also *end*[226] with a closing order.

The arbitral tribunal *issue*[227] a closing order when:

a) the claimant withdraws *their*[228] *claim*,[229] unless the respondent objects and the arbitral tribunal acknowledges that *the respondent has*[230] a legitimate interest in finally settling[231] the dispute;
b) the parties agree to terminate the proceedings;

---

209. "Abstains from invoking, without delay," has been replaced with "fails to timely object to."
210. "Its" has been replaced with "their."
211. "Shall" has been removed after "tribunal."
212. "Otherwise agreed by the parties" has been replaced "with."
213. "Be empowered" has been replaced with "also has the power."
214. "Decide" has been replaced with "settle."
215. "Conservatory seizures" has been replaced with "interim attachments." *See* the glossary, *infra*.
216. "Judicial sureties" has been replaced with "court-ordered securities."
217. "Shall rule" has been replaced with "rules."
218. "Pursuant to" has been replaced with "under."
219. "Absent such" has been replaced with "in the absence."
220. "Shall apply" has been replaced with "applies."
221. "Practices" has been replaced with "usages."
222. "Decide" has been replaced with "rule."
223. "Authorized it to do so" has been replaced with conferred such power on it."
224. "Procedure shall" has been replaced with "proceedings."
225. "It" has been replaced with "they," referring to the arbitral proceedings.
226. "Be terminated" has been replaced with "end."
227. "May issue" has been replaced with "issues."
228. "Its" has been replaced with "their."
229. "Request" has been replaced with "claim."
230. "There is" has been replaced with "the respondent has," "it" referring to the defendant, who, in the context from the original French version, can be the only person having an interest in the settling the dispute once for all.
231. "Finally settling" as used in the translated version above could be construed either as meaning "settling the dispute after a lenghty process" ("finalement réglé") or "settling the dispute once for all" ("définitivement réglé"); the latter is the most appropriate in the context and it would be good to find a better way of conveying that idea.

c) the arbitral tribunal finds that pursuing the proceedings has become, for any other reason, unnecessary or impossible;
d) the initial or extended arbitral time limit has expired;
e) there is *acquiescence to*[232] the claim, withdrawal from the proceedings, *or* settlement.

Article 17 The arbitral tribunal *sets*[233] the date on which the matter *will*[234] be deliberated.

After this date, no other claim may be introduced or argument[235] raised.

No remarks may be presented; nor may any *exhibit*[236] be submitted unless at the express and written request of the arbitral tribunal.

Article 18 The deliberations of the arbitral tribunal *are*[237] confidential.

CHAPTER 4: THE ARBITRAL AWARD

Article 19 The arbitral award *is*[238] rendered in accordance with the procedure and the forms agreed[239] by the parties.

Absent any such agreement, the award *is*[240] rendered by a majority vote when the tribunal is composed of three arbitrators.

If the parties *reach*[241] an agreement during[242] the arbitral proceedings, they may ask the arbitral tribunal to issue an award by consent. Such award *has*[243] the same status and[244] effect as any other award *ending the dispute.*[245]

Article 20 *In addition to the operative part,*[246] the arbitral award *must* contain:

a) the last and first names[247] of the arbitrator*(s)*[248] *who*[249] rendered the award;

232. "An acknowledgement of" has been replaced with "acquiescence to." *See* the glossary, *infra*.
233. "Shall set" has been replaced with "sets."
234. "Shall" has been replaced with "will."
235. "S" has been removed at the end of "argument."
236. "Document" has been replaced with "exhibit."
237. "Shall be" has been replaced with "are."
238. "Shall be" has been replaced with "is."
239. "Upon" has been replaced after "agreed."
240. "Shall be" has been replaced with "is."
241. "Come to" has been replaced with "reach."
242. "The course of" has been removed after "during."
243. "Shall have" has been replaced with "has."
244. "Shall have the same" has been removed after "and."
245. "Bringing the dispute to an end" has been replaced with "ending the dispute."
246. "Apart the holding" has been replaced with "in addition to the operative part." *See* the glossary, *infra*.
247. The order of last and first names has been aligned with the following paragraph of the section for consistency.
248. "Arbitrators" has been replaced with "arbitrator**(s)**" to reflect the original French version "du ou des arbitres," i.e., "the arbitrator" in case of a sole arbitrator tribunal or "the arbitrator**s**" as plural where there was a panel of three arbitrators.
249. "Having" has been replaced with "who."

b) its date;
c) the seat of the arbitral tribunal;
d) the *last, first and*[250] *corporate names*[251] of the parties, as well as *their domicile*[252] or registered office;
e) *if applicable,*[253] the last and first names of counsel or any person *who has*[254] represented or assisted the parties;
f) the statement of the respective *claims and arguments of the parties,*[255] as well as the procedural history.

The arbitral award must *be reasoned.*[256]

If the arbitral tribunal has been empowered by the parties to *rule*[257] as *amiable compositeur, it must be*[258] mentioned.

Article 21 The arbitral award *is*[259] signed by the arbitrator or arbitrators.

However, if a minority of them refuses to sign the award, such refusal *must* be mentioned and the award *has*[260] the same effect as if *it had been signed by all the arbitrators.*[261]

Article 22 The award discharges the arbitral tribunal of the dispute.

Nevertheless, the arbitral tribunal has[262] the power to interpret the award or to *correct any*[263] material errors and omissions affecting it.

Where the tribunal[264] has omitted to rule *on a claim,*[265] it may *remedy the situation*[266] by rendering an additional award.

In *either case,*[267] *the*[268] request must be made within thirty (30) days from the notification of the award. The tribunal *has*[269] forty-five (45) days to *rule.*[270]

250. "The last and first names and" has been replaced with "the last, first and."
251. "Trade names" has been replaced with "corporate names." *See* the glossary, *infra.*
252. "Headquarters" has been replaced with "their domicile."
253. "As the case may be" has been replaced with "if applicable."
254. "Having" has been replaced with "who has."
255. "Claims of the parties, their pleas and" has been replaced with "removed after their."
256. "State the reasons on which it is based" has been replaced with "be reasoned."
257. "Decide" has been replaced with "rule."
258. "This shall be" has been replaced with "it must be."
259. "Shall be" has been replaced with "is."
260. "Shall have" has been replaced with "has."
261. "All the arbitrators had signed it" has been replaced with "it had been signed by all the arbitrators."
262. "The arbitral tribunal shall nevertheless have" has been replaced with "Nevertheless, the arbitral tribunal has."
263. "Rectify" has been replaced with "correct any."
264. "It" has been replaced with "the tribunal."
265. "Upon a head of claim" has been replaced with "on a claim."
266. "Do so" has been replaced with "remedy the situation."
267. "In one or the other events mentioned above" has been replaced with "in either case."
268. "A" has been replaced with "the."
269. "Shall have" has been replaced with "has." Also, "a period of" has been removed after "has."
270. "Render a decision" has been replaced with "rule."

If the arbitral tribunal cannot be reconvened it *falls*[271] upon the competent *court*[272] in the *State Party*[273] to *rule.*[274]

Article 23 As soon as it is rendered, the arbitral award has *res judicata* effect regarding the dispute it settles.

Article 24 The arbitral tribunal may, *if the* provisional enforcement of the award has been requested, *grant it or reject it* by a reasoned decision.[275]

CHAPTER 5: RECOURSE AGAINST THE ARBITRAL AWARD

Article 25 The award *is*[276] not subject to opposition, appeal or *cassation.*[277]

It may be subject to *a motion for annulment,*[278] which must be *filed*[279] before the competent *court*[280] in the *State Party.*[281]

However, the parties may agree to waive the annulment action against the arbitral award provided *the latter*[282] is not contrary to international public policy.

The decision of the competent *court*[283] in the *State Party*[284] *on the motion for annulment*[285] may only be appealed *in cassation*[286] before the Common Court of Justice and Arbitration.

The arbitral award may *be*[287] the subject of *third-party opposition*[288] by any *person*[289] before the *court*[290] of the *State Party*[291] which *would have had jurisdiction*[292] *in the absence of*[293]arbitration and when that award *prejudices his rights.*[294]

271. "Will fall" has been replaced with "falls."
272. "Jurisdiction" has been replaced with "court."
273. "Member State" has been replaced with "State Party."
274. "Decide" has been replaced with "rule."
275. "The tribunal may grant provisional enforcement of the award if this has been requested, or may reject the request through a reasoned decision" has been replaced with "The arbitral tribunal may, if the provisional enforcement of the award has been requested, grant it or reject it by a reasoned decision."
276. "Shall" has been replaced with "is."
277. "Any opposition, or appeal on factual or legal grounds" has been replaced with "opposition, appeal or cassation."
278. "An annulment action" has been replaced with "a motion for annulment."
279. "Lodged" has been replaced with "filed."
280. "Jurisdiction" has been replaced with "court."
281. "Member State" has been replaced with "State Party."
282. "it" has been replaced with "the latter," to reflect the original French version "celle-ci," referring to the award.
283. "Jurisdiction" has been replaced with "court."
284. "Member State" has been replaced with "State Party."
285. "Regarding the annulment action" has been replaced with "on the motion for annulment."
286. "On points of law" has been replaced with "in cassation."
287. "Become" has been replaced with "be."
288. "Opposition" has been replaced with "third-party opposition."
289. "Third-party" has been replaced with "person."
290. "Jurisdiction" has been replaced with "court."
291. "Member State" has been replaced with "State Party."
292. "Been competent" has been replaced with "had jurisdiction."
293. "If there was no" has been replaced with "in the absence of."
294. "Is prejudicial to its rights" has been replaced with "prejudices his rights."

It may also be *the subject of*[295] a *motion*[296] for revision before the arbitral tribunal due to the discovery of a fact likely to have a decisive influence on the settlement of the dispute and which, before the rendering of the award, was unknown to both the arbitral tribunal and the party requesting the revision. *Where*[297] the arbitral tribunal *can*[298] no longer be *convened,*[299] the *motion*[300] for revision is brought before the *court*[301] in the *State Party*[302] which would have *had jurisdiction*[303] in the absence of arbitration.

Article 26 The *motion for annulment*[304] *is admissible only:*[305]

a) if the arbitral tribunal has ruled without an arbitration agreement or *on a null or expired agreement;*[306]
b) if the arbitral tribunal *has been*[307] *improperly*[308] composed, or the sole arbitrator was *improperly*[309] appointed;
c) if the arbitral tribunal *has ruled*[310] without *complying with the mission entrusted to it;*[311]
d) if the *adversarial principle*[312] has been *breached;*[313]

295. "Subject to" has been replaced with "the subject of."
296. "Request" has been replaced with "motion." *See* the glossary, *infra.*
297. "When" has been replaced with "where."
298. "May" has been replaced with "can."
299. "Reconvened" has been replaced with "convened," because while "reconvene" means to convene again after a short break, the word used in the original French version "réuni" means to convene.
300. "Request" has been replaced with "motion."
301. "Jurisdiction" has been replaced with "court."
302. "Member State" has been replaced with "State Party."
303. "Been competent" has been replaced with "had jurisdiction."
304. "Annulment action" has been replaced with "motion for annulment."
305. "Shall only be permitted" has been replaced with "is admissible only" because the original French word "recevable" means "admissible" in Legal English. (Nicholson & Stevenson, 2004); (Saint Dahl & Boudreau, 2007).
306. "Based on an agreement that is void or expired" has been replaced with "on a null or expired agreement."
307. "Was" has been replaced with "has been."
308. "Irregularly" has been replaced with "improperly."
309. "Irregularly" has been replaced with "improperly."
310. "Ruled" has been replaced with "has ruled."
311. "Conforming to the mandate with which it has been entrusted" has been replaced with "complying with the mission entrusted to it."
312. "Principle of due process" has been replaced with "adversarial principle," because the due process is a wider legal concept that encompasses adversarial proceedings. Thus, due process does not designate adversarial proceedings only and its use here could be confusing. (*See Black's Law Dictionary* online, https://thelawdictionary.org/due-process-of-law/).
313. "Not been respected "has been replaced with "has been breached."

e) if the arbitral award is contrary to international public policy;[314]
f) if the award *is devoid of any reason.*[315]

Article 27 The *motion for annulment*[316] *is admissible*[317] as soon as the award is *rendered.*[318] It *ceases*[319] to be if it has not been *filed*[320] within one month from the notification of the award *with*[321] *exequatur.*

The competent *court*[322] *rules*[323] within three (03) months of its *referral.*[324] *If that court*[325] fails to *rule*[326] within *that*[327] time period, it is *divested*[328] of the case and the action may be brought before the Common Court of Justice and Arbitration within the next fifteen (15) days. The latter must *rule*[329] within a maximum[330] of six months of *referral.*[331] In that case, the *time limits*[332] specified in the Rules of procedure of the Common Court of Justice and Arbitration *are*[333] reduced by half.

Article 28 Except where the provisional enforcement of the award has been ordered by the arbitral tribunal, the *filing*[334] of the annulment action *stays the*[335] enforcement of the award until[336] the competent *court*[337] in the *State Party*[338] or the Common Court of Justice and Arbitration, as the case may be, has *ruled.*[339]

That court[340] *also has jurisdiction*[341] to rule on a dispute concerning the provisional enforcement.

314. "Or" has been removed after ";" because it does not exist in the original French version.
315. "Fails to state the reasons on which it is based" has been replaced with "is devoid of any reason."
316. "Annulment action" has been replaced with "motion for annulment."
317. "Shall be permitted" has been replaced with "is admissible."
318. "Made" has been replaced with "rendered."
319. "Shall cease" has been replaced with "ceases."
320. "Exercised" has been replaced with "filed."
321. "Having received the "has been replaced with "with."
322. "Jurisdiction" has been replaced with "court."
323. "Shall render a decision" has been replaced with "rules."
324. "Seizure" has been replaced with "referral."
325. "When said jurisdiction" has been replaced with "if that court."
326. "Render a decision" has been replaced with "rule."
327. "This" has been replaced with "that."
328. "Discharged" has been replaced with "divested" because, "discharged" seems to refer to a jury. Alternatively, we could use "removed."
329. "Render a decision" has been replaced with "rule."
330. "Time limit" has been removed after "maximum."
331. "Its seizure" has been replaced with "referral."
332. "Deadlines" has been replaced with "time limits."
333. "Shall be" has been replaced with "are."
334. "Exercise" has been replaced with "filing" because in French, "exercer une action en justice" means "to file a lawsuit."
335. "Shall suspend" has been replaced with "stays the."
336. "Such time that" has been removed.
337. "Jurisdiction" has been replaced with "court."
338. "Member State" has been replaced with "State Party."
339. "Rendered a decision" has been replaced with "ruled."
340. "Jurisdiction" has been replaced with "court."
341. "Shall also be competent" has been replaced with "also has jurisdiction."

Article 29 In the event of *the*[342] annulment of the arbitral award and *unless*[343] the[344] annulment is based on the fact that the tribunal *has* ruled without an arbitration agreement or on a void or expired one, it rests upon the most diligent party, if *they*[345] so wishes, to initiate *new arbitration proceedings*[346] in accordance with this Uniform Act.

CHAPTER 6: RECOGNITION AND ENFORCEMENT OF ARBITRAL AWARDS

Article 30 The *arbitral* award *is enforceable only*[347] by virtue of an *exequatur* decision issued by the competent *court*[348] in the *State Party.*[349]

Article 31 *Recognition*[350] and *exequatur*[351] of the arbitral award *assume*[352] that the party *availing itself of the existence of the award*[353] establishes the existence of the arbitral award.

The existence of the arbitral award *is*[354] established by the production of its original[355] accompanied by the arbitration agreement or copies of these documents meeting *the requirements for*[356] their authenticity.

If[357] those documents are not written in *the official*[358] language(s) of the *State Party*[359] where the *exequatur* is *requested,*[360] the party *must*[361] submit a *certified translation*[362] by a translator registered on the list of experts established by the competent *courts.*[363]

Recognition and exequatur[364] *are*[365] denied *if*[366] the award is manifestly contrary to *an* international public policy *rule.*[367]

---

342. "An" has been replaced with "the."
343. "Save when" has been replaced with "unless."
344. "Said" has been removed after "the."
345. "It" has been replaced with "they."
346. "A new arbitration proceeding" has been replaced with "new arbitration proceedings."
347. "Shall only be subject to enforcement" has been replaced with "is enforceable only."
348. "Jurisdiction" has been replaced with "court."
349. "Member State" has been replaced with "State Party."
350. "The" has been removed before "recognition."
351. "Enforcement" has been replaced with "*exequatur,*" which was used here in the original French version.
352. "Presume" has been replaced with "assume."
353. "Relying on it" has been replaced with "availing itself of the existence of the award."
354. "Shall be" has been replaced with "is."
355. "Award" has been removed after "original."
356. "Conditions required to establish" has been replaced with "the requirements for."
357. "Where" has been replaced with "if."
358. "One of the original" has been replaced with "the official."
359. "Member State" has been replaced with "State Party."
360. "Demanded" has been replaced with "requested."
361. "Shall" has been replaced with "must," used in the original French version.
362. "Translation certified" has been replaced with "certified translation."
363. "Jurisdiction" has been replaced with "court."
364. "The" has been removed before "recognition" and "*exequatur.*"
365. "Shall be" has been replaced with "are."
366. "When" has been replaced with "if."
367. "A rule concerning international public policy" has been replaced with "an international public policy rule."

The State court,[368] *to which* a request for recognition or *exequatur has been referred,*[369] *rules*[370] within *a period which may not exceed* fifteen (15) days from the day of *referral.*[371] If at the end of this time limit the court[372] has not *issued its order,*[373] *exequatur is deemed*[374] to have been granted.

When[375] *exequatur is*[376] granted, or in the case of silence *of the referral court*[377] within fifteen (15) days as *mentioned above,*[378] the most diligent party *refers to*[379] the *chief* clerk[380] or the competent authority in the *State Party*[381] in order to *affix the executory formula*[382] upon the original of the award. The *procedure relating to the request for exequatur*[383] is not adversarial.[384]

Article 32 The decision which rejects[385] *exequatur can*[386] *be challenged*[387] *only*[388] before the Common Court of Justice and Arbitration.

The decision granting[389] *exequatur is*[390] not[391] subject to any appeal.

However, the annulment action of the arbitral award[392] automatically *entails* an appeal against the decision granting[393] *exequatur* within the limits of the referral of the competent *court*[394] of the *State Party.*[395]

---

368. "National jurisdiction" has been replaced with "state court."
369. "Seized by a request for recognition or *exequatur*" has been replaced with "to which a request for recognition or exequatur has been referred."
370. "Shall render a decision" has been replaced with "rules."
371. "Its seizure" has been replaced with "referral."
372. "Jurisdiction" has been replaced with "court."
373. "Rendered its decision" has been replaced with "issued its order" because the expression "la juridiction n'a pas rendu son ordonnance" used in the French original version, specifies the type of ruling, i.e. an ordinance.
374. "Shall be presumed" has been replaced with "is deemed."
375. "The" has been removed after "when."
376. "Has been" has been replaced with "is."
377. "From the jurisdiction seized by the request for *exequatur*" has been replaced with "of the referral court."
378. "Above-mentioned" has been replaced with "mentioned above."
379. "May seize" has been replaced with "refers to."
380. "Head clerk" has been replaced with "chief clerk," referring to the "Greffier en chef" in French-speaking legal systems.
381. "Member State" has been replaced with "State Party."
382. "Fix the formal *exequatur*" has been replaced with "affix the executory formula."
383. "*Exequatur* procedure" has been replaced with "procedure relating to the request for *exequatur.*"
384. "Contradictory" has been replaced with "adversarial."
385. "The" has been replaced after "rejects."
386. "Shall" has been replaced with "can" to reflect the wording of the original French version.
387. Here also, "challenge before the Common Court of Justice and Arbitration" refers to a "petition for cassation" or "appeal in cassation," known in French as "pourvoi en cassation."
388. "Only be subject to appeal on points of law" has been replaced with "can only be challenged."
389. "The" has been removed after "granting."
390. "Shall" has been replaced with "is."
391. "Be" has been removed after "not."
392. "Shall" has been removed after "award."
393. "He" [the] has been removed before "*exequatur.*"
394. "Jurisdiction" has been replaced with "court."
395. "Member State" has been replaced with "State Party."

Article 33 The dismissal of the annulment action[396] automatically *entails the validity of the arbitral*[397] award *and*[398] the decision *granting*[399] *exequatur.*

Article 34 *Arbitral*[400] awards rendered on the basis of rules different from those provided for in this Uniform Act *are*[401] recognized in the *States Parties* under the conditions provided for by international conventions possibly applicable and, in the absence thereof, under the same conditions as those provided in this Uniform Act.

CHAPTER 7: FINAL PROVISIONS

Article 35 This Uniform Act *serves as*[402] the *law relating to arbitration*[403] in the *States Parties.*

It *is applicable*[404] only to arbitral proceedings commenced after its entry into force.

Article 36 This Uniform Act, which *repeals*[405] the *Uniform Act on Arbitration of*[406] March 11, 1999, *will* be published in the OHADA Official Gazette within sixty (60) days from its *adoption.*[407] It *will* also be published in the Official Gazette of the *States Parties.*

It *comes into*[408] force ninety (90) days after its publication in the OHADA Official Gazette.

Conakry, November 23, 2017.

396. "Shall" has been removed after "action."
397. "Validate the" has been replaced with "entails the validity of the arbitral."
398. "As well as of" has been replaced with "and."
399. "Having granted" has been replaced with "granting"; and "the" removed before "*exequatur.*"
400. "The" has been removed before "arbitral."
401. "Shall be" has been replaced with "are."
402. "Shall be" has been replaced with "serves as."
403. "The arbitration law" has been replaced with "the law relating to arbitration."
404. "Shall apply" has been replaced with "is applicable."
405. "Abrogates" has been replaced with "repeals." NB: "abrogates" is right but "repeal" is preferable for style clarity.
406. "Arbitration Uniform Act dated 11 March 1999" has been replaced with "Uniform Act on Arbitration of March 11, 1999."
407. "Approval" has been replaced with "adoption," a term that also applies to the legislative process (*see* Collins Dictionary ... online https://www.collinsdictionary.com/dictionary/english/adopt [accessed Sept. 13, 2019 at 04:56] and is used to describe the legislative process by the European Union (https://ec.europa.eu/info/law/law-making-process/adopting-eu-law_en [accessed Sept. 13, 2019 at 04:52].
408. "Shall enter into" has been replaced with "comes into."

APPENDIX IV

Reduction of Time Limits Before the CCJA

The amended Article 27 paragraph 2 of the Uniform Act on Arbitration (UAA) provides that when the CCJA is called upon to rule on the motion for annulment of an arbitral award, the "the time limits specified in the Rules of procedure of the Common Court of Justice and Arbitration are reduced by half."

Likewise, Article 29.4, paragraphs 1 and 2 of the CCJA Regulation on Arbitration provide that when a motion for annulment of an arbitral award governed by the CCJA Rules if filed before the CCJA, the Rules of Procedure before the CCJA apply and the time limits set in those are halved.

In the absence of precision by the OHADA Legislator, it is appropriate to present those time limits provided for in the Rules of Procedure of the CCJA and likely to be applied in a procedure for the annulment of an arbitral award brought before the CCJA. Where necessary, it will be specified which of those time periods are applicable or not, bearing in mind that with regard to the procedure in matters of the annulment of arbitral awards (governed either by the UAA or by the CCJA Arbitration Rules) brought before the CCJA, the Rules of Procedure of the latter constitute the general text and the specific provisions of the UAA or the CCJA Regulation on Arbitration constitute the specific texts which will depart, if necessary, from the Rules of Procedure of the CCJA, but only with respect to the motion for annulment before the CCJA.

1. General Time Limit for Referral to the CCJA (Article 28 of the CCJA Rules of Procedure)[1]

By reference to Article 14 of the Treaty, Article 28 of the the CCJA Rules of Procedure lays down the general rules for a referral to the CCJA. *In the context of the OHADA*

1. Article 28.1 of the CCJA Rules of Procedure states at para. 1 that "When the Court is *referred to* by one of the parties to the proceeding through the appeal in cassation provided for in the third or fourth paragraph of Article 14 of the Treaty, the appeal *must* be *filed at* the Registry within two (2) months of the notification of the *challenged* decision by the attorney of the petitioner under the conditions set forth in Article 23 … .": https://www.ohada.org/attachments/article/1838/CCJA_Procedural_Rules_Reviewed-EN_Unofficial_Translation.pdf [accessed Apr. 25, 2020, at 08:26].

Arbitration Rules, the motion for the annulment of an award under Article 27 of the UAA of the CCJA Arbitration Rules amounts to a "decision not subject to appeal rendered by any court of the States Parties in [any matter raising issues relating to the application of the Uniforms Acts and Regulations under the Treaty]" within the meaning of Article 14 of the Treaty. This is the appeal in cassation for which the OHADA Legislator has set the statute of limitations of two months from the service of the challenged decision, which in this case, will be the arbitral award. If this period were to apply in this case, it would be reduced by half and would, therefore, be *one month*.

However, the statute of limitation under Article 28 of the Rules of Procedure (general text) of the CCJA does not have to be taken into account for motions filed under Article 27 of the UAA since the Legislator has already set a specific time limit of *fifteen days* from the expiry of the three months-period allocated to the national competent courts to rule on the motion for annulment. Thus, there is no need to resort to the reduced time limit of Article 28 for a referral to the CCJA in the event of failure of the competent court to rule on the action for annulment.

There is also no need to resort to the time limit under Article 28-6 of the CCJA Rules of Procedure[2] since there is no specific time limit set by the Rules. In the absence of a specific time frame provided set, the CCJA Registry should set a time limit that would be half the average time allocated to the parties in the context of Article 28-6 of the CCJA Procedure Regulations. As a result, Article 28 of the CCJA Rules of Procedure does not appear to have any particular impact in an action for the annulment of an award brought before the CCJA under Article 27 of the UAA.

Since Article 29.3 paragraph 1 of the CCJA Regulation on Arbitration has set a specific statute of limitation (of two months running from the notification of the award for filing a motion for annulment), which happens to be the same under Article 28 of the CCJA Rules of Procedure, the time period of two months mentioned at said Article 28 will not apply to the motion filed under Article 29.3 of the CCJA Regulation on Arbitration.

2. Time Limit for Filing a Response (Article 30 of the CCJA Rules of Procedure)[3]

This provision gives a period of three months to a party to a cassation appeal before the CCJA to file a response. This period must be reduced by half, namely forty-five days in the case of the motion for annulment of an arbitral award brought before the CCJA under Article 27 of the UAA and Article 29.4 of the CCJA Regulation on Arbitration. This would comply with the six-month time limit allocated to the CCJA for adjudicating on this matter.

---

2. Article 28.6 of the CCJA Rules of Procedure states that "If the appeal does not *comply with* the conditions laid down in this Article, the *reporting judge sets* a reasonable time limit for the *regularization of* the appeal or *the filing of the exhibits* mentioned above. Failing this regularization or submission within the time limit, the Court *must* rule on the admissibility of the appeal."
3. Article 30 of the CCJA Rules of Procedure states at para. 1 that "Any party to the proceedings before the National Court may *file* a statement of defense within a period of three (3) months from the *service* of the appeal *in cassation*."

3. Time Limit for Asking the President of the CCJA the Permission to File an Additional Brief (Article 31 of the CCJA Rules of Procedure)[4]

Article 31 of the CCJA Rules of Procedure grants a period of fifteen days to a party to a cassation appeal before the CCJA to ask its President for permission to file an additional brief (in reply, rejoinder, etc.). This period runs from the date at which the party seeking permission was served the brief to which they want to respond with the contemplated additional brief. This period must be halved to seven and a half days; however, for the proper administration of justice, it seems appropriate to reduce it to eight days for the motion for annulment of an arbitral award filed before the CCJA. Thus, within the framework of such a procedure, any party wishing to respond to the opposing party's submissions must submit their request to the President of the CCJA within eight days of receiving the brief to which they wish to respond.

4. Time Limit for Raising an Objection (Article 32 of the CCJA Rules of Procedure)[5]

Article 32 deserves special attention. It states in paragraph 1 that "Any objection to the jurisdiction of the Court or to the admissibility of the action must be raised within the time limit set for the filing of the first [brief or exhibit] emanating from the party raising the objection … ." The most likely cause is that in which the defendant to an action for annulment brought before the CCJA would raise an objection. In this case, the defendant will have to raise their objection within the same reduced period of forty-five days (half of the three-month period under Article 30 of the CCJA Rules of Procedure for the defendant to produce a response, which would constitute in this case their first pleading).

4. Article 31 of the CCJA Rules of Procedure states that:

> The appeal and the statement of defense may be supplemented by a reply brief and a rejoinder or by any other brief, when the President, either sua sponte or following an application to that effect within a period of fifteen (15) days from the serving of the statement of defense or reply, deems it necessary and expressly authorizes it.
>
> When the President authorizes the filing of a reply or a rejoinder, or any other brief, he shall set the timeframe for the submission.

5. Article 32 of the CCJA Rules of Procedure states that:

> 1. Any *objection* to the jurisdiction of the Court or to the admissibility of the appeal must be raised within the time limit set for the filing of the first procedural document [or brief] by the party raising the *objection*. The Court can rule separately on the objection or attach it to the merits.
> 2. When the Court manifestly lacks jurisdiction to hear the appeal, or when the appeal is clearly *inadmissible* or *devoid of merit*, it may, at any time, by a reasoned decision, declare itself incompetent, declare the appeal inadmissible or reject it.

5. Time Limit for Abatement of the Proceedings (Article 44 *ter* of the CCJA Rules of Procedure)[6]

Article 44 *ter* of the CCJA Rules of Procedure sanctions the lack of diligence by parties for two years by the abatement of the proceedings. If a motion for annulment of an arbitral award under Article 27 of the UAA or Article 29 of the CCJA Regulation on Arbitration is referred to the CCJA and the parties do not perform any diligence, the issue of whether there can be an abatement of the proceedings under section 44 *ter* above must be answered. In other words, does the fact that the CCJA is "locked up" within six months oblige it to rule after six months even if the parties do not react? Would this be a mandatory time period, requiring the CCJA to rule, sua sponte if needed, after six months, even if it were to dismiss the motion, or will the proceedings be abated? The wording of Article 27, paragraph 2 of the UAA, and Article 29.4 of the CCJA Regulation on Arbitration suggests that the CCJA must resolve the dispute on annulment within six months of referral. Thus, it does not seem plausible that the one-year statute of limitations under Article 44 *ter* will ever be relevant for annulment proceedings before the CCJA since it has to settle those issues within six months with is exactly half of the allotted time under Article 44 ter.

However, it might be considered that the CCJA is obliged to rule only if the case is ready for hearing. This requires that the parties take the necessary steps after the filing of the motion. Trial belongs to the parties and not the judge, which is why the OHADA Legislator provided under Article 27 of the UAA that "the appeal may be brought before the CCJA." The parties are free and must, therefore, express their desire to have their dispute resolved. Their inaction may imply that they do not wish to proceed with the trial, and in the absence of due diligence by the parties, abatement is necessary. The CCJA has not been put in a position to judge, and it cannot be criticized for not having ruled during the allotted time, especially since the OHADA Legislator has not set any specific penalty for noncompliance with this time period. Consequently, it might also be considered that the abatement of the proceedings under Article 44 *ter* of the Rules of Procedure may take place but with a reduced period of one year (initial period of two years reduced by half), in accordance in Article 27, paragraph 2 of the UAA and Article 29.4 of the CCJA Regulation on Arbitration. This last hypothesis seems noncompliant with Article 27, paragraph 2 of the UAA, and Article 29.4 of the CCJA Regulation on Arbitration, and it remains to be seen in the future how they will be implemented by the CCJA which will have the last word.

6. Article 44 *ter* of the CCJA Rules of Procedure states that "The proceedings *are* abated when none of the parties *performs due diligence* for two (2) years from the last procedural *step*. The abatement *does* not terminate the suit; it only *terminates* the proceeding *without making procedural steps already taken enforceable or allowing parties to avail themselves of them.*"

6. Time Limit for Filing a Request for Intervention (Article 45-2 of the CCJA Rules of Procedure)[7]

Article 45 of the Rules of Procedure allows a State Party to the Treaty or any other person with an interest in the preservation of their rights to support the claims of one of the parties. This request for intervention must take place within three months of the publication under Article 13-6[8] of the Rules of Procedure. The notice, the publication of which is required under Article 13-6, is intended to inform the public of the existence of a dispute before the CCJA likely to determine a person or a State which would have an interest in intervening in the proceedings. This publication does not seem to be currently effective,[9] and it may be difficult for the parties to be informed in time of the existence of a dispute before the CCJA, which could have an impact on the deadlines, since the time period under Article 45 paragraph 2 of the Rules of Procedure runs from the publication mentioned in Article 13-6.

In accordance with Article 27 paragraph 2 of the UAA, the motion for intervention must be filed within forty-five days (initial three-month period reduced by half) from publication. In the absence of proof of publication, and by analogy with the calculation of the time limit for a referral to the CCJA, it could be considered that no time limit can run against a person who wishes to intervene in the proceedings before the CCJA in the absence of the publication under Article 13.6 of the CCJA Rules of Procedure, like the CCJA held in *Lell v. Société Camerounaise de Transformation*,[10] and *Hajjar v. La Société Nationale d'Assurances et de Réassurances, Incendie, Accidents, Risques Divers*.[11] The setting of the time limit under Article 45.6 of the Rules of Procedure is left to the discretion of the President of the CCJA, and it would suffice for the latter to grant a shorter period of time than he would normally have granted in such a case.

---

7. Article 45 of the CCJA Rules of Procedure states that:

> 1. States Parties to the Treaty may intervene in cases submitted to the Court. Anybody interested in supporting the claims of one of the parties for the conservation of his rights shall also be entitled to intervene.
> 2. The request for intervention *must* be *filed* within three (3) months of the publication *under* paragraph 6 of Article 13 of these Rules.

8. Article 13.6 of the CCJA Rules of Procedure states that "A notice *is* published in the OHADA Official Journal stating the date of the *filing* of the motion instituting proceedings, the names, and domiciles of the Parties and the subject of the dispute … ."
9. However, efforts have been made recently and a considerable amount of information are regularly published on the Official website of the Organization, including the schedules of hearings of the CCJA. For example, *see* https://www.ohada.org/index.php/fr/ohada-au-quotidien/role-des-audiences-publiques-de-la-cour-ccja [accessed Apr. 25, 2020, at 22:24].
10. By transposition, Lell v. Société Camerounaise de Transformation, N° 002/2006, Decision, [C.C.J.A.], 2e ch., (Mar. 9, 2006), http://www.ohada.com/jurisprudence/ohadata/J-07-09.html, finding that, in the absence of service of the challenged judgment, the statute of limitation had not run against the applicants.
11. Hajjar v. La Société Nationale d'Assurances et de Réassurances, Incendie, Accidents, Risques Divers, N° 079/2006, Decision, [C.C.J.A.], Ass. plen., (Apr. 29, 2015), http://www.ohada.com/jurisprudence/ohadata/J-16-191.html, holding that, in the absence of production of the evidence of an act establishing the proper service of the appeal in cassation, as required under Art. 28 of the CCJA Rules of Procedure, the time limits for appeal have not begun to run and the objection of inadmissibility raised by the defendant must be disregarded.

7. Time Limit for Filing a Request for Revision of a Judgment (Articles 49.4 and 49.5 of the CCJA Rules of Procedure)[12]

In accordance with Article 27 al. 2 of the AAU, the time periods of three months to submit a request for review, which run from the discovery of the new fact (Article 49.4) and ten years beyond which no review can be formed (Article 49.5), must respectively be reduced by half, that is to say, forty-five days and five years. The CCJA will probably have to decide whether the ten-year time period at Article 49.5 of its Rules of Procedure must be halved or not.

8. Time Limit Because of Distance (Articles 459.4 and 49.5 of the CCJA Rules of Procedure)[13]

Article 25.5 of the CCJA Rules of Procedure states that "Procedural delays, due to the distance, shall be established by a decision of the Court and published in the OHADA Official Journal." Under the prescriptive Decision N° 002/99/CCJA of February 4, 1999 made by the CCJA under Article 25.5 of its Rules of Procedure, all the time limits under the Rules of Procedure are increased, due to distance, for parties who do not have their usual residence in Ivory Coast (the State party hosting the CCJA), by twenty-one days for Central Africa, fourteen days for West Africa and thirty days for Comoros. The extension of the statute of limitations due to the distance applies to any party to a case before the CCJA whose residence is not in Ivory Coast,[14] even if such party is represented by an attorney domiciled or residing in Ivory Coast.[15] It also applies to the initial petition referring a case to the CCJA as well as the statement of defense and any other brief filed before the Court (reply brief, replication, rejoinder, etc.).[16] The CCJA constantly applies these rules and has awarded fourteen days to parties from Western

---

12. Article 45 of the CCJA Rules of Procedure states that:

    1. States Parties to the Treaty may intervene in cases submitted to the Court. Anybody interested in supporting the claims of one of the parties for the conservation of his rights shall also be entitled to intervene.
    2. The request for intervention *must* be *filed* within three (3) months of the publication *under* paragraph 6 of Article 13 of these Rules.

13. Article 45 of the CCJA Rules of Procedure states that:

    1. States Parties to the Treaty may intervene in cases submitted to the Court. Anybody interested in supporting the claims of one of the parties for the conservation of his rights shall also be entitled to intervene.
    2. The request for intervention *must* be *filed* within three (3) months of the publication *under* paragraph 6 of Article 13 of these Rules.

14. Afriland First Bank v. Société Hôtelière du Cameroun, N° 203/2017, Decision, [C.C.J.A.], 2e ch., (Nov. 23, 2017).
15. Eyike v. Banque Internationale du Cameroun pour l'Epargne et le Crédit, N° 140/2016, Decision, [C.C.J.A.], Ass. plén., (Jul. 14, 2016), http://www.ohada.com/jurisprudence/ohadata/J-17-80.html.
16. Société Générale de Banques au Cameroun v. Essoh, N° 057/2005, Decision, [C.C.J.A.], 2e ch., (Dec. 22, 2005), http://www.ohada.com/jurisprudence/ohadata/J-06-44.html.

Africa (Benin,[17] Guinea,[18] Niger[19]) and twenty-one days to parties from Central Africa (Cameroon,[20] Gabon,[21] Chad[22]).

It remains to be seen whether the time limits because of distance will also be reduced when the CCJA is handling a motion for annulment of an arbitral award filed under Article 27 of the UAA, and the CCJA itself will probably have to determine this issue.

17. Adjovi v. Daoudalawal, N° 036/2016, Decision, [C.C.J.A.], 1e ch., (Feb. 29, 2016), http://www.ohada.com/jurisprudence/ohadata/J-16-238.html.
18. Bah v. Diallo, N° 061/2008, Decision, [C.C.J.A.], 1e ch., (Dec. 30, 2008), http://www.ohada.com/jurisprudence/ohadata/J-10-35.html.
19. Oumarou v. Harouna, N° 087/2019, Decision, [C.C.J.A.], 1e ch., (Mar. 28, 2019).
20. Afriland First Bank v. Société Hôtelière du Cameroun, N° 203/2017, *supra*, Appendix IV, fn. 14.
21. Aboghe v. Banque Internationale pour le Commerce et l'Industrie du Gabon, N° 029/2010, Decision, [C.C.J.A.], 1e ch., (Apr. 29, 2010), http://www.ohada.com/jurisprudence/ohadata/J-11-73.html.
22. Esso Exploration and Production Chad Inc v. Ressourcium International SARL, N° 037/2012, Decision, [C.C.J.A.], 2e ch., (May 3, 2012).

Bibliography

Bako, P. J.-B. (n.d.). *L'influence de la jurisprudence de la CJUE sur l'interprétation juridictionnelle du droit communautaire ouest-africain (CEDEAO-UEMOA)*. Retrieved March 2020, from L'influence de la jurisprudence de la CJUE sur l'interprétation juridictionnelle du droit comhttp://www.ceje.ch/files/4114/6218/2918/Geneva_JMWP_07-Bako.pdf

Black, H. C. (n.d.). *Black's Law Dictionary Free Edition*. Retrieved from The Law Dictionary: https://thelawdictionary.org

Born, G. (2009). The Principle of Judicial Non-Interference in International Arbitral Proceedings. *University of Pennsylvania Journal of International Law, 30*(4), 1020.

Bühler Michael W., G. A.-S. (2018). Le défi de la complémentarité entre le juge et l'arbitre dans l'espace OHADA. *Penant, n° 904, 2018*(904), 275-295.

Bühler, M. W. (2018). Out of Africa: The 2018 OHADA Arbitration and Mediation Law Reform. *Journal of International Arbitration, 35*(5), 517-540.

Canada, D. o. (n.d.). *Legistics. Present Indicative*, https://canada.justice.gc.ca/. Retrieved from https://canada.justice.gc.ca/: https://canada.justice.gc.ca/eng/rp-pr/csj-sjc/legis-redact/legistics/p2p3.html.

Carroll, R. M. (1991). Quasi-Judicial Immunity: The Arbitrator's Shield or Sword. *Journal of Dispute Resolution, 1991*(1), 30-31.

Cécile, C. (2014). Les mesures provisoires dans le nouveau droit français de l'arbitrage: à la recherche d'une complémentarité vertueuse entre arbitre et juge étatique. In J.-F. v. J. van Compernolle, *L'arbitre et le juge étatique* (pp. 282-328). Brussels: Bruylant.

Christophe, T. (2009, July 21). *Mais jusqu'où ira-t-on? Après les arbitres et les centres d'arbitrage, on s'en prend au juge de l'annulation … . Les Petites Affiches*(144), pp. 20-22.

Common Court of Justice and Arbitration. (2018). *Guide d'Arbitrage de la CCJA-OHADA* (2 ed.).

David Hacking, S. B. (2017). *"Ethics in Arbitration: Party and Arbitral Misconduct," In Defining Issues in International Arbitration*, Oxford University Press. Retrieved

April 2017, from www.lordhacking.com: http://www.lordhacking.com/Documentation/Hacking%20&%20Berry%20-%20Ethics%20in%20Arbitration%20April%202016.pdf.

Edition Francis Lefebvre. (1996, November). *Revue de Jurisprudence de Droit des Affaires, RJDA 11/96 n° 1414.*

Emmanuel, G. (2001). Transnational Law: A Legal System or a Method of Decision Making?. *Arbitration International, 17*(1), 59-71.

Federal Aviation Administration. (n.d.). *What's the Only Word That Means Mandatory? Here's What Law and Policy Say about "Shall, Will, May, and Must."* Retrieved from www.faa.gov/about/initiatives/plain_language/articles/mandatory/: https://www.faa.gov/about/initiatives/plain_language/articles/mandatory/

Fouchard, P., Gaillard, E., & Goldman, B. (1999). *Fouchard, Gaillard, Goldman on International Commercial Arbitration* (Kluwer Law International).

Gaillard, E. (2020, February). Nouvelles Réflexions sur la Sociologie de l'Arbitrage. *Procédures* (2), 35-37.

Garner, B. (2009). *Garner on Language and Writing* (1st ed.. American Bar Association).

Garner, B.A. (2009). *Black's Law Dictionary* (WEST).

Garside, M. (2020). *Major Countries in Worldwide Cobalt Mine Production from 2014 to 2019.* Retrieved from www.statista.com: https://www.statista.com/statistics/264928/cobalt-mine-production-by-country/

HarperCollins Publishers. (n.d.). www.collinsdictionary.com. Retrieved from: https://www.collinsdictionary.com

Huchet, G. (2009, March-April). Impartialité de l'arbitre et contrôle de l'ordre public international par le juge de l'annulation: confirmation de position. *Gazette du Palais*, pp. 1309-1311.

International Trade Center. (2018). *La Médiation et l'Arbitrage dans l'Espace UEMOA. Recueil des Lois et Pratiques.* Retrieved from www.intracen.org: http://www.intracen.org/uploadedFiles/intracenorg/Content/Publications/Receuil_arbitrage_final_Low-res.pdf

Katz, J.-D. (2010). Dictionnaire Juridique, Politique, Economique et Financier. Anglais-Américain-Français. Paris.

Kay, A. (2018, November 22). *5-Top Tantalum-Mining Countries.* Retrieved from https://investingnews.com/daily/resource-investing/critical-metals-investing/tantalum-investing/2013-top-tantalum-producers-rwanda-brazil-drc-canada.

Kodo Mahutodji Jimmy Vital, A. N. (2016). The CCJA as a Regional Arbitration Institution. In O. Emilia (Ed.), *The Transformation of Arbitration in Africa: The Role of Arbitral Institutions* (pp. 47-59). The Netherlands: Kluwer Law International.

Kodo, M.J., Al Dabbagh, H., & Boismain, C. (2019). *Code Pratique OHADA. Traité, Actes uniformes et Règlements Annotés.* Levallois-Perret, France: Editions Francis Lefebvre.

Lohoues Oble, J. (2002). Traité du 17 Octobre 1993 Relatif à l'Harmonisation du Droit des Affaires en Afrique. In J. Issa-Sayegh, P.-G. Pougoué, & F. M. Sawadogo,

OHADA: Traité et Actes Uniformes Commentés et Annotés (2nd ed., pp. 27-66). Poitiers, France: Juriscope.

Maury, F. (2015, December 9). *Affaire Getma-Guinée: les arbitres répondent.* Retrieved March 2020, from www.jeuneafrique.com: http://www.jeuneafrique.com/285543/societe/affaire-getma-guinee-les-arbitres-repondent/

Maury, F. (2016, December). *Affaire Getma-Guinée: les arbitres répondent.* Retrieved from www.jeuneafrique.com: http://www.jeuneafrique.com/285543/societe/affaire-getma-guinee-les-arbitres-repondent/

Mercadal, B. (2019). *Modèle Universel de Contrat d'Affaires.* Levallois-Perret: Francis Lefebvre.

Mercadal, B., Agboyibo, Y., & Kodo, M.J. (2011). OHADA Member States. In Y. Aubin, L. De Longeaux, & J.-C. Vecchiatto (eds.), *International Bank and Other Guarantees Handbook: Middle East and Africa* (pp. 411-454) (Kluwer Law International).

Merriam-Webster. (n.d.). *Merriam-Webster.com Dictionary, Merriam-Webster, https://www.merriam-webster.com/dictionary/.* Retrieved from www.merriam-webster.com: https://www.merriam-webster.com/dictionary/judge%20delegate.

Mustill, M. J. (1988). The New Lex Mercatoria: The First Twenty-five Years. *Arbitration International,* (4).

Nicholson, K., & Stevenson, A. (2004). *Harrap's Law Dictionary. English-French.* Chambers Harrap Publishers.

OHADA. (1997, November 1). *Official Journal of OHADA*(4).

OHADA. (1999, May 8). OHADA Official Journal. *OHADA Official Journal, No 8, May 15, 1999,* 21-22.

OHADA. (2016, November 24). *Official Bulletin of OHADA, November 24th 2016.* Retrieved from www.ohada.org: http://www.ohada.org/index.php/en/component/content/article?id=1848:official-bulletin-of-ohada-special-edition-nov-2016

Payne, J. (n.d.). *The False Imperative,* http://www.ncsl.org/. Retrieved May 3, 2020, from www.ncsl.org: http://www.ncsl.org/legislators-staff/legislative-staff/research-editorial-legal-and-committee-staff/volume-xxvi-issue-2-the-false-imperative.aspx

Rogers, C. (2016). *When Arbitrators and Institutions Clash, or The Strange Case of Getma v. Guinea.* Retrieved from www.kluwerarbitrationblog.com: http://kluwerarbitrationblog.com/2016/05/12/when-arbitrators-and-institutions-clash-or-the-strange-case-of-getma-v-guinea/

Rubino-Sammartino, M. (2020, February 7). *Links amongst venue, Lex Fori and jurisdiction to set aside proceedings.* Retrieved March 2020, from Www.lexology.com: https://www.lexology.com/library/document.ashx?g=64771aad-d5b4-4800-9f1c-51085c8ccdfe.

Saint Dahl, H., & Boudreau, T. (2007). *Dahl's Law Dictionary. Dictionnaire Juridique Dahl, Français-Anglais* (3d ed. William S. Hein & Co).

Seraglini, C. (2009). Mauvais procès quant à l'impartialité d'un magistrat. *Juris Classeur Prériodique (JCP) E,* p. 1781.

Sponseller, M. A. (1993). Mark A. Sponseller, Redefining Arbitral Immunity: A Proposed Qualified Immunity Statute for Arbitrators, 44 Hastings L.J. 421 (19 *Hastings Law Journal, 44*(2), 438-439.

Truli, E. (2006). Liability v. Quasi-Judicial Immunity of the Arbitrator: The Case Against Absolute Arbitral Immunity. *American Review of International Arbitration, 17*(3), 16.

Tumnde, M.S. (2012). OHADA as Experienced in Cameroon: Adressing Areas of Particuliar Concern to Common Law Jurists. In C.M. Dickerson (ed.), *Unified Business Law for Africa: Common Law Perspectives on OHADA* (2nd ed., pp. 81-95) (GMB Publishing).

UNIDA. (2010, March 4). *Newsletter, OHADA.com.* Retrieved from www.ohada.com: http://www.ohada.com/newsletter.php?news=04032010-848#

Voser, N., & Anya, G. (n.d.). Revision of Arbitral Awards. *ASA Bulletin Special Series*(38), 43-74.

Woodworth, A. T., & Adams, A. A. (2020). *Publication Manual of the American Psychological Association* (7 ed.).

Xavier, D. (2009). Arbitrage: impartialité du juge de l'annulation et ordre public international. *Recueil Dalloz*(13), pp. 880-881.

Yakubu, J. A. (2009). Community Laws in International Business Transactions. In C.M. Dickerson (ed.), *Unified Business Law for Africa: Common Law Perspectives on OHADA* (GMB Publishing).

Glossary

A

Acquiescence: Acquiescement
Address for service[1]: Domicile élu; élection de domicile
Adoption[2]: Adoption (d'un traité, des Actes uniformes)
Adversarial principle[3]: Principe du contradictoire
Appellant (person lodging an appeal against a judgment before a higher Court)[4]: Appelant
Appellee (person against whom an appeal is filed before a higher Court)[5]: Intimé(e)
Application for recusal: Demande de récusation
Appoint: Commettre (un expert); Nommer (un arbitre)
Arbitration agreement: Convention d'arbitrage
Arbitration Bylaws (The June 2, 1999 Arbitration Bylaws of the CCJA): Règlement Intérieur de la CCJA en matière d'arbitrage du 2 Juin 1999
Arbitration clause: Clause compromissoire
Arbitration Rules: Règlement d'arbitrage
Argument: Moyen (de cassation)
Articles of association[6] (of a corporation): Statuts (d'une société ou association)
Attachment of real estate: Saisie immobilière
Authentic instrument[7]: Acte authentique
Award (arbitral): Sentence (arbitrale)
Award by consent: Sentence d'accord parties
Award of damages: Condamnation aux dommages-intérêts

---

1. Harrap's. Jean Daniel Katz.
2. https://www.unicef.org/french/crc/files/Definitions.pdf.
3. https://www.ilo.org/dyn/triblex/triblexmain.showList?p_lang = en&p_keyword_id = 157.
4. (Black, s.d.).
5. *Id.*
6. https://thelawdictionary.org/articles-ofassociation/.
7. (Saint Dahl & Boudreau, 2007).

B

Brief (Law): a case: Dossier, cause. nb: à ne pas confondre avec "brief" qui exprime la brièveté de quelque chose. Donc par exemple, un " bref exposé des faits" devrait être traduit par "summary statement"
Business name[8]: Dénomination sociale
Bylaws: Règlement Intérieur

C

Capacity: Qualité
Cassation: Cassation
Certified copy: Copie certifiée conforme
Claimant: Demandeur
Common Court of Justice and Arbitration: Cour Commune de Justice et d'Arbitrage
Company name[9] (cf. corporate name): Dénomination sociale
Competent court: Juridiction compétente
Competent judge for interim measures (with power to hear urgent applications)[10]: Juge des référés
Condition precedent[11]: Condition suspensive
Contradictory reasons[12]: Motifs contradictoires
Consent award (cf. award by consent)
Conservatory measures: Mesures conservatoires
Corporate name[13]: Raison sociale

D

Deciding *ex aequo et bono*: Statuer en *amiable compositeur*
Decline jurisdiction: Se déclarer incompétent(e)
Demurrer[14]: Fin de non-recevoir
Devoid of merit[15] (cf. lacking merit)
Dies a quo (date of the start of an event)[16]: Point de départ d'un délai
Dies ad quem (date of the conclusion of an event)[17]: Dernier jour d'un délai
Double degree of jurisdiction: Double degré de jurisdiction

8. (Nicholson & Stevenson, 2004).
9. (Katz, 2010).
10. (Nicholson & Stevenson, 2004).
11. *See Black's Law Dictionary*, online https://thelawdictionary.org/due-process-of-law/.
12. https://eur-lex.europa.eu/LexUriServ/LexUriServ.do?uri=OJ:C:2005:031:0027:0028:EN:PDF.
13. (Black, s.d.); (HarperCollins Publishers, s.d.).
14. *Id.*; (Katz, 2010).
15. (In re Marriage of Flaherty (1982) 31 Cal.3d 637, 649): https://law.justia.com/cases/california/supreme-court/3d/31/637.html, setting the subjective standard for determining a frivolous appeal as whether a reasonable person would agree the appeal was totally *devoid of merit*.
16. (Black, s.d.).
17. *See Black's Law Dictionary*, online https://thelawdictionary.org/due-process-of-law/.

E

En banc (Court sitting): Assemblée plénière
Evidentiary documents: Documents probants; preuve par documents
Executory formula[18]: Formule exécutoire
Exercise of judicial discretion (of a judge or arbitrator): Appréciation souveraine (du juge ou de l'arbitre)
Ex officio[19]: D'office
Exequatur certificate[20]: Attestation d'exequatur
Extract of the court record[21]: Extrait de plumitif

F

First and last instance (court sitting in first and last instance): Premier et dernier ressort (juridiction statuant en)
Foreclosure of a mortgage (cf. attachment of real estate)
Formal notification[22]: Mise en demeure
Fuctus officio[23]: Dessaisi
Full Court[24] *(cf. en banc)*

H

Hearing: Audience
Hearing of a party (or parties): Audition d'une partie (ou des parties)

I

If applicable[25]: Le cas échéant
In camera (hearing)[26]: A huis clos (audience)
Interlocutory judgment[27]: Avant-dire-droit (jugement); Avant-faire droit[28]
Interim attachments[29]: Saisies conservatoires

18. (Nicholson & Stevenson, 2004). (Saint Dahl & Boudreau, 2007). Great Britain: Convention providing for the reciprocal enforcement of judgments in civil and commercial matters, ... https://www.jstor.org/stable/2213595?seq = 1; http://www.legislation.gov.uk/uksi/1969/1063/made.
19. http://curia.europa.eu/juris/document/document.jsf?text = &docid = 224339&pageIndex = 0&doclang = EN&mode = req&dir = &occ = first&part = 1&cid = 1653625.
20. (Black, s.d.).
21. (Nicholson & Stevenson, 2004).
22. *Id.*
23. (Black, s.d.).
24. *See*: https://eur-lex.europa.eu/LexUriServ/LexUriServ.do?uri = OJ:C:2003:026:0015:0015:EN:PDF [accessed Mar. 27, 2020,at 14:27].
25. (HarperCollins Publishers, s.d.).
26. (Black, s.d.).
27. https://eur-lex.europa.eu/LexUriServ/LexUriServ.do?uri = OJ:C:2005:182:0041:0042:EN:PDF.
28. (Nicholson & Stevenson, 2004); (Saint Dahl & Boudreau, 2007).
29. Under Scottish law, *see*: https://e-justice.europa.eu/content_interim_and_precautionary_measures-78-sc-maximizeMS_EJN-en.do?member = 1.

Interim measures: Mesures provisoires
Interim order[30] (cf. Interlocutory judgment)
International trade *usages*: Usages du commerce international
Inter partes[31] (between the parties; in their presence. cf. adversarial principle): Contradictoirement (en présence des parties)
Investment instrument: Instrument relatif aux investissements
It is settled case law[32]: Il est de jurisprudence constante

J

Joinder of proceedings[33]: Jonction de procedures
Judge delegate[34]: Juge délégué
Judicial discretion[35]: Pouvoir souverain (du juge)
Jurisdiction clause: Clause attributive de competence

L

Lack of merit (argument lacking or devoid of merit): Infondé (moyen, argument)

M

Memorandum of Understanding[36]: Protocole d'accord
Memorial[37]: Mémoire
Minutes: Procès-verbal

N

Natural person: Personne physique
Notarial act[38]: Acte notarié

O

Objection to admissibility[39] (or objection of inadmissibility): Exception d'irrecevabilité:

30. https://documents-dds-ny.un.org/doc/UNDOC/GEN/N09/306/47/PDF/N0930647.pdf?OpenElement.
31. (Black, s.d.).
32. It is settled case law: https://eur-lex.europa.eu/LexUriServ/LexUriServ.do?uri=SEC:2008:2038:FIN:EN:PDF; https://eur-lex.europa.eu/legal-content/EN/TXT/PDF/?uri=CELEX:62005CJ0381&from=EN.
33. (Katz, 2010); (Nicholson & Stevenson, 2004).
34. (Merriam-Webster, s.d.).
35. (Osborn v. United States Bank, 9 Wheat 866, 6 L. Ed. 204: https://www.courtlistener.com/opinion/85451/osborn-v-bank-of-united-states/); *Black's Law Dictionary*.
36. (Katz, 2010).
37. *Id.*
38. (Nicholson & Stevenson, 2004).
39. M/V Virginia G (Panama v. Guinea Bissau), Case N° 19, Judgment of Apr. 14, 2014, ITLOS Rep. 2014, 4, 93, https://www.itlos.org/fileadmin/itlos/documents/cases/case_no.19/judgment_published/C19_judgment_140414.pdf

Obligation of means[40]: Obligation de moyens
On its own motion (cf. ex officio; sua sponte)
Only be appealed *in cassation*[41] before the Common Court of Justice and Arbitration: N'est susceptible que de pourvoi en cassation devant la CCJA
Operative part (the) (of a judgment or an arbitral award): Dispositif (d'un jugement ou d'une sentence)
Overrule (a judgment): Casser (un jugement)
Overturn (cf. overrule)

P

Perform due diligence: Accomplir des diligences
Petition for interpretation, correction to or supplementation[42] of the award: *Recours en interprétation, rectification ou complément de sentence*
Prescriptive Decision (of the CCJA): Décision à caractère normatif (de la CCJA)
Process (to)[43]: Instruire (une affaire)
Prong (of an argument): *Branche (d'un moyen)*
Provisionnal measures: Mesures provisoires
Provisional attachments[44] (cf. interim attachments)

Q

Quash (a judgment: cf. overrule)

R

Recusal: Récusation
Referral: Saisine
Registered office: Siège social[45]
Reply brief (or replication)[46]: Mémoire en réplique
Reporting judge (the judge appointed to write the opinion of the court in a case): Juge rapporteur
Restricted formation (of the CCJA): Formation restreinte (de la CCJA)
Respondent: Défendeur
Rules of procedure of the CCJA: Règlement de procédure de la CCJA

40. https://eur-lex.europa.eu/LexUriServ/LexUriServ.do?uri=COM:2004:0207:FIN:EN:PDF [accessed Mar. 27, 2020, at 23:31].
41. "On points of law" has been replaced with "in cassation." Se pourvoir en cassation is translated by "lodge an appeal in cassation" (Katz, 2010).
42. (Garner, 2009).
43. (Katz, 2010).
44. In the Netherlands, *see* http://www.abld.nl/70/meer/syllabus/provisional-attachment.
45. (Nicholson & Stevenson, 2004).
46. (Black, s.d.).

S

Statement of defense: Mémoire en défense (ou en réponse)
Statement of rejoinder[47] (The second pleading on the part of the defendant, being his answer of *matter of fact* to the plaintiff's *replication*): Mémoire en duplique
Submission agreement: Compromis d'arbitrage
Sua sponte[48] *(cf.* ex officio*)*

T

Taking of evidence[49]: Administration de la prevue
Terms of reference: Acte de mission

U

Unqualified acceptance: Acceptation sans réserve

47. *Id.*
48. (Saint Dahl & Boudreau, 2007).
49. https://eur-lex.europa.eu/LexUriServ/LexUriServ.do?uri = OJ:C:2007:140:0013:0014:EN:PDF.

Cases and Precedents

OHADA Member States' Lower Courts Cases

OHADA Member States Courts' of Appeal Cases

CCJA Cases

Accor Afrique v. L'Etat Togolais, N° 064/2020, Decision, [C.C.J.A.], 3e ch., (Feb. 27, 2020) 148, 149

Africof v. Banque Islamique de Guinée, N° 080/2017, Decision, [C.C.J.A.], 1e ch., (Apr. 27, 2019) 206

Agence pour la Sécurité de la Navigation Aérienne en Afrique et à Madagascar v. Snack Bags, N° 011/2015, Decision, [C.C.J.A.], 2e ch., (Apr. 2, 2015) 181

Airtel Gabon v. 2JTH-Gabon, N° 203/2018, Decision, [C.C.J.A.], 3e ch., (Nov. 22, 2018) 134, 137, 168

Area Assurances v. Proassur, N° 195/2019, Decision, [C.C.J.A.], 2e ch., (Jun. 27, 2019) 57

ARNO c/ Libya Oil Cameroun, N° 006/2014, Decision, [C.C.J.A.], Ass. Plen., (Feb. 4, 2014), http://www.ohada.com/jurisprudence/ohadata/J-15-97.html 133

Ascot Commodities v. Dieye, N° 125/2016, Decision, [C.C.J.A.], 2e ch., (Jun. 23, 2016), http://www.ohada.com/jurisprudence/ohadata/J-17-66.html 70

Atlantique Télécom v. Planor Afrique, N° 016/2009, Order, [C.C.J.A.], (Aug. 19, 2009), http://www.ohada.com/jurisprudence/ohadata/J-10-187.html 198

Atlantique Telecom v. Planor Afrique, N° 041/2010, Decision, [C.C.J.A.], 1st ch., (June 10, 2010), http://www.ohada.com/jurisprudence/ohadata/J-11-85.html 18

Attijari bank Senegal v. Senegal, N° 002/2009, Order, [C.C.J.A.], (Jan. 1, 2009), http://www.ohada.com/jurisprudence/ohadata/J-16-93.html 198–199

Banque Internationale pour l'Afrique Occidentale—Côte d'Ivoire v. Societe Ivoirienne de Produits et de Negoce, N° 059/2005, Decision, [C.C.J.A.], (Dec. 22, 2005), http://www.ohada.com/jurisprudence/ohadata/J-06-36.html 3

Barou Entreprise des Travaux v. Société d'Exploitation des Mines d'Or de Sadiola, N° 040/2009, Decision, [C.C.J.A.], 1e ch., (Jun. 30, 2009), http://www.ohada.com /jurisprudence/ohadata/J-10-78.html 169

Benin Control v. Etat du Bénin, N° 103/2015, Decision, [C.C.J.A.], Ass. plén., (Oct. 15, 2015), http://www.ohada.com/jurisprudence/ohadata/J-16-96.html 77, 128, 141, 159, 164, 196, 197

Canac Sénégal v. Transrail, N° 082/2014, Decision, [C.C.J.A.], 2e ch., (May 22, 2014), http://www.ohada.com/jurisprudence/ohadata/J-15-173.html 65

Commercial Bank of Cameroon v. Archidiocèse de Yaoundé, N° 242/2018, Decision, [C.C.J.A.], 2e ch., (Nov. 29, 2018) 30, 100, 129, 135, 138, 157

Compagnie d'Opérations et de Reconditionnement Industriel v. Kabore, N° 120/2018, Decision, [C.C.J.A.], 1e ch., (May 31, 2018). 206

Compagnie Malienne pour le Développement des Textiles v. Société Inter Africaine de Distribution, N° 160/2016, Decision, [C.C.J.A.], Ass. plen., (Dec. 1, 2016), http://www.ohada.com/jurisprudence/ohadata/J-17-100.html 16, 22, 131, 143, 160, 164

Connexion Marketing v. Synergie Gabon, N° 027/2010, Decision, [C.C.J.A.], 1e ch., (Apr. 29, 2010) 135

Côte d'Ivoire Telecom v. Publistar, N° 015/2003, Decision, [C.C.J.A.], (Jul. 1, 2003), http://www.ohada.com/jurisprudence/ohadata/J-04-109.html 4

Société Camerounaise d'Opérations Maritimes v. Express Transport Khalifa, N° 060/2017, Decision, [C.C.J.A.], 1e ch., (Mar. 30, 2017) 110, 138

Société Construction métalliques Ivoiriennes v. Fraternité Saint Jean-Eudes d'Abatta, N° 062/2012, Decision, [C.C.J.A.], 3e ch., (Jun. 7, 2012), http://www.ohada.com/jurisprudence/ohadata/J-14-167.html 60, 124, 125

Societe d'Exploitation Hôteliere et Immobiliere du Cameroun v. Societe Generale de banques au Cameroun, N° 012/2003, Decision, [C.C.J.A.], (Jun. 19, 2003), http://www.ohada.com/jurisprudence/ohadata/J-04-104.html 4

Société de Manufacture de Caoutchouc de Côte d'Ivoire v. May, N° 012/2005, Decision, [C.C.J.A.], 1e ch., (Feb. 24, 2005), http://www.ohada.com/jurisprudence/ohadata/J-05-357.html 67

Societe des Huileries du Benin v. Societe Nationale pour la Promotion Agricole, N° 06/2011, Order, [C.C.J.A.], (Dec. 21, 2011), http://www.ohada.com/jurisprudence/ohadata/J-13-178.html 198

Société Générale Burkina Faso v. Nare, N° 012/2019, Decision, [C.C.J.A.], 1e ch., (Janv. 24, 2019) 130

Société Générale d'Electricité Ferroviaire du Congo v. Airtel Congo, N° 099/2009, Decision, [C.C.J.A.], Ass. plén., (Oct. 30, 2014), http://www.ohada.com/jurisprudence/ohadata/J-15-190.html 90

Société Générale de Banques en Côte d'Ivoire v. Kobenan Tah, N° 075/2016, Decision, [C.C.J.A.], 2e ch., (Apr. 21, 2016), http://www.ohada.com/jurisprudence/ohadata/J-17-24.html 50

Société Générale de Banques en Guinée v. Hann, N° 067/2015, Decision, [C.C.J.A.], Ass. plén., (Apr. 29, 2015), http://www.ohada.com/jurisprudence/ohadata/J-16-67.html 205

Societe Inter Africaine de Distribution v. Compagnie Malienne pour le Developpement des Textiles, N° 01/2015, Order, [C.C.J.A.], http://www.ohada.com/jurisprudence/ohadata/J-16-199.html 198

Société Inter Africaine de Distribution v. Compagnie Malienne pour le Développement des Textiles, N° 020/2013, Decision, CCJA, Ass. plen., (Apr. 18, 2013), http://www.ohada.com/jurisprudence/ohadata/J-15-20.html 131, 172, 183, 185, 197

Société Ivoirienne de Raffinage v. Bona Shipholding LTD, N° 029/2007, Decision, [C.C.J.A.], Ass. plen., (Jul. 19, 2007), http://www.ohada.com/jurisprudence/ohadata/J-08-241.html 52, 97

Societe Nationale pour la Promotion Agricole v. Societe des Huileries du Benin, CCJA, N° 04/2011, Decision, CCJA, 1e ch., (Jun. 30, 2011), http://www.ohada.com/jurisprudence/ohadata/J-12-137.html 163

Société Nationale Pour la Promotion Agricole v. Société des hydrocarbures du Bénin, N° 045/2008, Decision, [C.C.J.A.], Ass. plen., (Jul. 17, 2008), http://www.ohada.com/jurisprudence/ohadata/J-09-83.html 68, 111–113, 126, 163

Société Navale Guinéenne v. Société Africaine de Commerce, N° 047/2010, Decision, [C.C.J.A.], 2e ch., (Jul. 16, 2010), http://www.ohada.com/jurisprudence/ohadata/J-12-95.html 70

International Courts' Cases

French Cases

US & Canadian Cases

UK & Other Common Law Cases

Table of Legislation

Statutes

Treaties

Index

NOTE: The numbers in italics refer to page references of footnotes and list of abbreviations.

www.ingramcontent.com/pod-product-compliance
Lightning Source LLC
La Vergne TN
LVHW020644300926
849161LV00004B/804